THE USBORNE
HISTORY
OF
BRITAIN

Written by
Ruth Brocklehurst
with Henry Brook, Kate Davies, Hazel Maskell,
Conrad Mason, Abigail Wheatley,
Rachel Firth, Rob Lloyd Jones, Felicity Parker & Fiona Patchett

Illustrated by
Ian McNee and Giacinto Gaudenzi
with Dai Evans, Inklink Firenze, Adam Larkum & Lyn Stone

Designed by
Stephen Moncrieff
with Mary Cartwright, Anna Gould,
Tom Lalonde, Steve Wood, Stephen Wright,
Hannah Ahmed & Brenda Cole

Digital design by John Russell
Picture research by Ruth King

Edited by Jane Chisholm

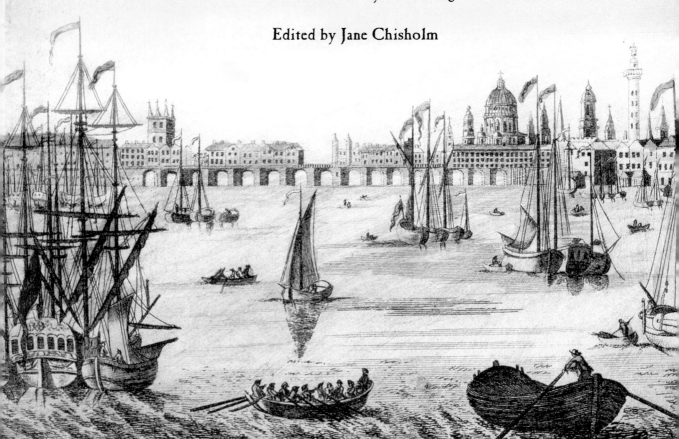

THE USBORNE
HISTORY OF BRITAIN

Contents

7   The people of Britain

11   Prehistoric Britain

29   Roman Britain

87   The early Middle Ages

119   The Middle Ages

177   Tudors and Stuarts

235   The Georgians

293   The Victorians

351   The early 20th century

393   The Second World War

451   Post-war Britain

475   Factfile

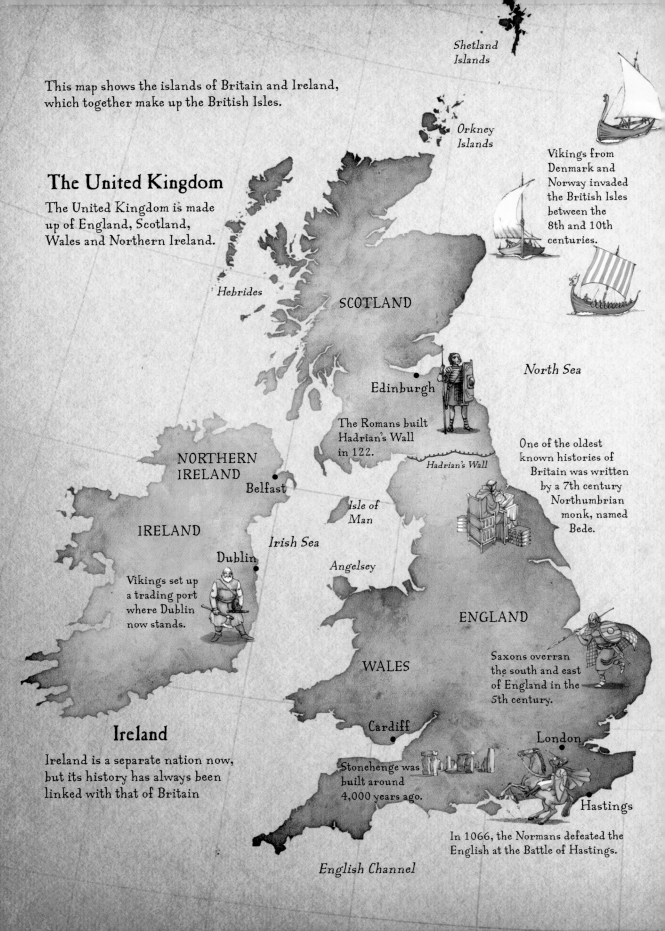

This map shows the islands of Britain and Ireland, which together make up the British Isles.

Shetland Islands

Orkney Islands

Vikings from Denmark and Norway invaded the British Isles between the 8th and 10th centuries.

The United Kingdom

The United Kingdom is made up of England, Scotland, Wales and Northern Ireland.

Hebrides

SCOTLAND

North Sea

Edinburgh

The Romans built Hadrian's Wall in 122.

Hadrian's Wall

One of the oldest known histories of Britain was written by a 7th century Northumbrian monk, named Bede.

NORTHERN IRELAND

Belfast

Isle of Man

IRELAND

Irish Sea

Dublin

Angelsey

ENGLAND

Vikings set up a trading port where Dublin now stands.

Saxons overran the south and east of England in the 5th century.

WALES

Ireland

Ireland is a separate nation now, but its history has always been linked with that of Britain

Cardiff

London

Stonehenge was built around 4,000 years ago.

Hastings

In 1066, the Normans defeated the English at the Battle of Hastings.

English Channel

THE PEOPLE OF
BRITAIN

Since the earliest times, the history of Britain has been shaped by different peoples, languages and cultures. Tribes have moved about; new kingdoms have risen while others have fallen; and raiders and settlers have arrived from across the seas.

While some changes have taken place gradually and peacefully, others have come about suddenly and violently through wars and conquests by foreign invaders.

Invasions

The first major takeover was by the Romans, who ruled Britain from the 1st to the 4th century. Later, people called Saxons, then Vikings, took charge. The final bloody conquest came when the Normans landed, in 1066, defeating the English at the Battle of Hastings.

None of these conquering powers ever managed to impose their rule on the whole of the British Isles, so they made a stronger impact on life in some regions than others. But each new invasion brought new people, customs and languages to the land.

Britain BC

Some of the dates in this book are shown with the letters BC. This means they are from the time before the birth of Christ, over 2,000 years ago. Dates in this period are counted backwards. So, the bigger the number BC, the longer ago it is.

Emerging nations

Although they still had much in common, people in different regions began to see themselves differently from one another. And so, the separate nations of England, Ireland, Scotland and Wales gradually emerged. Through wars, trade and royal marriages, the relationships, and the borders, between these countries have changed many times over the centuries, though England has dominated for most of the time.

Britain wasn't invaded again after 1066, but from Tudor times, British explorers and traders began to look to the wider world to discover what was out there, and see how they could profit from it.

Empire and after

By the 18th century, the British were setting up trading colonies all around the world. Eventually, the colonies came under British rule, as part of Britain's growing empire. By the end of Queen Victoria's reign, the empire was so vast that almost a quarter of the people in the world considered themselves British – even if they had never set foot on the British Isles.

During the 20th century, many men from the empire fought bravely for Britain in the First and Second World Wars. By the end of the century, the empire had been dismantled, and its countries had become independent, though most kept strong ties with Britain.

New arrivals

Through the centuries, Britain has provided a home to immigrants from all over the world, some seeking work and a better life, others escaping war or persecution in their own countries.

After the Second World War, the government invited people from the old empire, especially from India and the Caribbean, to live and work in Britain. They came in their thousands, all adding to the rich cultural variety of Britain today, as well as ever-changing ideas about what it means to be British.

"Rule, Britannia!
Britannia, rule the waves!
Britons never, never,
never shall be slaves!"

These lyrics from the 1740 anthem *Rule Britannia!* reflect the patriotic belief held by many British people during the 18th and 19th centuries that their powerful navy and vast empire made them invincible.

PREHISTORIC BRITAIN

The story of life in Britain goes back to a time before people knew how to read and write, in an era known as prehistory. Although Britain's earliest inhabitants didn't write anything down, they did leave other clues behind. Traces of their houses, their tools and ornaments, and sometimes even their bodies, have survived down the ages. They help to build up a picture of how people lived in Britain from around 700,000 years ago.

The Ice Age

From around 700,000 years ago

Getting warmer

During the Ice Age, the weather kept swinging from very cold to warm – though this happened very slowly, about every 100,000 years. Plants, animals and people could only survive in Britain in the warm periods.

When early people first set foot in Britain, things were very different from today. It was a period when temperatures swung between extremes. For thousands of years at a time it was bitterly cold. The sea that now divides Britain from the continent of Europe wasn't there, as much of the water was frozen into ice. Rivers of ice criss-crossed the land, and people, animals and plants just couldn't survive.

But, every hundred thousand years or so, the weather grew warmer and the ice melted. Plants grew, attracting herds of animals, such as mammoths, deer and wild horses, cattle and pigs. They walked to Britain on the dry land that connected it to Europe.

Around 400,000BC

Around 300,000BC

Around 200,000BC

In 2003, archaeologists discovered rare Ice Age art in caves at Creswell Crags in Nottinghamshire. Outlines of deer, wild cattle and bird-like creatures survive, carved into the cave walls.

Hunting and gathering

The first people arrived in Britain on foot, following the animals. They needed animals to survive – they ate their meat and used their skins for clothes. But many animals were huge and fierce, and people only had simple hunting tools, such as pointed wooden spears.

So they chased animals for long distances to tire them out, or scared them into bogs or off cliffs, to make killing them easier. They also made use of any animals they found that were already dead.

12

This saved the effort of hunting. But the hunters of the Ice Age didn't just eat meat. They also caught fish and gathered shellfish, wild nuts, fruits and roots. They twisted plant stems and leaves to make rope and twine. And, to help with all these tasks, they made themselves tools from wood, bone and stone.

On the move

Because they relied so much on wild animals, Ice Age hunters didn't have fixed homes. They moved around, following herds as they migrated in search of the best grass. At night, people slept in caves – if any were handy – or in shelters made of things they found nearby. But, every hundred thousand years or so, the cold weather returned again, the ice expanded to cover more of the land, and people and animals had to leave once more.

Stone tools

Early hunters chipped stones into a variety of shapes to help them with different jobs.

For cutting and scraping, they used roughly shaped pebbles...

...for piercing and chopping, they worked stones into thin points...

...and they used tiny flakes for any delicate jobs.

These Ice Age hunters have chased a huge mammoth into a bog, to confuse and exhaust it. They are finishing it off with wooden spears.

During the warmer periods of the Ice Age, people in Britain also hunted hippos, rhinos and elephants.

Stone Age hunters

From around 12,000 years ago

Ice and stone

The time when people used stone for most of their tools is often called the Stone Age. Confusingly, in Britain the Stone Age began during the Ice Age. But it continued long after the Ice Age had ended.

Around 12,000 years ago, the weather gradually began to get warmer and the Ice Age came to an end. Over thousands of years, water from the melted ice drained into the ocean, sea levels rose and water crept over low-lying land. The islands we now call Britain were separated from mainland Europe for good. The warmer weather encouraged a wide variety of plants and trees, and great forests grew, providing food and shelter for many animals such as wild pigs, cattle and deer and also for people.

Seasonal movers

The people who lived in Britain at this time were the ancestors of British people today. Now that a rich array of animals, roots, berries, fish and birds were flourishing across the country, people didn't have to travel very far to collect what they needed. Every year they moved between just a few campsites, according to which season it was, choosing places where they would have plenty to eat at that time of year.

What's for lunch?

As well as hunting for fish and meat, ancient people gathered wild foods that still grow in Britain today, including hazelnuts, elderberries, acorns and shellfish such as limpets and mussels.

14

This scene shows a seasonal campsite near a river. Hunters are collecting fish and shellfish, hunting animals and gathering berries and nuts. People returned to sites like this year after year.

Tools and techniques

Around this time, hunters developed sophisticated techniques and tools for hunting and finding food. They attached stone or bone blades to handles made from wood, to create very effective axes and spears – and even arrows, to use with bows.

They wove baskets and fish nets, sewed clothes from leather and skins, hollowed canoes out of tree trunks, and made themselves sturdy shelters from wood and animal skins. They even learned how to tame young wolves, to help them with hunting, and eventually they bred these into domestic dogs.

Bones and stones

Ancient hunters attached blades made from bone, deer antler or stone to wooden handles.

Harpoon with bone points

Arrow with stone head

Hatchet with stone head

15

Early farmers

Around 6,000 years ago, a totally new way of life arrived in Britain. Farming had begun in the Middle East 4,000 years earlier, when people first started to breed animals and grow plant crops for food. This gave them a much more reliable food supply than hunting and gathering wild food. So, gradually, farming know-how spread north and west into Europe, as groups of people showed each other how to make new farming tools and traded special breeds of pigs, sheep and cattle, and crops such as wheat and barley.

From around 6,000 years ago

Farming tools

These stone tools belonged to early farming people in Britain. They are around 5,000 years old.

This sickle-shaped blade was used to harvest crops.

These two stone axes would each have had a wooden handle.

Axes like these would have been used for chopping wood and other things.

New technology

Farmers from mainland Europe probably brought the first farm animals and crop seeds to Britain by boat around 6,000 years ago, along with farming tools, such as sickle-shaped stone blades for harvesting crops and stone grinders for making flour. Farming quickly spread all over the British Isles, and the hunting and gathering way of life came to a sudden end.

Farming meant that people no longer had to travel to find enough food. So, instead of camping in temporary shelters, they settled down, building houses from wooden planks or, sometimes, stones. And, because they didn't have to carry everything with them, they could make and store heavier, more elaborate equipment: pottery jars for cooking and storage, and large, delicately-shaped stone tools.

Food for thought

Now that people were making pottery jars and bowls, it was easier for them to store food. They could also cook new, sustaining foods such as porridge.

Changing the landscape

Farming quickly transformed the landscape of Britain. Grassland and fields soon began to replace forests, as farmers cut down more and more trees, opening up permanent clearings where they could grow their crops and raise their animals.

Groups of farmers also worked with each other to make their mark on the landscape in other ways, too. They banded together to construct miles of wooden trackways to provide safe paths through boggy areas. They piled up circular earth banks to create massive enclosures, which they may have used for protection, for herding animals, or even for religious ceremonies. And they also buried their dead in huge, eye-catching earth mounds, and under massive stone slabs carefully balanced on top of one another.

Firm footing

The long trackways built by early farmers to cross boggy ground may have looked like this one, made from split tree trunks, supported on smaller wooden posts.

One trackway found in Somerset, in southern England, ran for almost 2km (over a mile).

These huge stone slabs were set up by early farmers close to the east coast of Ireland. They mark the place where the farmers' dead relatives were buried.

Beakers and bronze

It wasn't long before the next big change swept across the land. By 4,500 years ago, things made from metal began to arrive in Britain. Metalworkers overseas were making small blades and ornaments using copper, gold and, later, bronze – which is a mixture of copper and other metals. But now, they started to bring these things, and their metalworking skills, over to Britain. This marked the start of the period in Britain known as the Bronze Age – though, for most of it, bronze was very rare and precious.

From around 4,500 years ago

Metalworking

To make things from metal, Bronze Age metalworkers found rocks containing gold or copper.

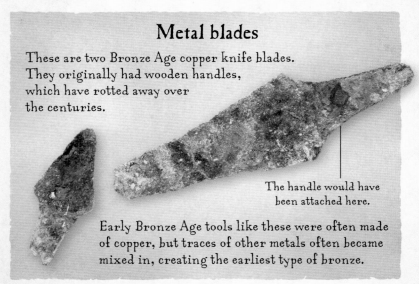

Metal blades

These are two Bronze Age copper knife blades. They originally had wooden handles, which have rotted away over the centuries.

The handle would have been attached here.

Early Bronze Age tools like these were often made of copper, but traces of other metals often became mixed in, creating the earliest type of bronze.

They crushed the rocks and then heated them in a furnace like this one, to extract the metal.

Next, metalworkers poured the molten metal into specially shaped hollows carved into pieces of stone.

Trading and raiding

Soon, people in Britain discovered rocks that contained metal, and learned how to extract it and turn it into tools and ornaments for themselves. But by now, all kinds of new goods, ideas and people were arriving in Britain. It's even possible there was a big invasion around this time by groups of people from the parts of Europe that now make up Germany and the Netherlands – but experts aren't sure.

Personal power

Whether or not Britain was invaded at this time, it was certainly changing. Soon, powerful individuals were thrusting themselves forward as leaders. Their groups competed against each other to trade the new metal tools and ornaments. The successful leaders made sure they were seen with plenty of these metal accessories, and were quick to adopt other new trends from mainland Europe, too. They started using a new kind of decorated drinking pot, known as a beaker, which was probably reserved for use only during special ceremonies and feasts.

Before long, the fashionable beakers were being made all over Britain. When they died, wealthy people were even buried with their beakers, metal knives and gold ornaments, to show how well-off and sophisticated they were. Now, important people were often buried alone, which was a new thing in the Bronze Age. Before this, many people were usually buried together.

This scene shows the funeral of a Bronze Age man. His most treasured possessions – beaker pots and metal tools – are being buried with him.

Buried treasure

In 2002, at Amesbury near Stonehenge in southern England, archaeologists found a Bronze Age body surrounded by an incredible array of grave goods.

A beaker pot

Five beaker pots lay around the man, along with copper knives, archery accessories, metalworking tools and two gold hair ornaments – the earliest gold objects found in Britain.

Gold hair ornaments

Bronze Age people often covered graves like this one with a rounded mound of earth, to mark the place where their relative was buried.

Mysterious monuments

As well as farming, working metals, making pottery and trading goods, Britain's Stone Age and Bronze Age people also found time to build some of the largest and most impressive monuments ever made. There are a few clues as to why people built these vast structures, but much about them is still shrouded in mystery.

From earth to stone

The simplest monuments were made of earth. People dug ditches using picks and shovels made from antlers and bones. Then they piled up the earth using baskets and ropes. Sometimes they made tall, pointed mounds, like hills; at other times they built banks enclosing flat circular or rectangular spaces.

More complex monuments were created by fixing big, upright timbers or stones into the ground. These were often arranged in ring shapes or lines, sometimes with other big stones or timbers laid flat on top of the uprights.

Mighty mound

Silbury Hill in Wiltshire is an earth monument built around 4,500 years ago. It's the biggest prehistoric mound anywhere in Europe.

To make a mound this vast, around 500 people would have had to work every day for 10 entire years.

Stonehenge, in the South of England, was in use from around 5,000 to 3,600 years ago.

The first monument on the site was a vast circular earth bank enclosing a flat space. Later, huge timber structures were erected within the banks. Later still, these were replaced by stones from as far away as Wales.

No one knows for sure how Stone Age and Bronze Age people managed to lift such huge stones into position for their monuments. But we do know that they shaped the stones using only simple stone tools, and that they dragged some stones for hundreds of miles using only ropes and log rollers.

The big question is, why on earth did they bother?

The changing seasons

Ancient farmers may have made monuments to mark out their territory. But perhaps they also created them to celebrate the changing seasons. Many of the earth banks, timber posts and stones were arranged to point to the position of the sun at important times of year, such as midwinter and midsummer. As the people of Bronze Age Britain depended on farming for their food, the sun and the changing seasons would naturally have been the most important things in their world.

Shape and raise

At Stonehenge, people used balls of hard stone to shape the stones and chip notches into them, to lock them together.

Then they pulled on some stones with ropes to raise them upright...

...and lifted up others using timber frames and levers, to sit on top.

Both the standing stones and the earlier earth banks at Stonehenge are arranged to face the parts of the sky where the sun rises at midsummer and sets at midwinter.

Troubled times

As the centuries passed, farming continued, but what changed life in Britain most was trade. The people who controlled the best trade routes with mainland Europe grew rich and strong, and the most powerful individuals displayed their wealth by wearing showy gold ornaments and throwing lavish feasts.

But the new riches also bred new conflicts, as different groups tried to grab more wealth, status and territory for themselves. On top of this, the weather was changing. Plunging temperatures and rising rainfall left farmers struggling to grow the crops they had always relied on. No wonder tensions between communities were getting worse.

This scene shows some late Bronze Age warriors who have just raided a rival settlement.

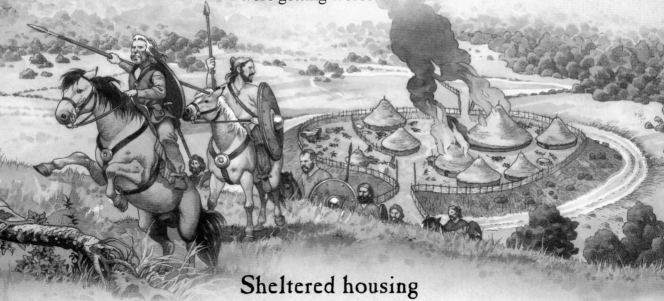

Horseback raids like this one were a common way for warriors to plunder cattle and other valuable goods.

Sheltered housing

So, instead of building monuments together, people began to create enclosures to keep raiders from rival groups out. Some covered whole hilltops, but others protected the homes of just a few families. People farmed in fields outside the walls, but stored their crops in pits within the enclosures, and herded their animals inside when raids threatened.

Glittering prizes

All this protection was matched by developments in weapons, as bronze swords, axes and spears were made in new and ever more streamlined shapes. But it was the spectacular gold ornaments and accessories created for the rich and powerful that best showed off the metalworkers' skills. They made gold jewels, capes and cups, which were probably used in special ceremonies and feasts that demonstrated the wealth and prestige of those who took part.

Horse power

Horses had been around in Britain for thousands of years, but it was only now that they became vital for transport and warfare. At first, people used horse-drawn carts to transport heavy goods. Important people also rode in carts, although this could be rather uncomfortable. So, gradually, people who could afford horses began to ride them instead, which was quicker and more comfortable. It also had special advantages for warriors: horseback fighters were speedier and had more height on their side than those on foot.

Splashing out

Around this time, as weather conditions were worsening, people in Britain started throwing valuable metal items into lakes, rivers and bogs. Experts think the metal goods were gifts to persuade the gods to send better weather.

The Iron Age

By around 2,650 years ago, people in Britain were starting to produce some tools and weapons from a new type of metal – iron. Iron is difficult to work, as it has to be heated to very high temperatures. But it can be used to make much stronger and sharper tools than bronze. So the introduction of iron was a big leap forward. It marked the end of the Bronze Age and the start of the Iron Age in Britain, though bronze was still used for some tools, weapons and ornaments.

Iron Age Britons continued to create defended hilltop enclosures. They were bigger and more complex than the Bronze Age ones had been, often with several rings of defences, and they are usually known as *hillforts*.

This Iron Age hillfort, known as Maiden Castle, is in Dorset, in the south of England. It's defended by massive earth banks, which would originally have been topped with wooden stakes.

In rockier parts of the country, hillforts had stone walls.

Place of safety

Iron Age hillforts had many uses: as storage depots for huge amounts of food, as homes for many people, and as workspaces for craft activities. They may even have been used as trading places or for religious ceremonies, as well as providing shelter for people who lived nearby in times of danger – and there were certainly plenty of those.

Tribes at war

People lived in groups, or tribes, each led by a powerful chief and defended by a band of fierce warriors equipped with sharp iron spears, large shields and swift war chariots pulled by ponies. Women were an important part of each tribe. They fought alongside men in the most vital battles, and some were even tribe leaders, too. Rival tribes were quite capable of capturing each other's hillforts and burning them to the ground, as a way of gaining more territory and goods for themselves.

Overseas contacts

But Iron Age Britons didn't spend all their time quarreling. All the different tribes spoke similar, Celtic languages, and so did many of the tribes living in the areas we now know as France and Spain. It was easy for all these people to understand each other, so when they weren't fighting, they often traded news, goods and fashions.

So, all across the northern part of mainland Europe, Celtic-speaking people shared a similar way of life. They wore the same kinds of clothes and ornaments, and they probably believed in the same gods, too.

A warrior's weapons

Iron Age warriors carried several different weapons adapted for different uses.

A long sword was for slashing at the enemy.

An iron-tipped spear was for throwing...

...and a wooden shield was for protection.

Living languages

People still speak Celtic languages today in Scotland, Wales, Ireland and Brittany, in northern France.

Celtic culture

Word of mouth

As well as composing and reciting poems, Celtic bards also had to boast about their tribe's chief, and think up creative ways of insulting his enemies – as entertainment during feasts.

Celtic tribes across Europe loved story-telling and they composed their own poetry, even though they didn't know how to read or write. Every self-respecting tribe had its own poet, or *bard*. It was his job to make up new poems about his tribe's most famous victories. He also learned old poems by heart so he could recite them from memory.

Celtic Britons also adorned their pottery, metalwork and ornaments with curves and spirals, or animal designs. They wore boldly patterned clothes made from wool dyed in bright shades. Those who could afford it also wore heavy gold ornaments – from rings and brooches to huge neck rings called *torcs*. They even decorated their bodies with bright blue war paint to intimidate their enemies in battle.

Celtic people in Britain and mainland Europe also shared a religion. They believed in many gods and goddesses, who each took care of a different aspect of the natural world, such as trees, stones or water.

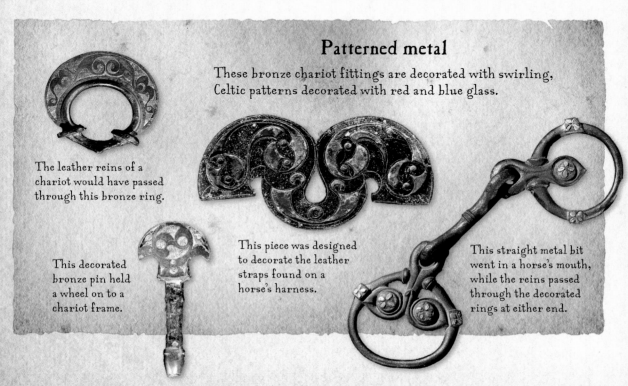

Patterned metal

These bronze chariot fittings are decorated with swirling, Celtic patterns decorated with red and blue glass.

The leather reins of a chariot would have passed through this bronze ring.

This decorated bronze pin held a wheel on to a chariot frame.

This piece was designed to decorate the leather straps found on a horse's harness.

This straight metal bit went in a horse's mouth, while the reins passed through the decorated rings at either end.

The Druids

Religious leaders known as Druids were in charge of sacred ceremonies, where they offered valuable things as sacrifices to please their gods. This might mean throwing precious ornaments into a lake, or burying them.

Druids may even have killed people as sacrifices. A number of Iron Age bodies bearing marks of a violent death have been found in bogs across Britain and other parts of Europe. These may have been victims of the Druids.

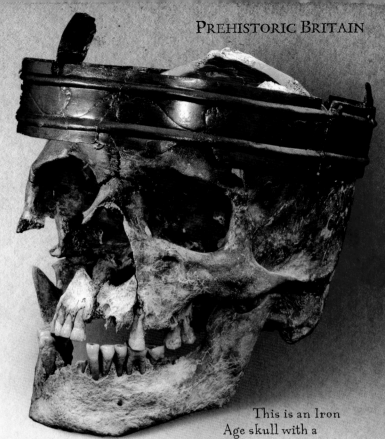

This is an Iron Age skull with a bronze crown, and it may have belonged to a Druid. His body was buried with the crown, an iron sword and a wooden shield.

Closer and closer

Celtic tribes were also famous for their trading. Even in the British Isles, cut off from mainland Europe by the sea, ships arrived regularly from as far away as the Mediterranean Sea, bringing fine pottery, wine, glassware and coins to exchange for British goods. Greeks and Romans were among the explorers and visitors, and some wrote down their impressions, creating the earliest written records about Britain.

Contact with the Romans was soon to change British life forever. At first, tribal leaders just traded goods such as grain, cattle, metals, animal skins and hunting dogs with the Romans. Later, tribes began to capture people from rival groups to supply the Romans with slaves. But soon they realized that what the Romans really wanted was Britain itself.

Tin Islands

A Greek explorer named Pytheas sailed all around Britain in 330BC, setting out from the South coast of France.

The ancient Greeks called Britain the *Kassiterides* or *Tin Islands*, because they sailed there mainly to buy the tin that was mined in Cornwall.

55-410

ROMAN BRITAIN

Around 2,000 years ago, life in Britain was dramatically shaken up when a powerful force invaded from across the sea – the Romans came, saw and, eventually, conquered.

From their magnificent city of Rome, the Romans had built up a mighty army and conquered more and more land until they ruled over the biggest empire of ancient times. For 400 years, most of Britain was part of that empire – daily life, culture, language and even the British landscape would never be the same again.

HIBERNIA
(Ireland)

CALEDONIA
(Scotland)

BRITANNIA

This map, based on one from the 2nd century, shows what the Romans thought the British Isles looked like. You can also see the names the Romans used for the different parts of the British Isles.

Romans invade

By 58BC the Romans dominated the Mediterranean region, from the deserts of North Africa and Syria to the Pyrenees. In the lands beyond Italy, which they called the provinces, the Romans imposed not only their laws and their hefty taxes, but also their way of life and their language, Latin.

The expanding empire

The great Roman army general Julius Caesar and his troops were fighting to secure the Roman province of *Gaul* (France). Britain, which the Romans called *Britannia*, lay tantalizingly close, on what many Romans believed to be the edge of the world. To capture these lands would surely be to conquer the world. But Caesar had practical motives too.

Britain was reported to be rich in gold and silver and its tribesmen disorganized and quarrelsome. Added to this, some southern Britons were supporting rebels in Gaul who were resisting Roman rule. Caesar calculated that conquering both Britain and Gaul would be a tremendous boost to his career – at a minimal risk.

Caesar attacks!

When Caesar first invaded Britain in 55BC, storms drove part of his army back to Gaul. He won some battles in the southeast of the country, but was surprised by the Britons' skilled use of chariots in combat. It was not the easy fight he had expected. Gales wrecked many of his ships on the beaches where they had landed and he was forced to retreat.

Caesar returned the next year, in 54BC, but he soon had to go back to Gaul to deal with a revolt. This wasn't the last the Britons would hear of the Romans, though. Nearly a hundred years later, Roman forces invaded again and eventually conquered all but the highlands of Scotland.

In the year 40, an insane Roman Emperor, Caligula, wanted to invade Britain. But he stopped at the French coast, where he ordered his men to collect shells to prove his 'conquest' of the sea!

British warriors watch from the cliffs of Kent as Caesar's army approaches.

According to some stories, Caesar brought 800 warships with him in 54BC.

Tribal Britons

The Romans weren't very impressed by the tribesmen of 1st century Britain. They saw the Britons as barbarians – often drunk and always fighting. While the Romans had been busy conquering a vast empire, building magnificent cities and developing a sophisticated culture, the people of Britain were leading a simpler rural life.

This bronze helmet is a fine example of British Iron Age metalwork – but it was probably made for show, rather than for fighting.

British living

Most Britons lived in small settlements in distinctive round houses made from wood plastered with mud, dung and straw. Even their fortifications – huge hilltop fortresses, called hillforts – were simply made from earth and wood or piled-up rocks.

This helped to confirm the Romans' view that Britain was a primitive and uncivilized place. What they didn't appreciate was that the Britons had a thriving culture, were highly skilled in many crafts including metalworking, and had trading contacts all over northern Europe.

When archaeologists at Butser Ancient Farm, in Hampshire, reconstructed these round houses, they found them surprisingly warm and weatherproof.

Round houses didn't have windows, so they were built with the doors facing east, to let in the morning sun.

A divided land

Because people in Britain and northern Europe, including Gaul, spoke a group of similar, Celtic languages, they could understand each other easily, and had much in common. But they had little sense of belonging to one nation, as they lived in separate tribes that often competed – and even fought – against one another.

After Caesar's attempted invasions, southern British tribes had much closer contact with the Romans in Gaul. Some tribes even paid taxes to Rome, in return for protection.

But one tribe, the Catuvellauni, led by an ambitious chief called Caratacus, began to capture more and more territory from surrounding tribes. Around the year 40, Verica, the king of the Atrebates tribe, fled to Rome to ask for help. This gave the Romans the excuse they needed to invade Britain again.

This map shows the different tribal areas in 1st century Britain.

Claudius conquers

The Emperor Claudius brought several war elephants to Britain as part of his army. The local people must have been terrified.

After Julius Caesar, the Roman empire was ruled by a series of emperors. In the year 41, Emperor Caligula was assassinated by members of his own army, who then declared his uncle Claudius the new emperor. To avoid Caligula's fate, Claudius did his best to win the respect and loyalty of his army and his people.

When King Verica appealed to Rome for help, Claudius seized his chance. He was determined to prove himself a strong ruler by conquering Britain once and for all.

This scene shows a British hillfort under siege. The wooden fortress is protected by rings of deep ditches and massive earth mounds up to 24m (80ft) high.

Roman archers shoot flaming arrows into the hillfort, to burn it down.

Britons hurl rocks at their attackers.

This smaller catapult, like a crossbow, is called a *scorpio*.

Roman soldiers use their shields to form a protective shell, known as the *testudo*, or tortoise.

Huge catapults, like this one, called a *ballista*, shoot boulders and heavy iron-tipped bolts over great distances.

34

River raids

Claudius ordered a massive number of troops – around 40,000 in all – to invade Britain. They landed on the southeast coast and marched inland until they reached a river. Caratacus and his army were waiting for them on the other side.

While both armies prepared for battle, the shrewd Roman general, Plautius, sent a team of crack troops downstream, with special instructions. They swam quietly across the river on horseback, to launch a surprise raid on the Britons. Meanwhile, the rest of the army crossed the river upstream, also unnoticed, and attacked the Britons from behind. It was a decisive Roman victory.

Britons under siege

Next, another general, Vespasian, advanced along the south coast, and laid siege to as many as 20 British hillforts. During these sieges, the Romans would surround the forts and subject them to merciless missile attacks, pounding the wood and earth walls with huge stones and bolts from massive catapults – until the Britons were forced to surrender.

Roman victory

Once most of the south was in Roman hands, Vespasian sent for the Emperor. Barely four months after the invasion began, Claudius and his legions marched in to capture the Catuvellauni stronghold at Colchester. Just two weeks later, Claudius returned to Rome, to a hero's welcome. There was a triumphal procession through the city to celebrate his conquest of *Britannia*.

"I had horses, men and weapons: is it any wonder I was unwilling to lose them? Just because you Romans want to rule everyone, does that mean everyone should accept slavery?"

Speech by Caratacus, imagined by the Roman historian, Tacitus, in his book, *The Annals*.

Freedom fighter

Caratacus was eventually caught and paraded through the streets of Rome in chains. But Claudius was so impressed with his dignity, he gave him his freedom.

Battling Boudicca

Over the next 30 years, the Romans gradually conquered most of southern England, but they often met fierce opposition. To help keep order, the Romans gave local tribal leaders jobs in government and allowed them to keep their land, in return for their loyalty.

But the Romans soon learned that they couldn't control the British against their will. In the year 60, they faced an uprising so serious that it nearly spelled the end of Roman rule.

Trouble brewing

One of the British leaders who was loyal to the Romans was Prasutagus, King of the Iceni tribe in East Anglia. On his deathbed, he divided his kingdom between his daughters and the Roman emperor. But the Roman authorities ignored his wishes, seizing the Iceni lands and all their possessions. When Prasutagus' wife Boudicca protested, she was whipped in the middle of the village and her daughters were raped. The Queen was furious – this was war!

Boudicca immediately raised a vast rebel army of men, women and children – all keen to drive out the occupying forces. They headed for Colchester, the Roman capital, and ransacked the city, killing thousands of people and destroying anything that represented Rome.

Then they turned on the Roman cities of *Londinium* (London) and *Verulamium* (St. Albans), and burned them to the ground in a ferocious assault.

This British warrior's shield was found in the Thames at Battersea in London. It dates from just before the time of Boudicca's rebellion.

Legends say that, after Boudicca's defeat, she and her daughters poisoned themselves to avoid being captured by the Romans.

The last battle

Meanwhile, most of the Roman army in Britain was hundreds of miles away in northern Wales, fighting another rebellious group, the Druids. When news of Boudicca's revolt came through, the army rushed back to deal with it.

Boudicca's 200,000 troops far outnumbered the Romans' 10,000, but the Britons stood little chance against the professional Roman fighters. The Romans advanced in tight formation, wading through the Britons, who turned and fled. It was a chaotic bloodbath in which Roman chroniclers claimed 80,000 Britons died.

Trapped

Boudicca's fleeing fighters were hemmed in by their own wagons, where their families had parked to watch the battle.

Hill

10,000
Romans

Forest

Forest

200,000
Britons

British wagons

The Britons sound elaborately shaped bronze war trumpets as they charge into battle.

The most important warriors ride on swift war chariots. Some women fight beside the men.

Military might

The key to the Romans' success in conquering so much of Britain so quickly was the virtually unstoppable power of their army. Not only was it the largest military force of its time, but its men were the most strictly organized, best equipped and most highly trained fighters of their day.

At its largest, the Roman army had over 300,000 men. To keep such a vast fighting machine running like clockwork, it had to be strictly regimented. So it was divided into units called legions. Each legion had over 5,000 foot soldiers, or legionaries, organized into groups of 80, known as centuries. With a clear chain of command, every man knew his place and exactly what was expected of him.

Roman legionaries were led into battle by officers with large banners.

A soldier's life

Legionaries were the elite soldiers of Roman times. To be eligible, a man had to be over 17, literate, tall and very fit. At first, only Roman citizens – men born in Rome or Italy – could become legionaries; non-citizens were known as auxiliaries.

In return for 20-26 years' service, a legionary earned a good wage and learned a trade, such as engineering or medicine. If he proved brave and loyal, he could rise up the ranks to become a *centurion*, the officer in command of a century.

Boot camp

When they joined up, all legionaries were issued with a kit that gave them the cutting edge over their enemies. Each man had a short sword called a *gladius*, a dagger and a spear-like javelin. For protection in battle, legionaries were given a metal breastplate, a helmet and a large curved shield. They also carried cooking utensils and tools for building temporary battle camps.

Roman soldiers had to keep super fit. As well as perfecting their javelin throwing, swordcraft and tactical moves, they also went on three training marches a month, marching over 30km (18 miles) in just five hours.

No wonder the average legionary went through three pairs of boots a year!

Roman soldiers carried swords and large shields, like the ones shown here.

A general commanded several legions.

A legate was in charge of a legion.

A centurion led a century (80 men).

A legionary was a citizen foot soldier.

A cavalry officer fought on horseback.

A non-citizen fighter was called an auxiliary.

This bronze helmet was found at the site of Ribchester Roman Fort, in Lancashire. A soldier would have worn it for training exercises.

This aerial photograph shows the remains of Housesteads Roman Fort in Northumberland. You can still see the outline of some of its buildings inside the fortified outer walls.

Keeping the peace

Once Roman rule was established in Britain, the role of the army changed from an invading force, to a peacekeeping one. Now its main job was to defend the country against attacks from hostile tribes and to enforce Roman law. Soldiers kept in training, and they also had non-military duties, working as engineers, accountants, cooks and vets. But, before they did anything else, they had to build themselves a fort.

Standard plan

The largest forts were almost like small towns, with everything the soldiers needed – from barrack blocks and bathhouses, to hospitals and stables. They all followed the same rectangular plan, which meant men could always find their way around – whether they were in Manchester, Mainz or Mesopotamia. The three legions based in Britain lived in fortresses in Caerleon, York and Chester. But there were many other forts for smaller units dotted around the country.

Lookout tower

Originally, five barrack blocks and a workshop stood in this part of the fort.

Food store

Officers' headquarters

Hospital

Commanding officer's house

Settling down

Many soldiers made friends with the locals, teaching them the Roman way of life, but adopting British customs too. When they retired, they often settled near their old forts, and even married local women.

Over time, British and Roman cultures became more and more mixed. Britons could also become 'Romanized' by joining the army themselves. For some, this was a chance to travel and experience life in other parts of the empire.

Tongue twister

Many British towns that grew on the sites of Roman forts – such as Manchester, Colchester, Gloucester and Leicester – have name endings derived from *castrum*, the Latin word for fort.

Letters from home

A treasure trove of hundreds of written records has been found in the ruins of the Vindolanda Roman Fort at Chesterholm. These provide an amazingly detailed picture of the daily lives of soldiers in Roman Britain.

Among the documents that have survived are duty rosters that describe soldiers working as shoemakers, brewers, builders and medics. There are also letters sent to and from soldiers. They include party invitations, deals with local traders – and even a letter from a mother sending her soldier son socks and underpants from home.

Barrack blocks

Main street

Main gateway

There were more barrack blocks here.

Latrines (communal lavatories)

Roman soldiers sent to Britain had to adapt to the chilly climate. This razor handle, shaped like a legionary's leg, shows the thick socks that soldiers wore under their sandals.

41

Road works

According to the proverb, all roads lead to Rome. This was literally true in the Roman empire, as the Romans built roads out from their capital city to each new territory they conquered. They were used to good, straight roads, but the only ones in Britain were dirt tracks. So, the army started right away on a massive campaign of building, to provide a brand new network of over 16,000km (10,000 miles) of roads.

This scene shows a Roman engineer using a device called a *groma*, to make sure he plots a straight course for a new road. He looks along the *groma* arms to make sure the next marker is in a straight line with the previous one.

Straight forward

Roads were vital for governing the province, as they helped troops to march quickly to wherever they were needed. They also made it much easier and faster to send messages between the forts, and to transport supplies. Eventually, there were roads connecting all the Romans forts and towns. Even today, several of the most important main roads in Britain still follow the routes of the original Roman ones.

Roman roads usually followed the most direct route possible, which often meant they went in a straight line. In fact they're famous for being incredibly straight – although they did bend around immovable obstacles such as marshes or steep hills.

Gravel sandwich

This diagram shows the layers of materials the Romans often used when building roads in Britain.

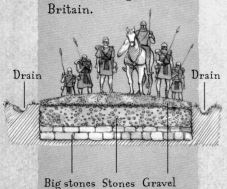

Drain   Drain

Big stones   Stones   Gravel

The engineer's assistant adjusts the position of the marker as instructed by the engineer.

The soldiers who built the roads used special surveying equipment to help them lay out a straight route. Then, construction work began. The work team dug a deep ditch, to make room for strong foundations. Then they filled it with layers of differently sized stones, all packed down tightly. The finished road had a humped surface with ditches on either side, so that rainwater would run off and drain away.

Finished roads were measured carefully, to give an accurate idea of how long it would take to travel along them. The Romans calculated distances in Roman miles, which were 1,000 paces long – equivalent to just under a modern mile, or around 1.5km.

Building bridges

To complement their extensive network of roads, the Romans also needed bridges to carry them safely across Britain's many rivers. During campaigns, when time was short, they made temporary bridges by fastening together a line of boats and placing a wooden walkway on top. More permanent bridges were constructed from wood or stone. Roman soldiers tested their stability by marching across them in formation.

This is a Roman milestone from Wales. Stones like this one, showing the distance to nearby towns or forts, were placed every mile along Roman roads.

43

Town life

To the Romans, the only civilized way to live was in towns. But the Britons didn't have any, so the Romans got building. Like Roman forts, every town followed a similar design. Streets were laid out in a grid, dividing the town into blocks known as *insulae*. At the heart of every town was the *forum*, a busy market square where people met to do business and catch up on the news. The *forum* was lined with shops on three sides. On the fourth side stood the Roman equivalent of the town hall, the *basilica*.

This scene shows the bustling market square, or *forum*, of a regional Roman town.

The town council held its meetings in this building, the *basilica*.

British temple

Town houses

A wealthy Roman would have lived in a large, luxurious town house, or *domus*. But most people lived in small houses in the *insulae*, working in trades and services. They sold their wares – from metalwork and pottery to meat and bread – from shops at the front of their houses, and lived at the back or upstairs.

Law and order

The Romans divided Britain into regions called *civitates*. Each had a main town with a council of local leaders in charge of taxes, law, public buildings and roads. By involving Britons in local government, the Romans hoped to avoid rebellions. During the 3rd century (years 200-300) many towns had walls built around them. These weren't just for protection; they showed off a town's importance and helped soldiers to control the traffic going in and out.

Roman temple

In an *insula*

This cutaway view shows how traders' houses in the Roman *insulae* were divided up. Families lived in the upper rooms...

...and used the lower rooms as workshops and trading outlets.

Retirement homes

Some towns, known as *coloniae*, were built to house Roman army veterans, and served as regional capitals. Colchester, York, Lincoln and Gloucester were all *coloniae*. Soldiers were given land there as part of their pensions.

Bathtime

Clean routine

Britons had always washed with soap, but instead the Romans rubbed perfumed oil into their skin.

Then they exercised to work up a sweat and scraped off the oil, sweat and grime using a curved tool called a *strigil*.

Strigil

Oil

The focus of social life in every Romano-British town was its public bathhouse. There, for a small fee, people could scrub and scrape, pamper and preen, and wash away the cares of the day. They could also work out in the exercise yard, unwind with a massage or catch up on the gossip over a relaxing game of dice.

The bathhouse consisted of a series of rooms of different temperatures. The bathing ritual usually began with a dip in a tepid pool in a room known as the *tepidarium*. The bather then moved to the steamy *calderium* to soak in a hot tub. Finally, the routine was finished with a refreshing swim in the cold, outdoor pool or *frigidarium*.

The Roman baths at Bath can still be seen today, although much of the building was reconstructed in the 19th century.

Many wealthy people paid slaves to do their scrubbing and scraping for them.

Aquae Sulis

One of the most magnificent bathhouses in Roman Britain was in the spa town of *Aquae Sulis*, now called Bath, where cleanliness and godliness came together – literally. Long before Roman times, Britons had visited its hot spring to worship Sulis, the water goddess of healing and wisdom.

The Romans linked Sulis with their own goddess, Minerva, who also had healing powers. So they built a temple by the sacred spring and dedicated it to Sulis-Minerva.

Later, a large bathhouse was added to the temple, using the naturally heated water from the spring. People visited from all over Europe, making Bath one of the liveliest and holiest towns in Roman Britain. Even today, the spring in the Roman baths is so hot you can see the steam rising from the water.

These Roman dice were found in the remains of a Roman bathhouse in London. Other games similar to backgammon were popular bathtime amusements.

Civil engineering

Roman forts, roads, bridges and towns were impressive enough. But Roman builders and engineers also equipped their great stone buildings and settlements with an array of gadgets that were all designed to make life safer, cleaner and much more comfortable. To the Britons, Roman technology must have seemed the ultimate in civilization.

Clean and clear

Running water was a basic necessity for the Romans. They invested a great deal of time, energy and ingenuity in finding reliable ways to transport it from mountain springs and streams down to their forts, towns and even their most important houses.

Back in Rome, water was brought to cities in stone-built channels, known as aqueducts, which were often raised on monumental stone arches. But in Britain, aqueducts were more modest channels that snaked along the ground and were often made from wood. Within towns, water was distributed in wooden pipes joined together with metal. The water supplied public drinking fountains, baths in public bathhouses and public toilets.

Built in stone

In some parts of Britain, people already used local stone to make buildings, but the Romans did things on a much grander scale. By gluing stones together with cement, they could make their walls much higher and thicker. They also built arches, which the Britons had never seen before.

Water works

As well as aqueducts and pipes, the Romans used other inventions to move water around in Britain.

They built chains of buckets, turned by big wooden wheels, to lift water up from the bottom of wells...

...and they created sturdy stone-built sewers under their streets, to take all their waste water away.

But the Romans weren't always so clever. They sometimes made water pipes from lead, which probably gave them mild lead poisoning.

Fire down below

Many Roman-style buildings in Britain had under-floor central heating, provided by a *hypocaust* system. This was a furnace that circulated hot air through specially constructed spaces under the floors and within the walls. *Hypocaust* heating was used for grand private houses and for bathhouses in towns and forts. Well-off people could also pay for tiled floors and even window glass to make their homes snug and bright.

Sea safety

The Romans also built tall lighthouses near their most important ports. These were sturdy towers with a place at the top for lighting a fire to guide ships safely in and out of ports at night.

During the daytime, the towers doubled as lookout stations, where soldiers could keep watch for pirates and raiders. To the Britons, it must have seemed that the Romans had tamed the elements.

This is a Roman lighthouse, which still stands on the coast at Dover in Kent. The orangey lines are clay tiles, laid in layers to strengthen the stone walls.

London town

The area occupied by Roman Londinium is now the financial district of modern London, known as The City.

This is an artist's impression of London in 120. Most of the city grew up on the north bank of the Thames, but a small trading settlement also developed on the south bank.

Londinium

London didn't exist before the Romans came to Britain; it was no more than a few farms scattered along the River Thames. But when Claudius invaded in 43, his men built a bridge across the Thames and put up a fort to guard it. Soon, local traders and craftsmen settled near the fort and a town grew up on the north bank of the river.

In Roman times, the Thames was wider than it is today, and deep enough for ships to sail right up to the bridge, where a port was built. This made the river a useful trading link between Britain and the rest of the empire. Within ten years, London – which the Romans called *Londinium* – had established itself as a thriving, cosmopolitan merchant town.

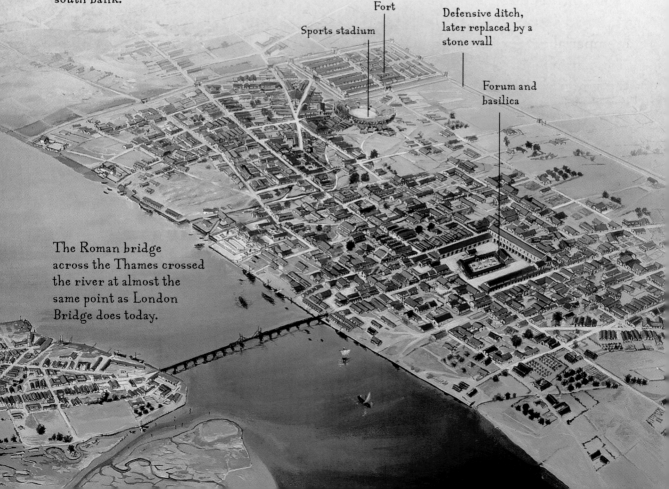

Sports stadium

Fort

Defensive ditch, later replaced by a stone wall

Forum and basilica

The Roman bridge across the Thames crossed the river at almost the same point as London Bridge does today.

Britain's first capital

Another town that grew rapidly during the early days of Roman rule in Britain was Colchester. In 49, the Romans had made it into a *colonia*, a town for Roman settlers and ex-soldiers. It soon became the first capital of the Roman province of Britain.

Then, in the year 60, Colchester and London were burned to the ground by Boudicca and her rebels. Both towns were quickly rebuilt, but Colchester's old tribal connections made it politically unstable. London, sited on the Thames, was more convenient for trade and transportation. So, gradually the Romans moved their headquarters to London.

Imperial London

By the turn of the 1st century, building work had begun to transform London into an imperial city, boasting a grand basilica and a forum even larger than Trafalgar Square. Later, an imposing city wall was added, to defend the capital. At the heart of the country's commercial and political life, London flourished and became one of the great cities of the Roman empire.

Power base

A few Roman emperors did visit Britain, but most of the time the province was run by a governing council, based in London. It was led by a governor, who was head of the army and chief justice. But to make sure he didn't become too powerful, the emperor appointed another official, called a *procurator*, to collect taxes and control the country's finances.

Luxury imports

Londinium was a destination for merchant ships importing goods that weren't made in Britain. Here are some of the things they brought:

Wine, olive oil and fish sauce from Italy and Spain

Glossy red pottery from France

Fine glass from Germany and Italy

Perfumes and spices from Egypt and the Middle East

Some experts think this mountain in northeast Scotland, Bennachie, is the site of Agricola's great Scottish victory. The Romans called Scotland *Caledonia*.

Welsh blade

This Roman sword was found in the Roman fort of Segontium at Caernarfon in north Wales. The fort was first occupied in 77.

The Roman peace

Once the Romans had settled in southern Britain and introduced the Roman way of life, they felt fairly secure. In return for benefits such as running water, regular markets and a reliable justice system, the local people were expected to cooperate with their new governors and obey Roman laws. They were still allowed to run their own tribes and follow their own religions – but on Roman terms.

The Romans had used this same system to bring peace and stability to the rest of their empire. It was so effective that this period became known as the *pax Romana*, or Roman peace. The Romans moved swiftly and ruthlessly against anything that threatened this peace. They had learned their lesson from the horrors of Boudicca's rebellion.

North and west

In the year 71, when the Brigantes tribe began to create unrest in northern England, the Romans reacted fast. The Roman army marched north, defeating the Brigantes and building forts in the area to strengthen their position. This gave them a secure base for pushing further north and west.

Agricola's army

But the most decisive move came in 77, with the arrival of a new Roman governor named Julius Agricola. He led a series of bold campaigns, finishing off the last lingering resistance from the Brigantes and advancing across Wales and Scotland.

Agricola moved his troops forward at an amazing pace, coordinating the movements of soldiers on foot, on horseback and even on ships, so that they all met up at the right time and place for their next attack. He also took advantage of British fighting skills, allowing Britons to join his troops if they had proved themselves loyal to Rome.

The tide turns

By 83, Agricola's troops had won a great victory in the northeast highlands of Scotland and had secured their control over a large area. They even began to look at Ireland with eager eyes, convinced that Rome could go on expanding forever. But not all of these gains were to last.

In 84, Agricola was called back to Rome by the emperor, Domitian. Some Romans believed that Domitian was jealous of Agricola's achievements. But perhaps he simply realized that Agricola was spreading his troops too thinly across too wide an area in Britain, creating serious problems for the control of the province.

Whatever the real reason, many Roman troops also left Britain at this time to defend other parts of the empire. The Romans withdrew from Scotland, and never gained as much ground there again. But at least they had strengthened their grip on Wales and England.

Agricola's campaign

We know a lot about Agricola because his son-in-law, a Roman writer named Tacitus, wrote about his career.

According to Tacitus, Agricola won over British chiefs by teaching them about Roman customs.

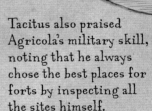

Tacitus also praised Agricola's military skill, noting that he always chose the best places for forts by inspecting all the sites himself.

Agricola died suddenly in Rome. Tacitus believed that he had been poisoned by the emperor Domitian out of jealousy.

Hadrian's Wall

Many Romans saw their withdrawal from Scotland as a temporary setback. There was no reason, they thought, why they couldn't keep extending their territory in Britain until they had conquered the whole island.

But in the year 117 there was a new Roman emperor, Hadrian, and he had other plans. He spent more than two thirds of his rule in the provinces and believed it was more important for the Romans to strengthen and defend the land they already had, than to conquer new territories. In 122, he visited Britain, where he set his ideas in stone.

Stonewalling

Hadrian realized that the fierce northern tribes weren't about to give up their land easily. Their constant attacks on the Romans were also draining valuable time and resources from the army. So Hadrian ordered a fortified frontier wall to be built, to protect Roman Britain. This allowed the army to control who crossed the border. It was also a potent symbol of the power of Rome.

Building the wall

Hadrian's wall was built from the materials that were available nearby.

Where stone was scarce, the builders mounded up earth and covered it in turf – earth and grass.

Elsewhere, the wall was built in longer-lasting stone blocks. Stone was also used to replace the turf section later on.

Much of Hadrian's Wall survives today, and can still be seen snaking its way across the north of England.

Hadrian's legacy

Hadrian's Wall was the largest structure in the Roman empire and an impressive feat of engineering. It was 120km (75 miles) long, stretching right across the country, between the rivers Tyne and Solway. Along the wall there were sixteen forts, with smaller forts, called milecastles, every Roman mile in between. There were lookout turrets too, so soldiers could keep watch and pass messages between forts if they spotted trouble.

Within months of Hadrian's death in 138, his successor, Antoninus Pius, attacked Scotland again. By 142, he had captured southern Scotland, so he began building a new frontier wall across the country. The 'Antonine Wall' was about half the length of Hadrian's and was mostly built from blocks of turf, instead of stone. But, less than 20 years later, local tribes rebelled, forcing the Romans back behind Hadrian's Wall. This remained the northern frontier for the next 250 years.

This head is all that's left of a 2m (6.5ft) tall statue of Hadrian that stood in London in around 122.

This section of Hadrian's Wall leads to Housesteads, one of the best preserved forts.

Tin trade

Throughout the ancient world, Cornwall was famous for producing tin. But the Romans had tin mines in Spain that were easier for them to get to, so they never really bothered with the Cornish mines.

This scene shows the village of Chysauster in Cornwall. The Britons who lived here piled up stones to make the walls of their round houses, and were probably from the Dumnonii tribe.

Life on the edge

Hadrian's Wall marked the official limit of the Roman empire in Britain. Beyond it, the tribes of Scotland were free from Roman interference, in theory at least. But even inside the wall, parts of Wales and the far west and north of England were so remote, that they gained little from the advantages of Roman civilization, even though the Romans were technically in charge.

Distant corners

While Britons in the south of England had adopted many of the Roman ways, tribes in the wilder parts of the west and the north continued to live much as they had before the Romans arrived. The main difference was they were no longer allowed to carry weapons.

Most still lived in round houses on small settlements and raised animals and grew crops for a living. Beyond the few Roman roads, travel was still slow and difficult, and people stayed close to home, only dimly aware of events in the wider empire.

Border country

When it came to the native Britons, both inside and beyond the boundaries of the empire, the Romans were generally prepared to live and let live. But local tribes just to the north of Hadrian's Wall could expect swift Roman raids if they stepped out of line – even if they didn't, the Romans kept a careful watch on them. If they wanted to trade with the Romans, they had to cross the wall, give up their weapons and pay taxes to the Romans on all their goods.

Free Caledonia

Further north into Scotland – the land the Romans knew as *Caledonia* – the tribes were harder to control. There, the Romans resorted to bribery, trade and diplomacy. They paid the more powerful tribal leaders with money, luxury gifts and privileges so that they wouldn't stir up trouble.

This gradually caused great changes in the region. The Romans never succeeded in conquering these tribes, but over time they began to merge together under just a few powerful leaders recognized by the Romans. This made them stronger, but their old way of life had come to an end – for good.

Painted people

One of the most powerful groups to emerge in Scotland were a people known by the Romans as *Picts*, or *painted ones*, because of the tattoos they were supposed to have had on their skin. The Picts were farmers who lived in central and northern Scotland, and were known for their ferocious raids on Roman-held areas of Britain.

"Let us, at the first encounter, prove what heroes Caledonia has in reserve – untouched, unconquered, ready to fight for freedom without regret."

Speech by Calgacus, a Scottish tribal leader, imagined by the Roman historian Tacitus, in his book, *Agricola*.

This standing stone was carved by Pictish craftsmen, and shows Pictish warriors, some of them on horseback.

Market forces

The new Romanized lifestyle in most of Britain led to an industrial boom, as craftsmen and merchants rushed to meet the demand for new products from around the Roman empire. The road system boosted local trade, making it easier than ever before to move goods around the country. International trade flourished too, as British products could now be transported as far away as Syria or Africa, in exchange for exotic foreign produce. The Roman empire soon became one great marketplace.

All at sea

The Romans had a vast fleet of merchant ships to transport goods all around the empire. Roman sailors didn't have any instruments to help them to navigate the seas. So they judged their position by the sun, moon and stars, and consulted books which recorded the best routes and times to travel. Storms were a terrible danger for the Romans' small wooden merchant ships, so they tried to sail only during the calmer spring and summer months. Pirates were also a constant worry. Even so, it was often quicker and easier to transport goods by sea than overland.

Checks and balances

Fair trade depended on everyone using the standard, Roman system of weights and measures throughout the empire. So roman merchants weighed their goods carefully, using special scales they carried with them. Legionaries also inspected the weights used in the markets to make sure that customers weren't being cheated by unscrupulous traders.

Roman coins

The same money was used all over the Roman empire, which made trade fairer and easier. Here are some of the most common coins.

A gold *aureus* – the most valuable Roman coin

A silver *denarius* – there were 25 in an *aureus*

A bronze *sestertius* – there were 4 in a *denarius*

A bronze *dupondius* – there were 2 in a *sestertius*

A copper *as* – there were 2 in a *dupondius*

A bronze *semis* – there were 2 in an *as*

A copper *quadrans* – there were 4 in an *as*

Made in Britain

One of the main reasons the Romans invaded Britain was for the metals mined there. In Roman Britain these were used to make everything from coins to army helmets and pipes for plumbing. Industries, such as pottery and the wool trade, also grew under the Romans. Most British goods were sold locally, but some were exported. One of the most prized British exports was a hooded cloak called a *birrus Britannicus.*

Map key

This map shows where different goods came from around the empire. Roman lands are shaded green.

- Grain
- Olive oil
- Wine
- Salt
- Cloth
- Pottery
- Metals
- Glass
- Wood
- Marble
- Purple dye
- Hunting dogs
- Cattle
- Horses
- Wild animals

> "The climate is objectionable, with its frequent rain and mists, but there is no extreme cold."
>
> The Roman historian Tacitus, who wrote about Britain and its history in the 1st century.

Far from home

It wasn't only goods and money that passed between Britain and the remotest corners of the empire. People also came and went — whether it was soldiers sent to Britain to keep the peace, traders bringing exotic goods, or British slaves shipped out as a profitable export.

Many of the legionary soldiers, administrators and traders who came to Britain were from Rome itself. For them it must have seemed a wet, chilly and distant land — and some complained about the clouds of mosquitoes that swarmed through the marshy land of the Thames in summer, and the illnesses they carried with them.

World travels

The Roman army also brought in extra troops, known as auxiliaries, from other parts of the empire, including Gaul, Spain, Germany, North Africa and the Near East. Later, fewer Romans wanted to sign up for the army. So troops from as far as Romania and Assyria arrived to join the British legions, while British recruits were sent to Spain, Armenia and Egypt, as well as to Rome itself.

Apart from soldiers, all sorts of other people chose to settle in Britain — from traders to people with special skills, such as doctors and teachers from Greece and sculptors from Gaul. But probably the largest numbers of people moving through Britain were slaves.

This is a carving of a legionary soldier, found in London. He may have come from Rome. You can see the warm cloak wrapped close around his neck.

60

These are Roman slave chains, found in Kent.

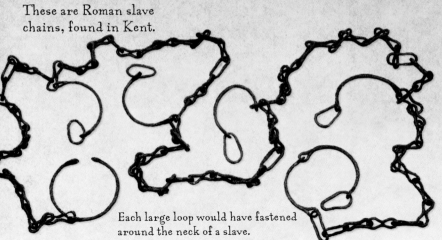

Each large loop would have fastened around the neck of a slave.

The slave trade

In many parts of the world in Roman times, it was common to use slaves for the dirtiest, most difficult and dangerous jobs. But the Romans turned slavery into an international business. When Julius Caesar conquered Gaul, he brought back a million people with him as slaves. They would have been sold at slave markets in Rome and throughout the empire.

The Romans made slaves of anyone they captured in war, but they also made some criminals into slaves as a punishment. When times were desperately hard, some Britons probably sold their relatives or even themselves as slaves.

Sometimes being a slave wasn't so bad. Those with useful skills might get comfortable jobs with kind families or in government. But others were so badly treated they ran away, or died from working in terrible conditions. We know very little about British slaves, as most Romans didn't think slaves were worth mentioning in their written records.

Slave stories

A tombstone from South Shields shows that Regina, a British slave woman, was happily married to a merchant who had come all the way from Palmyra in Syria.

A strip of wood found at Hadrian's Wall preserves a letter sent by a slave named Severus. He wrote to another slave, Candidus, about buying food supplies for a feast.

A wooden tablet found in London records the sale of Fortunata, a slave woman from northern France. She was bought by another slave who had a high-up job in the government of Britain.

61

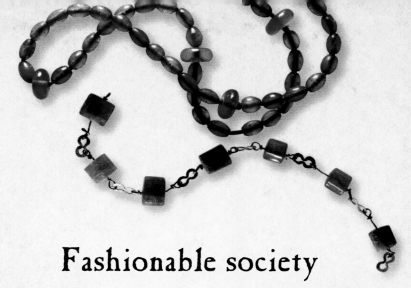

All that glitters

Men and women all piled on the jewels. Accessories like these gold rings showed off your wealth and status.

But brooches and pins weren't just fashion statements – they kept your clothes on. This dragon brooch in a Celtic design would have fastened a cloak.

Fashionable society

Romano-British society had a strict pecking order, which showed in the way people dressed. Slaves, who didn't count as citizens and had no rights, wore very simple clothing, and ordinary citizens dressed little better than their slaves. But people with wealth and power liked to flaunt it, adorning themselves with the finest fabrics and the most glittering gems.

Whatever their age, sex or social status, all Romano-Britons wore a basic garment called a tunic. It was made from two rectangles, or T-shapes, of woollen or linen cloth, sewn at the sides and shoulders, often tied around the waist with a belt or cord.

Celtic chic

Before the Romans came along, the Britons had their own style of dress. While the Romans wore plain clothes in sober shades, the Britons liked bold stripes and plaids, in as many gaudy shades of russet, yellow, blue and purple as possible. They decorated their clothes with embroidered designs and fastened them with large, decorative brooches and belt buckles.

Under Roman influence, Britons began to dress more like their new rulers, but they still kept some of their native styles too, adding distinctive Celtic touches to Roman outfits.

Power dressing

For formal events, men wore a *toga*, a large semicircle of cloth, draped carefully over the tunic. *Togas* were complicated to put on, and so heavy that men had to walk very slowly in them. This looked dignified, but it wasn't very practical – so *togas* were usually only worn by rich men with a leisurely lifestyle. A *toga* was a status symbol. Most men wore undyed *togas*, but politicians were allowed to wear a *toga* with a purple band. Only the emperor could dress all in purple.

The purple stripe on this man's *toga* shows he is a politician.

The woman having her hair done wears a dress called a *stola* over her tunic.

The head of this bone hairpin shows a very elaborate hairstyle that was considered the very height of fashion in the 1st century.

Hairdressing

The Roman emperor and his wife, the empress, set the trends right across the empire. Under Roman rule, men were usually clean-shaven and cut their hair short. But when Emperor Hadrian was depicted on a coin wearing a full beard, many men copied his style.

Women's hairstyles usually involved sweeping long hair into a bun. Slave girls spent hours styling their mistresses' hair in more and more elaborate buns, sometimes using hair pieces, decorated with hairpins and piles of false curls.

Sports and spectacles

To keep their subjects happy and loyal, Roman emperors and officials put on spectacular public shows in every town. These entertainments were often staged as part of public holidays or religious festivals and included plays and chariot races. But most popular of all were the sensational, often very violent, sporting shows, known simply as the games.

The games were held in a large stadium on the edge of town, often with enough seats for the entire local population. A day at the games began with a grand procession of all the performers around the oval arena. This was followed by animal fights, mock hunts, wrestling matches, public executions and finally gladiator combats.

This is how Caerleon Amphitheatre, in South Wales, may have looked during the 2nd century. It has enough seating for an audience of 6,000.

Outside the main arena, people buy snacks and trinkets or watch other entertainments.

Special guests, including local politicians, sit in an enclosed area, where they can enjoy the best views of the games.

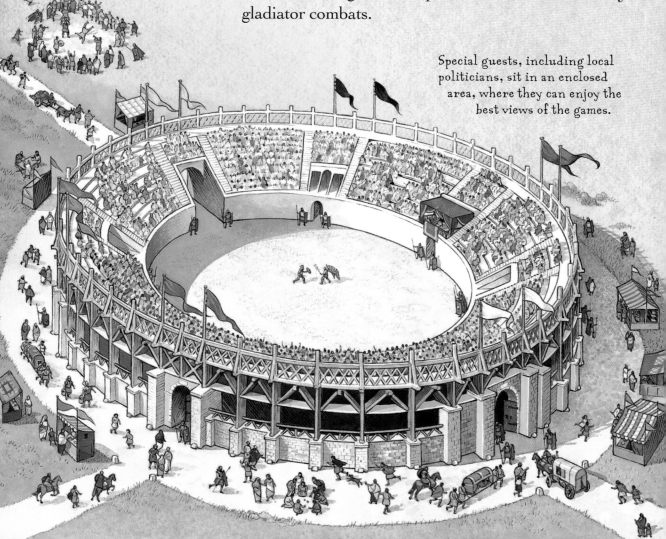

Gladiators

The highlights of the games were undoubtedly the gladiator combats. Gladiators were slaves or prisoners, specially trained to fight. Equipped with different weapons and costumes, they were pitted against each other, and sometimes against animals too.

Gladiators were the superstars of Roman times. If they won enough contests, they could win their freedom. But it was a brutal and bloody sport; gladiators were expected to fight to the death.

This mosaic is from Rudston villa, near Hull. The chariot racer is waving a palm leaf, showing he has won.

High drama

Theatrical shows were another popular form of public entertainment in Roman times. Plays known as tragedies told classical tales of the gods, while comedies were about ordinary people and could be very rude. To compete with the thrill of the games, these dramatic performances included all kinds of special effects, music, dancing and sometimes very realistic violence.

A day at the races

The Britons were skilled in the use of chariots in warfare, so they probably relished the Roman sport of chariot racing for entertainment. Racers hurtled around a large track at breakneck speeds, crashing into one another to try to throw their rivals off course.

The worst collisions, known as shipwrecks, were often fatal. But the violence wasn't always limited to the racetrack. Charioteers raced in teams and serious arguments and even brawls often broke out between fans of opposing sides.

Different strokes

There were several types of gladiators, with different costumes and weapons.

A *murmillo* had a sword, a shield and a helmet with a fish crest.

A *retiarius* fought with a net and a trident.

A *Thracian* had a curved dagger and a small, round shield.

A *Samnite* had a sword, a shield and a helmet with a visor.

65

Gods and goddesses

The official Roman religion was made up of many gods and goddesses. As long as the Britons worshipped the Roman gods, they were free to follow as many other religions as they liked. So, they kept their own local gods alongside Roman ones, as well as adopting exotic cults from all corners of the empire.

The Romans had themselves adopted most of their gods and goddesses from the Greeks, but changed their names to Roman ones.

Each god and goddess was said to control a different aspect of life. The king of the gods was Jupiter. People prayed to Mars for success in war, to Minerva for wisdom, and to Venus for love. Many emperors were even declared gods when they died, and statues and temples to them were built all over the empire. Praying to them was a mark of respect for the Roman rulers.

This is how the temple to the Emperor Claudius in Colchester would have looked before it was destroyed by Boudicca's army in the year 60.

The base of this temple is still standing today, under Colchester Castle. The castle was built on top around a thousand years after the temple was destroyed.

People gather outside the temple for public ceremonies – most of the time, only priests are allowed inside.

Sacred rituals take place at an altar, where offerings are burned to the gods.

Mix 'n' match religions

Like the Romans, the Britons also
worshipped many gods and goddesses.
Some Roman settlers adopted these local
gods, often matching them to Roman gods
with similar characteristics. Over time, the
identities of these gods became blurred and
new ones emerged, combining aspects of native
and Roman gods.

Sacred rituals

Religious rituals took place at temples that housed
statues of the gods. On a special holy day there was a
procession of priests and musicians playing on pipes
and tambourines. When they reached the temple, an
animal – oxen, goats and chickens were common
offerings – was sacrificed on an altar outside. People
also gave other, simpler gifts to the gods, including
cakes, wine and money.

This is part of a
bronze sculpture of
Sulis-Minerva found at
Bath. Her identity
combined Sulis, a local
water nymph, and
Minerva, the Roman
goddess of wisdom.

Exotic cults

Roman soldiers came to Britain from all corners of the
empire, bringing their religions with them. These
included devotion to mother goddesses, such as
Isis from Egypt and Cybele from Turkey.
Mithras, the Persian god of light, was
particularly popular with soldiers and
merchants, because he stood for discipline
and fair play. Only men could worship
Mithras. They met in underground
temples, where they underwent all kinds
of initiation rituals, including being locked
in a tomb for several hours.

The Druids

The Romans accepted
the Britons' religion,
but not their priests,
the Druids.

In the year 60, the
legions stormed
Anglesey, the
Druids' holy
island, and
killed
almost all
of them.

67

God's work

In the 5th century, Patrick, a Romano-British Christian, sailed to Ireland to spread Christian teachings. He became St. Patrick, the patron saint of Ireland.

This is a reconstruction of Lullingstone Roman Villa, in Kent. The side has been cut away so you can see the church inside. The walls are decorated with paintings of religious images and symbols.

Early Christians

Gradually, many people began to lose faith in the state gods and goddesses. Instead, they turned to new religions brought to Britain by Roman soldiers from the Middle East. The most popular was Christianity. Unlike previous religions, this new faith had strict rules on how its followers should live, and it offered them life after death.

Christianity began about 2,000 years ago when a Jew named Jesus started preaching in Judea, a small Roman province in the Middle East. After he died, his followers continued to teach his ideas. By the end of the 2nd century, Christianity had spread right across the Roman empire.

The Romans banned this new religion and persecuted Christians for refusing to worship the Roman emperor or the state gods. Christians risked flogging, prison and even execution if they were caught. But many continued to meet and worship in secret. Some of them even set aside a room in their home to use as a church.

In the cellar, historians found what they think is a pre-Christian shrine.

These painted figures from the house church at Lullingstone show how early Christians prayed, with their arms outstretched.

Dying for the cause

In the early 3rd century, a soldier named Albanus was beheaded after giving shelter to a Christian priest who was fleeing persecution. He was probably the first Romano-Briton to have died for his faith. Many years later, Albanus was made a saint and his town, *Verulamium*, was renamed St. Albans.

The most brutal persecution took place a century later, when Emperor Diocletian ordered the deaths of thousands of Christians across the Roman empire.

A Christian emperor

In 306, there was a new emperor, named Constantine, who was sympathetic to Christians. He ended the persecution and later became a Christian himself. Gradually Christianity gained more and more followers, then in 391, the emperor Theodosius declared it the official Roman faith. Although some people still believed in the old gods, it became illegal to worship them and many old temples were turned into churches.

This mosaic, from a Roman villa in Dorset, is the oldest picture of Jesus Christ in Britain. Behind him are the first two letters of Christ's name in Greek.

Country life

During the Roman occupation, dozens of new towns and army forts were built around Britain. The thousands of people who lived in them didn't have the time or space to grow their own food. But the new road network made it much easier and quicker for farmers to transport their produce to these new consumers. For the first time, farming became big business.

Farming innovations

To supply the growing demand, agriculture became more intensive. Farmers began to rotate their crops – planting a field with corn one year and beans the next – to keep the soil rich. The Romans developed more efficient tools and brought new ideas about fertilizers, land drainage and animal breeding.

New food

The Romans introduced the Britons to many new vegetables, including...

cabbages...

carrots...

lettuce...

...and onions.

Before this, Britons mainly ate bread, stews and porridge.

This scene shows how a Romano-British farm estate would have looked in the 2nd century.

Only an exceptionally wealthy family could afford a palatial *villa*, like the one on this hilltop.

Grand designs

Before Roman times, Britain's farmland was divided into small farms, owned and farmed by individual families and tribes. But, as farming became more commercial, many wealthy landowners bought up huge estates. The peasants no longer owned their own land, but rented homes on the estate they farmed. This social system lasted in England and Wales for the next thousand years.

As farms grew, so did the farmers' houses. Soon after the Roman invasion, many of them began to adopt a more Roman lifestyle, replacing their round houses with rectangular huts in the Roman style, with extra floors, verandahs and annexes. By the late 2nd century, many of these farmhouses had become lavish mansions, which the Romans called *villas*.

The chase

Hunting was central to country life in Roman Britain, both as a sport and for catching food.

This mosaic from Chedworth Roman Villa shows a hunter carrying a deer's antler and a hare. Hunters also chased wild boar and birds.

Pigeons are kept to use as food in winter.

Bees are kept in beehives for their honey.

Oxen do heavy work.

Hens and ducks are kept for their eggs and meat.

Feasting and fun

Whether they lived in a sprawling villa in the countryside or a large town house, known as a *domus*, Roman Britain's rich and famous lived in homes that were luxurious, even by today's standards. For men such as government officials and merchants, it was important that their homes reflected their wealth and status. So they had opulent living rooms, stylish dining rooms and formal courtyard gardens.

"Two measures of beans, 20 chickens, 100 apples if you can find good ones, 200 eggs if they're not too expensive, fish sauce, a measure of olives..."

A shopping list of food for Roman soldiers, found at Vindolanda fort

Home entertainments

Wealthy Romans loved to show off their beautiful homes by throwing extravagant dinner parties that began early in the evening and could last long into the night. Guests removed their sandals at the door and had their feet washed by a slave, before being shown to their places. They ate reclining on cushioned couches arranged in a horseshoe shape in the dining room.

The meal opened with appetizers such as salads, eggs, oysters and sardines. For the main course, fish, meat and poultry were served, often with strong sauces made from fish or spiced fruit. This was followed by fruit, nuts and honey cakes, all washed down with plenty of wine.

On the menu

As well as many types of meat, seafood, grain, fruit and vegetables still widely eaten today, the Romans also ate some dishes that were exotic, to say the least.

1,000 larks' tongues

Stuffed dormice

Sea urchins

Music and dancing

Hosts often hired performers to entertain their dinner guests with music and dancing. Some rich Romans did learn how to play musical instruments, but they thought it was undignified to play in public. So most professional musicians and dancers were slaves. The instruments they played included pipes, lyres (small harps) and tambourines.

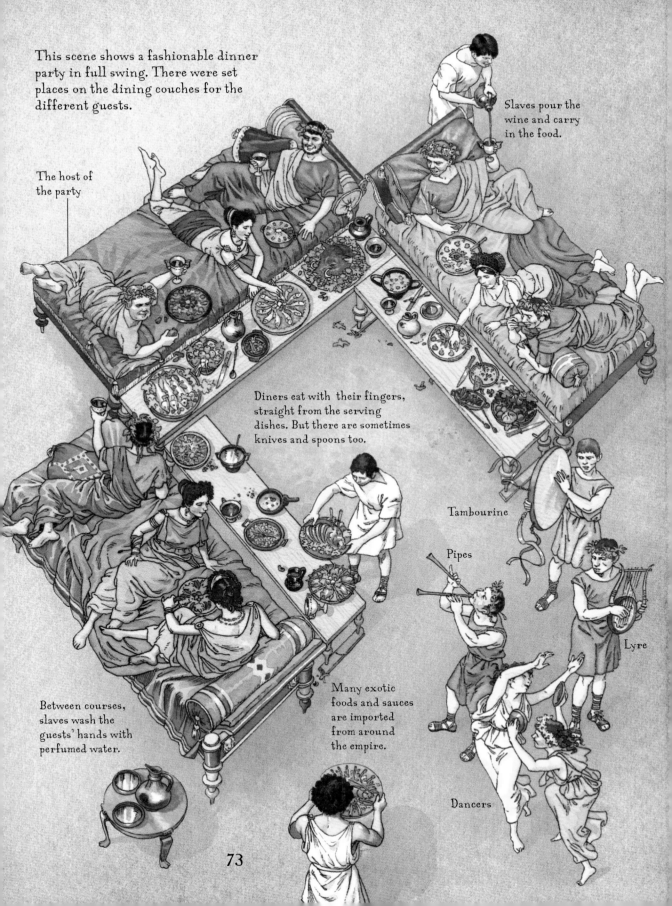

This scene shows a fashionable dinner party in full swing. There were set places on the dining couches for the different guests.

Slaves pour the wine and carry in the food.

The host of the party

Diners eat with their fingers, straight from the serving dishes. But there are sometimes knives and spoons too.

Tambourine

Pipes

Lyre

Between courses, slaves wash the guests' hands with perfumed water.

Many exotic foods and sauces are imported from around the empire.

Dancers

73

Family affairs

In the days before the Romans came, some British women, like Boudicca, held powerful positions. But under Roman rule a woman's place was far more limited. She was expected to stay at home and look after the family.

A typical Romano-British household was made up of the head of the family – the *paterfamilias* – his wife and children and his sons' wives and children. It was the father's duty to lead the rituals that marked the most important events in family life: births, marriages and deaths.

The fragrant plant myrtle, shown here, was often used to make wedding garlands.

In this Roman wedding scene, the *pronuba* (usually the mistress of the house or the bride's mother) is presiding over the ritual clasping of the couple's hands.

Married life

When a Romano-British girl was about 13, her family arranged a marriage for her. Wedding customs varied, but some British families adopted the Roman way of getting married. On the morning of a typical Roman wedding, the bride dressed in a long white tunic with a saffron-yellow veil over her head. Then the family decked the house in ribbons and garlands of flowers.

Wedding vows

When the groom and the guests arrived, a priest sacrificed an animal to the gods. After signing the marriage contract, the bride and groom joined their right hands to say their vows. The ceremony was followed by a feast and a procession to the groom's house.

74

When a child is born

A wife's main duty was to produce lots of children – preferably boys who might bring prosperity to the family. Childbirth was a risky business in Roman times, and shrouded in mystery. During pregnancy, women prayed to the gods for safe delivery of a healthy baby.

When a baby was born, it was placed at the feet of the *paterfamilias*, who lifted it up as a sign that he welcomed it into the family. At nine days old, the baby was named and given a lucky charm, called a *bulla*, to ward off evil spirits.

Ancient medicine

In Roman times, people knew little about how the body works or what causes diseases. Most doctors worked for the army and could only perform very basic operations. So, if a member of the family fell ill, he or she was usually treated by a friend with a little knowledge of herbal remedies. Many people thought sickness was a punishment from the gods. So they tried to find a cure by chanting spells or praying to particular gods with special healing powers.

Funeral fashions

When a person died, the family chanted a funeral song while the body was washed and clothed.

The body was carried to the cemetery outside the town walls, followed by mourners and musicians.

Sometimes, the body was cremated and the ashes put into a pot, like this one decorated with a face.

All these herbs were used to make medicines in Roman times.

Fennel was supposed to calm the nerves.

Sage was used in cough mixtures.

Rosemary was used in remedies for bad eyesight.

Mustard seeds were used to treat snakebites.

Lemon balm was believed to cure headaches.

Growing up

Being a child in Roman times probably wasn't much fun. As soon as they were old enough, most boys were sent to work, while their sisters stayed at home to learn how to spin wool, weave, sew and cook. But, if the family could afford it, at the age of seven, boys and a few girls were sent to a school called a *ludus*.

Before the Romans came, the Britons taught their children by word of mouth, passing on stories, poems and songs about the heroic deeds of their ancestors. Instead of writing these stories down, they learned them all by heart. And because they didn't keep written records of their history and literature, this meant British scholars, such as the Druid priests, were able to keep their learning and ideas secret from outsiders.

Text messages

But after the Romans arrived teaching was based on writing. Paper hadn't been invented yet, so there weren't any books. Instead, children read the works of Roman and Greek authors from large scrolls, made from papyrus reeds. But papyrus was expensive, so they used other surfaces to write out their lessons.

The youngest children tried out their letters by scratching them onto old bits of broken pot. When they were older, they used a pointed tool, called a *stylus*, to scratch words onto a wooden tablet coated with wax. Once the tablet was full, pupils used the flat end of the *stylus* to smooth out the wax, ready to start again. Older children sometimes also wrote on thin sheets of wood, using metal pens dipped in ink.

This scene shows a typical Roman school, known as a *ludus*.

A teacher was called a *pedagogus*. Many were slaves from Greece.

Older students read history and literature from scrolls...

...wrote on wax tablets

...and did sums on a counting frame, or *abacus*.

Younger children scratched letters onto bits of broken pot.

Great expectations

Most children finished school at age 11. But boys from affluent families went on to advanced studies at a school called a *grammaticus*. There, they were groomed for high-flying careers in law or politics. Their lessons included Greek and Roman literature, history, geography and mathematics. Another important subject was public speaking, or rhetoric, which the Romans considered a crucial skill for any official job.

Marbles and games pieces were made from glass, bone or pottery.

The word

To be successful in Roman times, the Britons didn't just need to learn how to read and write; they also had to learn a new language. Lessons were taught in Latin, the official Roman language of government, law, the army, business and trade. In the towns, younger people picked up Latin and passed it on to their children, but Celtic languages were still common at home and in rural areas.

This is a selection of Roman pens, wooden writing tablets and an ink pot with its owner's name, *Iucundus*, scratched onto it.

Child's play

But childhood in Roman Britain wasn't all work and no play. Many children had simple toys, such as dolls, model animals and marbles, which they often had to make for themselves. They also played games that would be familiar today, including dice, board games, hide-and-seek, ball games and hopscotch.

77

Tiny tiles

Decorative floors known as *mosaics* were often laid in grand homes and public buildings. They were made up of thousands of tiny glass, stone or pottery tiles, or *tesserae*, set in concrete.

Designs ranged from simple geometric patterns and borders, to elaborate scenes from ancient myths.

Complex designs were put together in wooden frames in the craftsmen's workshops. These were set in position, then simpler sections were completed on site.

This floor mosaic, from Bignor Roman Villa in Sussex, shows Venus, the goddess of love. The style is typically Roman.

Arts and crafts

Wealthy Romano-Britons loved to fill their homes with beautiful things. They paid highly skilled craftsmen to produce mosaics, sculptures, and beautiful artifacts that we can still admire today.

Artistic styles in Roman Britain combined two very different traditions. The British style was usually abstract, with intricate curved patterns. The Romans, on the other hand, liked to depict the gods, people and nature. Under Roman influence, British craftsmen began to illustrate the same subjects as the Romans, but often using a more decorative style.

This huge dish has the head of the sea god Neptune in the middle. At over 60cm (23in) across, it's the most spectacular piece from a hoard of Roman silverware found by a farmer at Mildenhall in Suffolk in the 1940s.

The treasure was buried at the end of the 4th century, like many other Romano-British hoards. Perhaps people hid things to keep them safe from raiders.

Sculpture

There were many uses for sculptures in Roman Britain. Government officials employed skilled sculptors to produce grand, larger-than-life statues of Roman emperors and dramatic carved battle scenes to grace town squares and public buildings.

At the market, ordinary people could buy small mass-produced statuettes of gods to place in shrines in their homes. Sculptors also applied their skills to decorating people's gravestones with pictures of the dead person at work or with their families.

Gorgeous glass

By the 1st century, the Romans had learned how to blow and shape molten glass to make anything from a simple jar to an exquisite drinking goblet. Plain glass bottles were manufactured cheaply in bulk. Precious glass objects could be made from tinted, engraved or even gilded glass. They were used at elegant dinner parties or put in people's graves as funeral offerings.

This delicate glass jug was discovered in a Roman grave in Buckinghamshire.

Ruling Britannia

In the 180s, trouble flared up once again in Britain, and once again it came from the north. The tribes of Scotland had been reasonably peaceful for 20 years, but now they crossed Hadrian's Wall to invade Roman territory. The Roman army in Britain crushed the rebellion, and the emperor Commodus was so pleased with the victory that he gave himself the title *Britannicus*, meaning Conqueror of Britain.

Power struggles

But this unrest had come at a time when Roman power was weakened by political turmoil back in Rome. By 192, Commodus had been assassinated, and power struggles continued over the next century, as rivals competed to become emperor. Meanwhile Britain, and its strong Roman army, had become an attractive prize for those aiming for total control of the Roman empire.

Divide and rule

After Commodus' death, legions from the different Roman provinces each proclaimed their own leader as the new emperor of Rome. One of them was the British governor, Clodius Albinus, but he was beaten to the top job by Septimius Severus, a general from Africa.

Severus arrived in Britain in 208 and spent three years sorting out all the problems. To prevent future governors becoming too powerful, he split Britain into two provinces: *Britannia Superior* and *Britannia Inferior*. They had a governor each, based in London and York.

80

This is a Roman painting showing the emperor Septimius Severus with his wife Julia Domna and his two sons, Caracalla (on the left) and Geta.

You can see that Geta's face has been scraped off. This is because, after Septimius Severus died, Caracalla killed Geta and had all traces of him wiped out. Caracalla then declared himself emperor.

Rebel empire

After Severus died, the empire was plunged into civil war again. The fighting went on for fifty years and became known as the Anarchy. During this turbulent period, Britain, Gaul, Spain and lower Germany broke away to form an independent Gallic empire. It lasted 14 years until 273, when a strong emperor, Aurelian, brought the provinces back under Roman control.

Minted

During the Anarchy, steep price rises and high taxes drove some people to forge counterfeit coins. Aurelian made reforms to prevent this. Like many Roman emperors, he also used the coinage to boost his public image. Every coin showed his portrait on one side and publicized his latest achievements on the other. This showed the people who was boss and kept them up-to-date with the news.

This gold coin shows Aurelian on the front...

...and his victory over the rebel provinces on the back.

81

New invaders

Near the end of the 3rd century, tribesmen from northern Germany, called Saxons, launched a number of pirate raids on ships in the North Sea. To protect themselves from further raids, the Romano-Britons built a string of forts along the coast from Brancaster in the east all the way to Portchester in the south. They called it the Saxon shore.

Compared to the usual Roman forts, the Saxon shore forts varied a lot in shape, their walls were higher and thicker, and they had more lookout towers.

Emperor of Britain

Carausius, a Roman admiral in charge of the fleet in the English Channel, was responsible for building some of the Saxon shore forts. But in 286 he was accused of keeping some of the Saxon pirates' bounty for himself. To avoid being punished, he seized control of Britain and proclaimed himself Emperor. While the Saxon shore forts kept the Saxons out, they probably helped Carausius to fend off the Romans too, for a while.

The Saxons' name is thought to have come from the weapon they used – a type of knife known as a *seax*.

Portchester Castle, near Portsmouth, is one of the Saxon shore forts built by Carausius in the 280s.

In this photograph, you can also see a castle (in the bottom left corner) and a church that were built inside the Roman walls in the 12th century.

Carausius and his independent British empire held out for ten years – until the Romans invaded and recaptured Britain. This time, the Romans divided the land into four provinces, with new capitals at Cirencester and Lincoln.

Imperial York

In 306, the emperor Constantius, who had been leading the Roman army in Britain, died in York, surrounded by his family. His son Constantine was immediately declared emperor by his troops in York – although he had to return to Rome and fight a rival before he could take control of the empire. Like Commodus before him, Constantine took the title *Britannicus*, showing that he had won a victory in Britain, though history doesn't record the details.

The trouble continues

For the emperors after Constantine Britain became more and more of a problem. They had to face increasing attacks from beyond the frontier, as well as rebellions inside the province. But Britain wasn't the only part of their empire that was causing concern.

By the end of the 4th century, Roman power over western Europe was starting to decline. A succession of weak emperors and attacks on the frontiers had taken their toll. So the Romans began to withdraw troops from Britain in order to defend other parts of their empire. Even the city of Rome itself was under threat. Finally, after four centuries, Roman rule in Britain came to an end.

Eboracum

The city of York – known to the Romans as Eboracum – in the north of England was made the capital of *Britannia Inferior* in the 3rd century.

It was unusual that Constantine was declared emperor there – normally the only city where this could take place was Rome.

But Constantine wasn't the first emperor to spend time in York. The earlier emperor, Septimius Severus, spent three years ruling the empire from York, until he died there in 211.

Despite the turmoil elsewhere, Britain was still peaceful and prosperous in the first half of the 4th century. Craftsmen were building lavish villas and creating fine mosaics and furnishings to put in them.

Decline and fall

By the beginning of the 5th century, the Saxons had intensified their raids in the south of Britain. The north was also under increasing attack too, from Caledonians and Picts from Scotland and tribes from Ireland breaking through Hadrian's Wall. In 410, Rome itself was overrun by Germanic tribes. The emperor, Honorius, told Britain it would have to fend for itself.

Although Roman rule was over, the Roman way of life lingered on in parts of Britain for the next 150 years. But gradually, more and more people started leaving the towns to live in the country, and once-grand public buildings were falling into disrepair. In the north and west, little changed. People continued to live as they had before the Romans, keeping their languages and culture alive.

But, in the 5th and 6th centuries, southern Britain came under new influences. Invading tribes of Saxons, Angles and Jutes, from what is now Germany, settled down and formed their own kingdoms. It was the beginning of a new age for Britain.

This is a modern painting showing a gang of Saxon raiders attacking a walled city in Roman Britain.

Map of Roman Britain, 43-410

This picture map shows the most important Roman landmarks, towns and roads in Britain.

- **Legionary fortress**
- **Major fort**
- **Saxon shore fort**
- **Villa**
- **Temple**
- **Capital**
- **Major town** – *colonia* or *civitas* capital (with Roman name)

Inchtuthil

Antonine Wall

Bearsden   Bar Hill

Newstead

CALEDONIANS AND PICTS

Carrawburgh   Wallsend

Housesteads   Chesters

Hadrian's Wall

Birdoswald   Corbridge   South Shields

Vindolanda   Newcastle-upon-Tyne

Hardknott

Ambleside

BRIGANTES

Aldborough (*Isurium Brigantum*)

Rudston

York (*Eboracum*)

Brough (*Petuaria Parisorum*)

Anglesey

Caernarfon (*Segontium*)

Chester (*Deva*)

Wroxeter (*Viroconium Cornoviorum*)

DRUIDS

Lincoln (*Lindum*)

Brancaster

Caistor (*Venta Icenorum*)

Leicester (*Ratae Coritanorum*)

Burgh Castle

BOUDICCA AND THE ICENI

CARATACUS AND THE CATUVELLAUNI

Fosse Way

Ermine Street

Watling Street

Colchester (*Camulodunum*)

Walton Castle

Carmarthen (*Moridunum*)

Gloucester (*Glevum*)

Caerwent (*Venta Silurum*)

Chedworth

Woodchester

Cirencester (*Corinium*)

Caerleon (*Isca*)

Lydney

Uley

St. Albans (*Verulamium*)

London (*Londinium*)

Bradwell-on-Sea

Canterbury

Reculver

Richborough

Cardiff

Bath (*Aquae Sulis*)

Silchester (*Calleva Atrebatum*)

Lullingstone

Dover (*Dubris*)

Low Ham

Winchester (*Venta Belgarum*)

Lympne

Hinton-St-Mary

Bignor

Pevensey Castle

Exeter (*Isca Dumnoniorum*)

Dorchester (*Dumovaria*)

Brading

Fishbourne

Portchester Castle

THE EARLY MIDDLE AGES

After the Romans left Britain, chaos ruled for some time. Local leaders vied with each other to control their land and people, and to fight off wave upon wave of bloodthirsty raiders who arrived in ships to take valuables, people and land for themselves.

But gradually, strong local leaders emerged and began to create order, organizing huge armies and bringing back civilized skills such as reading and writing once again. Over time, smaller territories merged together under these great leaders, and the British nations we know today – England, Ireland, Scotland and Wales – were slowly formed.

The Dark Ages

When the Romans left Britain, history went with them. Or, to put it another way, Britain more or less disappeared from written history. As the Roman system of government broke down, all its form-filling and letter-writing gradually vanished. People in Britain just didn't see the need to write things down any more. And because there are so few writings from this period, it's difficult to know exactly what was happening.

Without a clue

Many of the other clues that usually help historians, such as objects or buildings, are also missing. Once the sturdy Roman buildings and tools had fallen apart, people had to rely on cheap, flimsy materials such as leather and wood, which often rot down quickly leaving no trace. Because historians are more or less in the dark about what was going on at this time, it's sometimes known as the Dark Ages. But the little that is known suggests it was a dark time for Britain, too.

These spearheads survived from the Dark Ages because they were made from iron. The handles are modern.

This scene shows some early raiders arriving in Britain. They struck coastal settlements first and then gradually worked their way inland.

Invasions

The few people who did keep a record of events had a grim story to tell. They wrote of devastating invasions during the 5th century, from around the year 450. Things soon became so bad, they reported, that much of southern and eastern Britain was occupied by three groups of invaders. They came from the areas we know as Scandinavia and Germany and some writers named them as the Saxons, the Angles and the Jutes.

Record keeper

The most detailed account of these invasions that survives was written by a monk named Bede around the year 730, more than 300 years after the invasions began. He reported that the Jutes ended up living on the Isle of Wight and the part of the mainland opposite it. The Angles took over the area we now know as East Anglia and the lands to the north of it. The Saxons gave their name to the areas they occupied: Sussex for the South Saxons, Wessex for the West Saxons and Essex for the East Saxons.

True or false?

Historians now think that the story Bede recorded may not have been correct in all its details, and this isn't too surprising given that he hadn't even been born when these events took place. But, generally, what he wrote about the invasions was fairly accurate.

It's also clear that the British tried their hardest to stop the invaders. The story of their resistance quickly became the stuff of legend, woven around the mysterious figure of King Arthur…

Making books

During the Dark Ages, some of the only people who wrote things down were Christian monks living together in isolated communities known as monasteries.

They couldn't get hold of many of the writing materials the Romans had used, so they treated cow and sheep skins to create smooth sheets, known as vellum or parchment.

They wrote using pens made from feathers and ink made from parts of oak trees. Then, they sewed up the pages into books. Some of these books still survive today.

King Arthur

Experts are fairly sure that there never was a British leader called Arthur. But some of them think that stories about Arthur may preserve a faint memory of a long-forgotten leader who united the British against the invading Angles and Saxons.

Scholars from Wales were the first to mention Arthur in writing. They wanted to show that the British had put up a good fight against the invaders, even though they lost in the end. Later writers added characters such as Lancelot and Gawain, and tales like the Holy Grail, to create long and complex stories.

Making a point

Arthur has often been used to score political points. For example, the Tudor family, who took the English throne in 1485, claimed they were descended from King Arthur to support their shaky claim to the crown. Even today, heirs to the British throne, including Prince Charles and Prince William, have Arthur as one of their names, in memory of the great king.

This 14th century picture illustrates a popular story about how the young King Arthur pulled a magic sword from a stone to prove he was the rightful King of England.

This is how the story of Arthur took shape...

Around 550

A priest from Wales named Gildas writes about a general called Ambrosius, who led the British to victory against the Angles and Saxons. It's possible the name 'Ambrosius' was mistaken for 'Artorius' or 'Arthur' by later writers.

Around 830

A writer known as Nennius, who was probably from Wales, writes of a powerful military leader called Arthur who won many battles against the Angles and Saxons.

Around 1130

A Welsh writer named Geoffrey of Monmouth describes how a king named Arthur defeated the Saxons and united Britain, with the help of Merlin the magician.

1160-90

Chrétien de Troyes, a French writer, writes many stories about Arthur and his knights, including Lancelot, Gawain and Percival. He describes Arthur's court at Camelot and the Quest for the Holy Grail.

1344

King Edward III decides to bring back the noble traditions of King Arthur. He holds a tournament called a 'Round Table' at Windsor Castle.

1469-70

Sir Thomas Malory, an English writer, completes his book telling the whole story of Arthur from beginning to end. In 1485, this becomes one of the first books to be printed in Britain.

1485

Henry Tudor becomes King of England. His family claims to be descended from King Arthur, to help to prove their right to the throne.

1691

Poet John Dryden and composer Henry Purcell write the first opera about King Arthur.

1840-1900

Many stories, poems and pictures about King Arthur are created by writers including Alfred Tennyson and Mark Twain and artists such as Gustav Doré and William Morris.

1960

'Camelot' the musical is produced by Alan Jay Lerner and Frederick Loewe. In 1967, it's released as a film, too.

1982

Prince William is born and named William Arthur Philip Louis.

91

New kingdoms

Whatever resistance there really was to the invasions, it didn't work. Clearly, the newcomers wanted to stay. Some experts think they may have been driven out of their homelands on the coast of Germany by rising water levels.

By around 600, the south and east of Britain were permanently occupied by people who brought with them their own types of housing, clothing and ornaments, their pagan religious beliefs and their Germanic languages. They changed Britain forever, and played a vital role in shaping the English language that we speak today. These people are often known as the Anglo-Saxons.

A divided land

But the Britons didn't just melt away. For the ones who lived in the south and east, being taken over by an invading force wasn't anything new. After all, the Romans had settled most heavily there, too. So, many Britons probably stayed on in these areas, perhaps working for the newcomers and gradually adopting their language, religion and way of life. Over time, several kingdoms – run by different groups of Angles and Saxons – emerged there.

But in the western parts of Britain and in the north of England, Celtic-speaking Britons stayed in control. They were probably joined by Britons fleeing the south and east.

Further north, the Picts, who had managed to resist even the Romans, controlled much of what is now Scotland. The exception was the kingdom of Dalriada, which was run by the Celtic-speaking tribe known as the Scots, who had come over from Ireland.

This map shows the different regions and the most important kingdoms in Britain around the year 600.

Pictish kingdoms
Celtic kingdoms
Anglo-Saxon kingdoms

Resistance movement

The Celtic kingdoms who were still free from the invaders kept in close contact with each other. Although the people in different areas now spoke variations of the Celtic languages, they still understood one another. They also shared many customs – including their religion, Christianity. Some of them even revived ancient Celtic traditions, to show the Anglo-Saxons they were proud to be British.

In the west of England, Britons rebuilt old hillforts first used by their Iron Age ancestors, patching up the walls with stone from crumbling Roman buildings nearby. They also adapted the traditional swirling style of decorations first used in the Iron Age, using them to decorate not only traditional metalwork but also new Christian books. So, alongside their ancient crafts, they preserved the skills and beliefs they had learned during the Roman occupation. Eventually, both the Britons' stylish craftwork and their religion had a huge impact on Anglo-Saxon culture.

Meanwhile, in the south and east of England, a very different way of life was taking shape.

Rich grave

British tribes probably hated and feared the Anglo-Saxons, but they still traded with them. We know this because British goods were found in the rich burial of an Anglo-Saxon king found at Sutton Hoo in Suffolk.

The king was buried in a ship with lots of his possessions. He was probably Redwald, a ruler of the East Angles, who died around the year 625.

This hanging bowl was among the finds in the Sutton Hoo ship burial. It is made of beaten metal, with decorations of red, blue and green enamel and glass.

It was probably made by British metalworkers and given to the Anglo-Saxon king, perhaps as a gift or as part of an exchange.

93

The Anglo-Saxons

The Anglo-Saxon invaders were born fighters. They started fighting as soon as they jumped off their ships, and gradually battled their way inland, taking more land as they needed it.

This picture from a late Anglo-Saxon book shows two farmers at work, harvesting their crops with huge tools known as scythes.

A farming life

But fighting was just one part of life for Anglo-Saxons. Once they had some land, most of them settled down to live peacefully as farmers. An ordinary Anglo-Saxon farmer usually owned a small piece of land – the right size to grow enough food for one family. This amount of land was known as a *hide*, and the man who owned it was known as a *ceorl* (say *churl*).

Ceorls and their families grew wheat, oats and barley, peas and beans, and raised pigs, sheep, goats and cows. They lived near their fields in houses made from sturdy wooden frames, finished with mud and reeds. A man who owned more than five hides of land was known as a *thegn* (say *thane*). Thegns had bigger farms and bigger wooden houses, known as halls. And above the thegns was the king.

"Ten vats of honey, 300 loaves of bread, 42 measures of ale, two cows or ten sheep, ten geese, 20 hens, ten cheeses, one measure of butter, five salmon, 100 eels..."

List of goods collected from every 10 families each year for the king, from a 7th century Anglo-Saxon law code.

Living like a king

The king lived off food and goods collected from each ceorl and thegn in the kingdom. Administrators assessed what each landowner should pay, based on how much land he owned and what he produced on his farm. It might sound as though the king had an easy life, but it wasn't a job for the faint-hearted. Only strong fighters became kings, and they might be challenged or killed by anyone who thought that they weren't up to the job.

The king lived in a large and ornate hall, along with his bravest and most loyal thegns. He took the lead in any fighting, helped by his thegns – and he had to reward them regularly with lavish feasts and gifts of fine weapons, rich jewels and land, to make sure they stayed with him.

Sometimes kings also swore their loyalty to other, more powerful kings nearby. This meant that the lesser king had to support the greater one in fighting, and give him valuable gifts. So, all in all, being a king was a very expensive business. No wonder Anglo-Saxon kings were always raiding each other's territory for more loot and land.

This scene shows a powerful Anglo-Saxon thegn giving a huge feast in his hall. The guests are eating meat cooked on the central fire and drinking ale, while a poet entertains them with stories set to music.

Week days

The Anglo-Saxons named days of the week after their important gods:

Tiw's day (Tuesday) Tiw was the god of bravery and fighting.

Woden's day (Wednesday) Woden was the chief of the gods.

Thor's day (Thursday) Thor was the god of war and thunder.

Friya's day (Friday) Friya was the goddess of love and beauty.

This is a 7th century Anglo-Saxon box lid, carved with gods and heroes. It also features writing in letters known as *runes*. You can see them above the figure on the right with the bow and arrow. They spell his name, *Aegil*.

The English language

Unlike the Celtic-speaking Britons, some of whom understood Latin and could read and write, the Anglo-Saxons only spoke a Germanic language, and they weren't great readers or writers. But the Anglo-Saxon language gradually spread. After many shifts and changes, it became the English language that's spoken across much of the world today. Many words in modern English point back to the Anglo-Saxons – for example, some of the days of the week are still named after their gods.

Beliefs and customs

Unlike the Christian British, the Anglo-Saxons were pagans and prayed to many different gods who, they believed, were in charge of rocks, trees and other aspects of nature.

The Anglo-Saxons had strict rules about how to behave, and a strong sense of family loyalty, even to very distant relatives. For example, if any member of their family was murdered, they felt it was fair to kill someone from the murderer's family, unless they received some money in compensation. Laws set out the amount of compensation money for different types of victim – more for thegns, a little less for ceorls, and less again for women and the lowest of the low, slaves.

Pecking order

Most Anglo-Saxon women had fairly limited lives. They were in charge of spinning and weaving thread, sewing and caring for clothes, furnishings and bedlinen. They also brewed and served drinks such as ale and *mead*, a strong drink made from fermented honey.

Slaves had even fewer rights. Some were born into slave families; others were captured in wars. They had to help with all the hardest and dirtiest jobs.

Farming and fighting

On the other hand, free Anglo-Saxon men had very active lives. They were farmers, but they also hunted for meat, using dogs to track down deer and wild boar and hawks to hunt pigeons and other birds. They had to be ready to fight whenever necessary, and they paid for their weapons themselves. All fighters carried long spears with iron points, and sometimes they also had sharp iron battle axes or swords.

This magnificent iron helmet is decorated with bronze, gold, silver and jewels. It probably belonged to an Anglo-Saxon king, and may have acted as his crown, as well as his helmet. Only very wealthy warriors had helmets.

Clothes and fashion

Both Anglo-Saxon men and women wore loose-fitting tunics woven from wool or linen, gathered with a belt at the waist. Women's tunics came down to their ankles, but men wore knee-length tunics with cloth leggings underneath. For extra warmth, people wore cloaks fixed in place with metal brooches. They had leather shoes and bags.

Even kings just wore more luxurious versions of the same clothes and accessories.

Dressing up

The Anglo-Saxons wove cloth from wool and linen, dyed with plant juices. Their clothes were warm and practical, but they piled on lots of ornaments too.

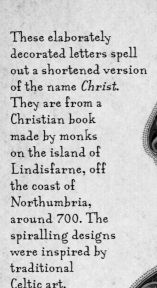

These elaborately decorated letters spell out a shortened version of the name *Christ*. They are from a Christian book made by monks on the island of Lindisfarne, off the coast of Northumbria, around 700. The spiralling designs were inspired by traditional Celtic art.

Saint David

Christians in Wales were too busy fighting the Anglo-Saxons to try to convert them. During one battle, a religious leader named Dewidd is supposed to have told the Britons to attach leeks to their hats, so they could see each other more clearly on the battlefield. Dewidd is now known as Saint David and the leek is a Welsh national emblem.

Christianity returns

By the late 6th century, the Anglo-Saxon kingdoms were becoming more organized. But Christians in Ireland and Italy were worried because the Christian Britons had been pushed aside by the new, pagan settlers. So Church leaders decided to send missionaries to Britain, to try to convert the Anglo-Saxon kings to the Christian faith. They hoped that the ordinary people would then follow, too.

Holy island

One of the first missionaries to make an impact was an Irish monk named Columba. He converted the Pictish people in the north of Scotland and, around 563, he set up a monastery on the tiny island of Iona off the northwest coast. As the Christian message spread, Irish monks moved south and set up new monasteries in Essex (in southeast England) and Wessex, Northumbria and Mercia (see map on page 105).

Moving south

Meanwhile, Roman monks were targeting the south of Britain on the orders of their leader, the Pope. In 597, a monk named Augustine arrived in Kent to meet the king, Aethelbert.

At first, Aethelbert thought the monk would try to cast magic spells on him, but he soon changed his mind and was baptized as a Christian. Augustine set up a monastery at Canterbury in Kent and became the first Archbishop of Canterbury – a job that still exists today. There were baptisms in Essex too, and several monasteries were founded, including one in London.

Little angels

Augustine is supposed to have had his first sight of Anglo-Saxon people at a slave market in Rome. The fair skin and hair of some young slaves made Augustine exclaim that they were *angels*, not *Angles!*

Double trouble

By the late 7th century, Christianity had spread across Britain and there were monasteries and churches everywhere. Monks, nuns and priests taught people about Christianity, but also about all the skills they had preserved since Roman times: reading and writing, the Latin language, painting and the art of building in stone. The Anglo-Saxons were grateful – with this knowledge, they could run their kingdoms more efficiently and build magnificent palaces.

But unfortunately the monks from Irish and Roman monasteries argued about the right way to do things, and a huge row blew up when they couldn't agree how to fix the date for Easter each year. In 664, they held a meeting at Whitby Abbey to try to settle their differences. The Roman monks won the day, and Christians across Britain agreed to be guided by the teachings of the Pope in Rome.

This photograph shows the ruins of Whitby Abbey in Yorkshire. It was first founded in 657 by an Anglo-Saxon nun named Hild. She was still in charge when Roman and Irish Church leaders held discussions there in 664.

The rise of Mercia

Even though Anglo-Saxon kings now welcomed Christian monks, this didn't mean they always followed their teachings. In fact, some kings were proving that ruthless violence was a very effective way of making themselves richer and more powerful.

For King Aethelbald of Mercia – who ruled from 716 to 757 – receiving gifts and services from less powerful kings nearby was no longer enough. He started calling himself not just King of Mercia, but King of the South English. To prove it, he began to act as though he ruled Kent and London too – but other kingdoms resisted him.

This photograph shows part of Offa's Dyke, a huge earth wall along the boundary between England and Wales.

The dyke was finished during the reign of King Offa of Mercia, and was so huge that sections of it still survive today.

King Offa

Aethelbald's successor, Offa, went even further. During his reign, from 757 to 796, he expanded Mercia hugely by capturing land from nearby kings. In the end, he more or less took over all the Anglo-Saxon kingdoms, except for Northumbria and Wessex.

So that no one would challenge him, he had many of the lesser Anglo-Saxon kings killed and took the title of 'king' away from others. He also tried hard to conquer the people of Wales, fighting many battles against them. But their mountainous country and steady resistance defeated him.

Building barriers

Both Aethelbald and Offa needed to be very organized to keep control of such large territories. They kept lots of written records, and came up with new ways of defending their land. For example, they made it compulsory for all landowners to help them build a series of massive new fortifications. Soon, defensive earth banks and ditches were springing up around Mercia's important settlements. A vast earth wall was also built between England and Wales, to prevent attacks from the Welsh side. It is known as Offa's Dyke and much of it is still standing today.

Money man

Offa also decided to start producing coins. His silver pennies had his portrait on them, and were some of the first coins to be used in Britain since Roman times. They must have seemed very impressive, as most people weren't used to coins – they just exchanged one type of goods for another.

New money

This silver penny issued by King Offa of Mercia has his portrait stamped on the front. You can see the back of the coin too.

Offa also issued this gold coin. The design copied gold coins from the Middle East. The front is shown on the left.

Offa's wife, Cynethryth, had her portrait on the front of some coins, like this one. The back of the coin is on the right.

Trade, language and learning

During the 8th century, trade was on the increase across Europe, and Anglo-Saxons seized their opportunities. Coins were now widely used. They made trade easier for everyone, because people knew how much each coin was worth, and were sure they weren't being cheated. Carrying the small, light coins was also much simpler than exchanging goods for other goods that might be bulky or easily spoiled.

A series of trading ports sprang up all around the coasts of northwest Europe and southeast England at this time. The Anglo-Saxons called them *wics*, and this word is still part of place names such as Sandwich on the south coast. Other *wics* were at Southampton, also on the south coast, and at London, Ipswich and York on the east coast. There, locals and merchants from all over Europe could trade goods with one another.

Men of letters

It wasn't just trade that was becoming more international. Thanks to monks, Latin had caught on in the Anglo-Saxon kingdoms as the language for anything official. This was useful, as people in other parts of Europe understood it too. Educated Anglo-Saxons wrote to people all over Europe.

Letters still survive that were sent by King Offa of Mercia to Charlemagne, King of the Franks, a people who lived in the areas that are now known as France and Germany.

Charlemagne also corresponded with Alcuin, an Anglo-Saxon scholar from Northumbria, whose fame for learning and wisdom had spread across Europe. In the end Alcuin went to live at Charlemagne's court and became one of his most trusted advisers.

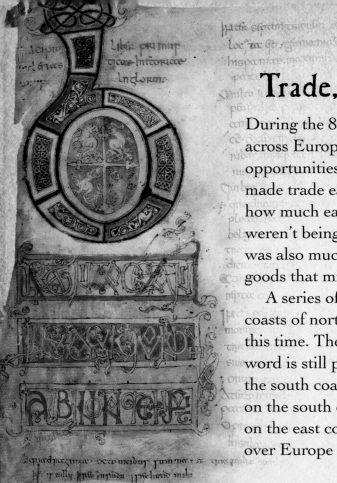

This is part of the opening page of a history book completed in 731 by Bede, the Northumbrian monk and historian. His history of England covered the period from the time of the Romans up to his own day.

Historians still rely on Bede's work today, although parts are now thought to be inaccurate.

Coming together

All over Britain, people were borrowing ideas from other cultures, too. While Latin was used for international communication, the Anglo-Saxon language was developing. Poets began composing poems with a distinctly Anglo-Saxon feel, but inspired by stories and verse styles from northern Europe. The most famous poem to survive is named *Beowulf* after its hero, and records his heroic battles with monsters and dragons.

Metalworkers, carvers and painters were bringing together the delicate interlacing patterns found in Celtic-speaking areas with bold Anglo-Saxon designs, to produce ornaments in an intricate new style.

In *Beowulf*, the hero kills a terrible marsh-monster named Grendel with his bare hands.

Drifting apart

But, across Europe people were also becoming more aware of their own separate cultures. People from the Celtic-speaking areas we now call Ireland, Cornwall, Wales and Scotland were in close contact with each other, but their languages were continuing to develop along separate lines. Although these places were divided up into many different kingdoms, the more powerful ones were now organizing joint forces to resist the Anglo-Saxons.

So Britain was beginning to split itself up into the separate regions we recognize today.

This magnificent silver, gold and amber brooch was made around the year 700. It combines styles from England, Germany, Ireland and Scotland.

Raiders from the sea

This scene shows a Viking raid on a monastery. The raiders are stealing valuable objects, capturing or killing the locals, and destroying buildings.

In around 789, three long, low ships appeared off the coast of Wessex. As they came into shore, the local official rode out to greet the newcomers. Without a second thought, the men from the ships killed him. This was only the first in a series of bloody raids by attackers who stripped settlements of valuables, killed anyone who stood in their way and then sailed off.

These fearsome attackers were warriors known as Vikings. They came from the areas we now call Norway, Denmark and Sweden. For the next 60 years or so, shiploads of Vikings arrived in the spring and summer to seize everything they could carry away on their boats. When they left, they often burned or wrecked anything they couldn't take with them.

People in Britain didn't know what to do. It was no good gathering an army to fight off the Vikings, as no-one knew where or when the next raid might be. Instead, they prayed for help, but this didn't seem to make any difference. In fact, the Vikings often targeted churches and monasteries for their precious ornaments, killing the monks and burning their books. Some people thought God had abandoned them.

From bad to worse

Then, in 851, things changed. For the first time, the Vikings didn't sail away at the end of the summer. Instead, they camped near their boats for the winter, living off the spoils of their summer raids, so as to be in place for the next round of raids in the spring. It wasn't long before they decided to stay for good.

By the mid-860s, the Vikings were planning to conquer Britain. A huge army of Danish Vikings landed in 865. By 870, they had conquered Northumbria and East Anglia, weakened the once-powerful kingdom of Mercia, and were preparing to attack Wessex.

At the same time, a band of Vikings from Norway was attacking and settling along the northwest coast and in parts of Ireland.

In just a few years, the Vikings had conquered much of Britain. They must have seemed unstoppable. But who were they?

✝ monasteries targeted in Viking raids

Iona

Lindisfarne

Jarrow

Northumbria

York

Mercia

East Anglia

Wessex

This map shows the main late 9th century Anglo-Saxon kingdoms. The areas that are now Scotland and Wales were unconquered by the Vikings.

These metal heads of Viking weapons were found in London. The wooden handles are modern.

105

The Vikings

The lands that the Vikings came from were criss-crossed by rivers and lakes, and bordered by seas. Surrounded by all this water, the Vikings had become master shipbuilders and navigators. They sailed their ships far around the world, often following the migration routes of birds and fish.

By the 9th century, they had outgrown their homelands and were seeking new places to live. They struck out across Europe, Africa and Asia, and the most intrepid even reached as far as North America. Many modern place names are reminders of their travels – Greenland was named by Viking explorers, and Russia gets its name from the Rus tribe of Vikings.

Many Viking warships had dragon heads like this one at the front, to scare their enemies.

Sailing the seas

The designs for Viking ships had been perfected by generations of expert shipbuilders. Their fast, streamlined ships were made from wooden planks held together by iron rivets, and were coated with tar from pine trees.

Viking warships, called *longships*, could be rowed up rivers to attack towns and villages inland.

Merchant ships, called *knorrs*, had a pit in the middle to hold goods.

When a powerful Viking died, his body was put in a ship with his most valued treasures. Then the ship was buried or sent out to sea, sometimes in flames.

Earning a living

Many Vikings were merchants, and their trade routes spanned much of the known world. They carried furs, slaves and amber to the east to trade in the huge city of Constantinople (now Istanbul) and crossed deserts to reach the Arabian city of Baghdad. Then they returned laden with silver, spices, silk and other luxury goods.

Other Viking trading posts lay closer to home. Remnants of key settlements have been found under Dublin in Ireland, and beneath the northern English city of York – known as *Jorvik* by the Vikings.

Viking York

Thousands of Viking objects have been found in York, including clothing and shoes made from leather and other fabrics, utensils such as wooden cups, and a range of intricate metal knives and ornaments. Visiting merchants would have traded these wares for goods from overseas.

Waste from Viking food was also discovered, including bones of animals and fish, and seeds from fruit and vegetables. Archaeologists even uncovered some human skeletons. Experts have used computer imaging techniques to build a picture of what a Viking face might have looked like, based on one of the skulls.

Brothers at arms

Although the Vikings and Anglo-Saxons were now at loggerheads, they had much in common. Both groups were made up of farming people and warriors intent on conquering new lands. The Viking religion was also very similar to the one the Anglo-Saxons had followed before they converted to Christianity.

Viking gods

The Vikings believed in many gods and goddesses. Here are some of the main ones:

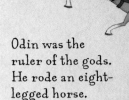

Odin was the ruler of the gods. He rode an eight-legged horse.

Thor carried a hammer, and drove across the sky in a thundering chariot.

Freya was the goddess of love and death. She had a magic cloak made of falcon feathers, which she could use to fly.

Alfred the Great

Having conquered Northumbria, East Anglia and much of Mercia, the Viking raiders now turned their attentions to Wessex.

One cold winter day in January 871, King Aethelred of Wessex rode out to meet the Viking army that was poised to attack on the frosty Berkshire Downs. He was accompanied by his forces, and his younger brother Alfred. They won the battle that followed – but it was only the start of what would be a long and bitter struggle between the Vikings and the Wessex kings.

It's thought that this jewel was ordered by Alfred himself. A pointer was probably attached to it for following words in a book while reading. During his reign, Alfred tried hard to revive reading and writing skills.

Not-so-great chef

A legend tells of how Alfred met a peasant woman while he was hiding. Not knowing who he was, she left him in charge of cooking some cakes. But Alfred was thinking about the kingdom's problems and let them burn.

Disaster strikes

In the spring of 871, Aethelred died. At the same time, a horde of Viking reinforcements arrived from Denmark. Alfred, now King of Wessex, tried his best to fight them off, but he spent the first year of his reign on the losing side of skirmishes. Eventually he gave in, and paid the Vikings not to attack Wessex again.

Christmas carnage

This break in the fighting didn't last long. In 876, a Danish leader called Guthrum headed another Viking attack on Wessex. This time, Alfred managed to drive them off.

But, less than two years later, Guthrum launched a surprise attack on Alfred and his followers, who had just finished celebrating Christmas. The Wessex forces were taken completely off-guard, and many were killed. Alfred himself only just managed to escape, by running away and hiding in marshland.

Turn of the tide

Alfred spent several desperate months
in the marshes, on the move with only a
few followers. But he worked tirelessly
to gather support, and by May, he was
ready to take on the Vikings again. He
rallied his forces, and they set off to face
Guthrum's army.

It was the Vikings' turn to be caught
unawares. They fled the battle, and
surrendered two weeks later. Alfred
agreed peace terms, on the condition that
Guthrum became a Christian. Guthrum
promised not to attack Wessex again, while
Alfred accepted that Viking settlers were in
England for good. The two leaders also set a
boundary between their lands. Alfred's land lay
to the west of it, and the Vikings' lay to the east.

Leader of the English

The Viking part of England became known as
the Danelaw, because of its Danish customs and
culture. Meanwhile, Alfred was rearranging
his army into a better fighting unit. He also
ordered a fleet of ships, and built fortified
towns. With his strengthened forces, he was
able to keep Wessex safe from Viking attacks.

Other Anglo-Saxon leaders began to look
to Alfred for leadership too. To break down
barriers between different kingdoms, Alfred
developed the idea of a united England.
Under his influence, the Anglo-Saxons began
to call themselves *Angelcynn* – the English.

Alfred is remembered as the
greatest Anglo-Saxon king.
This statue of him was put up
in Winchester, his capital, one
thousand years after his death.

United kingdoms?

The Scottish island of Iona was the burial place for many early Scottish kings, including Kenneth MacAlpin.

Before the 9th century, most of Britain was made up of fairly small kingdoms. But during the Viking raids, many of these began to join forces. So, gradually, larger kingdoms began to emerge.

Destiny's stone

A flat piece of rock called the Stone of Destiny was used in king-making ceremonies in the new Scottish kingdom of Alba. Before that, it was probably used by Pictish kings. Some legends trace it back to the Bible.

Picts and Scots

For centuries, the most northerly region of Britain had been divided mainly between the Picts and the Scots. But in the late 8th century, a Scots king called Constantin MacFergus gained control over the Picts too. However, his dynasty wasn't to last, partly as a result of the devastating Viking raids.

In around 850, a Scots king called Kenneth MacAlpin again brought the Picts under a single rule with his own kingdom of Dalriada. As his united subjects struggled against the Vikings, their shared plight drew them closer together. Under Kenneth's descendants, this kingdom became known as Alba, and it formed the core of what later became Scotland.

Divided Wales

In the 9th century, Wales was made up of separate kingdoms. Gwynedd was the most powerful. From the 840s onward, the King of Gwynedd, Rhodri Mawr (or Rhodri the Great) came to rule most of Wales through marriage, inheritance and probably conquest, too. But when he died, his kingdom collapsed. Just under a century later, Hywel Dda (or Hywel the Good), did the same, but his kingdom didn't survive his death either.

Becoming English

In England, Alfred's descendants carried on fighting the Vikings, and bit by bit they captured portions of the Danelaw. In 927, Alfred's grandson Athelstan finally conquered Northumbria, becoming the first king of a united England. Northern resistance continued for a while, but by the time Alfred's great-grandson Edgar the Peaceful became king in 959, the kingdom of England was well established.

Irish Vikings

Ireland was divided into kingdoms interspersed with Viking settlements, including the prosperous town of Dublin. There was fierce fighting across Ireland for over a century. But by the mid 10th century the Irish and the Vikings had begun to trade with each other, and even intermarry.

Making laws

During Hywel Dda's reign, the first Welsh laws were beginning to be written down. After his death, Hywel was remembered as a lawmaker.

This map shows the main 9th century kingdoms in Britain, and some Viking cities in Ireland. The southern boundary of the Danelaw is shown in red. Further north, the boundary was less fixed.

Pictish kingdoms

Iona
Dalriada

Northumbria

Dublin

Gwynedd

Powys   DANELAW

Dyfed   Mercia

Cork

ANGLO-SAXON ENGLAND

Wessex

This is a photograph of Corfe Castle in Dorset, which stands near the site of Edward's murder.

The young King Edward was murdered while he was visiting his half-brother Aethelred, who had been staying near Corfe with his mother, Aelfthryth.

One story claims that Aelfthryth herself stabbed her stepson to death, so her own son could be king.

Unready, unraed

Aethelred is often called *the Unready*. Some people think this is because he failed to cope with the Vikings. But in fact, it's based on the early phrase *Aethelred Unraed*, which actually meant Aethelred the Ill-Advised.

The new raiders

Edgar the Peaceful ruled England for over twenty years. He was a strong ruler, and it was a time of peace and stability. The Viking raids had ended, and the raiders' descendants had mostly been absorbed into the new English nation. But when Edgar died in 975, things began to unravel. He left two young sons by different mothers – Edward and Aethelred, aged around 12 and 9. Edward succeeded his father, but many nobles wanted Aethelred as king instead. Just three years after his coronation, Edward was murdered by Aethelred's supporters.

Aethelred became King, but the first decades of his reign were difficult. He was a bad judge of character, and the advisers that he picked often turned out to be greedy and corrupt. Meanwhile, many people were outraged over the murder of Edward, who became known as Edward the Martyr.

To cap it all, Danish Vikings resumed small-scale raids along much of the southern English coastline. Then, in 991, a massive fleet of Viking ships set sail for England.

The Vikings victorious

The Viking fleet landed near the town of Maldon, where they were met by an army from Essex. Despite a valiant effort, the English lost the battle. In desperation, Aethelred paid the Vikings to leave.

But no matter how much Aethelred paid, the raiders kept coming back. Eventually, he started to look for other ways to keep them away. After raids, the Vikings often sheltered with the Normans, descendants of earlier Vikings who had settled in France. To stop this, Aethelred made an agreement with the Duke of Normandy that they would support each other against their enemies. Aethelred sealed the deal in 1002 by marrying the Duke's sister, Emma.

Aethelred also took drastic measures at home. He issued orders for all Danes in England to be murdered. The slaughter is said to have enraged the Danish King, Swein Forkbeard, who invaded England. In 1013, after years of fighting, he forced Aethelred into exile in Normandy, and declared himself King of England.

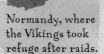

Maldon, the site of the first major battle.

Normandy, where the Vikings took refuge after raids.

This is a reconstruction of a Viking longship. According to the *Anglo-Saxon Chronicle*, the Viking fleet that landed at Maldon was made up of 93 ships like this.

King Canute

With Aethelred forced into exile and Swein the new King of England, the war seemed to be over. But it wasn't long before fighting broke out again.

Swein's reign turned out to be very short. He died in February 1014, just a few months after claiming the crown. His Danish army quickly proclaimed his young son Canute to be the new King of England, and he began to gather support across central England.

Meanwhile, further south, the English nobles had invited Aethelred to return as King – but only on the condition that he treated his subjects better. Humiliated but determined to take back what he believed was his, Aethelred agreed, and turned his attention to driving out the Danes. He caught them unprepared and succeeded in forcing Canute back to Denmark.

A family affair

Even with Canute gone, Aethelred faced problems at home. Many of his northern subjects had Viking ancestors, and may still have been resentful of his murder of the Danes. Some had also been supporters of Swein and Canute. Their anger came to a head early in 1015 with a huge rebellion, led by Aethelred's own son Edmund who was protesting against corruption in his father's court. By the summer, Edmund was widely accepted as the lord of the north.

Then, in August, Canute invaded England. Edmund put his differences with his father behind him to fight off the invasion. But in April 1016 Aethelred died and Edmund became King. He was far more successful at resisting the Vikings than his father had ever been, and he became known as 'Edmund Ironside' for his strength and courage.

> "We richly deserve the misery that we're suffering, and we must work hard to please God if things are going to start getting better."

Archbishop Wulfstan of York said this in a sermon in 1014. He believed that the suffering caused by the Vikings' return was a punishment from God.

Treason

Edmund's rebellion was probably aimed at a corrupt nobleman called Eadric Streona, which means the Grasper. Eadric had become the power behind the ageing king, but he later betrayed Aethelred to the Danes. Eadric ended up being executed by Canute for his treachery.

This illustration of Canute was drawn during his lifetime. It shows him with his wife Emma, presenting a cross to a monastery in Winchester.

Canute and Edmund

After months of fighting, Canute finally won a major victory in October 1016. But he didn't want to anger Edmund's many supporters, so he agreed to split the kingdom with Edmund. The pair also agreed that when one died, the other would inherit his land.

This agreement probably wouldn't have lasted, but Edmund died just a month later, and Canute became the King of all England.

From conqueror to king

At first, many people were unwilling to accept Canute's rule, so he had to control his subjects with an iron grip. But he also tried to win them over, by giving gifts to the churches, bringing back the popular laws of Edgar the Peaceful, and marrying Aethelred's widow Emma. These policies paid off, and he became well-liked. He also inherited the kingdom of Denmark, and soon his empire covered Norway and parts of Sweden too.

Turning the tide

A story tells of how Canute's nobles thought he had godlike powers. Weary of denying it, he took his throne to a beach and ordered the tide not to come in. Of course, he got wet, and his nobles saw he was just human.

115

Trouble ahead

Canute's reign over England was peaceful, and lasted nearly twenty years. But his death in 1035 led to a crisis that spelled the end for his own line of Viking conquerors, and for Alfred's ancient House of Wessex.

Succession struggles

Canute had wanted his entire empire to pass to his son Harthacanute after he died. But Harthacanute couldn't travel to England to be crowned. He was in Denmark dealing with urgent political problems, caused by his Norwegian subjects. Many English nobles were wary of making him king while he was overseas, so they invited Harold, another of Canute's sons, to rule until Harthacanute's return. But they had misjudged Harold, who soon seized the crown for himself.

It was 1039 before Harthacanute could leave Denmark to deal with his half-brother. Yet another battle for England seemed to be looming. But, by the time Harthacanute arrived, Harold had fallen ill and died. Soon after, Harthacanute was accepted as King.

This picture shows Queen Emma being presented with a book, while her sons Edward and Harthacanute look on. Emma was influential at court, and played a key role in gathering support for her sons and herself.

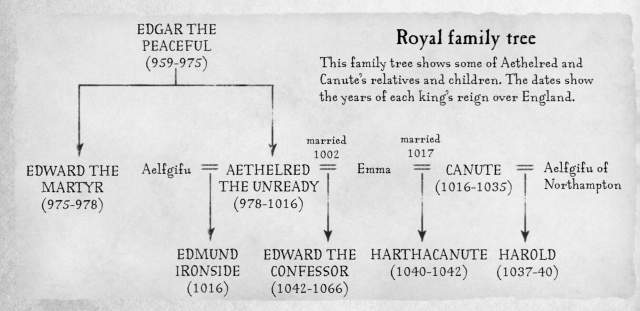

Royal family tree

This family tree shows some of Aethelred and Canute's relatives and children. The dates show the years of each king's reign over England.

EDGAR THE PEACEFUL (959-975)

EDWARD THE MARTYR (975-978)

Aelfgifu = AETHELRED THE UNREADY (978-1016) = Emma (married 1002)

Emma = CANUTE (1016-1035) (married 1017) = Aelfgifu of Northampton

EDMUND IRONSIDE (1016)

EDWARD THE CONFESSOR (1042-1066)

HARTHACANUTE (1040-1042)

HAROLD (1037-40)

Reunited brothers

One of Harthacanute's first acts as King was to order his treacherous half-brother's body to be dug up and thrown into a bog. But he was much kinder to his last surviving half-brother, Edward, son of Aethelred and Emma. Edward had grown up in exile in Normandy, but now he was invited to return to England. When Harthacanute died in 1042, Edward succeeded him.

Wessex's dying spark

Edward was accepted gladly by ordinary people, but he never got on with his nobles, and was more at ease with Norman friends. Nevertheless, his reign was prosperous, and the first real towns started to emerge.

But the peace came to a sudden end in 1066, when Edward died. With no children or close relatives, the throne was up for grabs, and plenty of contenders stepped forward to claim it. The three main players were Harold Godwinson, a powerful English noble fresh from battlefield victories; Harald Hardrada, King of Norway; and William, Duke of Normandy. The scene was set for a mighty power struggle.

Saintly Edward

Edward was deeply religious, and was made into a saint after he died. He became known as Edward 'the Confessor' – a name given to someone who lived a holy life.

This section from the Bayeux Tapestry shows Edward's body being carried to Westminster Abbey, which he founded. God's hand is shown above, pointing to the new building to bless it.

PORTA·TVR·CORPVS·EADWARDI·REGIS·AD·ECCLESIAM·SCI PETRI APĽI

THE MIDDLE AGES

In 1066, the Normans invaded and conquered England, marking the start of a new era. Along with their ruthless fighters, the new Norman kings brought French culture and language, binding England and France with strong political ties that lasted for several centuries. These changes had their effects on life in Wales, Ireland and Scotland too.

But kings didn't have it all their own way. Changes in technology, vast wars and terrible diseases such as the Plague all had their impact on ordinary people, who repeatedly rose up to express their anger and frustration. It was the people, as much as their leaders, who changed the course of history in medieval Britain.

hIC EXEVNT:CABAL

The Norman Conquest

The Bayeux Tapestry

The Bayeux Tapestry is a huge embroidered cloth that tells the story of the Norman conquest of England, in pictures. It's about 50cm (20 inches) wide and over 70m (230ft) long.

It was made for the Normans shortly after 1066, by English women. Because it was designed for the winning side to celebrate their victory, it may not be entirely truthful.

One bright October morning in 1066, near Hastings on the English south coast, two armies – the English and the Norman – were poised, ready to fight. The battle that followed was decisive, as it brought in a whole new line of rulers from France.

A few months earlier, Edward the Confessor, King of England, had died suddenly, leaving no heirs. There were three strong contenders for the throne: Harold Godwinson, a powerful English lord; Harald Hardrada, King of Norway; and William, Duke of Normandy, in France. The King's council of chief advisers – known as the Witan – wanted to settle the matter as quickly as possible.

So when Harold claimed that, on his deathbed, Edward had named him as his heir, they had him crowned the very next day.

From the outset, Harold was expecting trouble from his rivals – especially William. So he positioned an army all along the south coast, ready to defend against an attack from Normandy.

DENAVIBVS : ‑ ET HIC:MILITES: FESTINA VERVNT:HESTI

A waiting game

They waited all summer, but nothing happened. The
army was just about to disband when shocking news
came – Hardrada had invaded northern England. At
once, Harold and his army charged north, moving so
quickly they were able to surprise the enemy. At the
Battle of Stamford Bridge, in Yorkshire, the
Norwegians fought fiercely, but the English defeated
them, decimating their troops and killing Hardrada.

Normans invade

But the English had barely started celebrating when
yet more disastrous news arrived. William and his
army had crossed the English Channel with a
huge fleet. They had invaded southern
England, and set up camp at Hastings.
Exhausted from the battle, Harold
mustered his troops, and sped
back south to meet the
invasion force.

This is a section of the
Bayeux Tapestry. It
shows the Normans
landing near Hastings,
and unloading their
horses. The Normans'
expertise in fighting on
horseback would give
them a crucial advantage
against the English.

The Bayeux Tapestry
depicts a comet that
appeared in 1066. Many
people thought it was a
warning of terrible
things to come.

121

The Battle of Hastings

"Look, I am here, and with the grace of God I will win the day!"

William is said to have spoken these words during the battle, when gossip spread that he had been killed. He pushed back his helmet, crying out to his men to encourage them and to prove that he was alive.

The two armies came face to face near Hastings, on October 14, 1066. It was to be a hard-fought battle. William's men had better training and equipment. They included archers and horsemen. Harold's soldiers were exhausted from fighting in the north only days earlier. But they held a strong position at the top of a hill, where they formed a wall with their shields, which the Norman soldiers found impossible to penetrate.

The armies became locked in a stalemate, until William came up with a plan that changed the course of the battle. He ordered his army to pretend to run away. When some of the English soldiers gave chase, the Normans turned around, slaughtering the English and riding triumphantly through the front line.

This photograph shows a reenactment of the Battle of Hastings.

122

As soon as they had broken through the English ranks, the Normans easily overcame Harold's troops. Harold himself was killed, and the Normans declared a victory.

But the Battle of Hastings didn't mark the end of the Norman Conquest. William and his troops faced strong resistance from English lords as they advanced from Hastings to London for his coronation on Christmas Day, 1066. Even then, William was far from secure in his position and his soldiers remained on their guard. During the ceremony, they heard the sound of cheers from nearby houses, and mistook it for the start of a riot. They panicked, and set the houses on fire. Eyewitnesses reported that William was shaking with fear as the crown was put on his head.

A bloody battle

No one knows exactly how Harold was killed, but the Bayeux Tapestry shows him with an arrow in his eye, and being hacked from his horse by a Norman knight.

After his victory, William built an abbey named Battle as a memorial to the dead. The altar is positioned on the spot where Harold is said to have been killed.

Knights

One of the things that helped the Normans conquer England was the special training of their warriors on horseback. At this time, horses were so expensive that if an English fighter had one he would ride to the battlefield, but fight on foot. Fighting on horseback might have given him some extra height for throwing his spear and thrusting his sword, but it wouldn't have made enough difference to risk a valuable horse.

But Norman warriors had developed a highly effective new technique. Holding their spears firmly under their arms, they rode straight at their enemies, delivering a devastating blow with all the weight of the horse and rider behind it. This new tactic changed the course of battles, and transformed the way wars were fought for the next 500 years.

Battle gear

As well as specially strengthened spears, known as *lances*, knights also fought with swords, axes and clubs known as *maces*. They fended off enemy blows using big shields.

For extra protection, knights wore helmets, reinforced shirts and sometimes special guards for their arms and legs. They were also trained to fight on foot, as well as on horseback.

This is a painting from around 1250. It shows a knight on horseback wounding another knight with his lance.

All the knights shown here are wearing protective clothing known as chain mail. It was made by linking many small iron rings.

Noble fighters

The men who fought like this quickly took on almost legendary status. The awe-struck English called them *knights*. At first, any man who could afford a horse and put in the training could be made a knight. But soon knights started being chosen mainly from the families of other knights. These families were known as the *nobility*, because they were supposed to have *noble* qualities of bravery and loyalty. Before long, almost all noble boys became knights as the first step of their careers – even if they went on to become lords, bishops or kings later.

As well as fighting, knights had a vital role in running the country too. The king trusted them above everyone else. He chose his most important knights to become lords and officials, and divided up his land between them. In return, they promised to keep the peace in their areas, to help to run the law courts, and to fight for the king for part of each year, bringing plenty of knights with them.

In turn, the lords then divided up their lands among their knights, who promised to fight for their lord and guard his castles for part of each year. In England, the Normans started to put this system in place soon after William was crowned.

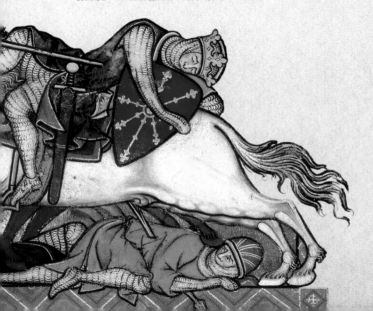

Training

Boys started training to be knights from a young age – sometimes as early as age seven. First of all, a boy became a *page*, and was sent to live with the family of a famous knight. He fetched, carried and learned about horses.

Next, he became a knight's personal assistant, or s*quire*. He took care of the knight's battle gear, and learned how to handle weapons for himself.

Finally, if he did well, he was made a knight at a special ceremony. The king or another famous knight tapped him with a glove or sword and gave him a sword and other gifts.

Lords and castles

Even once he'd been crowned King of England, William couldn't relax. For the next five years, his army was constantly on the move, trying to keep on top of rebellions that erupted up and down the country – some of them even led by disgruntled Norman lords.

At first, William told English lords and church leaders that they could keep their titles and lands if they swore to be loyal to him. But many of them kept on attacking the Normans and William soon realized that he couldn't trust them to keep their word.

The new order

By 1086, there were very few English lords left – William had replaced almost all of them with his own men. The land was now divided up between Norman lords, each with his own knights and soldiers to help keep the peace in his area – by force if necessary.

They had a great new invention to help them: the castle. The Normans began building castles as soon as they arrived in England.

Northern terror

The most serious English rebellions were in the winter of 1069, in the north of England. William hit back hard – with what came to be known as the Harrying of the North.

It's not certain exactly what happened, but some claimed that William's troops had destroyed everything in their path – houses, crops and animals – while the terrified locals fled, dying in their thousands from starvation and cold.

In this picture, the massive stone tower of a new Norman castle is being built. Norman stonemasons are in charge, but the fetching and carrying is done by English workers.

Stonemasons work in shelters known as lodges.

Stone is brought by cart from local quarries.

Mixing mortar

Castle building

The earliest castles were simple structures of wood and earth, designed to give fighting troops shelter and good views of approaching enemies. But, soon, stronger, more permanent castles were springing up all over the country. They were intended to keep the new Norman lords, their knights and their followers safe as they tried to impose their rule.

Castles could be spectacular, with vast courtyards enclosed by thick walls, and massive stone towers that housed huge halls for feasting, many bedrooms, toilets and even running water. They were status symbols as well as a safe places. Big and small, wood and stone, castles continued to be built all through the Middle Ages. But everyone building a castle had to get special permission from the King before they started.

Motte and bailey

The Normans created many castles with massive earth mounds, known as *mottes*. Next to the mound was a fortified area, or *bailey*.

This type of castle is often known as a *motte and bailey*.

The walls have outer layers of carefully cut stone. The middle is filled in with rubble and mortar.

Chepstow Castle, perched on a cliff above the Wye River, in Wales, was first built in 1067, by William Fitz Osbern. He played a key role in the Norman Conquest and, as Earl of Hereford, was one of William's marcher lords.

Borderlands

In 1066, the frontiers between England, Scotland and Wales weren't fixed, so territories in the border regions – or marches – often changed hands. But now that William had the English crown, he wanted to push out his frontiers and gain power over the people beyond. At that time, Wales was divided into five kingdoms, each ruled by a warrior prince. In Scotland, however, power was more centralized. Although King Malcolm III had less control over some parts of the country than others, he was far stronger than any of the Welsh princes.

Princes and kings

At the start of the Middle Ages, 'prince' was a title given to the ruler of a small kingdom, or principality. It was only later that the title of prince came to mean 'son of the king'.

Marcher lords

As the most powerful ruler in Britain, William expected the King of Scotland and the Welsh princes to recognize him as their overlord. This meant they had to swear loyalty to him and provide him with money and soldiers, in return for his protection. Some were more cooperative than others. So, to defend his lands and keep the locals in check, William posted his most loyal and capable lords in the marches. He also gave these marcher lords powers most other lords weren't allowed: they could make laws, keep their own armies and build castles without asking him first.

Normanizing Wales

From the outset, William instructed the marcher lords near Wales to invade the lands of any disloyal Welsh princes and replace them with loyal Normans. The Normans extended their territories deep into Wales and built several castles, including Chepstow in the south, Rhuddlan in the north and Cardigan and Pembroke in the far west.

This didn't happen without a fight, although the Welsh weren't simply conquered by violence. In some places, the Normans brought their rule and their way of life to Wales by building towns and monasteries and encouraging settlers who were used to Norman ways to live there.

Canmore

To the north, King Malcolm III, also known as Malcolm Canmore, had taken advantage of the upheaval during the Harrying of the North to raid Cumbria and Northumbria. William decided to deal with Canmore personally. So, in 1072, he took an army and a fleet up to Scotland. The two kings met at Abernethy, where Canmore was forced to swear allegiance to William, and to hand over his son Duncan as a hostage.

After Canmore's death, the frontier between England and Scotland was officially set for the first time, though this didn't stop further Scottish raids into England. At the same time, the Scots court came under more Norman influence, as Canmore's sons married English women and English replaced Gaelic as the language of government.

English exiles

During the Norman Conquest, many English nobles took refuge in Wales and Scotland. Among them was Edward the Confessor's great-neice Margaret, who married Malcolm Canmore. Scholarly and devout, she set up an abbey at Dunfermline, and was later made a saint.

Map of 11th century Britain

☐ Marcher lordships

☐ Early Norman castles in Wales

SCOTLAND

• Abernethy

Northumbria

☐ Newcastle
Cumbria ☐ Durham

ENGLAND

Rhuddlan
☐ ☐ Chester

☐ Shrewsbury

WALES ☐ Hereford

☐ Cardigan
☐ ☐ Chepstow
Pembroke
Cardiff

This is the Domesday Book. It contains very detailed information about who owned what at the time of the Conquest.

Domesday

One of the main reasons William had for taking over England was the country's wealth. He knew that the English kings had very efficient systems for collecting taxes. Now that he was in charge, William wanted to find out exactly who owned what, and how much they might owe him.

So, he sent out officials to every county in the kingdom, to put together a new and more thorough record, to make sure all of the facts were absolutely accurate and up-to-date. All the information was written down carefully, and then copied out into a great book.

Understandably, the English were very alarmed at such a detailed enquiry into their land being made by a hostile King. It felt to them like having their souls weighed up on Judgement Day, so they called the book *Domesday*.

"He had everything investigated so thoroughly that there was not one single yard of land nor one cow or pig that was left out."

An entry about William's Domesday survey in the *Anglo-Saxon Chronicle*, a record of events written by medieval English monks.

130

Lords of the land

But although the Normans now owned the land, they left many English systems in place. For example, tax collecting and the law courts carried on much the same, and most English people continued to live as they had before 1066.

At this time, 90% of people were peasants, who lived in the countryside and raised crops and animals for a living. Different peasants had different arrangements with their landlords – some were free, meaning they could come and go as they liked and choose who they wanted to work for. But most peasants had to stay in the place where they were born and work for whoever owned the land for a few days each week. There were also some slaves, who had very few rights at all.

Most peasants continued to rent their land from a lord, or to work for him on his land, just as they had done before 1066. Everyone also continued to hand over a tenth (or *tithe*) of their produce to the Church, and to pay taxes to the King. This enabled the King, his lords and religious leaders to live in comfort and devote their free time to fighting wars, managing the Church and running the country.

Difficult times

But the Norman lords had come to England to get rich. So, they could be harsh landlords, demanding more from their peasants than ever before. Some peasants could barely afford these extra payments, while others, who had never had to work on their lords' land before, were suddenly made to do so.

For slaves, though, life became better. By 1100, the Normans made most slaves into normal peasants, who had to stay on their land, but had more rights.

Pecking order

Some peasants were worse off than others. Usually, this was because their ancestors had also been worse off – there wasn't much they could do to change things.

Free peasants farmed land for themselves and helped the landlord with hunting and organizing other peasants.

Peasants known as *villeins* farmed a little land for themselves, and helped the landlord with planting and harvesting.

Cottars farmed plots so tiny, they couldn't produce enough to feed their families.

Serfs were slaves who worked for the landlord all the time, but at least they were fed by him too.

Country life

Life in a medieval village could be hard. Peasants worked in the fields from dawn till dusk whenever there was work to do. Diseases and bad weather could wipe out their crops, and even in good years it could be hard to store up enough food to last through the winter.

But many medieval villages were well organized, to help everyone to make the most of the land. There were a few streets lined with houses, each with a small garden for growing fruit and vegetables.

Some nearby woodland was set aside for gathering firewood and some grassy areas were left for putting sheep and cattle out to graze. There were also two or three large fields around the village for growing crops. These fields were divided up again to form many strips, and each peasant had a few strips to farm.

Daily bread

In the Middle Ages, bread was the most important food. Well-off people ate fine white bread made from wheat flour, while poorer people ate coarser bread made from less expensive grains such as barley, or even from ground beans.

A mill was essential for grinding grain into flour. Around the time of the Conquest, people used the power of fast-flowing streams to turn their mills. But by around 1180, windmills like this one were being built.

Mills were expensive, so only landlords could afford to build them. They charged the local peasants to use the mill, and millers often made fat profits.

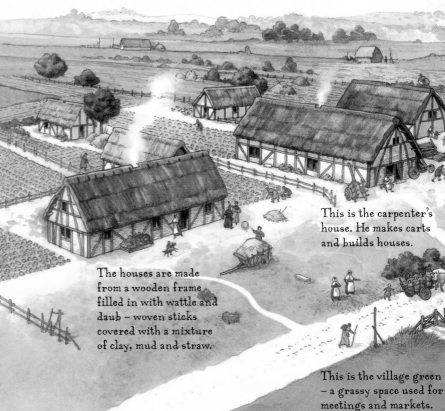

This is the carpenter's house. He makes carts and builds houses.

The houses are made from a wooden frame filled in with wattle and daub – woven sticks covered with a mixture of clay, mud and straw.

This is the village green – a grassy space used for meetings and markets.

The strips were allotted carefully, so that no one peasant had all good ones or all bad ones. Everyone agreed what to plant in each field each year – usually wheat or barley. They often left one field bare, so it would be more fertile the following year. And they sold any extra produce at local markets, to earn some money.

Not everyone spent their time growing crops. Often, the villagers appointed someone to care for all the sheep, pigs or cattle. Some peasants were carpenters, blacksmiths or cloth weavers, who sold their goods and services to the other peasants. So, even though they had to give part of their produce, their time and their money to their landlords and pay Church tithes, some peasants did well, and even became quite rich.

This scene shows a medieval village surrounded by fields. Peasants spent most of their lives in villages like these, but they did visit markets in nearby towns or villages.

Everyone grinds their grain into flour at this watermill, built by the landlord.

Shepherd

Beehives

Blacksmith

Vegetable patch

Church

This barn is for collecting all the produce paid to the Church as tithes.

Money lending

During the Middle Ages, many Christians believed they shouldn't profit by lending money. So they borrowed money from Jewish merchants, who were allowed to do this.

William the Conqueror encouraged Jewish merchants to settle in England, to help build up trade and wealth.

This painting of an English town was made around 1320-40. You can see the town walls enclosing houses and a large church. The poles sticking up from some of the houses are trade signs, to show everyone what kind of goods are sold there.

Towns and trade

When the Normans took over, there were only about a hundred towns in England, and by today's standards, they were very small. But they were growing in size and number. People from the countryside brought their surplus produce to town to sell at markets, and some moved into the towns permanently to learn trades or to work as servants for rich merchants.

As towns grew, trade also flourished. Markets boosted dealings in all kinds of goods, from grain and animals to dairy produce and salt. Craftsmen set up workshops to make and sell everything from bread to cooking pots, shoes, cloth, tools and ornaments.

Many newcomers had a better life in towns than they would have had in the countryside. The lords who owned the land where towns were built did well too. They charged the townspeople rent and collected their own fees on the goods sold at markets.

Trading places

By far the biggest town at this time was London. Its docks heaved with merchant ships coming and going. Many smaller towns held a special market, or *fair*, once a year to attract traders from near and far.

The Normans had many contacts in northern Europe, particularly in France, which was a source of goods such as wine. Other luxuries that couldn't be made in England, such as fine cloth and top-quality metalware, were shipped in. In turn, English merchants exported goods such as tin and most of all, wool, to the Continent.

But towns also had their downsides. Some traders tried to maximize their profits by selling shoddy wares or tampering with their weights and measures. And in many towns overcrowding, overflowing waste, house fires and thieves made life dangerous and unpleasant for everyone.

Making the rules

To try to keep things fair, clean and safe, important citizens banded together to set rules for their towns. Some formed trade associations, or *guilds*, and set standards for goods and trading.

Others set up town councils with mayors to organize market tolls, local law courts and repair and building work.

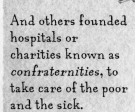

And others founded hospitals or charities known as *confraternities*, to take care of the poor and the sick.

Anarchy

William II was known as William Rufus, which means *red*. He probably had red hair, or maybe a ruddy complexion.

In 1087, William the Conqueror died and his territories were divided among his sons. Robert, the eldest, became Duke of Normandy. The middle son, William, became King of England. But there was no land left for the youngest son, Henry. This division wasn't popular with anyone. Robert and William fought constantly over each others' land, and Henry often joined in, too.

Then, in 1100, William II died after a hunting accident. Henry was with him at the time, and some experts wonder whether he had a hand in his brother's death. Either way, Henry was crowned King of England three days later. By 1106, he had defeated his brother Robert and become Duke of Normandy, too.

Heirless Henry

After that, King Henry settled down to a peaceful rule. But tragedy struck in 1120, when his son and heir was drowned in a shipwreck. Henry wanted his daughter Matilda to succeed him, so he made his nobles promise to accept her as their next ruler. Then he married her to a powerful French lord, Geoffrey of Anjou. But, Henry's nephew, Stephen – also a grandson of William the Conqueror – thought the throne should be his.

When Henry died in 1135, Stephen rushed to London and had himself crowned before Matilda had a chance. Once Stephen was officially King of England, many lords felt there was little they could do about it, even though they had promised to help Matilda. But she wasn't prepared to give up that easily.

Sensing that Stephen was in a weak position, the Welsh rose up against English settlers in Wales, while King David of Scotland invaded northern England and grabbed Northumbria.

Family line

This family tree shows how Stephen and Matilda were related to William the Conqueror.

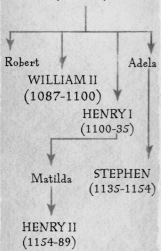

WILLIAM
THE CONQUEROR
(1066-87)

Robert | Adela

WILLIAM II
(1087-1100)

HENRY I
(1100-35)

Matilda | STEPHEN
(1135-1154)

HENRY II
(1154-89)

The dates show the years of each king's reign.

Cousins at war

Things really fell apart when Matilda and her forces landed in England to fight Stephen for the crown. They fought up and down the country, in Normandy and other parts of France. This bitter civil war lasted for most of Stephen's reign and is known as the Anarchy.

Sometimes Stephen had the upper hand, sometimes Matilda, but the ordinary people suffered most. Many were killed in the fighting, while others were forced to build castles for the opposing forces or were tortured for information. Thousands more died of starvation because no-one could grow or distribute food properly.

Finally, in 1148, Matilda retreated to France. It looked as if she had finally given up. But when Stephen's son and heir died in 1153, he realized that Matilda would win in the end. He signed a treaty leaving the crown of England to Matilda's son, Henry. Now at last there would be peace.

"And so it went on for nineteen years while Stephen was King...the land was laid waste and people said openly that Christ and his saints were asleep."

An entry about the Anarchy in the *Anglo-Saxon Chronicle*, a record of events written by medieval English monks.

During fighting at Lincoln, Stephen's forces were so desperate, they took over the cathedral as a base for attacking the castle opposite it. This photograph of Lincoln Cathedral is taken from the walls of the castle.

Family names

Historians usually refer to Henry II and his brothers as the Angevins, because their father, Geoffrey, came from Anjou, in France.

Later, the family became known as the Plantagenets, possibly because Geoffrey wore a sprig of broom (*planta genista* in Latin) in his hat.

This is a medieval picture of Henry II.

Henry Plantagenet

Matilda's son Henry was already Duke of Normandy, Count of Anjou and Duke of Aquitaine when he became King Henry II of England in 1154. His vast realm stretched from the Scottish borders to the south of France, and later he would also count Ireland as part of his domain. Henry was arguably the most powerful monarch in Europe at that time, and he was determined to stay that way.

Taking control

Having come to the English throne out of a period of civil war, Henry's first task was to restore order and strengthen his authority. He earned the nickname 'Castle Breaker' because he had a number of castles pulled down, which had been built without royal permission during the Anarchy.

Henry considered himself to be the overlord of the rest of Britain. So he quickly set about reclaiming territory that the Scots and the Welsh had seized from the English during the turmoil of the civil war. King David's son, Malcolm IV of Scotland, reluctantly co-operated, returning Northumbria to English rule.

But the Welsh put up more of a fight. In 1163, Henry demanded that the Welsh princes recognize him as their overlord. Many refused, so he launched a massive invasion. It was a disaster. Despite having a far bigger army, the English knights struggled against heavy rains in hilly terrain, and were soon beaten into a retreat.

Into the Pale

Like Wales, medieval Ireland was divided into many small kingdoms. When one of the Irish kings appealed to Henry to help him put down a local rebellion, Henry sent over the English nobles who had been pushed out of Wales. Led by the Earl of Pembroke – nicknamed 'Strongbow' – the English knights soon crushed the rebels and began to colonize part of Ireland, which became known as the Pale. Realizing that they were becoming too independent, Henry sailed to Ireland in 1171, and made the English settlers swear loyalty to him. Many Irish kings joined them, but they didn't see Henry as their king.

The Anglo-French connection

Relations between Henry and Louis VII of France had been strained from the start. Henry married Eleanor of Aquitaine, Louis' ex-wife, and gained a huge area of central France as a result. In effect, he controlled more French land than Louis. As Louis was anxious to prevent him from gaining any more power, this often led to conflict between the two monarchs.

With so much territory to control and defend, Henry spent much of his 35-year reign on the move, crossing the English Channel as many as 28 times. London was the cornerstone of his empire, but the French cities of Rouen, Chinon and Poitiers served as regional capitals.

French was the language of government and nobility across Henry's empire. But many of his ordinary subjects spoke English, Gaelic and other different regional languages. Henry knew better than to impose foreign languages and customs on them. As long as they accepted his rule, they could live as they pleased.

France in the 12th century

■ Land held by Henry II

■ Land under the control of the kings of France

"Now in England, now in Normandy, he must fly rather than travel by horse or ship."

King Louis VII of France was amazed at the speed with which Henry II moved around his empire.

Murder in the cathedral

One of the main ways Henry II enforced his rule in England was through the law. He reorganized the legal system and set up new courts around the country. He believed that, as King, he should have the final say in all matters of justice. But this led to an explosive row with the Church, and one man in particular: Thomas Becket.

Becket was the son of a wealthy London merchant. He was clever and ambitious, with a taste for the finer things in life. He rose to power at the royal court to become one of Henry's closest advisers, and even led military campaigns for the King. Then, in 1162, he was appointed Archbishop of Canterbury, the head of the Church in England. From then on, he ate only simple food and exchanged his expensive clothes for coarse robes. But the greatest change was in Becket's relationship with the King.

Taking sides

During the Middle Ages, almost everyone in England belonged to the Catholic Church, led by the Pope in Rome. So, Becket's loyalty was not only to Henry, but also to the Pope. The Church also had its own law courts, and when Henry tried to bring churchmen who had committed crimes to justice in his courts, Becket stood in his way. The dispute became more and more heated until Becket, fearing for his life, fled to France.

When Becket returned to England, he expelled from the Church all the bishops who had taken the King's side. It was the last straw for Henry. Exasperated, he raged, "Will no one rid me of this troublesome priest?" Four knights took him literally, and rode to Canterbury to execute the King's wishes. On December 29, 1170, they stormed the cathedral and murdered Becket.

By the book

A new set of laws that applied to the whole of England was produced during Henry's reign. At the time, the laws only applied to freemen – most peasants were still at the mercy of their lord.

Many lawyers now see this as the basis of today's English Common Law.

"There are two principles by which the world is ruled: the authority of priests and the royal power. The authority of priests is greater..."

Thomas Becket in a letter to Henry II, 1166

Saints and sinners

The murder caused an outcry, and the Pope declared
Becket a saint. As penance for his part in the killing,
Henry walked to Canterbury to visit Becket's tomb,
wearing only a sackcloth, then he was flogged, naked,
at the door of the cathedral. The King's humility
won him forgiveness from the Pope and restored
his reputation with the public.
But the legal dispute
was never resolved.

This is an illustration
from an English
manuscript from
around 1200. It is one
of the earliest surviving
pictures of Thomas
Becket's murder in
the cathedral.

The Crusades

Henry II recovered quickly from the Becket affair. But the end of his reign was neither happy nor peaceful. He spent it fighting his sons Richard and John, who were both angry at the way he planned to split his territories between them when he died. And to complicate matters, in 1187, the Pope announced a Crusade.

Holy wars

Crusades were wars fought by European Christians against people who didn't follow the Catholic faith. The First Crusade started in 1095, when Pope Urban II urged western knights to drive out Muslims who lived in the Holy Land – the area of the Middle East where Jesus Christ had spent his life. But the Holy Land, and especially the city of Jerusalem, were holy places for Muslims too, so things were bound to become nasty.

The response to the Pope's call was overwhelming. Thousands of ordinary men, women and children as well as knights set off from all over Europe by land and sea. Many died of starvation, fatigue and disease along the way, and more were killed in fierce fighting when they got there. But, by sheer luck, one group of crusaders managed to capture Jerusalem in 1099.

Crusader king

In 1187, Jerusalem was retaken by the brilliant Muslim leader Salah al-Din – known to the crusaders as Saladin. The new Pope, Gregory VIII, called for another expedition, to regain Jerusalem. Although they were at loggerheads, King Henry and his son Richard agreed to join the Crusade. But before they set off, Henry died and Richard was crowned.

Good out of evil

The Crusades encouraged religious hatred at home, as well as in the Holy Land. In 1189 and 1190, angry mobs attacked and killed Jewish people living in London and York. But Crusaders may also have learned from the sophisticated Muslim culture. New ideas and skills came into Europe at this time, such as...

more accurate maps...

the Arabic way of writing numbers...

...and more silks and spices than ever before.

King Richard headed for Jerusalem right away. He and Saladin were both brilliant military leaders. They respected each others' abilities and almost managed to negotiate a truce. Meanwhile, Richard and his troops made great advances. But in 1192, news arrived that Richard's brother, John, had started a rebellion back in England. Richard knew England needed him.

This 14th century manuscript painting shows a bloody battle between crusaders, on the right, and Muslim fighters.

A king's ransom

Richard's journey back home was a disaster. First, he was shipwrecked, then captured by Duke Leopold of Austria. The people of England had to pay a vast ransom to have Richard freed, and the country suffered for years after handing over a massive pile of silver. But Richard didn't enjoy his freedom for long. He went straight to France, to try to win back land the French had seized while he was away. And in 1199, during a siege, he was hit in the shoulder by an arrow, and died.

Lionheart

King Richard was known as Richard the Lionheart. He was probably given this nickname because of his bravery. But one story told that he put his arm down a lion's throat and tore out its heart.

143

Journey of faith

The furthest most people ever went from their homes was when they went on a spiritual journey, called a pilgrimage.

Pilgrims visited churches and holy places where saints were buried, or where holy objects called relics were kept.

Casket for Saint's remains

Pilgrims enter niches to pray

Many pilgrims brought back souvenirs, such as badges, as mementos of their trips.

Religious life

The Catholic Church played a central part in daily life in medieval Britain. Most people went to church regularly, and their entire year was shaped by religious festivals that took place throughout the year. These included Easter in spring, Whitsun in summer, and Christmas in winter.

Men of the Church

The local priest was a vital member of every community. Priests had some land in the village fields, and collected tithes, so they were usually better off than the other villagers. As well as performing religious services, they were expected to look after the people in their area. They visited the elderly and the sick, and sometimes taught local boys.

Seeing is believing

A church was the social hub of the community as much as a place of worship – a meeting place where friends could catch up on the latest news. But walking into one could be an awe-inspiring experience. People believed that building a church was a way to praise God. So, the more elaborate and impressive, the better.

Church services were conducted in Latin, which most people didn't understand. In fact, many priests didn't have enough education to know what they were saying themselves. They simply learned the words by heart, then repeated them. So, the meaning of church services had to be communicated to the congregation in other ways. Churches were filled with beautiful paintings, sculptures and stained glass windows that illustrated important stories from the Bible.

144

This sculpture shows the Three Kings visiting the baby Jesus Christ and his mother, Mary. It is one of many alabaster (a kind of stone) sculptures that were produced near Nottingham and shipped all over Europe.

A church could choose from a selection of different scenes, or even slot several of them together in a wooden frame to make an impressive display.

Chantries

Some rich people paid for a chantry – a fund to pay for a priest or two to pray for the souls of the dead. These prayers were said at an altar in a parish church, or in a special small chapel built into the side of the church.

Spectacular services

To impress the congregation even more, the services themselves were filled with elaborate rituals, visual spectacles and inspiring music. Bells were rung at certain points to let people know that something particularly important was happening. The clergy wore richly woven and embroidered robes, and used beautiful objects, such as silver chalices, to give parishioners a sense of the grandeur and importance of the Church. A choir sang prayers set to music, as the congregation listened.

This photograph shows Merton College, part of Oxford University. The tower belongs to the chapel.

Scribes

Monks who produced hand-lettered manuscripts worked in a writing room known as a *scriptorium*. One monk working alone would have taken about a year to copy out the Bible.

Learning

There was a strong connection between education and the Church in medieval Britain. Some men dedicated their lives to religion by becoming monks, usually living apart from the rest of society in religious communities known as monasteries. Monks spent most of their time praying, working or studying, and lived by strict rules – they had to give up most of their possessions, ate plain food, avoided comfort and weren't allowed to marry.

During the Early Middle Ages, monasteries were the main places of learning, as monks preserved and copied out ancient texts handed down from ancient scholars. Their books, known as *manuscripts*, were hand-written and often richly illustrated, or *illuminated*. These books took a lot of work, so they were extremely valuable: a single book could be worth around the same as an entire field of wheat.

Wider knowledge

The first schools were set up to educate future monks and priests. There was a greater demand for educated parish priests, as people expected them to understand the Bible and to be able to preach sermons. Men seeking well-paid jobs outside the Church needed to know some Latin, too, to make legal records, or to keep accounts. Boys could get a basic education at elementary schools, called song schools, and soon all towns and a few villages had grammar schools which provided an advanced education in Latin.

Some boys went on to higher education. The universities of Oxford and Cambridge were established by the beginning of the thirteenth century, followed by one at St. Andrews in Scotland in 1413. Young men usually entered university when they were around fourteen years old, and studied for six years. They took lessons in subjects including philosophy, religious studies, geometry, algebra and music, to prepare them for careers in the Church.

But university graduates didn't just become parish priests or monks. They often found work as clerks, government officials, or school teachers, instead.

Going for gold

During the Middle Ages, a few men began conducting experiments into the natural sciences and *alchemy* – the science of turning lead, and other base metals, into more precious metals, such as gold. Among them, was a monk named Roger Bacon. Although he and his fellow alchemists never achieved their aim, they did make many discoveries about the properties of different metals. Bacon was also the first person to record making a rainbow by shining white light through glass.

Marvellous medicine

Doctors studied ancient Greek and Arabic medical texts about herbal remedies and other treatments. But some medicines worked better than others...

Doctors gave patients willow bark to treat fevers. This eventually led to the development of aspirin, a drug widely used today.

Leeches, a kind of blood-sucking worm, were used to draw blood from patients who were thought to have the wrong balance of fluids in the body.

Some unscrupulous doctors charged a fortune for medicines that might not work, by claiming that they included rare and expensive ingredients.

The first parliament

When Richard I died in 1199, he had no official heir, so his brother John became King of England. But King John seemed to do everything wrong. He lost some of England's territories in France, imposed harsh laws and taxes and accused his lords of plotting to overthrow him. He also angered the Pope, who cast him out of the Church and suspended all church services in England.

By 1214, the English lords had lost patience. They raised an army and cornered King John, asking him to sign an agreement limiting his power and giving them more say in government. It was known as *Magna Carta*, or the great charter. When John later tried to wriggle out of it, the lords hit back. In 1216 they invited Louis, the heir to the French throne, to London to take over. John fled and died a few weeks later.

The Great Council

With John dead, the English lords turned to his nine-year-old son, Henry, who was crowned in October 1216. Louis withdrew soon after. Because the King was so young, the lords had to help with government. But when Henry III came of age and took over for himself, the lords missed their power. They also grew uneasy that Henry's French wife and relatives were distracting him from English matters. They decided *Magna Carta* wasn't enough. So, in 1258, they demanded that Henry summon a Great Council of lords and bishops to help him decide all important matters.

Henry agreed, but he soon went back on his word and a civil war broke out. Simon de Montfort, Earl of Leicester, who was married to the King's sister, led the lords' forces. They rode to victory against the royal troops at the Battle of Lewes in 1264.

This is a copy of *Magna Carta*, made in 1225. Although King John revoked the document, most of his successors agreed to it. Many people today see *Magna Carta* as the first step on the road to democracy in Britain.

"No free man shall be arrested or imprisoned...or outlawed or exiled or victimized in any other way...except by the lawful judgement of his peers or by the law of the land."

Magna Carta, article 39

King in chains

Henry III was thrown in prison, and Earl Simon ruled in his place. To prove he had wide support, he called a Great Council of loyal followers, to back him up. For the first time in the Great Council's history, Earl Simon included wealthy townsmen and knights as well as bishops and lords. Never before had non-nobles been involved in government. This marked the origin of the House of Commons.

But Edward, the King's son, came to his father's aid. He raised an army in the Welsh marches and in 1265, defeated the lords at the Battle of Evesham, where Earl Simon was killed. Henry III was back on the throne, and was later succeeded by his son.

Edward I was careful to show his respect for the terms of *Magna Carta* and continued to consult the Great Council. In 1295, he summoned the biggest council ever, made up of barons, clergy, knights and townspeople. It later became known as the Model Parliament – England's first parliament.

Talking shop

The word *parliament* comes from the French word for *talking*. It meant a gathering to talk about important issues. Now, Parliament is the place where Britain's House of Commons and House of Lords meet to discuss things.

This illustration from a 16th century manuscript shows Edward I in the Model Parliament. King Alexander of Scotland is seated to the left of the throne and Prince Llywelyn of Wales on the right. On the outside are bishops, clergy and townspeople.

Profit and persecution

Edward also profited by persecuting Jewish merchants and their families, who had been in England lending money to people since the Conquest.

In 1275, he forbade all Jews from making a profit by money-lending, and in 1290 he expelled them from the country, seizing their land and property.

This is Beaumaris Castle. Edward ordered it to be built on the strategically important island of Anglesey in North Wales in 1295, as part of his total conquest of Wales.

Law of the land

Edward I was a crafty ruler. He was careful to be seen to consult Parliament, but he often ignored its advice. And though he reformed many laws to make them less complicated, he advanced his own interests, too.

In 1274, Edward set up an enquiry into who owned what land, and how the country was being run. It was partly designed to make the law clearer, and partly to check up on dishonest officials. But the King's main motive was to discover how much land and power he could claim back from his lords, who he believed had illegally taken land rights from him. He also set up heavy taxes to pay for his wars at home and overseas. Meanwhile, Edward had set his sights on other prizes.

The Welsh princes

There had been tensions in Wales ever since the Norman Conquest. The Welsh princes – leaders of the different regions of Wales – were supposed to swear loyalty to the English king. But by the time Edward I came to the throne, one Welsh prince had become more powerful than the rest. Llywelyn ap Gruffydd (say Griffith) had taken the title Prince of Wales.

Stubborn resistance

Llywelyn steadfastly refused to swear loyalty to Edward and even invaded English territory. So, in 1277 Edward led over 15,000 men to North Wales, Llywelyn's home ground. This show of strength convinced Llywelyn to sign a peace treaty. This treaty stripped him of many of his lands, but still left him as Prince of Wales.

But in 1282, Llywelyn's brother, Dafydd led a full-scale uprising in Wales. This time, Edward set off not just to invade Wales, but to conquer it completely. There was fierce fighting as Edward's army advanced against the Welsh forces, but the English had the upper hand. Llywelyn was killed in battle and the Welsh surrendered. Dafydd was later captured and executed.

In 1284, Wales officially became part of England, and many Welsh laws were replaced by English ones. Edward left workmen building a series of fine stone castles to defend his newly-won territory.

But the Welsh had still not given up. In 1294, there was yet another uprising, led by the Welsh people themselves. Once again, the fighting was fierce, but by 1295, Edward had triumphed – in Wales at least.

This medieval English manuscript shows Llywelyn ap Gruffydd meeting his death at English hands. No one knows exactly how Llywelyn died – some accounts say he was tricked by the English; others that he fell in battle, fighting bravely.

The Stone of Destiny

In 1296, Edward I seized John Balliol's crown and the Stone of Destiny, on which Scottish kings had been crowned since the 9th century, and took them to London.

The stone was housed in a specially built throne in Westminster Abbey. All English (then, after 1603, British) monarchs have been crowned on the throne ever since.

In 1950, a group of students stole the stone and took it to Scotland, but it was soon found and returned to Westminster.

In 1996, the stone was returned to Scotland. It's now on display in Edinburgh Castle.

Do, or die

Unlike the Welsh, the Scots had managed to get along with the English relatively peacefully. But in 1286, King Alexander III of Scotland died in a riding accident. Four years later, his only heir, his infant granddaughter Margaret, died too. This left Scotland with no clear heir to the throne, and set off a chain of events that led to war between the two nations.

Taking control

A number of lords stepped up to claim power, but there were two leading contenders: Robert Bruce and John Balliol. To avoid a civil war, the Scots asked Edward I to help them to decide whose claim was the strongest. Edward chose Balliol, but only after Balliol had promised to recognize the English King as his overlord.

But, as soon as Balliol was crowned, Edward began demanding money and soldiers, and interfering in Scottish legal cases. The Scots were furious. In 1295, they made a treaty with France to help them throw Edward off. It was the start of the 'auld alliance' – a long-standing friendship between Scotland and France.

Fighting for Scotland

The English took it as a declaration of war and invaded Scotland in 1296. Edward's armies laid waste to southern Scotland. Balliol was forced to surrender, stripped of his crown and taken prisoner. Edward's message was clear: he wanted Scotland to be ruled by England from now on.

But the following year, the Scots rebelled. Led by a nobleman named William Wallace, Scottish forces defeated the English at the Battle of Stirling Bridge.

In 1298, Edward invaded again, beating the Scots at Falkirk. For the next few years, Edward mounted attacks every summer, gradually wearing down his opponents. In 1304, the Scottish nobles finally accepted defeat. Only Wallace refused, but he was captured, taken to Westminster and hanged.

Bruce and Bannockburn

But Scottish independence didn't die with Wallace. In 1306, Robert Bruce, the grandson of the earlier Robert Bruce, was crowned King of Scotland, and launched attacks on the English in Scotland. The following spring, Edward I died. His son, Edward II, didn't pick up the fight straight away. This gave Bruce time to build up support and retake much of Scotland.

By 1314, Edward II could no longer ignore the threat. He led a huge army to Scotland and the two forces met in June at the Battle of Bannockburn. Against the odds, it was a major victory for Bruce, but it wasn't until 1328, that the English finally recognized Bruce's kingship and Scotland's independence.

This is a picture, from 1327, of the Battle of Bannockburn.

The English knights far outnumbered the Scots, who mostly fought on foot. But the Scots won, partly because the battlefield was boggy, which made the fighting extremely difficult for the English horsemen.

"Lay the proud usurpers low!
Tyrants fall with every foe!
Liberty's in every blow!
Let us do, or die!"

In his 1794 poem, *Scots Wha Hae*, Robert Burns imagines Robert Bruce addressing his men before the Battle of Bannockburn.

French knights line up
to charge at the English.

French armies had many
knights. They relied
on powerful cavalry
charges to win battles.

Fighting France

In 1327, Edward II was deposed and killed by
his wife, Queen Isabella. Their 14-year-old son
was crowned King Edward III. For a few years,
Isabella was in charge, but at the age of 17, the
ambitious Edward locked up his mother and
began to rule for himself. Determined to prove
himself a stronger ruler than his father, he invaded
Scotland, in an attempt to reconquer the country. He
soon defeated Bruce's successor, David II, then he
turned to France.

The French throne

Lions and lilies

When Edward III
claimed the throne of
France, he changed his
royal coat of arms. He
added the French *fleur-
de-lys* – lily flower –
to the three
lions of
England.

Soon after Edward's coronation, King Charles IV
of France had died, and was succeeded by his cousin,
Philip. But Edward's mother Isabella was Charles's
sister, and Edward thought that, as Charles's nephew,
he had a better claim to the French throne than Philip.

In 1340, war broke out, and Edward openly claimed
the crown of France for himself and his heirs. The first
big battle was at sea, near the town of Sluys. The
English won, gaining control of the English Channel,
and the rest of the war was fought on French soil.

Great victories

Edward soon proved himself a brilliant general. At the Battle of Crécy in 1346, his troops won a great victory. His son, the Black Prince, was just as successful. At the Battle of Poitiers, he even captured King John of France, Philip's successor. In 1360, the French had to sign the Treaty of Bretigny, giving up more than a quarter of their land to the English. Edward died in 1377, but the war wasn't over. Fighting continued, on and off, for the next 76 years, and the conflict is now known as the Hundred Years' War.

Secret weapon

Most of Edward's army was made up of longbowmen. Longbows could shoot arrows faster, and were easier to carry, than the heavy crossbows used by French archers.

Crécy

At the Battle of Crécy, Edward III used his longbowmen to devastating effect. Here you can see what happened.

- 🛡 English longbowmen
- 🛡 English knights
- 🛡 French crossbowmen
- 🛡 French knights

1. At the start of the battle, Edward arranged his soldiers at the top of a hill. They were outnumbered, but had a better position.

2. Philip commanded his crossbowmen to advance and fire, but they were beaten back by the English longbowmen.

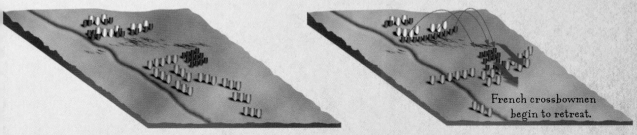

French crossbowmen begin to retreat.

3. The French knights charged over their own crossbowmen. English longbowmen rained arrows on the knights, halting the attack.

4. Some French knights reached the English battle line, but they were defeated by English knights on foot. The rest of Philip's army fled.

French knights retreat.

This is a painting from France, showing a mass burial of Plague victims.

Mystery illness

Even today, experts disagree about what caused the Plague. Most think that it was carried by fleas that lived on rats and bit humans.

Rats were a constant problem in the Middle Ages. Many people owned cats, but they still couldn't get rid of all the rats.

Plague

In the late 1340s, a terrible plague swept out of Asia and into Europe, wiping out nearly half the population. It arrived in Britain in 1348, and spread through the land with terrifying speed. The first signs were a high fever and black, foul-smelling boils – at first on the armpits, groin and neck, and then all over the body. Usually, victims died within 48 hours – but sometimes they dropped dead within minutes.

The wrath of God

No one knew what had caused the Plague, or how to cure it. Most people believed it was a punishment from God, and that the only way they could be saved was by praying. Meanwhile, the graveyards filled up, and bodies were piled in long trenches. By the time it died down in 1349, the Plague had killed more than a third of the people of Britain. Over the next 30 years, there were several smaller outbreaks, killing many more.

Aftermath

The Plague had a big impact on those who survived. Some lost their faith in the Church, as many priests had died of the Plague, and some people thought this showed that God was punishing them. But many people became more religious. They gained some comfort from joining together in brotherhoods to worship particular saints, and marching through the streets in processions to show their faith.

Peasant problems

With so many dead, it was difficult to produce enough food, as there were few peasants left to work in the fields. Landlords needed all the help they could get, but some peasants tried to use the opportunity to demand better terms, or even ran away to find land and work elsewhere. So the landlords clamped down, forcing their peasants to work under the old conditions. This only made things worse.

The Statute of Labourers

There was also a terrible shortage of other types of workers. Surviving workers demanded more pay because they knew their employers were desperate, and some left their jobs to find better ones. In England, Edward III worried that this might lead to the breakdown of order. So in 1351, he introduced the Statute of Labourers, which limited wages to pre-Plague levels and tried to prevent workers from leaving their employers. But it wasn't enough. Soon, growing discontent among the poorest people would lead to bloodshed.

Perpendicular architecture

After the Plague, a new, simpler style of religious architecture developed in England, known as *Perpendicular*. Some experts think the Plague caused the change in style – either because many masons died and new ones took over, or because religious ideas were changing.

This is King's College Chapel in Cambridge, built in the Perpendicular style. You can see the strong, straight lines that gave the style its name.

John of Gaunt was the fourth son of Edward III.

Like his older brother, the Black Prince, John fought in the Hundred Years' War in France, but he won few victories.

While Edward lay dying, John took over the King's Council, effectively ruling the country. He won a reputation for bribery and corruption.

After the Peasants' Revolt, John left England to fight a war in Spain, leaving the 19-year-old Richard to rule England himself.

The Peasants' Revolt

In 1377, Edward III died. His son, the Black Prince, had died the year before, so the English crown passed to Edward's grandson, Richard II. The young King was only 10 years old at his coronation. Just four years later, he faced a terrifying crisis, which tested his courage to the limit.

For the first few years of his reign, England was effectively ruled by Richard's uncle, John of Gaunt. But he became very unpopular, especially when he introduced heavy taxes to pay for the war with France. In 1381, he brought in a poll tax, by which everyone paid the same amount, whether they were rich or poor. Most people were furious, and when officials tried to collect the tax, riots broke out all over the land. This was the start of a great uprising which became known as the Peasants' Revolt.

Wat Tyler

The Peasants' Revolt was sparked off by the poll tax, but there were bigger things at stake. For centuries, many people had felt that the social system in England was unfair. Now the poorest workers saw a chance to win their freedom. In Kent, a craftsman named Wat Tyler began gathering a huge crowd. His plan was to march on London, and demand that the King abolish the peasants' duties to their landlords.

When they arrived in London, Tyler's mob ran riot. They set fire to John of Gaunt's palace and killed the Archbishop of Canterbury. While many of King Richard's advisers panicked, the young King bravely agreed to meet the rebels and listen to their demands. At Smithfield, the 14-year-old King Richard II came face-to-face with Wat Tyler.

The end of the revolt

But while Richard and Tyler were talking, the Lord Mayor of London drew his dagger and stabbed Tyler to death. He said that he was protecting the King, but it was more likely that he had planned to get rid of the rebel leader. The peasants might have attacked, but Richard turned to them, calling out, "I will be your captain!" It was the most successful moment of his reign. With Tyler dead, the peasants went home, convinced that the King was on their side.

In fact, Richard did nothing to help them. The leaders of the revolt were rounded up and executed. But, in any case, life in Britain was gradually changing in the wake of the Plague, as landowners were starting to allow their peasants more and more freedom.

This picture tells the story of Richard's meeting with Tyler. Richard appears twice – in the foreground, he is shown watching the Lord Mayor strike Wat Tyler, and on the right, you can see him addressing the mob.

It is unlikely that Tyler's band would have been anything like as well equipped as they appear in this picture.

This exquisite painting was probably made in England around 1395, and is in the new 'international' style of art. It was made for the King, Richard II and shows him kneeling in front of three saints. Richard is praying and looking up to the infant Jesus, his mother Mary and a group of angels.

Literature and art

All through the Middle Ages, British musicians, architects, artists and writers were busy creating songs, buildings, paintings, carvings and poems. Although they drew inspiration from local traditions, they often used styles and techniques that were popular throughout Europe.

By the 14th century, a polished style, full of intricate patterns, elegant postures and details copied carefully from nature, had developed across Europe. It's often known as International Gothic. British architects and painters were now producing works very similar to those painted hundreds of miles away, while writers were experimenting with stories and styles from many different countries, too.

160

Native tongues

Up to this time, most writing had been in Latin, which only a few educated people could understand. But now, writers all across Europe were starting to compose works in their own languages. In Britain, poets such as Geoffrey Chaucer wrote poems in English that included local characters and events. Chaucer's most famous poem, *The Canterbury Tales*, describes his journey with a rowdy group of pilgrims to visit the shrine of Saint Thomas Becket at Canterbury Cathedral.

This picture of Geoffrey Chaucer was painted in the margin of a richly illustrated copy of *The Canterbury Tales* from around 1405.

Language and religion

But there was also a more serious side to writing in English. Ordinary people who didn't know any Latin could begin to understand what writers were saying. People soon realized what a huge impact this might have.

In 1382, a religious teacher at Oxford University named John Wycliffe decided that people didn't need priests to teach them about religion. He started to translate the Bible from Latin into English, so everyone would be able to understand it.

Church leaders were outraged, as they believed uneducated people should not be allowed to read the Bible and form their own opinions. They denounced Wycliffe and his ideas, and quickly clamped down on his followers, who were known as Lollards. Some of these rebels were even burned to death.

But, from this time on, British writers began to use English more and more often. And when an English Bible was eventually published in 1611, it was partly based on Wycliffe's work.

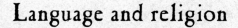

Printing press

For most of the Middle Ages, books were copied by hand. But in 1440, a German named Johannes Gutenberg invented a way of fixing together tiny metal letters and printing them onto paper. He produced Europe's first printed books.

In 1476, William Caxton set up Britain's first printing press. One of the first books he printed was *The Canterbury Tales*.

Medieval women

Men were officially in charge in medieval Britain and held all the top jobs – from kings and bishops to knights, lawyers and even village officials. So it's all too easy to forget the varied and important roles women played. Most medieval women got married and had children. But they were expected to work as well. This meant very different things for different women.

Learned ladies

As the Middle Ages went on, more and more people learned to read and write, including many women. Reading was a great help to women running households and businesses. Women were also encouraged to read prayers and other religious writings.

Ladies of leisure?

At the top of the social scale, queens had a great deal of power and influence. They usually had their own land and income and ran their own households. Queens were often important patrons, paying writers and artists to create great works of art. They could intervene in international politics, sometimes in ways that didn't meet their husbands' approval.

Lower down the scale, noblewomen took an active part in running their husbands' households, advising their husbands and taking the lead at feasts and ceremonies. When their husbands were away, or if they died, noblewomen often took charge, organizing vast estates, important business deals and even warring armies.

This is a medieval painting showing a group of nuns led by their abbess, on the left. They are holding music books, which they would have sung from during worship.

162

Jobs for women

The wives and daughters of businessmen and craftsmen often had a very active role in the family business. They helped out in the workshop as skilled weavers, dyers, bakers, leatherworkers or even blacksmiths – whatever the family trade was. And if a craftsman died, his wife often took over the business and ran it herself.

Poorer women often found work as servants, as assistants for craftsmen, working on farms, driving carts or even mending roads. All these jobs allowed women to earn a living, but also gave them a chance to meet people – including future husbands.

If they married, women often gave up paid jobs and helped in their husbands' work instead. Looking after children, cooking, cleaning and helping on the farm or in the workshop was a full-time job. But resourceful housewives could still make extra money by selling ale they had brewed, or spinning thread to be made into cloth.

For better or worse

Women of all social classes who didn't want to marry could become nuns. Better-educated nuns often rose to become powerful abbessess, running their own nunneries. So, many women had skilled jobs and did very well for themselves. But others weren't so lucky. Many men resented successful women and tried to prevent them from earning a living, by excluding them from craft guilds, or paying them less than male workers. Some Church teachings also made women's lives difficult. And, sadly, some women suffered at the hands of cruel employers, husbands or fathers.

Real women

Christina of Markyate was born around 1100 in Cambridgeshire. Her parents forced her to marry, but she went into hiding and eventually became a nun at Markyate. She was so famous, a book was written about her.

Margaret Paston was the widow of a 15th century Norfolk landowner, who left his affairs in disarray. Her letters still survive, asking for gunpowder and arrows, to defend Caister Castle from 3,000 armed men who were trying to claim it.

Margery Kempe was a married woman who lived in King's Lynn from around 1373 to 1438. She had religious visions, and made pilgrimages to Rome, Spain, and Jerusalem, leaving her husband at home.

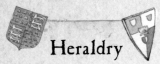

Heraldry

Knights' helmets covered their faces. This was confusing for anyone trying to work out who was who in a war or a mock battle. So knights started to display distinctive emblems on their shields and clothing.

Soon there were so many emblems, only specially trained men could remember which was whose. They were called *heralds* and the study of knightly emblems was known as *heraldry*.

Knights were proud of their emblems and passed them on to their sons and other family members. An English knight had this picture painted of himself with his wife, daughter and horse, all kitted out in his family emblems.

Noble pastimes

Among the nobility, women were considered important as an inspiration for men. People thought that loving a noble lady would inspire knights to be braver, more loyal and better-behaved. No one really knows how seriously most knights or ladies took this idea, but some certainly seem to have acted on it.

Some knights went on quests for adventure in the name of their lady-love. Others spent hours composing love-poetry, dancing and playing music to impress ladies – and other knights, too. But knights were also expected to fit in plenty of active pastimes, to keep them fit for fighting. Ladies were often involved in these activities, too.

Fighting for fun

Knights often fought in mock battles known as tournaments. In the early days, these could be bloody and chaotic, but rules were soon developed to stop them from killing each other, and knights started to wear special reinforced helmets and use blunted weapons.

Later tournaments often included a mock battle known as a *mêlée*, where two teams of knights fought each other in a designated area, under strict rules. One-to-one combats known as *jousts* were also popular at tournaments. Two knights charged at each other along a marked course. Points were awarded according to whether and where a knight managed to hit his opponent with his lance. A blow to the torso gained maximum points, while extra points were given to a knight who broke his rival's lance or knocked him off his horse.

This 15th century painting shows a joust between an English knight (on the left) and a French one.

The thrill of the chase

Hunting was another way for nobles to perfect their horseriding and weapon-handling, and there were many rituals involved. Noblemen were accompanied by servants whose job it was to find the prey and handle specially trained hunting dogs. Noblewomen often went too, but they sometimes watched rather than taking part. The most sought-after animals were reserved for nobles to hunt – strict laws forbade common people from catching the larger prey.

Different animals presented different challenges. Deer ran swiftly, so only the best dogs or archers could catch them. Wild boars weren't fast but they were strong and vicious, so hunters needed great timing and strength to spear them. After the hunt, the animals were taken home and eaten at great feasts.

Hawking

Women and men both joined in *hawking*, a type of hunting where specially trained birds of prey were used to track down and kill birds and animals such as partridges and hares.

Fun and games

Some sports and games have changed little over the years. Medieval men and women played a game similar to tennis. Players didn't use racquets – they hit the ball with their hands.

Those who wanted something more sedate could always take part in board games. Chess was one of the most popular, and was thought suitable even for noble ladies.

Football was popular among peasants, but very dangerous. There were no rules, and some players carried knives, which meant that tackling could be especially risky.

Merrymaking

Noble people weren't the only ones who had fun – on festival days throughout the year, everyone from a peasant to a prince would join in the celebrations.

Many of these were Christian holidays that are still celebrated today. At Christmas time, people decorated their houses with greenery and mistletoe, and tucked into huge meals. Meat and fish of all kinds were eaten, and feasting went on until January 6, which marked the day the Three Kings visited Jesus Christ. Instead of Christmas presents, people exchanged New Year gifts.

Some festivals with pagan origins were also celebrated, though not always with the approval of the Church. May Day was a celebration of the fertility of the countryside, and at various times in June, summer games led to much drinking, dancing and feasting. In the countryside, bonfires were lit, and burning wheels were rolled down the hillsides, while Londoners decorated their houses with bright garlands of flowers.

During festivals such as midsummer, the social structure was turned upside down. A peasant was declared Lord for the day, and was treated like a noble by the other villagers.

Strange shows

On the feast of Corpus Christi, commemorating Jesus Christ's last day on Earth, guilds of craftsmen would put on plays based on Bible stories, performed in the open air around towns. The craftsmen made props to promote their trades, and no expense was spared on special effects. An audience could watch Saint John the Baptist being beheaded, and be splashed with ox blood in the process. Another play called for the actor playing Judas to hang himself from a tree – one actor took his role so seriously that he nearly died.

Extreme eating

Nobles celebrated special occasions with particularly lavish feasts. The dishes were elaborately prepared, with sauces made from expensive spices and dried fruits. Leftover food was handed out to the needy, and rich people sometimes invited a few poor people to eat with them. But there was more to a feast than just the food. Dancers and acrobats kept the guests entertained, and musicians played throughout the meal. Sometimes the arrival of a spectacular dish was announced with a trumpet fanfare.

Asking for indigestion

The amount of food and drink consumed at royal feasts was staggering. Here is just some of what was ordered for the wedding celebration of Henry III's daughter Margaret in 1251:

25,000 gallons of wine
70,500 fish
7,000 hens
1,500 deer
68,500 loaves of bread

In this medieval painting, peasants are celebrating May Day by dancing to bagpipe music and wearing green branches in their hats.

The Welsh Prince

Ever since the Peasants' Revolt, Richard II's reign had gone downhill. He taxed the country heavily to pay for his lavish lifestyle, and heaped expensive gifts upon his friends. Meanwhile, he ignored Parliament, and made enemies among his most powerful nobles.

The usurper

Eventually Richard's cousin, Henry, Duke of Lancaster, led a rising against him. By this time, the King had lost all support. In 1399, he had to surrender the throne to his cousin, who became King Henry IV, the first Lancastrian king of England. Richard, meanwhile, was murdered in prison.

Unfortunately for Henry, he had no real claim to the throne. Richard's rightful heir was the Earl of March, the great grandson of Edward III. This made Henry a usurper. For his entire reign, he would face violent attempts to overthrow him.

Rebellion in Wales

Just one year after Henry took the throne, there was a major rebellion in Wales. It began as a dispute over land boundaries between a Welsh nobleman, Owain Glyndwr (say Glendower), and a marcher lord, Reginald de Grey. Henry sided with de Grey.

Furious, Glyndwr responded by sacking his rival's town, Ruthin. Before long, this local feud had become a full scale revolt against English rule. Welsh nobles flocked to join Glyndwr, and within a few months, they had proclaimed him Prince of Wales. The new Prince set about reclaiming Welsh lands from the English.

The Scottish succession

While Richard gave up the throne of England, there was a similar crisis in Scotland.

In 1402, Robert III's heir David was murdered by his power-hungry uncle. David's 12-year-old brother James had to flee the country.

But the ship was captured by pirates, and James was handed over to Henry IV of England.

James grew up in captivity, as the prisoner of the English King, while Scotland was ruled by his uncle. James took up the crown of Scotland in 1424, after marrying Joan Beaufort, the granddaughter of John of Gaunt.

Hotspur

Henry's English enemies saw the Welsh revolt as a chance to overthrow him, and joined forces with Glyndwr. Among the rebels was a fearsome warrior, Henry Percy, or 'Hotspur' as he was nicknamed. Hotspur was the King's cousin, and had actually been in charge of putting down the rebellion – until he had switched sides.

At the Battle of Shrewsbury in 1403, Henry IV's army caught Hotspur on his way to join up with the Welsh rebels. It was a bloody victory for the King and his son, Prince Henry, and Hotspur was killed in the battle.

Glyndwr's rebellion continued for years after the Battle of Shrewsbury, but gradually the King's forces won the upper hand. Glyndwr was forced into hiding, and after 1412 he was never seen again. To many people in Wales he is a national hero, and the last true Welshman to claim the title of Prince of Wales.

"I can summon spirits from the vasty deep"

Glyndwr appears in William Shakespeare's play *Henry IV part I* as 'Glendower'. In this play, his is portrayed as a mysterious figure, who claims that he can perform magic.

These actors are dressed as Owain Glyndwr and one of his knights. The emblems on the flag and other kit were adopted by Glyndwr from the 13th century Welsh ruler Llywelyn ap Gruffydd. They are still used by the Prince of Wales today.

Henry's longbows

Just like Edward III, Henry V knew that archers armed with longbows could win him victory in battle.

Longbows were very difficult to use, and so archers began practising from boyhood.

Henry's archers were mostly peasants, and so their victories over the French knights were also seen as victories over their social superiors.

They were not all English, though – many were from Wales. The Welsh were famous for their longbowmen.

By law, all men in England had to train at archery regularly.

Fields of France

In 1412 Henry IV died. He had spent most of his reign fighting off attempts to overthrow him – but his son would become one of the most popular kings in English history. When Prince Henry became Henry V, he set up law courts to bring criminals to justice. This won him many supporters. He also pardoned his old enemy Glyndwr. Then he turned to France, renewing the war that Edward III had begun.

War with France

There had been a truce between England and France since the reign of Richard II, but Henry believed that he had a right to the French throne. He had proved his military genius in the fight against Glyndwr, and in 1415 he set sail for Normandy, with an army of around 12,000 men. The campaign began badly. Henry's forces were weakened by a bout of dysentery, and he decided to retreat to the port of Calais. But, before he got there, he came up against a vast French army, near the village of Agincourt. Some historians think there were 40,000 Frenchmen – outnumbering the English by four to one.

The Battle of Agincourt

Just as at Crécy and Poitiers, the French army included thousands of knights, while most of the English soldiers were longbowmen. Once again, this proved decisive. The ground was wet and muddy, and the French knights quickly got bogged down. The English showered them with arrows, slaughtering thousands. It was a triumph for Henry. After Agincourt, he conquered Normandy, and married the French King's daughter.

Defeat

But Henry's victories were short-lived. Two years after his marriage, the great warrior King died, leaving behind him an infant son, Henry VI, to rule England and France. At the same time, the French were growing more determined to drive the English out of their country. Gradually, they won back the lands that Henry V had taken from them, until the only territory left in English hands was the port of Calais.

After a long campaign, the final battle of the Hundred Years' War was fought at Castillon in 1453, when a French army, equipped with cannons, defeated the English. After this, the English gave up trying to conquer France altogether. They soon had far more to worry about at home, where trouble was brewing.

Joan of Arc

Joan of Arc was a French peasant girl who had visions of saints. She encouraged the French Dauphin (heir to the throne) to fight the English, and even led French armies to victory in several battles.

In 1430, Joan was captured by the English, and burned at the stake on charges of heresy. After her death, she became a French national hero, and was made a saint.

This 16th century painting shows Englishmen killing French prisoners after Agincourt.

These two soldiers are counting money stolen from their victims.

Wars of the Roses

The fighting between the Yorkists and the Lancastrians later became known as the Wars of the Roses. The Yorkists often wore the emblem of a white rose, while the Lancastrians wore a red rose.

A family at war

Henry VI was just nine months old when he came to the throne, so England was ruled by a council of noblemen, who often argued among themselves. When the King was old enough to rule on his own, it soon became clear that he was not the great leader that his father had been. Henry VI was a gentle, religious man, who could not control his ambitious nobles. Worst of all, he suffered from bouts of insanity which left him unable to rule.

York and Lancaster

During one of these bouts, Richard, Duke of York, was chosen to rule England until the King's recovery. But when Henry took back power, the powerful and popular Richard led an army against him, defeated him, and carried on ruling the country. Henry's wife, Margaret of Anjou, was furious. She was determined to win back power for her husband, and set about raising an army of her own.

So began a violent civil war to decide who would rule England. On one side was Henry's family, the House of Lancaster, led by Margaret of Anjou. On the other was Richard's family, the House of York. Both sides had good claims to the throne, for both Henry and Richard were descended from Edward III.

EDINBURGH

Hedgeley — Moor 1464

Hexham — 1464

Towton 1461

YORK

—Ferrybridge 1461

Blore Heath 1459

Wakefield 1460

Losecote Field 1470

Ludford —Bridge 1459

Mortimer's Cross 1461

—Northampton 1460

Tewkesbury 1471

Edgecote Moor 1469

—St. Albans 1455

—St. Albans 1461

—Barnet 1471

LONDON

Battlefields

This map shows the most important battles, and which side won.

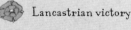 Lancastrian victory

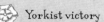 Yorkist victory

172

Edward IV

Battles were bloody, and power swung rapidly back and forth between the two families. At first the Yorkists won the advantage, capturing Henry and imprisoning him in the Tower of London. Then, at the Battle of Wakefield, they suffered a massive defeat and Richard himself was killed. His head was cut off and displayed in York, wearing a paper crown. But in 1461 Yorkists crowned Richard's son Edward IV. He finally defeated his enemies at the Battle of Towton, slaughtering thousands of Lancastrians.

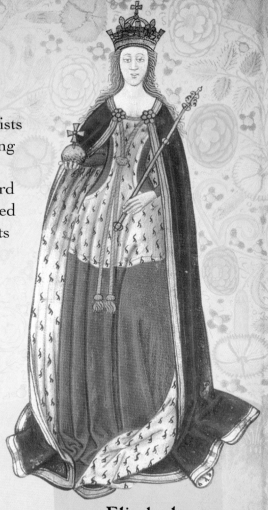

The Kingmaker

Shortly after his victory, Edward fell out with his greatest ally, Richard Neville, the Earl of Warwick. Neville had earned the nickname 'the Kingmaker' for his help in putting Edward on the throne. Now Edward hoped to ignore his ally and make his own decisions.

Neville switched sides, forced Edward to flee the country, and restored Henry to the throne. But Edward refused to give up, and soon returned at the head of an army. At the Battle of Barnet, he defeated Neville's forces, and Neville himself was killed.

Elizabeth Woodville

Edward IV married the beautiful Elizabeth Woodville in 1464.

At first, they kept their marriage secret, because Elizabeth was not from a noble family.

After the marriage was discovered, Elizabeth's relatives were given powerful positions in court. This angered Neville and many other nobles.

Peace

Edward was King again, and in 1471, it was announced that Henry had died in the Tower of London. For the next ten years the country was at peace. It seemed that the House of York had won, and that Edward's heirs would be the future kings of England. But it was not to be. When Edward died in 1483, his son and heir, Edward V, would be King for just two months.

Richard the villain

Under the Tudors, Richard III was portrayed as an evil usurper, and Henry as the man who saved England.

In the plays of the Tudor playwright William Shakespeare, Richard is a cruel, hunchbacked murderer with no remorse.

"I am determined to prove a villain."

A 16th century portrait of Richard III. In the Tudor period, it was changed to make him look like a hunchback.

The end of the line

Edward V was only 12 years old when he was crowned, and everyone feared that war would break out again. They were especially afraid that Elizabeth Woodville's ambitious family would try to seize control. In fact, it was not the Woodvilles who took power, but Edward IV's brother, Richard, Duke of Gloucester.

Richard III

Edward IV had chosen his brother to act as the King's protector, but Richard wanted the throne for himself. He locked up the young Edward, and his 10-year-old brother, the Duke of York, in the Tower of London. Then he had himself crowned Richard III.

As soon as he became King, Richard began executing his enemies without trial, and confiscating land. Many people suspected that he'd had his two nephews, the Princes in the Tower, murdered. When a young Lancastrian from Wales, Henry Tudor, claimed that the throne was rightfully his, both Lancastrian and Yorkist nobles flocked to support him. Everyone was anxious to be rid of Richard.

Invasion

Henry Tudor had been living in France, but in 1485 he crossed the English Channel with an army, to take the crown by force. Many of Richard's friends and allies deserted him, joining Henry. The King's only hope lay with one of the most powerful nobles in England, Lord Stanley. But Stanley refused to commit to either side, waiting to see which army was likely to win.

Many soldiers at Bosworth carried poleaxes – heavy wooden poles with metal heads. Some experts think that Richard was killed by one of these.

The Battle of Bosworth

On the morning of August 22, 1485, Richard and Henry faced each other at the Battle of Bosworth. On Richard's standard was his personal emblem, a White Boar, while on Henry's was a Red Dragon, a symbol of his Welsh roots. Meanwhile, Stanley's troops stood on a hill above the battlefield, ready to join in when it was clear who would win. In the end, Stanley entered the battle on Henry's side, and Richard was killed in the fighting.

The victorious Henry Tudor was crowned Henry VII, and married Elizabeth of York, Edward IV's sister, finally bringing together York and Lancaster. After years of chaos and bloodshed, the fighting was at an end. Henry was the first of a new line of kings and queens – the Tudors.

Dodgy claim

Henry Tudor claimed he had a right to be King, as a great grandson of Edward III. But many people had closer links to the throne – including the Princes in the Tower.

Some historians even think it may have been Henry who had them killed, rather than Richard III.

To strengthen his position, Henry claimed to be descended from King Arthur.

TUDORS & STUARTS

The 16th and 17th centuries were a time of momentous change in Britain. Under the Tudor monarchs, England and Wales were finally united, and the English gained control of parts of Ireland. The Tudors and the Scottish royal family, the Stewarts (later renamed Stuarts) also came together, through a marriage which later brought the two countries under one Stuart king.

It was an age of great religious upheaval, which eventually saw Protestantism replace Catholicism as the official faith in Britain. Many people's views of the world changed dramatically too, as adventurers explored new lands, and the arts and sciences flourished.

Elizabeth of York

King Henrye the seventh

This is a portrait of Henry VII and Elizabeth surrounded by York and Lancaster roses.

Henry created a new family emblem, the Tudor rose, by combining the white rose of York with the red rose of Lancaster.

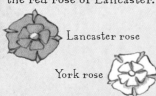

Lancaster rose

York rose

Tudor rose

The first Tudor

In 1485, Henry Tudor defeated King Richard III at the Battle of Bosworth, and became Henry VII, the first Tudor king of England. His victory ended 30 years of bloody civil war between two branches of the royal family – the Lancastrians and the Yorkists. Henry, who was a Lancastrian, brought the two sides of the family together by marrying Elizabeth of York. His reign promised a new period of wealth and stability in the kingdom.

Although he had married Elizabeth, Henry still feared that his Yorkist enemies might try to seize power. To strengthen his position, he took their estates, and had some of them executed for treason. He also brought in high taxes and banned nobles from raising their own armies. If they broke his laws, they were tried in a court, the Star Chamber, and fined heavily.

178

Plots and pretenders

Henry was right to be suspicious – he faced several Yorkist plots to overthrow him. Often his enemies were helped by the Irish and by the kings of Scotland and France, England's traditional enemies. In 1487, a group of Yorkists persuaded a boy called Lambert Simnel to pretend he was Richard III's nephew, the Earl of Warwick, who they believed had a stronger claim to the throne than Henry did. But the real Warwick was a prisoner in the Tower of London, and Henry paraded him through the streets to prove it. Simnel was arrested and sent to work in the royal kitchens as a punishment.

In 1491, a more serious threat came from a man named Perkin Warbeck, who pretended to be another of Richard III's nephews, Richard, Duke of York. It was thought that the real Richard had been murdered in the Tower of London, but Warbeck claimed that he had escaped from the Tower and fled abroad. He raised an army and invaded England. But he was defeated, and later hanged as a traitor.

James and Margaret

Among Warbeck's supporters was the Stewart king of Scotland, James IV. England and Scotland had often fought in the past, and the Scots sometimes sided with the French against England. But when Warbeck's plot failed, James decided it was time to make peace with the English.

To prevent further fighting, a treaty was signed, and in 1503, James married Henry's daughter, Margaret. This brought together the Stewart and the Tudor families. But the marriage didn't bring peace for long. Ten years later James IV was killed while fighting the English at the Battle of Flodden.

Tudor society

Henry kept close control over the nobles, but he still needed their support. They were at the top level of Tudor society.

Nobles were men with titles such as lord, duke and earl. They came from important families, which owned lots of land.

The gentry were wealthy, well-educated, and didn't need to work with their hands for a living. They included rich merchants and knights.

Yeomen farmers owned land, which they worked on themselves.

The lowest classes of society included 'tenant farmers' who rented land, farm workers, servants and beggars. This group made up 90% of Britain's population.

Henry VIII

In 1509, Henry VII died and was succeeded by his 18-year-old son, who became Henry VIII. The new King had a huge appetite for pleasure – eating too much, drinking too much, and spending most of the money that his father had saved on grand banquets and arrogant displays of power.

This portrait by Hans Holbein, a German painter, shows Henry in fine clothes and jewels, to show off his wealth and power.

Tudor tantrums

The young King was incredibly athletic, and often challenged the nobles in his court, known as courtiers, to wrestling or jousting competitions. Henry always won, of course – no one dared to beat him. The courtiers lived in constant fear of the King's childish moods. He often flew into sudden rages, thrashing them with sticks or bursting into tears.

As his reign wore on, Henry grew paranoid, believing that his courtiers would betray him, so he encouraged them to spy on each other. He executed some of his most trusted ministers simply because of lies that were spread by their rivals.

As this portrait shows, Henry VIII was an imposing figure of a man. Not only was he broad-chested, but historians believe he could have been as tall as 190cm (6ft, 4inches) at a time when people were, on average, shorter than they are today.

The King's Cardinal

At first, the most powerful minister in the land
was Henry's chancellor, Cardinal Thomas Wolsey.
He wasn't a noble, but he was hard working and
ambitious, and soon became the King's closest advisor.
At the height of his powers, Wolsey owned palaces,
and founded schools and colleges. Many courtiers
hated him for his wealth and his influence over Henry.

Henry's Great Matter

Henry married his brother's widow, Catherine of
Aragon, and they had a daughter, Mary. As Catherine
got older, Henry worried she would never have a son.
The problem became known in court as the King's
Great Matter. In around 1527, Henry fell in love
with one of his courtiers, Anne Boleyn. He wanted to
divorce Catherine so that he could marry Anne, and
have another chance to father a son.

But since England was a Catholic nation, divorces
had to be agreed by the Pope – and he wouldn't allow
it. Henry turned to Wolsey to find a solution. Wolsey
failed, and his enemies pounced. They accused him of
treason, and turned the King against him. Wolsey fell
ill and died in 1530, on his way to face the charges.

The break with Rome

Although Henry was a devout Catholic, he saw that
the only way to get the divorce he wanted was to
break away from the Roman Catholic Church. So he
ordered Parliament and Thomas Cranmer, Archbishop
of Canterbury, to declare him Supreme Head of the
Church in England, instead of the Pope. Now, he
could do whatever he liked.

Henry's six wives

Henry had six wives.
His first marriage,
to Catherine of
Aragon, ended
in divorce.

He had Anne Boleyn
executed on charges of
witchcraft and
adultery, after
she bore him
a daughter,
Elizabeth,
but no son.

Jane Seymour
was Anne Boleyn's
lady-in-waiting.
She died after
giving birth to
a son, Edward.

Henry divorced
his fourth wife,
Anne of Cleves,
deciding that
she was ugly.

He had
Catherine Howard
executed for
having affairs.

Catherine
Parr looked
after the old
King until
he died.

When Henry died in
1547, he spoke the
name of Jane Seymour,
the only wife that he is
said to have truly loved.

Henry's new powers

The Pilgrimage of Grace

Some people were angry with Henry's harsh treatment of the monks. In October 1536, an army of 30,000 people marched from the north of England in protest. It was known as the Pilgrimage of Grace.

Henry promised to consider their grievances, but as soon as the protestors had dispersed, he arrested their leaders and executed them.

Once Henry was in charge of the Church in England, he began using it to increase his own wealth. During the 16th century there were 850 monasteries in England, which were home to over 9,000 monks and nuns. They owned over a quarter of the country's land, which made them very rich. Henry decided to shut them down, and take their money.

The Dissolution of the Monasteries, as it became known, lasted four years, from 1536 to 1540. Led by Henry's new chancellor, Thomas Cromwell, the King's men looted the monasteries, stealing anything of value. Some of the buildings were burned to the ground. Others were simply left to crumble, the valuable lead stripped from their roofs, and beautiful stained glass windows smashed.

This is Fountains Abbey in Yorkshire. It was one of the many wealthy English monasteries that fell into ruin after being closed down.

Wales and Ireland

As well as making himself rich at the expense of the monasteries, Henry extended his power over Wales and Ireland – both Catholic countries. English kings had ruled over Wales for years, and Henry was of Welsh descent. But some areas were controlled by powerful Catholic nobles known as 'marcher lords' who made their own laws and appointed their own officials. Henry worried that after his break with Rome, the marcher lords wouldn't be loyal to him. So, in 1536, he united Wales and England, and brought in English Law for the Welsh.

One of Henry's titles was Lord of Ireland – but in fact he had little power there, and the Catholic Fitzgeralds, the leading nobles in Ireland, often rebelled against him. Henry sent in an army to restore order, and in 1541 he declared himself King of Ireland. But it made little difference. Many Irishmen deeply resented the English claims to their country, and they refused to break with Rome as Henry had done.

Solway Moss

Henry urged his nephew James V of Scotland (James IV's son) to break from Rome. But to his uncle's fury, James refused to do so.

Before long, England and Scotland were at war, and James sent a large army to invade England.

At the Battle of Solway Moss, the Scots outnumbered the English three to one. But they were so disorganized that the English quickly sent them fleeing from the battlefield.

The defeat broke James. He died two weeks later, and the crown passed to his baby daughter, Mary.

Wrestling kings

In 1520, Henry met Francis I of France at a huge peace conference named the Field of the Cloth of Gold. Everything went well, until Henry challenged Francis to a wrestling match.

Francis won, but the English said that he had cheated. The conference failed to prevent war from breaking out again.

Fortress England

When Henry came to the throne, the most powerful countries in Europe were Spain and France. England and France had always been enemies, and although Henry met the French king for a peace conference, the hostility continued almost throughout his reign.

But, after his break from Rome, Henry grew worried that the Catholic kings of both Spain and France were planning to invade England. So, using the stone from the abandoned monasteries, he built forts along the south coast to protect his country from attack.

The Royal Navy

Before Henry VIII, English kings had borrowed trading ships for battles, as they didn't have a navy of their own. But now Henry built up a huge fleet of ships to protect England.

The most formidable warship was named *Henri Grâce à Dieu* – it had five decks and over 200 cannons. But Henry was fondest of his flagship, the *Mary Rose*. In 1545, the *Mary Rose* set sail to fight the French. But it was so overloaded with cannons and men that it sank, with Henry watching in horror from the shore.

Blast from the past

Tudor ships were armed with incredibly powerful cannons, that needed teams of three or four people to load and fire. This was a dangerous job – the cannons sometimes blew up, killing the men who operated them.

This painting shows Henry's warship, *Henri Grâce à Dieu*, leaving England, carrying the King to the Field of the Cloth of Gold.

Working in the fields

Farm workers had to be ready to do whatever was asked of them. Their jobs were different at different times of year. The work included:

sowing seeds...

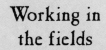

harvesting crops...

cutting back vines...

shearing sheep...

or building walls to mark out areas of land.

The Tudor countryside

While Henry and his troops were busy fighting the French, most people in Britain lived in rural areas, and rarely left the villages where they had been born. All kinds of people lived in the countryside, from wealthy nobles with large estates, to poor beggars who lived on village streets. But most country folk were farmers. They made their living by growing crops and grazing their animals. The poorest used 'common land' – land that was free to be used by anyone.

A farmer's life

Farmers spent almost all of their time working outside, while their wives stayed at home, preparing and preserving food, baking bread, brewing beer, and taking care of young children. By the time they were around seven years old, the children would begin work, too. Young girls helped their mothers in the house, and boys joined their fathers in the fields. Everyone had to work hard to provide food for the family. But however hard they worked, if the harvest was bad, everyone went hungry.

For the poorest farm workers, life was much the same as it had been during the Middle Ages. They lived in tiny, cold cottages. A few people had small glass windows, but most had to make do with bits of cloth or simple wooden shutters to keep out the cold. There was very little furniture. A table and some stools was all that most could afford. Often whole families lived together in a single room, which they shared with their animals – usually a few chickens, whose eggs they would sell. If times were hard, the chickens could be killed and eaten.

Market day

On market day, people set off for the nearest town, with produce to sell. For most, this was the furthest they went from home – roads were bumpy, muddy tracks, and thieves were everywhere. The market was a place to meet friends, attracting everyone in the area. There were also festivals and country fêtes, often on special days, such as Easter and Christmas.

Fun and games

For rich nobles, the countryside was like a playground. They enjoyed hunting deer with dogs, or bows and arrows...

...and hawking – using trained birds of prey to catch rabbits and pheasants.

Kett's Rebellion

Meanwhile, life was getting harder for the poorest farmers. In the 1500s, wealthy landowners began fencing off areas of common land for themselves. They wanted to make money by rearing sheep there, and selling wool. This process, called enclosure, left many people with no land to farm. Fences were torn down in protest, and in 1549, a farmer named Robert Kett gathered an army of rebels in Norwich, demanding that the enclosures be pulled down. The rebellion was brutally crushed by the Earl of Warwick.

This painting shows a fête in the village of Bermondsey.

Rebirth and reform

This is a detail from *The Ambassadors*, by the Renaissance painter Hans Holbein. The men, a merchant and a cleric, are surrounded by instruments of Renaissance learning.

In the middle of the floor, you can see a squashed image of a human skull – a reminder that death comes to everyone.

During the 15th and 16th centuries, a great cultural movement swept across Europe. This became known as the Renaissance – or 'rebirth' – because artists and writers rediscovered ideas from ancient Greek and Roman civilizations, and produced brilliant works of art and literature. At the same time, great thinkers and scientists came up with new ideas and discoveries that gradually changed people's lives.

Renaissance men

In England and Scotland, King Henry VIII and King James IV led the way as 'renaissance men' – well-educated in all fields of art and literature, and dedicated to learning.

Henry played several instruments, wrote music, and spoke French, Latin and Spanish. He invited great painters, like the German Hans Holbein, to the English court.

James was even more impressive. One great scholar of the Renaissance, the Dutchman Erasmus, said he had, "an astonishing knowledge of everything." Like Henry, James spoke several languages and was fascinated by the arts. He founded universities, and encouraged noblemen to send their children to school.

The Protestant Reformation

In Europe, meanwhile, trouble was brewing. A German monk named Martin Luther had begun to attack the Catholic Church, arguing that it needed to be reformed. His ideas soon became the basis for a new form of Christianity, called Protestantism.

Protestants claimed that the Church was rich and corrupt. They rejected the authority of the Pope, and believed that church services should be read in their own language, instead of Latin. Throughout Europe, Christians argued fiercely over religion.

Under the leadership of Henry and James, England and Scotland remained Catholic. But as books and pamphlets written by Protestants flowed into Britain, people began to move away from Catholicism. When Henry and James died, the next few years were dominated by struggles over whether England and Scotland would be Catholic or Protestant.

Printing ideas

New ideas spread fast, thanks to a method of printing, invented during the late Middle Ages by a German, Johannes Gutenberg.

His printing presses meant that books and pamphlets could be produced easily, and read aloud in public places.

During the Reformation, books helped to spread the word about Martin Luther and Protestantism.

Edward VI

This portrait shows Edward VI at six months old. He grew up to be an intelligent, serious boy, and oversaw big changes to the English Church.

Paintings, statues and stained glass windows were smashed or removed.

Church services were held in English, instead of Latin.

Thomas Cranmer, the Archbishop of Canterbury, introduced a Protestant prayer book to be used by everyone in England.

Religious turmoil

Henry VIII died in 1547, and the crown passed on to his nine-year-old son, who became Edward VI. Since Edward was so young, his uncle, the Duke of Somerset, was appointed to rule on his behalf. Under his uncle's influence, Edward made changes to the English Church, to bring it closer to the ideas of European Protestants.

The nine-day queen

But Edward became ill, and in 1553 he died, naming as his successor his 17-year-old Protestant cousin, Lady Jane Grey. When Jane was proclaimed Queen, Edward's Catholic half-sister Mary, who was next in line for the throne, was horrified. She gathered support, then marched to London, took power, and began preparing for her coronation. Jane was imprisoned in the Tower of London and later beheaded. She had been Queen for only nine days, and hadn't even been crowned.

A 19th-century painting of Lady Jane Grey's execution

Bloody Mary

As soon as she became Queen, Mary turned back the clocks. She made the Pope head of the English Church again, and freed Catholic priests whom Edward had imprisoned, locking up Protestant clergy instead. She also married a Catholic, the future King Philip II of Spain, despite many people's fears that this would give the Spanish power over England.

During the five years of Mary's reign, she had more than 300 Protestants burned alive at the stake. By the time she died in 1558, Mary was so unpopular among Protestants that they nicknamed her 'Bloody Mary' and celebrated the day of her death each year. Mary never had any children, so it was left to her Protestant half-sister, Elizabeth, to take the throne.

The Scottish Reformation

Meanwhile, north of the border, the Protestant Reformation swept through Scotland. At its head was a fiery preacher named John Knox, who attacked Catholicism in his sermons. In 1560, the Scottish Parliament voted in Protestantism as the country's official religion.

At this time, James IV's Catholic daughter, Mary, Queen of Scots, was living in France as the wife of the *Dauphin*, the heir to the French throne. It was here that she changed her name from 'Stewart' to 'Stuart' – to sound more French. When her husband died in 1560, Mary returned to her kingdom of Scotland, which had been ruled by her mother while she was away. But she found that her Catholic faith made her unwelcome. It seemed that in England and Scotland, the battle between Catholics and Protestants had been won by the Protestants – for now, at least.

The Book of Martyrs

After Mary's death, a man named John Foxe put together a *Book of Martyrs*, with accounts of Protestants who had been burned for their beliefs. A copy was put in every church to remind people of the horrors of Catholic rule.

Shown here in his clerical robes, John Knox was a fierce opponent of the Catholic Queen, and thought it was wrong for women to be monarchs.

191

Elizabeth I

Bloody Mary's half-sister Elizabeth was crowned
Queen of England in 1558. The daughter of Henry
VIII and Anne Boleyn, Elizabeth I became one of the
most successful monarchs in European history. She was
a brilliant politician and diplomat, and during her reign,
England became an important European power.
She made the country Protestant once
again, but she didn't execute Catholics
– unless they plotted against her.

Queen Elizabeth knew
how important it was
to look like a monarch.
Here, courtiers carry
her in a litter – a
finely decorated,
portable chair.

Elizabeth's courtiers

Elizabeth surrounded herself with a court of over 1,000 leading men, who flattered her with displays of dancing and recitals of love poetry. Some of them even kept their marriages secret, in case it upset her. These courtiers depended on Elizabeth for their wealth, as she could grant them land and titles. Those that she liked best, such as Robert Dudley, the Earl of Leicester, became very rich.

Elizabeth also made rules for her court, to create a strong image for the monarchy. Courtiers were never allowed to turn their backs on her. After speaking to her, they had to walk away backwards. Wherever the Queen went, trumpet fanfares announced her arrival.

Royal tours

Throughout her reign, Elizabeth went on regular tours, known as progresses, around the south of England, staying as a guest with chosen courtiers. She always made her host provide lavish entertainment for the entire court, saving her vast amounts of money. A visit from the Queen was a huge privilege, but it was so ruinously expensive that many courtiers dreaded her arrival.

The Virgin Queen

Elizabeth's chief advisors, known as the Privy Council, hoped that the Queen would marry and give birth to an heir. Many important men – including Philip II of Spain, her sister Mary's widower – wanted to win power by marrying her. But Elizabeth didn't want to share her position with anyone. Because she never married, she is sometimes called the Virgin Queen.

Royal beauty

Everyone wanted to look like the Queen. Women went to great lengths to copy her striking white makeup and red hair.

For the skin, they rubbed on a toxic mixture of white lead, vinegar and raw egg white. False veins were then painted on to make the skin look even paler.

They dyed or bleached their hair, or wore wigs – like Elizabeth herself.

Several of Elizabeth's teeth were rotten and black. Many women even copied this, rubbing their teeth with soot to make them black.

Elizabethan fashion

Queen Elizabeth probably got her dress sense from her father. He took great care over his appearance, and loved to dress up in fine clothing and jewels. But he became worried that some wealthy merchants were better dressed than his nobles – and he wanted everyone to be able to spot a noble. So he introduced new 'sumptuary laws' to control what clothing people wore. Nobles could wear materials and dyes that were banned for other people, however rich they were.

Young adults

Young boys and girls from noble families were dressed like small adults. Here, the children of Lady Tasburgh are dressed up to look just like Queen Elizabeth.

Their mother, standing at the back, is wearing an expensive black gown.

Dressed to impress

By the time of Elizabeth's reign, everyone wanted to show off by wearing elegant clothes. Elizabeth herself is said to have owned more than 250 gowns. A person's clothing was a way of displaying how rich and powerful they were. For instance, black dye was very expensive – so nobles wore black clothing so that people knew they were rich.

Dressed for work

While fashions moved quickly among nobles, little changed for the poorer people in society. Their clothes were made to work in, and so were much more practical. They were spun out of thick, itchy wool, and were usually brown, since this was the cheapest dye. Farmers often wore just a tunic, so they didn't get too hot.

Gentlemen of the court

Elizabeth's courtiers were the best dressed people in all of Britain. Male courtiers wore lots of layers, to make themselves look big and impressive. Some even wore shoulder pads and stuffed their clothing.

First they put on a shirt, and a coat called a doublet.

A jerkin went over the doublet.

A long gown or cloak went on top. This was often trimmed with fur.

On Sundays, every man wore a hat.

The doublet was fastened with laces. Buttons were just for decoration.

Ladies of the court

Ladies of the court were just as stylish as men. They dressed in richly embroidered gowns, made of heavy materials such as velvet. Underneath, they wore special undergarments to change the shape of their bodies.

A farthingale was a cone-shaped frame that pushed out the gown.

Many ladies wore a figure-hugging bodice to flatten their curves.

A pomander, a container of sweet-smelling spices, was hung from the waist.

Ladies had servants to help them dress.

Both men and women wore large, frilly collars called ruffs.

195

The Golden Age

At Elizabeth's court, art and culture flourished, and people called it a Golden Age. Poets such as John Donne and Edmund Spenser composed great works of literature. The Queen encouraged talented musicians to give concerts in private houses and playhouses. She also loved plays, and had performances put on at court specially for her entertainment.

Entertainment

In Tudor times, wealthy people enjoyed concerts, recitals, banquets and dancing.

Meanwhile, poorer people had their own entertainment. One common sport was bear baiting, in which people watched bears fighting with dogs.

People also held cock fights. Large bets were placed on which cock would win.

Plays became more and more popular during Elizabeth's reign. They were one of the few forms of entertainment that could be enjoyed by both rich and poor.

This picture shows Shakespeare's Globe playhouse with part of the wall cut away, so that you can see inside.

'Groundlings' pay a small price to stand and watch the play. Higher up, the seats are more expensive.

William Shakespeare

Elizabethan writers such as Christopher Marlowe and Ben Jonson produced brilliant plays that are still performed today. But the greatest writer of them all was William Shakespeare. He wrote at least 36 plays, acting in many of them, and he is now one of the most famous writers of all time.

Performances

Shakespeare put his plays on at the Globe, a playhouse in London that held up to 3,000 people. These performances were very different from modern productions. The actors had to shout to be heard over the noisy audience. Women were played by male actors wearing wigs and dresses. Actors in fight scenes used real weapons, and sometimes seriously injured each other. Cannons were sometimes fired on stage, and on one occasion, this set the building on fire.

'Gatherers' stand at the door with boxes to collect admission money.

Shakespeare's plays

Shakespeare's plays included romances, such as *Romeo and Juliet*...

"O Romeo, Romeo! Wherefore art thou Romeo?"

Tragedies like *Hamlet*...

"To be, or not to be: that is the question."

And dramatic versions of British history, such as *Henry V*...

"Once more unto the breach, dear friends!"

Moving to the towns

While Elizabeth's courtiers enjoyed new art, music and literature, life was getting harder for the poor people of England. The population had been rising during the Tudor period, and by the time of Elizabeth's reign, there weren't enough jobs to go around, especially in the countryside, where landowners were fencing off more and more land for their flocks of sheep.

Many people decided to pack their bags and head to the nearest town in search of employment. Swollen by these new arrivals, towns expanded rapidly, becoming dirty and overcrowded. Competition for jobs was fierce, and whole families were often forced into begging or stealing, just to stay alive.

Living in towns

Towns bustled with activity, and some people found work in new industries, such as glass and paper making, and book printing. Farmers could sell their produce in noisy open-air markets, and merchants traded all kinds of goods such as wool and iron. Exotic merchandise from all over the world flowed into ports such as London and Bristol – for the few who could afford it.

For most people, though, even soap was a luxury. There was no running water, and household waste was usually simply dumped in the street. Fleas, rats and flies were attracted to the crowded streets. The filth and vermin caused deadly diseases such as smallpox and tuberculosis to spread quickly. By 1600, London had a population of over 200,000. It was by far the biggest city in Britain, and one of the greatest trading cities in Europe. But it was also one of the filthiest places in the world.

The Poor Law

In England and Wales, the Elizabethan Poor Law made sure that all districts provided work for the poor, and shelter for those who couldn't work. The poor were divided into categories:

The 'impotent poor' were those who were considered too old, young or sick to work.

The 'able-bodied poor' were those who were unable to find work.

'Sturdy rogues' were those who could work but chose not to. They were thought to be lazy and dangerous, and were punished.

Crime and punishment

With so many townspeople jobless and desperate for money, crime was common. There was no real police force in the 16th century, but local constables enforced laws, and town magistrates handed out harsh punishments. Anyone found begging without permission was flogged, murderers and thieves were hanged, nobles who were accused of treason were beheaded and people who spoke against the Church could be burned alive.

Dishonest people were locked in a wooden frame called a pillory, where people could throw things at them.

This picture shows a typical town in Elizabethan England.

It was against the law to kill large birds such as ravens. They were needed to eat the waste in the streets.

Streets are narrow and dirty.

This farmer has come to sell bales of wool.

The market

A pickpocket

Market stalls

Most buildings have tiled roofs and are made of wooden frames filled with plaster.

Exotic goods

Elizabethan explorers brought back exotic goods that had never been seen before in England.

Sir Walter Raleigh brought back potatoes...

...but at first people tried to eat them raw.

Sir John Hawkins brought back tobacco...

...but his servant saw him smoking and poured water on him, thinking his master was on fire.

Exploring the world

In 1492, an Italian explorer named Christopher Columbus landed in America. At first, Europeans called it the New World, because they hadn't even known that it existed before. This was the start of a great age of European exploration. In 1498, the Portuguese explorer Vasco Da Gama found a sea route from Europe to the East Indies, which was rich with fine silks and spices.

Meanwhile, Spaniards were busy setting up colonies in the New World. By Elizabeth's time, their ships were sailing back and forth across the Atlantic Ocean, bringing home vast quantities of gold and silver from South and Central America, and the West Indies.

English adventurers

Envious of Spain's growing riches, Elizabeth encouraged her sailors to search for new lands and treasures too. Sir Walter Raleigh hunted for gold in South America, while Sir John Hawkins sailed from Africa to the New World, bringing African slaves to work in the West Indies. Elizabeth also gave her sea captains permission to attack foreign treasure ships, although this made them very unpopular with the Spaniards.

This is a replica of Francis Drake's flagship, the *Golden Hinde*.

Drake's progress

The blue line on this map shows
Drake's route around the world.

Europe

Asia

North
America

China

PACIFIC
OCEAN

West
Indies

PACIFIC
OCEAN

India

East Indies

South
America

Africa

ATLANTIC
OCEAN

Australia

New Zealand

Around the world

Among these captains was a man named Francis
Drake. He was so feared by the Spaniards that they
nicknamed him *El Draque* – the Dragon. To them he
was just a pirate. But to the English, he was a hero.

In 1577, Drake set sail across the Atlantic Ocean,
to plunder Spanish ships and settlements in South
and Central America. Some of his ships were lost in
stormy seas, but he continued on into the Pacific
Ocean, then to the East Indies and Africa, before
returning home laden with silver, gold and pearls that
he had looted from the Spaniards. The journey took
three years, but Francis Drake had become the first
Englishman to sail all the way around the world.

Elizabeth came to meet
Drake on board the
Golden Hinde, where
he was knighted for
services to his country.

Rival queens

In England, while Protestants were enjoying religious freedom, Catholics were being forced to pay fines, and were even banned from holding religious services. Most of them felt they could do nothing about this, but some were determined to turn England into a Catholic country again, and this meant replacing Elizabeth with a Catholic monarch. As it happened, there was an ideal candidate – Mary Stuart, Queen of Scotland, who was Elizabeth's cousin.

An early portrait of Mary, Queen of Scots. Catholic painters usually made her look beautiful, as she appears here, while Protestant artists made her look ugly.

Mary in Scotland

When Mary took up power in Scotland in 1561, after the death of her French husband, the Scots were suspicious of her. They were fiercely Protestant, and were scared that Mary might try to impose her Catholic faith on them. Since she had spent most of her early years in France, they also saw her as a foreigner, who knew nothing of their country.

Mary soon won them over. She married a handsome Scottish nobleman Lord Darnley, and although she held Catholic services for herself, she made no attempt to interfere with the country's religion. For a while, her subjects were content – but that quickly changed.

202

A murder for a murder

Within months of her marriage, Mary discovered that the dashing Lord Darnley was little more than a bullying drunkard. He grew jealous of his wife, and angry at her close relationship with her secretary, David Rizzio.

In 1566, Darnley joined a plot to kill Rizzio, and helped to stab him to death. Mary never recovered from the shock of this murder, and grew to hate her husband. A year later, Darnley was strangled to death, and most people thought that Mary was involved. There was a scandal, and Mary had to abdicate, and flee to England.

Catholic plots

As soon as Mary arrived in England, Catholics began plotting to put her on the English throne. Elizabeth had no choice but to keep Mary locked up. Her ministers advised her to execute Mary, but Elizabeth didn't want to kill a queen – especially her own cousin.

One of these ministers, Sir Francis Walsingham, ran a network of spies to uncover plots. A firm Protestant, he was desperate to prove that Mary was guilty of treason. In 1586, one of his spies gave him a coded letter from Mary to a Catholic plotter, in which she agreed to have Elizabeth killed. This finally convinced the Queen of England to have her rival beheaded.

Mary's pet dog went with her to the execution, hidden under her dress.

The Babington Plot

Mary was executed in 1587 for her part in the Babington Plot, masterminded by a wealthy young Catholic, Anthony Babington.

Babington planned for Elizabeth to be murdered and for a Spanish army to invade England.

But among the plotters was one of Walsingham's spies. He revealed that the plotters were sending messages to each other hidden inside beer barrels.

Babington and his conspirators were imprisoned, and put to death. Soon after that, Mary was tried and executed at Fotheringhay Castle.

The Spanish Armada

Almost immediately after Mary's execution, Elizabeth faced another threat, this time from Philip II of Spain. He had become angry about English raids on Spanish ships in the Caribbean, especially as his spies had found that Elizabeth was taking a share of the treasure herself. To add to his fury, she was also helping Protestants in the Spanish-controlled Netherlands to rebel against him. Philip turned on the Queen whom he had once wanted to marry, and decided to go to war.

Facing the Armada

Legend has it that when news reached England that the Armada was approaching, Sir Francis Drake was playing a game of bowls. He is supposed to have remarked casually, "we have time to finish this game, and beat the Spaniards too."

Elizabeth I delivered a great speech to the English army at Tilbury fort to encourage them to fight hard.

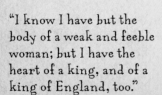

"I know I have but the body of a weak and feeble woman; but I have the heart of a king, and of a king of England, too."

Plans of attack

In 1587, Philip planned to send a vast fleet of ships, known in Spanish as an *armada*, to the Netherlands. There it would pick up a Spanish army of 30,000 men, and ferry them over the English Channel to invade England. But there was an unexpected setback. English spies discovered Philip's plans, and Sir Francis Drake raided the Spanish port of Cadiz, where the Armada was assembling. There, he burned many ships before they had even set sail. It is said that Drake boasted that he had singed the King of Spain's beard.

Fire ships

When the Armada finally set sail in July 1588, it was met by an English fleet led by Lord Howard of Effingham, with Drake as his vice-admiral. They hounded the Spanish ships as they sailed up the English Channel. The Spaniards took shelter in the French port of Calais, but in the dead of night, the English set fire to eight of their own ships and sent them crashing into the enemy fleet. This drove the Spaniards into the open sea, where the English were waiting to attack them.

Victory

On August 8, 1588, the rival fleets met at the Battle of Gravelines, near Calais. The English destroyed several Spanish ships, but could not defeat the Armada entirely.

Then, the next day, strong winds drove the Spaniards north, before they had a chance to pick up Philip's army in the Netherlands. They were forced to sail around Scotland and Ireland and back to Spain, with storms wrecking many of their ships along the way. In London, crowds cheered as Elizabeth gave a speech, thanking God for the victory. Many Protestants saw their success as a sign that God was on their side.

The Armada in Ireland

→ Route of the Armada

■ Spanish lands

Many Spanish ships were wrecked on the coast of Ireland. Around 5,000 Spaniards were drowned or killed by local Irishmen.

The English 'fire ships' were old or worn-out ships, loaded with firewood and tar. They caused little damage, but a lot of panic.

The cannons on the fire ships were loaded. There was no crew to fire them, but the flames set them off anyway.

Great Britain

England and Scotland remained two separate nations under James. But he was the first to use the term Great Britain, and he even created a new flag, the Union Jack, out of the English and Scottish flags.

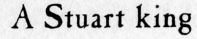

A Stuart king

In 1603, the great Queen Elizabeth died without any children, and the Tudor dynasty came to an end. Her successor was James VI of Scotland, the son of Mary Stuart. Now, he was also James I, the first Stuart king of England. For the first time, Scotland, England, Ireland and Wales were all ruled by the same monarch.

James and the English

The English were excited about their new king, but James soon made himself unpopular by surrounding himself with Scottish courtiers, and tactlessly ignoring English customs.

To make matters worse, James was a fierce defender of the Divine Right of Kings. This was the idea that a king's power came from God, and nobody could question his decisions. His ideas offended members of Parliament, who wanted more power in government.

The Gunpowder Plot

James loved to lecture his subjects. He called himself the "great schoolmaster of the whole land" – and he hoped to convert everyone to his Protestant beliefs. This upset some Catholics, who were disappointed that the son of Mary Stuart would not let them worship in peace. It wasn't long before a number of Catholics began plotting against the King.

One group came up with a particularly daring plan: to use gunpowder to blow up the Houses of Parliament, with James inside.

This portrait shows James in fine clothing. He was so scared of being assassinated that he had his clothing specially padded, in case he was stabbed.

A date to remember

But one of the conspirators warned a fellow Catholic, Lord Monteagle, to stay away from Parliament. Monteagle told the authorities at once. At midnight on the 5th of November, 1605, soldiers searched the cellars beneath the Houses of Parliament, and found Guido, or Guy, Fawkes, one of the conspirators, with barrels of gunpowder. The plotters were rounded up and hanged. The date went down in British history and is now celebrated every year with bonfires and fireworks.

Fighting with Parliament

Meanwhile, Parliament was getting more and more frustrated with the King, who loved to show off his royal power and fritter away money on his friends. This was especially offensive to a group of extreme Protestants known as Puritans, who thought that people should work hard and live a simple life. James's quarrels with Parliament grew more and more serious, and when his son, Charles, became King in 1625, the situation reached a crisis point.

Torture

After his arrest, Guy Fawkes was tortured in the Tower of London.

He was then made to sign his name on a confession, but was barely able to write.

Top: signature after torture
Below: signature 8 days later, after he recovered

This print shows the Gunpowder Plot conspirators. Their leader was Robert Catesby, who is second from the right. Guy Fawkes stands next to him.

Robert Winter
Christopher Wright
Iohn Wright
Thomas Percy
Guido Fawkes
Robert Catesby
Thomas Winter

Laud and the Puritans

William Laud tried to stamp out Puritanism. Puritan priests were horribly punished. One Puritan lawyer, William Prynne, was branded and had his ears cut off.

In 1620, a group of Puritans known as the 'Pilgrims' set sail for North America. They wanted to worship as they pleased, so they set up a colony there and named it New England.

In 1644, Prynne had his revenge. He oversaw the trial of Laud for treason. The next year, Laud was beheaded.

King or Parliament

Charles I was a shy, dignified young man, who stammered when he spoke. Like his father, James, he believed firmly in the Divine Right of Kings, and relied on his friends for advice. This infuriated many MPs, who thought that the King should consult them on important matters.

The Puritans in Parliament were also worried that Charles wanted to make England Catholic again, since the King was married to the Catholic French princess Henrietta Maria. They grew even more concerned when Charles appointed his friend, William Laud, as Archbishop of Canterbury. Although he was a Protestant, Laud hated Puritans, and brought in grand church ceremonies that seemed Catholic in style.

Charles in charge

Soon after coming to the throne, Charles needed to raise money to fight wars in Europe. But Parliament refused to help him. For a while, the King angrily dismissed Parliament every time its members argued with him, or tried to get rid of his advisors. Eventually, he grew so fed up that he sent the MPs home for good.

From 1629 to 1640, Charles ruled and raised money without calling Parliament. But this 'eleven years' tyranny' ended when he tried to introduce Laud's church ceremonies in Scotland, together with a new prayer book. Unfortunately for Charles, most Scots were Presbyterians. Their beliefs were similar to those of the Puritans, and they hated Laud's grand style of Protestantism. They also objected to Charles interfering in their country, because they saw him as a foreigner.

The National Covenant

In churches all over Scotland, angry mobs rioted and attacked clergymen. Thousands vowed to fight religious change, and signed the National Covenant, a document which attacked Laud's ideas. Charles had lost control, and before long the Scots were threatening war. In 1640, the King was finally forced to recall Parliament, and ask for money to raise an army.

This portrait by van Dyke show Charles I elegantly dressed. Many MPs disapproved of his extravagance, which cost the country a lot of money.

Parliament's revenge

The new Parliament knew that the King needed its help, and exploited the situation. Laud was arrested, together with the Earl of Strafford, one of the King's chief advisors. A group of MPs, led by the devout Puritan John Pym, brought in laws to reduce the King's powers. One law required him to call Parliament every three years.

The road to war

Charles was enraged by these plans to limit his authority. In January, 1642, he burst into the House of Commons and demanded the arrest of Pym and the four other leading MPs who had opposed him. But they had been warned and had already escaped. Charles left London, raised an army of Royalist supporters and declared war. His opponents, the Parliamentarians, prepared to fight against him.

Throughout England, families, villages and towns decided which side to join. The Civil War had begun.

The Civil War

This map shows which areas mainly supported Parliament and which supported the King at the outbreak of war in 1642.

Marston Moor, 1644 ✕
Preston, 1648 ✕

✕ Naseby, 1645

Edgehill, 1642 ✕

Oxford ●

London ●

For seven years, bloody battles raged between the Parliamentarians and the Royalists. The war involved almost everyone in Britain, and many families were torn apart by arguments over which side to join. Most Puritans fought for Parliament, while Catholics were mainly Royalists. The city of London and the navy sided with Parliament, which gave its armies a huge advantage. They had the wealth of the capital at their disposal, and could move troops by ship – which was much faster than marching by land.

 Under control of Parliament

Under control of Charles

✕ Battle site and date

This scene shows a re-enactment of the Battle of Edgehill, the first battle of the Civil War.

Cavalrymen fought on horseback.

Foot soldiers fought with long, pointed wooden pikes.

Musketeers used guns called muskets, which were heavy and could be used as clubs in hand-to-hand fighting.

'Push of pike'

In battle, large blocks of soldiers with pikes advanced and tried to push the other side back. If one side broke, most of them would be killed.

Hedgehog

When enemy cavalry attacked, foot soldiers formed a 'hedgehog' with the musketeers in the middle and the pikemen around the edges.

The fight for London

The King raised his standard at Nottingham Castle to declare war, but as soon as it was up, a gust of wind blew it over. Many saw this as a bad omen. All the same, Charles set about preparing to fight. He made Oxford his base, gathered his army, and headed for London. He was determined to capture the capital.

The first big battle took place at Edgehill. The Royalists were helped by Charles's nephew, Prince Rupert of the Rhine, who was a brilliant cavalry commander. But the Parliamentarians managed to stop the King's army from reaching London.

Marston Moor

Meanwhile, Charles's enemy John Pym made a deal with the Scots. They would send an army to join forces with Parliament. In return, Parliament would establish the Presbyterian Church in England. In 1644, the combined Scottish and Parliamentarian army met the King's Cavaliers at Marston Moor. It was the biggest and bloodiest battle of the war. The Royalists lost, and Parliament won control of northern England.

Roundheads and Cavaliers

Royalists called the Parliamentarian soldiers Roundheads, because they cut their hair short and wore round helmets.

The Parliamentarians called their enemies Cavaliers, after the French word *chevalier*, meaning a knight. They thought that Cavaliers were vain and arrogant.

Oliver Cromwell

Oliver Cromwell was a Puritan who became MP for Huntingdon in 1628. When war broke out he joined the army, and rose rapidly through the ranks. He led the Parliamentarian cavalry at Marston Moor and at Naseby.

Victory and defeat

After the Battle of Marston Moor, the Royalists were all but defeated. Charles had missed his chance to capture London and win the war, and now he was running out of money. His soldiers were mostly local troops who did not want to travel too far away from their homes, and this meant that he couldn't move his armies around freely.

Meanwhile, the Parliamentarian army was getting even stronger. An MP named Oliver Cromwell persuaded Parliament to create a 'New Model Army' made up of professional soldiers, who were fiercer and tougher than the untrained Royalist troops.

In 1645 the New Model Army was put to the test, when it faced the King's army at the Battle of Naseby. Cromwell's soldiers crushed their opponents, and the Royalists fled.

The Battle of Naseby was the end for Charles. Soon afterwards he gave himself up to the Scots, hoping for protection — but in 1647, they handed him over to Parliament. It looked as if the war had been won.

Unlike Charles, the Puritan Oliver Cromwell did not want to be flattered in paintings. This portrait shows him 'warts and all' — with a red face and a shiny nose.

The second war

Charles had one last chance to snatch victory from the jaws of defeat. While he was imprisoned at Carisbrooke Castle on the Isle of Wight, the King persuaded the Scots to change sides and join the Royalists. But it was all in vain. In 1648, the final battle of the Civil War was fought at Preston. It was another resounding victory for the New Model Army.

The King on trial

The leaders of the New Model Army thought Charles was too dangerous to be kept alive. They saw his alliance with Scotland as treason, and argued that he should be put on trial. But Charles claimed that the courts had no right to try the King.

A vote was held in Parliament to decide whether there should be a trial. That day, Cromwell's soldiers surrounded the House of Commons, keeping out any MPs they thought would vote against trying the King. Cromwell and his allies had already decided on the verdict: Charles was sentenced to death, and the monarchy abolished.

On January 30, 1649, King Charles I was beheaded outside the Banqueting House in London. There was no rejoicing. As the blow fell, the crowd let out a huge groan. Many sobbed openly.

Rule by Parliament

For the first time in a thousand years, the country had no monarch. Instead, it was ruled by Parliament, led by Oliver Cromwell, who had risen from the middle classes to become the most powerful man in the land. His rule came to be known as the Commonwealth.

Trial and execution

No one wanted to be the man to sentence Charles to death. In the end, John Bradshaw reluctantly agreed to be judge at the King's trial.

Bradshaw was so scared of being assassinated that he wore this hat, lined with steel, to stop bullets.

The day of Charles's execution was freezing cold. Proud until the end, he asked for an extra shirt to wear, so the crowd wouldn't think he was shivering with fear.

The Commonwealth

Although the King was dead, there were still many Royalists in Ireland and Scotland who hoped to put his son, Charles Stuart, on the throne. Cromwell dealt with them swiftly and brutally.

First, he took the New Model Army to Ireland, and killed thousands of Irish Royalists, many of whom were Catholic. Meanwhile, Scottish Royalists crowned Charles King of Scotland, and invaded England. Cromwell returned from Ireland and crushed them at the Battle of Worcester. Charles himself managed to escape to France, where he stayed in exile, waiting for a chance to return.

Lord Protector

With his opponents defeated, Cromwell gave himself the title of 'Lord Protector' and ruled England for five years, until his death in 1658. Just like Charles I before him, he often argued with Parliament and dismissed it. Unlike Charles, though, he had a powerful army on his side.

In 1655 there was yet another Royalist uprising, and Cromwell decided that he needed to keep a closer watch over his people. He divided England into 11 districts, each one ruled by a major-general. Then he set about enforcing Puritan values all over the land. He closed down inns and playhouses, and banned popular pastimes such as bear-baiting and traditional activities, including maypole dancing. People were fined for being drunk, for gambling, and even for playing sports.

Escape

After Cromwell won the Battle of Worcester, Charles Stuart had lots of adventures while trying to escape.

He cut his hair and pretended to be a woodsman.

He hid in 'priest-holes' – secret rooms in Catholic people's houses, used to hide priests in times of persecution.

He even spent a day hiding in an oak tree. Many pubs in England are named 'Royal Oak' in memory of Charles's hiding place.

Life under Cromwell

Most people were scared of Cromwell's army, and hated the dull Puritan lifestyle. The Lord Protector even banned Christmas and Easter celebrations, and replaced them with days of fasting.

But in many other ways life got much better. For one thing, Cromwell allowed people to worship in almost any way they wished. For another, many people were becoming richer, as overseas trade thrived – especially the trade in sugar and slaves with the West Indies.

When Cromwell died, his son Richard became Lord Protector. But Richard had nothing like his father's character, and he couldn't control Parliament or the army. Before long, the army took matters into its own hands, and invited Charles I's son back from exile in France, to become King Charles II. Oliver Cromwell had worked hard to make England into what he saw as a better place. But after his strict Puritan Commonwealth, almost everyone was excited about having a king on the throne again.

Puritan England

Cromwell stripped churches of decoration – paintings, statues and stained glass windows.

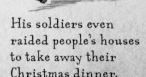

His soldiers even raided people's houses to take away their Christmas dinner.

This painting shows the Puritan family of Henry Chorley, a cloth merchant from Preston. Puritans wore simple, plain clothes, unlike the extravagant outfits of Charles I's court.

Crime pays

In 1671, a man named Colonel Blood disguised himself as a priest and tried to steal the Crown Jewels. When he was caught, he demanded to see the King.

Charles was so impressed by his bravery and his amusing stories that he not only pardoned him, but rewarded him with a pension and some land.

The Merry Monarch

Charles II couldn't have been more different from Cromwell. A fun-loving king, he soon earned the nickname the Merry Monarch. He was cultured too, and encouraged science, art, drama and music to flourish. Charles introduced champagne to Britain, reopened the playhouses that Cromwell had banned, and sparked a fashion for sailing when he and his brother raced their yachts down the River Thames.

Care-free and heir-free

The King was charming and good-looking, with an eye for the ladies. He was married to a Portuguese princess, Catherine of Braganza, but had a string of affairs with many different women. His mistresses produced 14 children between them, but none of them could be heir to the throne. The Queen didn't have any children, so Charles would be succeeded by his brother, James.

216

Problems with Parliament

At the beginning of his reign, Charles was careful to build a good relationship with Parliament, because he didn't want to risk another civil war. But soon he began to clash with MPs over religion. They wanted to make sure that the country would remain Protestant, and many believed that Charles was secretly a Catholic. Charles was certainly sympathetic to Catholics – he was trying to persuade Parliament to give them more rights, and his brother had converted to Catholicism.

Then, in 1670, Charles made a secret deal with Louis XIV of France. In exchange for money, he promised to become a Catholic and to help the French in their war against the Dutch. When gossip about the deal spread through Parliament, many MPs felt that Charles couldn't be trusted.

This painting shows Charles entering London the day before his coronation. He is wearing a tall hat and riding a white horse.

Party politics

James was even less popular than his brother, and some MPs were determined to stop him from succeeding to the throne. Politicians became so divided on the matter that they formed two political parties.

The MPs who supported James were called Tories, and those who were against him were called Whigs. They were the first political parties in Britain.

In this picture, the plague is depicted as a skeleton dancing on coffins, with London in the background.

"Ring a ring o' roses
Pocket full o' posies
Atishoo! Atishoo!
We all fall down."

This nursery rhyme is said to be about the Black Death. Victims would show symptoms such as red rashes on the body ("ring o' roses") and sneezing ("Atishoo!") before falling down – dead.

The plague

When Charles came to the throne, London was a dirty, overcrowded city. Rats thrived in the grimy conditions, and diseases spread very easily. In the summer of 1665, just four years into Charles' reign, London was ravaged by a deadly disease called the Bubonic Plague.

The plague germs were carried by fleas which lived in the fur of black rats. Fleas passed the plague, also known as the Black Death, to humans when they bit them. Within days of being bitten, black blotches and huge, painful lumps would appear on victims' bodies. Sometimes their fingers, toes and noses turned black and fell off. They would writhe in agony for days, vomiting and shaking, before they finally died.

"Bring out your dead!"

Nobody knew what caused the plague, or how to cure it, so anyone who showed symptoms was locked in their house with their family, and left to die. A red cross was painted on the door to warn others to stay away. Many people starved, as they could not leave their houses to find food. At night, men would roam the streets with huge carts, crying, "Bring out your dead!" Corpses were loaded up and driven away to enormous burial pits on the outskirts of the city.

Eventually, the cold winter weather killed off the fleas, and the plague began to die down. But the Black Death had killed 68,000 Londoners – around one in five of the population.

Doctors wore leather robes with hoods and gloves. Their masks had glass eyeholes and beaks stuffed with herbs, which were supposed to protect them from the plague.

Samuel Pepys

Much of what we know about the plague comes from the diary of Samuel Pepys. He was an MP and an administrator for the navy. He wrote in his diary almost every day between 1660 and 1669, and kept detailed notes on everything from his private life to public events, including the coronation of Charles II.

Pepys's diary tracks the spread of the plague, and gives a very personal account of the tragedy. On August 10, 1665, he rushed home to write his will, realizing that, "a man cannot depend upon living two days to an end." But by September 3, he was more concerned that his new wig would go out of fashion: "for nobody will dare to buy any hair for fear of the infection, that it had been cut off the heads of people dead of the plague."

Extracts from Samuel Pepys' Diary

June 7, 1665

This day...I did in Drury Lane see two or three houses marked with a red cross upon the doors, and "Lord have mercy upon us" writ there - which was a sad sight to me, being the first of that kind that to my remembrance I ever saw.

October 16, 1665

Lord, how empty the streets are, and melancholy, so many poor sick people in the streets, full of sores, and so many sad stories overheard as I walk, everybody talking of this dead, and that man sick.

November 22, 1665

I heard this day that the plague is come very low; that is 600 and odd - and great hopes of a further decrease, because of this day's being a very exceeding hard frost - and continues freezing.

London's burning

Just as people started to feel safe in London again, a second disaster struck. In the early hours of September 2, 1666, a fire started in a bakery on Pudding Lane, in the heart of the city. It was a hot, dry summer, with strong winds that fanned the flames. The Great Fire, as it became known, raged for four days, destroying four-fifths of London.

Panic spreads

At first, no one thought the fire was very serious. Sir Thomas Bludworth, the Lord Mayor of London, was irritated when he was woken in the middle of the night and told about the fire. 'Pish!' he said and, thinking the fire would be easy to put out, he went back to bed. But as he slept, the fire raged on. By morning, hundreds of houses had already been destroyed.

Most of the shops and houses in London were made of wood, and they were tightly packed together, so it was easy for the flames to spread. There was no fire service, and very few people had water in their homes to throw on the flames. Panic-stricken Londoners rushed to the river to fill buckets with water, but the fire was impossible to control.

"The stones of St. Paul's flew like grenades, the lead melting down the streetes in a stream, & the very pavements glowing with fiery redness, so as nor horse nor man was able to tread on them."

John Evelyn, a writer and gardener, describes the destruction of St. Paul's Cathedral during the Great Fire of London in his diary.

Londoners flee to the south side of the river to escape the flames, throwing their belongings into boats, in the hope that they'll survive the fire.

220

Tearing down the houses

King Charles insisted on pulling down as many buildings as possible to stop the fire from spreading to the Tower of London. The city's supply of gunpowder was kept there. If the fire had reached it, the consequences could have been catastrophic.

In the midst of the chaos, Pepys bumped into the Lord Mayor in the street, now wide awake. Pepys wrote that he cried, like a fainting woman, "Lord, what can I do? I am spent: people will not obey me. I have been pulling down houses, but the fire overtakes us faster than we can do it."

Lucky escape

Officially, only nine people died in the fire, but it is likely that there were many other deaths which went unrecorded.

The aftermath

By September 6, the fire had died down, and shaken Londoners began to return to the city.

But there was a silver lining to this tragedy: the fire killed the last of the rats and fleas which were carrying the plague, so the city was finally free of the Black Death.

This painting shows the Tower of London glowing in the light of the flames. Luckily, the fire never reached the Tower.

Wealthy Stuarts

Charles was determined to prevent such a fire from happening again, and so he ordered London to be rebuilt with stone, instead of wood. The architect Sir Christopher Wren was commissioned to design the new-look London. Narrow, winding streets were to be replaced with wide, paved avenues, but many of the plans had to be scrapped as there wasn't enough money to cover the costs. Even so, London was transformed. The most famous new landmark was Wren's magnificent St. Paul's Cathedral.

The rich get richer

This new London reflected the newfound opulence of England under Charles II. While life for the poor remained much the same, life for the wealthy was improving rapidly. After the dull lifestyle of the Commonwealth, those who could afford it took advantage of their new freedom.

Clothing became more elaborate, with large wigs and bright coats for men, and beautiful gowns and lace for ladies. Furniture was more finely carved, and upholstered with leather. For the first time, many houses were designed with separate rooms for living, eating and sleeping in. Charles's court, meanwhile, developed a taste for all things French – from clothing to art.

This portrait of Sir Christopher Wren shows St. Paul's Cathedral in the background. The arches and domes are in the Baroque style, influenced by Italian Renaissance architects.

Charles II in his finery. Men's clothing was similar to the clothing of Charles I's court, except that boots were replaced with stockings and buckled shoes.

222

Business booms

Trade flourished in the Stuart period, and a flurry of innovations made business easier. Envelopes, newspapers and insurance were all introduced for the first time. 1694 marked the foundation of the Bank of England (which was established to lend money to the government), and the appearance of the first English banknote.

In the early 1600s, coffee arrived in Britain. Coffee houses began springing up in cities from around 1650, and coffee gradually took over from beer as the nation's most popular drink. Coffee houses were soon fashionable places for men to meet and conduct business. At one point, Charles tried to close them all down, as he feared that plotters would use them as meeting places. But his subjects complained so bitterly that he relented.

This painting shows fashionable Stuart men socializing at a coffee house.

Trade triangle

Britain's wealth was largely thanks to booming trade overseas. The 'trade triangle' was most valuable. British merchants traded iron and guns for African slaves, and then sold them in the New World. Meanwhile, British ships brought home sugar, cotton and tobacco.

→ iron and guns
→ African slaves
→ sugar, cotton and tobacco

House and garden

For an average, well-off family in the mid-17th century, life revolved around the home. The father of the household often ran his business from a shop or workshop on the ground floor, and the mother looked after the running of the house. Children spent less time at home than their parents, as they were usually sent to be educated at a grander family's house. At midday, the whole household would come together in the wood panelled main room, or hall, to eat a large meal, and they would eat a lighter supper in the evening.

Houses were lit by fire and candlelight. Candles were very expensive, and few people could afford good quality beeswax candles. Most of the time they used cheap tallow candles, made of animal fat, which smelled unpleasant and filled the house with smoke.

Pretty but practical

Richer people had gardens, which provided a welcome escape from the filth and bustle of the town. Most gardens had decorative flowers and trees, and some had ornamental features such as fountains or sundials.

Many of the plants grown had practical uses, too — vegetables were grown alongside herbs for cooking and medicinal purposes. A garden also served as a place where laundry could be hung out to dry, firewood and water could be stored, and pens could be built to house pigs or chickens to provide extra food for the family.

How does your garden grow?

Herb gardens were usually planted in geometric beds and included plants which people believed to have medicinal properties. Here are a few plants that were popular in the 17th century, and the complaints they were supposed to cure:

The bitter herb wormwood was believed to keep away fleas and to relieve gout.

An infusion of marigolds was drunk to soothe the spirits.

Borage was said to drive away sorrow.

Feverfew was taken for headaches.

Bachelor's buttons buttercups were believed to cure insanity.

224

This is an illustration of a cloth merchant's house from around 1640. It has been cut away to reveal the different rooms and furnishings inside.

Servants lived in basic rooms known as garrets at the top of the house.

Bed chambers were often used for entertaining as well as sleeping.

The toilet, or privy, was housed in a shed behind the house. Waste went into a pit underneath, which was emptied at night by men called night soil men.

225

Isaac Newton

Sir Isaac Newton was the first person to suggest that science and mathematics could explain everything.

It is said that he came up with his theory of gravity when he saw an apple falling from a tree.

Newton also made important discoveries about light, and invented the mirror telescope to study the stars.

Newton's telescope

The rise of science

When the Great Fire happened so quickly after the plague, many people thought that it was the work of the devil – or a terrible punishment from God. In Stuart times, most people had to rely on religion, superstition or plain guesswork to try to explain the world around them. But, at the same time, intellectuals were making exciting scientific discoveries. Their work would have a huge impact on modern science.

The Royal Society

In the 1640s a group of scientists, including Christopher Wren and Samuel Pepys, began meeting to discuss ideas and perform experiments. They called themselves the Invisible College. By the 1660s, King Charles had officially recognized their work, and they became the Royal Society. Charles was so interested that he even helped out with some of the experiments. In 1675, he also set up the Royal Observatory in Greenwich, where astronomers studied the Sun, moon and stars. Their work was interesting, but it was also useful. For example, studying the stars helped them to tell the time and navigate at sea.

A true genius

In 1703, the Royal Society appointed a new president – Sir Isaac Newton, one of the greatest scientists of all time. One of his most important discoveries was that a force, which we call gravity, pulls objects towards the ground. He realized that gravity was what keeps the moon moving around the Earth. Newton was the first person to be knighted for scientific work.

Medicine

While Newton and the Royal Society were studying the natural world, doctors were learning more about the human body. Until the 1600s, little had been known about how the body worked, or what caused disease – the Church wouldn't allow dead bodies to be cut up and examined. Only one in ten people lived to be 40. Operations were done by 'barber surgeons' who set broken bones, as well as trimming hair. One common treatment was bleeding: cutting patients open to let out the 'bad blood' that they believed caused illness.

However, in the early 17th century, the Church finally allowed doctors to cut up corpses to learn more about the body. A physician named William Harvey made one of the most important medical discoveries of all, when he uncovered the secret of circulation. He realized that the heart is a pump, which makes blood flow around the body. Unfortunately, it took a long time for discoveries like this one to have a real impact, and treatments such as bleeding carried on long after Harvey's death.

Witch hunts

Despite new scientific knowledge, many people still believed in witches. In the 1640s, a lawyer named Matthew Hopkins came up with a test to identify witches. The accused was thrown into water. If she drowned, she was innocent. If she lived, she was thought to be a witch, and executed.

Inventions

Some Stuart inventions opened the way for a new industrial age.

1701 – Jethro Tull's seed drill plants seeds faster than by hand.

1705 – Thomas Newcomen's steam engine pumps flood water out of coal mines.

1709 – Abraham Darby discovers how to purify coal to make coke. Coke is used as a fuel in steel and iron production.

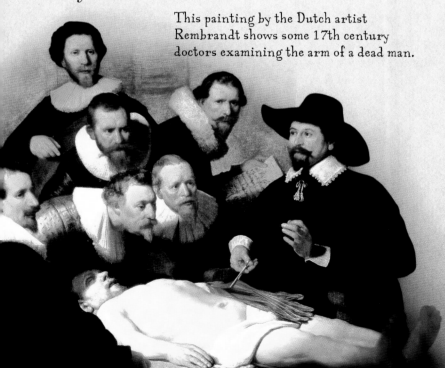

This painting by the Dutch artist Rembrandt shows some 17th century doctors examining the arm of a dead man.

A Catholic king

Charles II's extravagant lifestyle eventually caught up with him, and he died in 1685. He was succeeded by his brother James, who believed that God had put him on the throne to convert the country back to Catholicism. James refused to compromise with Parliament on matters of religion, and it wasn't long before this made him extremely unpopular with Protestant politicians – and the public.

This is a portrait of James II, wearing a curly wig that would have been the height of fashion at the end of the 17th century.

The Monmouth rebellion

Just four months into James's reign, the Protestant Duke of Monmouth – an illegitimate son of Charles II – led a rebellion against him, and tried to seize the crown. James's troops quashed the rebels, but it was a hollow victory. Monmouth was executed along with 300 other Protestant rebels, and a further 800 were shipped to Barbados as slaves. The brutal trials became known as the 'Bloody Assizes'. The King's harsh treatment of the defeated rebels made him more unpopular than ever.

Challenging the Church

In 1687, James tried to take the law into his own hands, issuing an order called the Declaration of Indulgence to abolish the laws against Catholics. Parliament refused to accept it, which made the King look weak and foolish, but he wouldn't give in.

He ordered the Declaration to be read out in every church, and when the bishops protested, he put them on trial. James was humiliated once again when his judges found the bishops not guilty.

The final blow

At first, James's critics could console themselves with the thought that he wouldn't be around for long. James was 52 when he came to the throne – an old man by the standards of the day – and, when he died, his Protestant daughter Princess Mary would be Queen. But, in 1688, everything changed. James's Catholic second wife, Mary of Modena, gave birth to a son named James. There was a new Catholic heir to the throne, and the Protestants were horrified.

Almost immediately, a group of MPs invited Princess Mary's Dutch husband, the Protestant Prince William of Orange, to invade. So, on November 5, 1688, William landed in Torbay with 15,000 men, forcing James to step down. James fled to France, and William and Mary were crowned King and Queen. This dramatic takeover became known as the Glorious Revolution.

The baby and the warming pan

Some people refused to accept that James's son was really his. Gossip spread that the baby had been smuggled into the Queen's bedroom in a warming pan.

This is a Dutch painting showing William of Orange landing in Torbay.

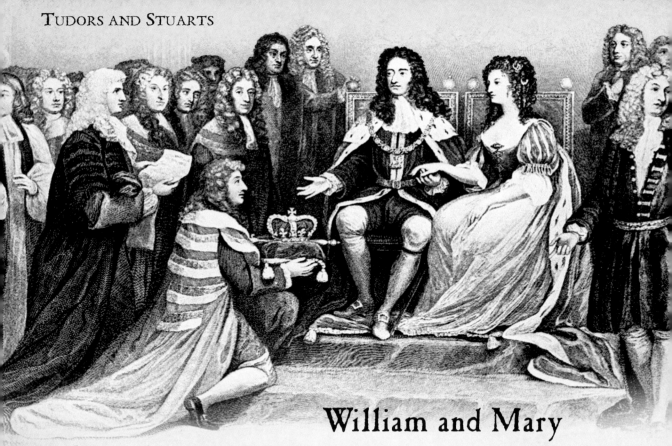

This picture shows William and Mary at their coronation.

"She seems to be of a good nature... she takes nothing to heart; whilst the Prince her husband has a thoughtful countenance, is wonderfully serious and silent, and seems to treat all persons alike gravely"

John Evelyn gives his impression of William and Mary in his diary.

William and Mary

William and Mary were appointed by Parliament to reign together. This put an end once and for all to the idea that kings and queens were appointed by God. In 1689, they agreed to limit the powers of the monarchy, with a Bill of Rights presented to them by Parliament. It stated that all future monarchs had to be Protestant, and that they couldn't keep an army or raise taxes without permission from Parliament, which would have to be called every three years.

The unpopular Dutchman

Mary was well-loved by the British people, but William soon made himself unpopular. He made no secret of the fact that he only wanted the throne so that British soldiers would fight in a war he was waging against the French. He spent most of his reign fighting in Europe, leaving Mary to rule alone.

The exile returns

The exiled James II still had support – especially among Catholics in Ireland and Scotland – and saw that he had one last opportunity to reclaim his crown. In 1689, he landed in Ireland and, with the help of French and Irish Catholics, tried to seize control from the English Protestants who had settled there. He managed to hold the town of Derry under siege, but his army was no match for William's disciplined troops. On July 1, 1690, William defeated him at the Battle of the Boyne. What's more, the King gave more land in Northern Ireland to the English Protestants, and Derry was renamed Londonderry. Beaten, James II fled to France and lived there in exile for the rest of his life.

Highland massacre

William didn't want to risk another rebellion. So, in 1692, he made the Catholic clans (families) of the Scottish Highlands sign an oath of loyalty to him. When the MacDonalds of Glencoe missed the deadline to sign, 38 members of their clan were massacred by a rival clan, the Campbells, under orders from the government.

William alone

In 1694, Mary died of smallpox, leaving William to rule alone. William was devastated by his wife's death, and said he had never found a single fault in her. As they had no children, Parliament passed an Act of Settlement in 1701, declaring that Mary's sister, Anne, and her heirs, would succeed to the throne. A year later, William died and Anne became Queen.

A shaky start

William and Mary's marriage did not begin happily. Mary was only 15 when her father forced her to marry William, who was 12 years older than her.

At nearly 1.8m (6 feet) tall, she towered over William, and she is said to have cried all the way through the wedding ceremony. But, against the odds, the couple gradually grew to love each other.

When William died in 1702, he was wearing Mary's wedding ring and a lock of her hair close to his heart.

Queen Anne suffered from gout – a painful disease which causes swelling in the joints – so she was rarely seen in public.

She had an attack of gout during her coronation, and had to be carried in a sedan chair.

The last Stuart

Queen Anne was a shy woman, whose reign was blighted by health problems and personal sadness. She was married to Prince George of Denmark, and was frequently pregnant, which made her health even worse. Anne gave birth to 19 children, but sadly none of them survived.

A challenge for Churchill

Early in Queen Anne's reign, Britain joined with Austria and the Netherlands in a war against France and Spain. A young general named John Churchill helped win a series of victories for the British, and became a national hero. Queen Anne rewarded him with a title, Duke of Marlborough, and a plot of land, where he built a palace called Blenheim, named after one of his most famous battles. His wife Sarah was Anne's closest friend, but eventually the two women fell out, and the Queen banished Churchill from public life.

Many generations of the Churchill family lived at Blenheim Palace. Sir Winston Churchill, Prime Minister during the Second World War, was born here in 1874.

The United Kingdom

It soon became clear that Anne would die without any children to succeed her. As some Scottish people still didn't accept the Act of Settlement, Parliament feared that the Scots might try to put James II's son, also called James, on the throne in Scotland. To prevent this, Parliament passed the Act of Union. In 1707, England, Scotland and Wales were united under one Parliament, and from then on the nation became known as the United Kingdom of Great Britain.

A new royal family

In 1714, Queen Anne died and the throne passed to the next in line: George, the son of Princess Sophia of Hanover, in Germany, and a great-grandson of James I. Parliament had become stronger during the Tudor and Stuart period, and the powers of the monarchy had gradually declined. But the country George now inherited was one of the most powerful in the world.

Praise from a pirate

Queen Anne's reign became known as the 'Golden Age of piracy', because so many pirates attacked ships journeying between England and America.

One of the fiercest was Englishman Edward Teach, who went by the name Blackbeard.

He named his flagship the *Queen Anne's Revenge* in the Queen's memory, shortly after her death.

THE GEORGIANS

In 1714, Queen Anne, the last Stuart monarch, died and the throne passed to her heir, George, Elector of Hanover. Over the next 100 years or so, the country was ruled by four Hanoverian kings named George, so this period is often known as the Georgian age.

It was a time when Britain became the world's leading naval power, laying the foundations of an empire in India, but losing another in America. The Georgians saw great advances in farming and the beginning of the Industrial Revolution. Meanwhile, political revolutions overseas rocked the old order, and led to social and political changes in Britain too.

A German court

The new King arrived in London with a host of German nobles, a German composer named Handel, and two German-speaking Turkish servants.

He also brought his two German mistresses with him. One was short and fat, and the other was tall and skinny.

Deeply unpopular, the women were nicknamed the 'Elephant' and the 'Maypole' by the British public.

A German king

George I was 54 years old when he first stepped on British soil, in 1714, to be crowned the nation's King. He was the ruler of the German state of Hanover, spoke only broken English and had little interest in British affairs. Many British people disliked the idea of being ruled by a foreigner, but as the great grandson of James I, and Queen Anne's closest Protestant relative, he was the best choice.

The Hanoverian had few kingly qualities to win the respect of his new subjects. It was said that his main interests were food, horses and women. He had a cruel streak too. Twenty years earlier, he had divorced his wife for having an affair. He forbade her from seeing their children ever again, and had her locked in a castle for the rest of her life. His son, the future George II, was nine years old at the time. He never forgave his father, and the pair argued constantly.

In this painting Handel (in red) is presenting his musicians to the King as they are rowed along the Thames. They are playing his composition *Water Music*.

Kings and queens

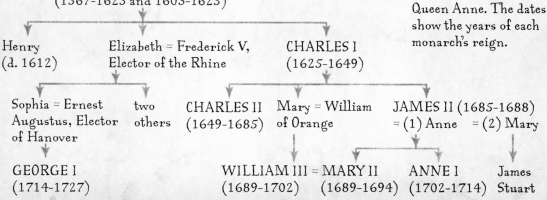

JAMES IV of Scotland and I of England
(1567-1625 and 1603-1625)

Henry
(d. 1612)

Elizabeth = Frederick V,
Elector of the Rhine

CHARLES I
(1625-1649)

Sophia = Ernest
Augustus, Elector
of Hanover

two
others

CHARLES II
(1649-1685)

Mary = William
of Orange

JAMES II (1685-1688)
= (1) Anne   = (2) Mary

GEORGE I
(1714-1727)

WILLIAM III = MARY II
(1689-1702)   (1689-1694)

ANNE I
(1702-1714)

James
Stuart

This family tree shows how George I and James Stuart were related to Queen Anne. The dates show the years of each monarch's reign.

A Scottish contender

There was another reason why not everyone in Britain warmed to their new King. Many believed that Queen Anne's half-brother, James Stuart, was the rightful heir. Parliament had opposed his claim to the throne because he was a Catholic. But some of his supporters – known as Jacobites – were prepared to fight to put the Stuart family back on the throne.

Matters came to a head after George I sacked a leading politician, a Scotsman named John Erskine, the Earl of Mar. In retaliation, Mar raised an army of Jacobites in the Scottish Highlands. In November 1715, Mar's army fought government forces at Sheriffmuir, near Stirling. But neither side won a clear victory.

It was only then that James arrived in Scotland from France, where he was in exile. But he came without an army, and when the Dutch sent forces to join the Hanoverians, the Jacobite rebellion collapsed. To prevent another rising, George I had five Jacobite leaders beheaded and posted large numbers of troops in Scotland. James fled back into exile, and never again posed a real threat to King George.

Jacobite dress

Being a Jacobite in Georgian Britain was almost like being a member of a secret society.

Many Jacobites wore a sprig of white heather, or a white feather in their hats, as a symbol of their loyalty to the Stuarts.

A Scottish Jacobite, Lord Nithsdale, was due to be beheaded for his part in the 1715 rising. But he escaped from the Tower of London by disguising himself as a female friend of his wife's.

237

Bigwigs

Georgian politicians were expected to dress formally in Parliament, which, according to the fashion of the day, meant wearing powdered wigs. It was also common for them to wear their swords.

A hair-raising incident was recorded where one MP's sword accidentally spiked and removed another's wig.

This Georgian illustration shows Robert Walpole standing to talk to the ministers of the Cabinet.

Walpole was a skilled and persuasive debater, but he was also known for his lack of tact and his crude manners. The look on the face of the bishop at the far right suggests he disapproves of something Walpole has just said.

A wily Whig

With the Jacobite threat dealt with for the time being, George I was free to get on with the business of government. But he took little interest in British affairs and, because of his poor English, he seldom met with his ministers. Instead, he left the Cabinet – a council of top ministers – to run the country, while he spent as much time as he could in Hanover.

Divided rule

There were two main political parties in Georgian Britain: the Whigs and the Tories. But a number of Tories had backed the Jacobites, and George made it clear that he would not allow them to take power. In fact, the Whigs would dominate Parliament for the rest of the 18th century. But without a real opposition, the Whigs began to fight among themselves. They split into two main groups, one behind the King, and the other behind his most bitter rival – his son, George.

Boom and bust

Then, in 1720, the government was nearly toppled by a financial crisis. A trading venture, called the South Sea Company, had been selling shares on the promise of vast profits. Thousands of people – from small investors to politicians and even the King – rushed to buy the shares, which immediately shot up in value. This frenzy became known as the South Sea Bubble – and in 1720 it burst. The company wasn't making the profits it had hoped for, the value of its shares crashed, and many investors were bankrupted.

Number 10

In 1735 George II gave the house at 10 Downing Street to Robert Walpole to live and work in.

It is still the official residence of the Prime Minister today.

The first Prime Minster

A shrewd, ambitious Whig named Robert Walpole, emerged to take charge of the situation. He rescued the government from collapse and stabilized the country's finances. With many of his opponents ruined when the South Sea Bubble burst, Walpole became the most powerful minister in Parliament. In effect, Walpole was Britain's first Prime Minister, although at that time the title was only used as a term of abuse.

In 1727, George I died in Hanover. He was little mourned in Britain, least of all by his son, who became George II. Walpole tried to keep taxes low by avoiding costly wars, but the new King was itching for glory on the battlefield.

In 1739, war broke out, first against Spain, then France. It was the end for Walpole. He resigned in February 1742 after 21 years in power – still the longest term of any British prime minister.

This is a detail from a painting of George II leading his troops against the French at the Battle of Dettingen. He was the last British king ever to go into battle.

This photograph shows the grand, Roman-style entrance to Stowe House, which was designed by the architect Robert Adam.

On tour

During the 18th century, it became customary for the young men (and sometimes their sisters) of wealthy families to go on a 'grand tour' of Europe.

Similar to a gap year, this was a long trip that took young adventurers to key cities and monuments, particularly in France and Italy, to learn about European culture.

Many returned home laden with works of art they had collected during their travels.

Landed gentry

With his great power, Robert Walpole was able to acquire a great fortune. And he spent much of it building Houghton Hall, a grand house on the site of his ancestral home in Norfolk. In the first half of the 18th century, much of the British countryside was in the hands of only a few hundred wealthy families – the 'landed gentry' – who dominated politics and business, and wanted their country homes to reflect their wealth, power and good taste.

Classical elegance

Houghton Hall was just one of many large 'stately homes' built, or rebuilt, by Georgian landowners. It was among the first to be designed in an elegant style that became fashionable in the 1730s, known as 'Palladian' architecture. Inspired by the ancient Roman temples and villas of Italy, this style used tall columns, geometric proportions and clean lines to create a commanding impression on the surrounding landscape.

Power houses

These great buildings were more than family homes. Some became places of learning, playing host to artists and poets. One of the most impressive stately homes was Stowe, in Buckinghamshire, which belonged to a leading Whig named Viscount Cobham. It became the headquarters for 'Cobham's Cubs' – a group of Whigs set up in opposition to Walpole.

A capable gardener

The grounds at Stowe were landscaped by a 26-year-old named Lancelot 'Capability' Brown, who went on to become the most sought after landscape gardener of the day. He earned his nickname because he could always see the "capability for improvement" in any garden.

Under his influence, it became fashionable to create country parks with wide, sweeping lawns, informal flower beds, lakes and striking features, such as statues, fake Roman ruins and temples. At Stowe, Cobham had more than 30 monuments and 50 statues installed.

Funny walls

Many stately homes were surrounded by a sunken wall known as a ha-ha. This kept out wild animals and trespassers, without interrupting the views of the countryside from the house.

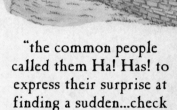

"the common people called them Ha! Has! to express their surprise at finding a sudden...check to their walk."

Robert Walpole's son Horace attempts to explain where the term 'Ha-Ha' came from.

Robert Adam

One of the most influential Georgian architects working in the Palladian style was a Scotsman named Robert Adam, whose portrait is shown here.

He designed many stately homes and public buildings, including Stowe, parts of the University of Edinburgh, and Kenwood House, in London.

Adam sometimes designed interiors too. This is one of his drawings for a reading room in a town house.

Theatrical satire

John Gay's play *The Beggar's Opera* was a huge box office hit in 1728. It included characters that satirized Robert Walpole and Jonathan Wild.

In this picture by a Georgian cartoonist Thomas Rowlandson, an excited mob is watching as two cocks fight to the death. Fights such as this were extremely bloody, as the birds were often fitted with razor-sharp spurs around their legs.

Sleazy living

Its stately homes may have looked genteel, but Britain in the 1720s and 30s was a violent, crime-ridden place. Extreme poverty and hunger drove some people to petty crime, simply to survive. Meanwhile, a number of politicians and public officials were involved in corruption scandals, as they abused their positions to gain even more wealth and power. Walpole himself was not above using bribery to get what he wanted.

Writers, such as Jonathan Swift, John Gay and Alexander Pope, and artists including William Hogarth and Thomas Rowlandson, used satire in their works to criticize the immorality they saw at all levels of society.

Social vices

Violent sports such as bear baiting, cock fighting and bare-knuckle boxing were all hugely popular, and spectators would add to the thrill of the fight by placing bets on the results. Coffee houses, inns and clubs provided ample opportunities for gambling at cards or betting on public events, births and deaths.

Drunk and disorderly

This picture is *Gin Lane*, by William Hogarth. It shows a destitute mother who is so drunk on gin that she has dropped her baby.

Cheap, strong gin became a popular drink in the early 18th century, and was wrecking people's lives. Religious leaders and politicians also feared that it was causing laziness and crime among the working classes.

Walpole's government tried to clamp down on the gin trade. But it backed down in 1743, after mobs began shouting "No gin, no King!"

But the gin problem got worse and worse, as the British were drinking 8 million gallons a year. So, in 1751, the Gin Act was brought in to limit the production and consumption of gin.

Organized crime

Georgian Britain was a pretty lawless place. Gangs of poachers roamed country estates and royal parks, hunting for animals to feed their families or to sell. Highwaymen, like Dick Turpin, lurked in country roads, robbing mail coaches and passers-by. Pirates raided trade ships, and smugglers secretly imported luxury goods – such as silks, tea and brandy – without paying taxes on them. But crime was worst in towns, where gangs of pickpockets and thieves operated.

There was no national police force, but local magistrates offered rewards to anyone who caught a criminal. A few people, such as Londoner Jonathan Wild, made a living as 'thief takers'. Until he was caught and hanged, he also made money sending out thieves to steal goods, which he then sold back to their unsuspecting owners.

Paying the price

Criminals who were caught faced severe punishments. Even pickpocketing could be punished by hanging.

Jack Shepherd was one of the most infamous petty thieves. He had been arrested several times, and escaped from prison each time before he was finally hanged, aged 22.

His escapades made him a local hero. Some 200,000 Londoners went to his hanging, hoping that he might even escape death.

The Stuarts' last stand

Only 30 years after the earlier Jacobite rising, James Stuart's dashing and charismatic son, Charles Edward Stuart, renewed the campaign to restore the Stuarts to the British throne. Fondly known by his supporters as 'Bonnie Prince Charlie', Charles landed in Scotland in July, 1745, to make his claim.

Bonnie Prince Charlie is often depicted as a handsome and romantic hero, as in this portrait. Here, his clothes are made from tartan cloth.

Rebel rousing

Bonnie Prince Charlie was joined by only a few Scottish clans. The French sent help, but it was too little and too late to make a difference. Even so, he had some success, capturing Edinburgh, and then marching south into England.

By December, the Jacobites had got as far as Derby, but they failed to muster enough support in England to risk advancing to London. King George may not have been very popular, but people had become used to life under the Hanoverians. With government troops hot on their heels, the Jacobite rebels fled back to Scotland, and eventually to the Highlands.

The final battle

On April 16, 1746, the two armies met at the Battle of Culloden Moor in the north of Scotland, near Inverness. Better trained and equipped, the Hanoverian troops outnumbered the Jacobites by around 9,000 to 6,000. The Jacobites were utterly defeated, in a battle that is said to have lasted less than an hour.

244

A wanted man

Charlie went on the run in the Highlands. The government sent troops to track him down, and even offered a £30,000 reward for his capture. But the Prince managed to avoid arrest, and his supporters took great risks to protect him, offering him food and shelter wherever he went. A woman named Flora MacDonald helped him to reach the Isle of Skye disguised as her maid. From there, a ship picked him up, and he sailed back to France.

In the aftermath, the government dealt harshly with the Jacobites. Around 3,500 were imprisoned, and many of them were transported to penal colonies overseas. Their leaders were charged with treason and executed. It was the Stuarts' last stand, and the last full-scale battle ever to be fought in Britain. Bonnie Prince Charlie died in exile. With his death all hope of restoring the Stuarts to the British throne ended for good.

This is a Georgian artist's impression of the Battle of Culloden, showing the Jacobites being defeated by the government's 'redcoat' troops in red uniforms.

Cracking down on the clans

For nearly 40 years after the Battle of Culloden, the British government banned people from wearing kilts and playing bagpipes. The ban was only lifted once politicians were sure the Jacobite threat was over.

Fat of the land

Just a few years after the Battle of Culloden, the Highlanders were dealt another blow. During the 1760s, Scottish landlords began to evict tenant farmers forcibly from their land, usually to replace them with sheep farming, which was more lucrative. Whole communities were uprooted, in what became known as the Highland Clearances. Many moved to towns in search of work, but many more emigrated to America.

The clearances were only a part of a series of changes to rural life and farming methods throughout Britain during the 18th century. Some historians now refer to these changes as the Agricultural Revolution.

Enclosures

Until the late 1600s, farming had changed little in Britain for hundreds of years. Most families grew their own food on narrow strips of land in big, open fields that belonged to wealthy landowners. They kept a few animals on common land, and some made a little money by spinning yarn, or weaving cloth at home.

But, from around 1750, more and more British landowners decided that they wanted to make their land more productive and to increase their profits. They took over the strips and made large fields enclosed by fences or hedges. Some cleared forests, drained marshes and took over common land, too.

The new enclosed fields were grouped together to make large farms. These were rented out, but at a much higher rate than before, which most farmers could not afford. This meant that many people no longer had anywhere to grow their food, and were forced to leave the villages where their families had lived for generations, to find work elsewhere.

Changing the landscape

This diagram shows an area of farmland made up of open fields, divided into strips. The strips are shown in the same shades as the cottage of the farmer who works on them.

Landlord

Below, the same area of land is divided into two profitable farms, after enclosure.

North Farm

South Farm

Modern methods

To make the most of their land, Georgian farmers began trying out new ideas and developing new machines to do some of the hard work for them. One of the most important machines was the seed drill, invented by an English farmer named Jethro Tull. Instead of scattering seeds over the ground by hand, the drill planted seeds carefully in the soil.

Traditionally, many farmers rotated their crops, planting a different crop in each field every year, and regularly leaving each field fallow (unplanted) to rest the soil. But Viscount Townsend learned from Dutch farmers that planting the resting fields with crops like turnips and clover instead, actually enriched the soil, as well as providing food for cattle during the winter.

Fat cows

Some farmers, including Robert Bakewell and Thomas Coke, began using only their best, biggest cattle, sheep and pigs for breeding.

These animals often had big babies, so livestock became significantly larger during the 18th century.

This is a Georgian cartoon, by James Gillray, of a country squire showing off one of his vast bulls.

247

Human cargo

Hundreds of slaves were crammed onto each slave ship – the more a ship's captain could carry, the more he would be paid.

Conditions on board were appalling. Slaves were chained up for the entire eight week voyage. More than a third died in transit from disease, thirst and hunger.

This plan made by a slave trader shows how slaves were tightly packed into a ship.

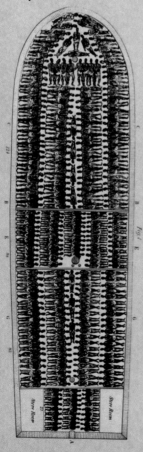

Trade and empire

Since Stuart times, British traders had been sailing around the world. They brought tea, textiles, gold and spices from China and India, and tobacco, cotton and sugar from plantations in North America and the Caribbean back to ports at London, Bristol, Liverpool and Glasgow. British manufactured goods, such as woven cloth, guns and iron tools, were then shipped to West Africa in return for slaves, who were transported across the Atlantic to work on the plantations.

This trade grew rapidly, making British owners of merchant ships, factories and plantations incredibly wealthy. By George II's reign, the British had set up many trading colonies around the globe.

Global power struggle

In 1756, a war broke out between Britain and France over colonial territories in India and America. This war was part of what later became known as the Seven Years' War. Fighting also took place in Europe with Britain, Hanover and Prussia on one side, against France, Austria, Russia, Sweden and Spain on the other. Because it was fought across three continents, many historians see this as the first ever global war.

Rivalry in America

By now, the British had many colonies along the east coast of America. But the French, who controlled much of the trade in Canada, built a series of forts along the Great Lakes, the Ohio River and the Mississippi, to try to encircle the British colonies and prevent them from expanding westward. Local skirmishes broke out, and at first the French had the upper hand.

Sending in the redcoats

Britain's Secretary of State was William Pitt, a politician who had risen to power as one of Cobham's Cubs. Determined to drive out the French, he built up the nation's army, nicknamed the redcoats, and sent a massive military expedition to America in 1758.

The British troops, along with American soldiers, began in New York and worked their way north. The first French fort they captured was Duquesne, which they renamed Pittsburg. From then on, the French forts fell to the British one by one. In the summer of 1759, they reached the French city of Quebec, in Canada.

Perched on a steep cliff above a river, with French troops on all sides, Quebec seemed impenetrable. But James Wolfe, a talented young general leading the British, had a plan. Under cover of night, he led 5,000 men in rowing boats downriver, where they silently scaled the cliffs to launch a surprise dawn raid on the French. Quebec was taken, and by 1760, the British controlled Montreal and most of Canada, too.

This painting shows the Battle of Quebec in 1759. Both General Wolfe and the French commander were wounded in the battle, and died soon after.

"I believe that I can save the country and that no one else can."

William Pitt believed that the French posed a dangerous threat, not only to Britain's colonies, but to Britain itself.

Dehli

Plassey •

BENGAL

Calcutta •

Chittagong

GAIKWAR

MARATHA TERRITORY

ORISSA

Bay of Bengal

INDIA

PESHWA

Bombay •

Indian Ocean

NORTHERN
SAKARS

HYDERABAD

Goa •
(Portuguese)

Arabian Sea

MYSORE

Seringapatam •

Arcot • Madras •

Mysore •

CARNATIC

Pondicherry •

CEYLON
(now Sri Lanka)

British in India

This map shows the
gradual spread of British
power in India during
the Georgian period.

Land under
British control by:

 1767

 1805

An Indian
soldier, or
sepoy, in the
British
East India
Company's
army uniform

Power in India

While Wolfe was fighting in America, the Seven
Years' War also spread to India, where the British
East India Company had set up trading posts in
Calcutta, Bombay and Madras. Thousands of
British settlers lived in these bases, governed by
the company and defended by its own army. At
this time, India was divided into many areas
ruled by local princes who often fought each
other. Meanwhile, the French set up bases at
Arcot and Pondicherry.

Now, the British and the French began to
take sides in local wars as they competed for
power in India. The first major British victory came
in 1751, when Robert Clive, a young East India
Company clerk, led a small force of 200 British soldiers
and 300 Indians to seize Arcot.

The Black Hole of Calcutta

In 1756, the ruler, or *Nawab*, of Bengal captured
Calcutta from the British. He took 146 prisoners and
locked them overnight in a small, hot cell, with little
ventilation and no water. Only 23 survived what has
gone down in history as the 'Black Hole of Calcutta'.

Gains and losses

Outraged, the British counterattacked. At the Battle of Plassey in 1757, Clive's army defeated the Nawab's much larger forces, who also had French support. This victory gave the British East India Company effective control of Bengal, and weakened the French hold on India. In 1761, the British captured Pondicherry, and two years later the Seven Years' War finally came to an end. The peace treaty that followed gave the British the upper hand in both America and India.

From then on, the British East India Company's prosperity grew steadily, as it gained more territories and privileges through wars and deals with local rulers. Eventually, the British government decided that India was too valuable to be left in the hands of a private company. So in 1784, it took control of all political decisions made in India.

It was Britain's first step on the road to building an empire in India.

This painting by Francis Hayman, shows Robert Clive meeting Mir Jafar, the commander of the army of the Nawab of Bengal.

At this meeting, Clive persuaded Mir Jafar to switch sides, and together they went on to defeat the Nawab of Bengal at the Battle of Plassey.

Textiles and technology

Around the same time that farming methods were improving at home and British trade was growing overseas, manufacturing in Britain began to change too. It was the beginning of what became known as the Industrial Revolution.

Cottage industry

These are two 'flying shuttles' designed by John Kay in 1733. Rollers at either end guide the shuttles across the loom.

At the start of the 18th century, people lived in the countryside. Britain already had a flourishing cloth industry, and it was this that led the way into the industrial age. Until the 1730s, most textile workers worked at home, spinning thread from wool, flax or imported cotton, and weaving it into cloth using basic spinning wheels and small looms.

But that all changed as new tools and machines were invented that made this work faster and more productive. First came John Kay's 'flying shuttle' which allowed threads to be thrown across the loom, rather than being passed through by hand. Not only was this quicker, but it also meant that weavers could make broader cloth.

This painting from the early 19th century shows the cotton mills and houses that were built for the factory workers at New Lanark in Scotland.

Factory life

As the weaving process became faster, hand spinners struggled to keep up with the demand. So, machines were invented that could spin more threads faster. Next, inventors developed new ways to use energy from water wheels to power bigger and better spinning and weaving machines. The new machines were costly to build and too big to use at home, so wealthy businessmen began to build factories to house them.

As other industries expanded in a similar way, factories sprang up around the country, especially in hilly areas in the north of England, where there were plenty of fast-flowing rivers to drive the water wheels. Traditional craftsmen couldn't compete with the new industries, so they were forced to leave home to find work in the factories. These also drew farmers who had become unemployed after enclosures. As towns soon grew around the factories, the old country life began to die out.

But the Industrial Revolution was more than a series of new inventions. The development of banking, increased foreign trade, improved agriculture and a rise in the population all played a part too.

Spinning yarn

Before the 18th century, most fabric in Britain was made from wool. But, as raw cotton from the West Indies and America became more readily available, the demand for cotton cloth grew – until it far outstripped that for wool.

A spinning wheel could only make one reel of thread at a time.

In 1764, James Hargreaves invented the hand-operated 'Spinning Jenny' which could spin 16 threads at a time.

Richard Arkwright took things a step further in 1769 with a water-powered spinning machine. In 1785, Edmund Cartwright made the first water-powered loom, which was later driven by steam.

Highways and waterways

British industry was also helped to grow by enormous improvements in transportation. At the beginning of the Georgian age, many of the nation's roads were no more than dirt tracks, full of potholes that became waterlogged and muddy as soon as it rained. But more and more merchants and manufacturers needed to transport goods around the country, and they were frustrated that the atrocious state of the roads was affecting their businesses. Something had to be done.

Turnpike trusts

Improving the roads would be expensive, so local parishes leased stretches of track to organizations called turnpike trusts. The trusts built thousands of miles of new roads, and repaired and maintained the old ones, sometimes making them straighter too. In return, they collected a fee, or toll, from people who used them. Tolls were collected at gatehouses built at either end of the turnpike roads.

TURNPIKE TARIFF

Horse with rider	1/2 penny
Cattle, sheep, pigs	1-2 pence
Coaches	2-12 pence
Wagons	from 5 pence

(There are extra charges for more horses and for narrow wheels, which make deep ruts in the road.)

Soldiers, mail coaches, funerals and local vicars travel for FREE.

This scene captures the bustling activity at the turnpike on Tottenham Court Road, on the outskirts of London, as people pass through the gate to pay their toll.

In this picture from 1792, a barge is pulled through a tunnel on the Thames and Severn Canal at Sapperton Hill in Gloucestershire.

Horse power

The Georgians relied so much on horses that there were millions more in 18th century Britain than there are today.

The new road system made travel easier and quicker than ever before. In 1720, it would have taken three days to reach London from Manchester. By 1770, the journey could be completed in a day. And, as the amount of traffic on the roads grew, engineers such as Thomas Telford and Robert Macadam developed methods of building stronger, smoother roads.

Heavy goods

But the horses and carts couldn't cope with the increasingly heavy loads of goods and raw materials, such as coal and iron, being transported around the country. Where possible, these goods were taken by barges along rivers; where there wasn't a river, a canal was dug.

One of the first Georgian canals was built by an engineer named James Brindley, in 1759. It linked the Earl of Bridgewater's coal mines in Worsley to his factories in Manchester. Over the next 50 years, a vast network of over 6,000km (3,720 miles) of canals was constructed across Britain. Along with the turnpikes – and, later, the railways – the canals transformed the country, and allowed Britain's trade and industry to flourish.

Horses drew coaches and carts along the roads...

...pulled farm machinery...

...and towed barges down the canals.

Thousands were also needed for the cavalry.

255

King and constitution

In 1760 George II died and was succeeded by his 22-year-old grandson, George. Unlike the two kings before him, George III was born and educated in Britain, and was fiercely proud to be British. In fact, he never visited Hanover. He would be King for 60 years – although in the last decade he was too ill to rule for himself – and was held in much affection by his people.

Home life

George III was quiet, shy and deeply religious. His father, Prince Frederick, had died when he was 12, so the main male influence in his childhood was his tutor, his mother's friend John Stuart, the Earl of Bute.

On Bute's advice, George married a German princess, Charlotte of Meklenburg-Strelitz, soon after he became King. It proved a very happy marriage. Unlike his predecessors, George was utterly faithful to his wife, and the couple had fifteen children together. They lived relatively modestly, eating a simple diet, and enjoying regular fresh air and exercise.

The King's Friends

Unfortunately, George's relations with Parliament were a lot more complicated than his family life. He disliked the way the Whigs had been allowed to dominate government since 1714, and was determined to take back some of the political power his predecessors had handed over to Parliament. A year after he came to the throne, George ousted Pitt and made Bute his Prime Minister. He also began replacing Whig politicians with his own supporters, known as the King's Friends. This didn't go down at all well in Parliament.

> "Born and bred in this country, I glory in the name Briton."
>
> A line from George III's coronation speech.

Regal deaths

Like his father before him, George II was always arguing with his son, Frederick, Prince of Wales. Prince Frederick spent much of his time gambling, playing sports and plotting against the King.

But he died before his father, of a brain haemorrhage, after being hit on the head with a cricket ball during a match.

George II suffered from constipation in later life. He died on the lavatory, from a heart attack brought on by over-exertion.

Political pressure

The King faced savage criticism from a troublesome politician, John Wilkes. In his newspaper, *The North Briton*, Wilkes claimed that the King's interference was unconstitutional, and accused him of lying in Parliament. Wilkes was arrested, but soon set free again. Twice, he was expelled from Parliament, then voted back in again, under the slogan 'Wilkes and liberty'.

The unpopular Bute resigned after less than two years and four Prime Ministers came and went in quick succession. George struggled to trust them, and they were frustrated that the King continued to consult Bute behind their backs. In 1770, George finally found his man in Lord North, who would remain in office for a decade.

After Wilkes criticized William Hogarth's work, the artist produced this unflattering portrait of him as a cross-eyed, satanic figure.

This family portrait from 1770 shows George III and Queen Charlotte with six of their children. The future George IV is on the left in red, and the future William IV is in blue.

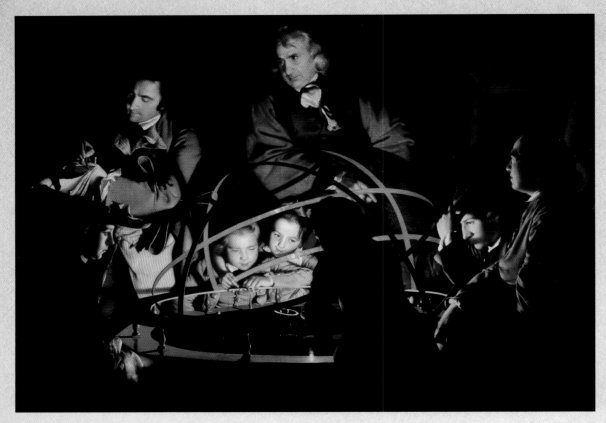

In this 1766 painting, *The Orrery* by Joseph Wright of Derby, a group gazes at a model of the Solar System while a scientist, in red, explains how it works.

"A wise man proportions his belief to the evidence."

Statements such as this earned the Scottish thinker, David Hume, criticism from religious leaders, who thought his theories contradicted their teachings.

The Age of Reason

As a boy, George III had been a slow learner, but as King, he was an enthusiastic patron of the arts and sciences, and an avid reader of all the latest ideas. He was fortunate to come to the throne at the height of an exciting period of scientific curiosity and discovery. It had begun during the 17th century, and was known as the Enlightenment, or the Age of Reason.

At its heart was an optimistic belief that by observing and exploring the world around them, and conducting experiments, scientists could shed new light on the mysteries of the universe. This theory was also applied to law, politics, economics and the arts, in the hope that all areas of human life could be improved by the powers of reason and common sense.

258

Scientific progress

British scientists made many new discoveries during the 18th century. Joseph Priestley, Joseph Black and Henry Cavendish identified the different chemicals that make up air and water. Humphrey Davy discovered that nitrous oxide – 'laughing gas' – could be used to put patients to sleep during surgery. He also invented a safety lamp for miners. In the field of medicine, William Smellie developed ways to make childbirth safer, and Edward Jenner introduced vaccination, to protect people against a deadly disease called smallpox.

In the know

Scientists formed societies, where they shared their latest findings, and they published them in pamphlets, newspapers and books. Many educated people were keen to stay informed. They read all the latest publications, invited guests to their homes to discuss the new ideas, attended public lectures and flocked to museums that were opening up around the country.

Collecting ideas

In 1753, a doctor named Sir Hans Sloane left his vast collection of books, manuscripts, natural history specimens and scientific instruments to the nation, on the condition that the government help to maintain it as a public museum – the British Museum.

Soon, other collectors, including George III, donated things to the museum's growing collection. The exhibits were classified and displayed according to their age, material or use. Often this helped to show a kind of progress from older, primitive forms to newer, more advanced examples.

From A to Z

Until the 18th century, there was no proper English dictionary, and there weren't any clear rules about English spellings or grammar.

So a journalist named Dr. Samuel Johnson began compiling a dictionary of the English language. After nine years' hard work, he finally finshed this great task in 1755. Published in two massive volumes, the dictionary was 2,300 pages long, with over 42,000 entries.

In 1768 the first edition of the *Encyclopaedia Britannica* was published in Edinburgh. It aimed to be 'a dictionary of the Arts and Sciences' with articles arranged from A to Z by subject on all fields of knowledge. It was by far the largest, and most comprehensive encyclopaedia of its time.

John Harrison designed this 'chronometer' in 1759. It was the most accurate watch of its day, and a vital tool for navigators who needed to know the exact time to calculate their position at sea.

Sailing the Pacific

In 1768, Captain James Cook, a navigator and explorer, set sail for the South Pacific on his ship, HMS *Endeavour*. He had two important missions. The first was to chart the transit of Venus over the Southern Ocean, near Tahiti. At that time, navigators relied on readings of the stars to calculate their position at sea. The Royal Navy hoped that these new readings would help British merchants to trade in new places.

Voyage of discovery

From Tahiti, Cook headed south, to carry out his second mission – to find and explore Australia, which had remained uncharted since Dutch sailors first reached its northern coast, in 1606. Cook was joined by a team of scientists whose task was to study the plants, wildlife, rocks and minerals in this new land. Among them was Joseph Banks, a young botanist (plant expert) who would later help George III set up the Royal Botanic Gardens at Kew.

James Cook and his men raise the British flag at Botany Bay in Australia.

These paintings show two of the plants Joseph Banks collected. The plant on the left was called *Banksia*, after the botanist. On the right is a breadfruit.

After stopping at New Zealand on the way, Cook eventually arrived on the east coast of Australia in April 1770, and claimed the country for Britain. He later named the place where he landed Botany Bay, after its extraordinary range of strange, exotic plants.

Nearly three years after the voyage had begun, the *Endeavour* returned to England. Cook had charted over 8,000km (5,000 miles) of coastline; and Banks brought back detailed notes, drawings and samples of over 1,000 new plants and animals.

Settling down under

From the 1780s, British people began to settle in Australia. Many were criminals, who were sent there to work by the British government. But others were farmers looking for land. By the 1830s, there were about 100,000 Europeans living there. The native Australians, the Aboriginals, suffered terribly as a result. Many were forced off their land, or killed; others died of diseases brought by the newcomers.

All at sea

About half of sailors went to sea unwillingly. Not enough men volunteered for the navy, so captains sent out 'press gangs' to force any man who worked at sea to serve.

The diet on board was poor, vermin and diseases were a constant problem and discipline was harsh. Anyone not following orders could be punished with a lash, known as a cat-o-nine-tails.

261

George III attends an exhibition at the Royal Academy in Somerset House in London.

The art establishment

By the beginning of the 18th century, more people were buying art than ever before. Painters were constantly trying to think of new ways to advertise their work to these new buyers.

Like many other professional groups, artists had started to band together into societies. The main one was the Royal Academy, founded in 1768 with the support of George III. Under the guidance of its first president, Joshua Reynolds, the Academy hit upon a revolutionary way to meet the massive new demand for art – it put on large exhibitions. Art-lovers thronged to these displays, eager to buy or commission paintings, or just to absorb the atmosphere. But the Academy didn't only sell art. It had a huge influence over fashionable society, and was able to set trends too. Its works were seen to be the height of good taste, a reputation it maintained by carefully picking its members, and training young artists to work in its preferred styles.

This is a self-portrait by Joshua Reynolds, who was president of the Royal Academy from 1768 until his death in 1792.

Bands of musicians

Music was also hugely popular all across Georgian Britain. Small groups of music-lovers formed over the country, to perform concerts or just to enjoy singing simple tunes known as 'glees'. Meanwhile, larger music societies formed in the cities, culminating in the founding of the Royal Academy of Music, in 1822.

Club rules

The academies could be a mixed blessing. Their powerful influence meant that their views on style and taste held sway, and attempts to break away could be stifled. One artist who felt frustrated was Thomas Gainsborough, a member of the Royal Academy who was well-known for his portraits. He longed to earn a living from his less conventional landscape paintings instead, but failed to find any support. Eventually he left the Academy in disgust.

"Rule, Britannia! Britannia, rule the waves! Britons never, never, never shall be slaves!"

The words for the patriotic anthem *Rule Britannia!* were written by a Scottish poet named James Thompson, and set to music by the composer Thomas Arne, in 1740.

Mr. and Mrs. Andrews is a portrait of a fashionable landowner and his wife on their country estate. Thomas Gainsborough painted it in 1748-49.

Grand designs

As trade prospered and factories grew, merchants and factory owners across the country felt the benefits. Their growing incomes allowed them to live more luxuriously, and they became members of a new 'middle class'. Some even made fortunes to rival those of the established landed gentry.

As the newly wealthy urbanites thrived, they looked for houses to match their growing status. Even the richest businessmen who owned grand country estates still needed a base in the city to conduct their affairs.

From the 1760s, the rising demand for elegant town houses led to the renovation and growth of many cities, including Edinburgh, London and Bath. Many ports, such as Bristol and Liverpool, also expanded to become thriving cities based on trade.

This picture shows part of The Circus in Bath, designed by John Wood and completed by his son. It was the first circular street to be built in Britain, and its dimensions were based on measurements Wood had taken at Stonehenge.

Urban planning

Georgian houses were designed to be regular and symmetrical, with clean lines and elegant facades. Tall and narrow, lots of these new houses were built side-by-side in long rows called terraces. As each house looked much like the next, for the first time, they were given numbers to tell them apart.

Many terraces sprang up as part of grand building projects. Carefully planned streets were laid out with curved crescents, squares, parks and wide streets designed for horse-drawn carriages. Whole sections of cities such as Edinburgh and Dublin were demolished to be rebuilt in this new style.

Famous architects

As more and more people were taking an interest in fashionable houses, many architects became household names. John Nash, Robert Adam and his brother James were celebrated for their work in London, and James Craig was the designer of much of the New Town in Edinburgh.

Windows and doors

Georgian houses had big windows, to let in lots of light. Nobody knew how to make large sheets of glass, so windows were made up of lots of little panes.

Doors were often flanked by classical-style pillars. They were topped with an intricate semi-circular window, called a fanlight.

Objects of desire

The richest families filled their homes with stylish items, made by the very best craftsmen.

This mahogany chair was created by Thomas Chippendale, one of the best-known Georgian designers.

Josiah Wedgwood owned a big factory where he produced pottery in a classical style.

This piece was based on a famous Roman vase, which showed scenes from ancient myths.

Items imported from Asia were very popular, such as this tea set from China. Sets like this were used by rich families to serve a tea, which had become the height of fashion.

Interior design

Buying a town house was only the first step to becoming a respectable city dweller. The next task was to furnish the inside in the fashionable manner. Georgian ideas of taste and style were firmly fixed, and even a small slip could ruin the image of elegance.

Furniture fashions

The Georgian style of furniture was much like the architecture – graceful and refined. Georgian tables, chairs, sofas, cabinets and sideboards were made from expensive woods, and most had thin legs and simple shapes. Understated classical patterns were carved into the wood, or displayed on cushions and coverings. Later, other influences crept in too, particularly from eastern Asia. This style of furniture had a dark background overlaid with gold, often showing an 'oriental' scene.

Furniture was usually made by individual craftsmen. The most famous designers released books of their patterns, so they could be copied by other manufacturers across the country.

Wallpaper and rugs

The rest of the house had to match the fine furniture. Fireplaces, doorways and even ceilings were richly carved. Floors were covered with oriental rugs, and walls were painted or decorated with wallpaper, which was the very latest fashion.

This picture shows a Georgian town house with one side cut away.

The servants' bedrooms are on the top floor. The owners' rooms are below.

The middle two floors hold the dining room and drawing room.

Servants use a separate stairway, which is much plainer than the main staircase.

The kitchen and laundry room are at the bottom of the house.

267

Poverty and principle

While the middle classes enjoyed the wealth and the luxury goods that the new industries brought, these came at a price. Most of the workers that kept the industries going had been forced to move to towns and cities, where they lived in over-crowded, filthy slums, on very low wages. Their plight mostly went unheeded, but some well-to-do citizens worked tirelessly to help them, often motivated by religious beliefs.

John Wesley gave over 40,000 outdoor services in industrial towns up and down the country. Poor workers made up most of his audiences.

A broad church

Migrants to the cities often stopped going to church. They lost their old ties to the Church, or found that busy urban churches had no space left, and many people thought that the Church wasn't doing enough to help them. So a preacher named John Wesley decided to take religion to the workers. He rode around the country giving open-air sermons, and later built churches where there weren't enough. Wesley and his followers became known as Methodists, and many were involved in charity work and social reform.

This picture shows the chapel of Coram's Foundling Hospital, where charity performances of Handel's *Messiah* were given regularly.

Sunday schools

There was no compulsory education in the 18th century, and most schooling cost money. Children from poor families worked long hours at paid jobs, so could spare neither the time nor the money for education. Appalled by conditions in the towns around her Somerset home, one writer named Hannah More set up a string of free Sunday schools, where local children received religious instruction and learned to read.

Saving the children

On his return to London, a sea captain named Thomas Coram was shocked by the sight of children living on the streets. Many were orphans, or had been abandoned by parents who couldn't afford to look after them. Coram set up a 'Foundling Hospital' for homeless children, and famous artists and musicians gave their support.

Reformers such as Wesley, More and Coram could only help a small number of those in need. Many of the poorest people had little power to improve their lives. If they couldn't pay their bills, they were sent to prison — and had to pay fees to wardens while they were there. Others starved on the streets.

Behind bars

To help the women and children in Newgate Prison, Elizabeth Fry set up a school and provided inmates with items so that they could knit and sew goods to sell.

She also made sure that the prisoners were given regular Bible readings.

Breaking the chains

"I have seen a negro beaten till some of his bones were broken, for only letting a pot boil over."

Equiano describes the cruel punishment of a slave in the Caribbean.

This picture shows slaves working on a plantation. They are taking sugar cane to a windmill to crush out the juice so it can be refined to make sugar.

The buying and selling of people as slaves had been going on since ancient times. But, by the 18th century, this trade had increased dramatically, generating great wealth for European merchants – and causing terrible suffering for the slaves. During the 1720s, British ships sailing from London, Bristol and Liverpool transported some 200,000 Africans to North America and the Caribbean. By the 1790s, that number had doubled.

Those who survived the dreadful voyage were then sold to work on plantations where they were made to work long hours, and often beaten. Many slaves tried to escape or rebel against their masters. A few were successful, but many were punished brutally.

As people in Britain began to hear of the harsh realities of slavery, some began to demand an end to the trade. They met opposition at first, but eventually slavery was abolished in Britain and throughout its colonies.

1760

A slave named Tacky leads a massive rebellion in Jamaica. Sugar crops are set alight and around 60 white people are killed. Tacky and 400 other rebels die or are executed.

~

Quaker leaders ban their followers from slave trading.

June, 1772

James Somerset, a slave, escapes from his owner in London. His case is taken to court, and he is declared a free man. Many people mistakenly take this to mean that slavery is now outlawed in England.

1774

Methodist preacher John Wesley publishes an anti-slavery pamphlet entitled *Thoughts upon Slavery*.

1787

Granville Sharp and Thomas Clarkson found the Society for the Abolition of the Slave Trade. They persuade MP William Wilberforce to be their spokesman in Parliament.

November 1781

The captain of a slave ship, *Zong* throws 133 slaves overboard alive, then files an insurance claim for their value. The case shocks many people into joining the fight against slavery.

1787

Josiah Wedgwood produces the Abolition Society's seal. It includes the motto, "Am I Not a Man and a Brother?"

1789

A former slave named Olaudah Equiano publishes his autobiography. It becomes a bestseller.

1789

Wilberforce makes his first anti-slavery speech to the House of Commons.

1792

Freetown, in Sierra Leone, west Africa, is established under British rule as a home for former slaves.

1807

The slave trade is abolished in Britain and its empire, but slave ownership continues in British colonies.

1831

A slave named Sam Sharpe leads a rebellion of over 2,000 slaves in Jamaica. British troops restore order, but the rebellion inspires people in Britain to renew the fight against slavery.

1833

Slavery is abolished in all British colonies.

The American Revolution

By the 1770s, many people in Britain's American colonies had become resentful of British rule. King George III's government enforced strict controls on trade to and from the colonies, and imposed increasingly heavy taxes on them, too. The colonists felt this was unfair. As they didn't have representatives in Parliament in London, they thought they should only pay taxes approved by their own governing assemblies. Many began to protest more and more vehemently against British rule, and some of these protests led to violence.

"We hold these truths to be self-evident that all men are created equal; that they are endowed by their Creator with certain inalienable rights; that among these are life, liberty, and the pursuit of happiness."

Lines from the Declaration of Independence.

Storm in a teacup

One of the most infamous anti-tax protests took place in 1773, after the British refused to remove import tax on tea.

Some colonists stopped buying tea in protest, but a party of men in Boston took things further. Disguised as Native Americans, they stormed a ship bringing tea into the port and threw its cargo overboard.

This protest became known as the Boston Tea Party.

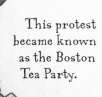

Congress signs the Declaration of Independence, July 4, 1776.

A united stand

In May 1775, representatives from 13 of the colonies met at the Congress of Philadelphia. They decided it was time to break away from British rule. So, they set up an army under the command of a soldier named George Washington. On July 4, 1776, Congress signed a document called the Declaration of Independence. This stated that the colonies were now an independent country – the United States of America.

Losing America

The British weren't going to give up without a fight. Their army was stronger and better trained than Washington's troops, and won several early battles. But, as the American troops grew tougher and more experienced, they became more successful. They also gained allies in the French, the Spanish and the Dutch, who saw the war as a chance to weaken British influence in America.

In 1781, after a fierce fight at the Battle of Yorktown, the war finally ended in victory for the colonies. Two years later, at the Treaty of Paris, Britain officially recognized the United States of America as an independent nation. In Britain, many people held George III to blame for losing America, and his Prime Minister Lord North was forced to resign.

Washington

The leaders of the United States soon began to build the foundations of their new country.

In 1789, George Washington was elected the first President of the USA.

His government, and all future US governments, followed the American Constitution, a set of laws written by a lawyer named Thomas Jefferson.

In this scene, British soldiers are defending their position from a makeshift wooden fort.

The Americans are fighting under their new flag. It has 13 stripes, one for each of the colonies.

273

Heads roll

In 1792, the French abolished their monarchy. The following year, they beheaded their royal family using a machine known as a guillotine.

This horrified many people in Britain, not least Queen Charlotte, who feared the same thing might happen in Britain.

The rights of man

After losing America, George III faced a difficult time with his ministers – until 1783, when he found a talented and supportive politician to lead his government. William Pitt the Younger – the 24-year-old son of William Pitt who had held power during the Seven Years' War – would be Prime Minister from 1783-1801, and 1804-6, steering the nation through a series of events that threatened to topple the King and his government.

The first of these came in November 1788, when the King suffered what his doctors described as a fit of insanity. He began talking gibberish and foaming at the mouth. His eyes became so bloodshot that one observer said they looked like currant jelly. The episode was short-lived, and by April 1789, George had returned to his royal duties. But a far more serious threat lay ahead.

Reason and republicanism

The Americans weren't the only people with revolutionary ideas. In France, writers Voltaire and Jean Jacques Rousseau had begun to apply Enlightenment principles to society, claiming that all people were equal and that the idea of a monarchy was irrational and outmoded.

An English writer, Thomas Paine, held similar views, and had taken part in the American Revolution. He published a pamphlet, entitled *Common Sense*, which argued for republicanism – government by the people, with an elected head of state instead of a monarch.

This cartoon, by James Gillray, depicts Thomas Paine as a dangerous man, spreading nonsense, anarchy and misery.

Revolution in France

In the summer of 1789, ideas were put into action as revolution broke out in France. At first, the French ruler, Louis XVI, was made to sign a new constitution that gave him only limited powers in government. But in 1792, the French abolished the monarchy altogether and declared their country a republic.

Thomas Paine celebrated the French Revolution in his pamphlet, *Rights of Man*. It became a bestseller, as many in Britain greeted the news from France with similar enthusiasm. But this turned to outrage and alarm in 1793, when the French royal family and hundreds of 'enemies of the revolution' were executed during a period known as the Reign of Terror.

Just as Pitt was debating how to react to the threat from across the Channel, the French declared war.

In this painting from 1793, Pitt the Younger stands in the House of Commons to announce the French declaration of war.

To prevent revolution breaking out in Britain, Pitt brought in emergency powers. Anyone who might pose a threat to national security was arrested. Thomas Paine escaped to France, but many political campaigners were imprisoned.

Rebellion in Ireland

This is a picture of the leading members of the United Irishmen.

Standing in the middle, hat in hand, is Robert Emmet. He was a young leader of the United Irishmen, who survived the 1798 rebellion by fleeing to France. He was later caught and executed for treason.

Two people to the right of Emmet, standing by the pillar, is Theobald Wolfe Tone. Tone was a Protestant lawyer who was deeply committed to improving the rights of Catholics.

Since the Battle of the Boyne in 1690, most of the land in Ireland had been owned by Protestants with close ties to Britain. Meanwhile, Ireland's Catholic majority had very limited rights. They couldn't vote, own land, educate their children or become politicians or lawyers.

Ireland had its own Parliament, but its decisions were highly influenced by the British government. Members of the Irish Parliament were coerced or bribed into voting the way that Britain wanted.

Demanding change

In 1791, a group of Catholics and Protestants joined to form the United Irishmen. Inspired by the American and French revolutions, they aimed to break away from Britain and form their own republic, with better rights for Catholics. One of the leaders, Theobald Wolfe Tone, went to ask the French for military support.

Revolution and reaction

In the spring of 1798, the United Irishmen launched an uprising. The French sent troops but they didn't arrive in time to help, and British forces were able to crush the rebellion at the Battle of Vinegar Hill in June.

Meanwhile, French troops landed in Mayo, on the west coast. But, despite a summer victory at Castlebar, they were also soon forced to surrender. Tone landed in Donegal with further French forces, but was captured by the British and committed suicide in prison.

A new kingdom

To prevent more uprisings, the British government decided to tighten its grip on Ireland. Pitt the Younger persuaded the Irish Parliament to disband. In return, he offered better rights for Catholics, and allowed Irish representatives to sit in Britain's Parliament in London.

In 1801, the Act of Union joined Ireland and Britain to form the new United Kingdom. But George III, who was a staunch Protestant, refused to pass the law giving Catholics their promised rights. Ashamed that he couldn't keep his word, Pitt resigned.

1606 flag

Irish flag

Union Jack

The Union Jack

In 1606, King James IV of Scotland and I of England had a new British flag made. It combined the flags of the two nations he ruled.

In 1801 the Irish flag was added – to create the British flag that is still used today, commonly known as the Union Jack.

Ireland in 1798

This map shows where the key battles and uprisings took place.

✗ Battle

✗ United Irish uprising

▇ Area of United Irish activity

▇ Area occupied by the French

ULSTER

DONEGAL

Antrim

Belfast

Ballynahinch

Killala

Sligo

MAYO

CONNACHT

Castlebar

Ballynamuck

Tara

LEINSTER

Dublin

The Curragh

Wicklow

Arklow

Gorey

Vinegar Hill

New Ross

MUNSTER

Wexford

Cork

Bantry

Napoleon and Nelson

The French failed to take the revolution to Ireland, but by 1797, they had defeated much of Europe. Much of their success was down to the skills of a charismatic general, named Napoleon Bonaparte, who was rapidly rising through the ranks.

Napoleon seemed unbeatable, but at sea he met his match in the British naval commander, Horatio Nelson. Nelson was convinced that the mighty Royal Navy could save the country and change the course of the war. In August 1798, his fleet destroyed the French navy in the Mediterranean, at the Battle of the Nile. From then on, he enjoyed a series of victories at sea.

By the turn of the century, Napoleon was effectively ruling France as a military dictator. There was a brief period of peace, but fighting broke out again in 1802.

Napoleon's rise to power

1769 – born in Corsica.

1782 – attends military school in Paris.

1793 – helps lead a siege at the French port of Toulon to defeat anti-revolutionary forces.

1796 – marries Josephine de Beauharnais, commands the French army in Italy, and forces Austria to make peace with France.

1798 – conquers Egypt in order to block British trade routes to India. He is later defeated by Nelson's navy at the Battle of the Nile.

1799 – disbands the French government, the Directory, and appoints himself First Consul – he is effectively a military dictator.

1804 – crowns himself Emperor Napoleon I.

This painting of the Battle of Trafalgar shows a fight between a French warship, on the left, and a British one, as they fire their cannons at each other.

Trafalgar

In 1803, Napoleon started gathering an army to invade Britain. But his soldiers couldn't cross the English Channel without naval support, and Nelson was determined that they would never get that far.

On October 21, 1805, Nelson's fleet met a combined French and Spanish force off Cape Trafalgar, near the southern tip of Spain. Using his three most powerful warships "like a spear to break the enemy line," Nelson sent the rival fleet scattering. In the hard-fought battle that followed, Nelson was shot and later died. But his tactic had paid off, and the superior skills and experience of Britain's seamen won the day.

Nelson's victory at Trafalgar removed the immediate threat of invasion, and encouraged other countries to stand up to France – but Napoleon wasn't beaten yet.

Nelson's column

Nelson served in the navy from the age of 12. He lost his right arm and the sight in his right eye in earlier battles, but was mortally wounded at Trafalgar. On hearing that the British were winning, his dying words were, "Thank God I have done my duty."

Nelson was immortalized with a giant 5.5m (18ft) statue of him, erected at the top of a 46m (150ft) high column. Nelson's Column, as the landmark is called, towers over Trafalgar Square in the heart of London.

Suited and booted

Wellington had his shoemaker modify his boots so that they were sturdy and comfortable in battle, but smart enough for evenings.

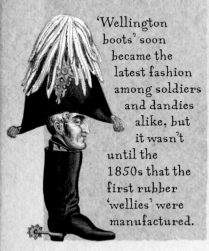

'Wellington boots' soon became the latest fashion among soldiers and dandies alike, but it wasn't until the 1850s that the first rubber 'wellies' were manufactured.

Wellington raises his hat aloft as a signal to his troops to advance, in this artist's impression of the Battle of Waterloo.

Wellington and Waterloo

By 1812, Napoleon had conquered most of western Europe. But his days in power were numbered, as Britain and many European countries formed a new alliance to beat him once and for all.

In June that year, he led a disastrous invasion of Russia. Badly equipped and ill-prepared for the harsh winter, of 600,000 men, only about 30,000 returned. Meanwhile, a British army, led by Arthur Wellesley, later the Duke of Wellington, helped to drive out the French from Spain and Portugal. These losses marked a turning point in Napoleon's fortunes. After several major defeats, he was captured in April 1814, and imprisoned on the Italian island of Elba.

The Hundred Days

A year later, Napoleon escaped and retook power in France for a brief period, known as the Hundred Days. In June, he led his armies to Belgium to face his enemies in what was to be the final, decisive battle at Waterloo.

Into battle

Two forces were assembled in Belgium, ready to do battle with Napoleon: an army of 89,000 men from the German state of Prussia, led by a veteran fighter, Field Marshal Blücher, and an allied force of 68,000 British, Dutch, German and Belgian soldiers under Wellington.

Napoleon's strategy was to launch lightning attacks on his opponents, before the two armies could join forces and outnumber his 71,000 troops. On June 16, he struck the Prussians at Ligny, forcing them to retreat. Thinking Blücher was defeated, Napoleon turned his attentions to Wellington on June 18, 1815.

A close-run thing

Wellington's men held a defensive position on a ridge of land, just south of Waterloo. At midday, the French opened fire, with a massive artillery barrage. Wellington ordered his men to stand firm. His foot soldiers formed tight squares behind the ridge, while his gunmen fired at Napoleon's advancing troops. There were heavy losses on both sides, but the French failed to break through the allied line.

Just as daylight was beginning to fade, the Prussians arrived, and the combined allied forces charged their opponents. The French were routed, and fled back to Paris. As the smoke from the cannons lifted, 25,000 French and 22,000 allied soldiers lay dead or wounded. Wellington later described the battle as "the closest-run thing you ever saw in your life."

His empire in tatters, Napoleon finally surrendered to the British in July. His defeat ended French domination of Europe for good.

Island exile

After his defeat at Waterloo, Napoleon was sent to live in exile on the tiny, remote island of St. Helena in the South Atlantic Ocean.

Thousands of miles from anywhere, with no means of escape, Napoleon died on the island on May 5, 1821. His doctor claimed he died of stomach cancer, but some historians believe he might have died as a result of arsenic poisoning.

This cartoon shows Napoleon in his earlier island exile, on Elba.

Romantic hero

This portrait shows the English poet Lord Byron in Albanian costume. He spent time in Albania, Greece and Turkey when he was 21.

He later returned to Greece, to help in the nation's fight for independence. But he caught a chill there, and died aged 36.

This moody, romantic landscape painting by John Constable is of Derwentwater, in the Lake District.

Mad, bad and dangerous

While the Napoleonic Wars were raging, an artistic movement, known as Romanticism, swept across Europe too. Partly inspired by revolutionary politics, and partly reacting against ideas of the Enlightenment, Romantic poets, painters and composers began to explore new styles and new sources of inspiration.

Radical politics

One of the first English Romantics was William Blake. He studied at the Royal Academy, then worked as a printer and engraver, publishing his own poems, which he also illustrated himself. A supporter of Thomas Paine and the revolutions in America and France, many of his poems expressed his passionate beliefs in social equality and creative freedom.

As an idealistic young man, the poet William Wordsworth spent time in France during the early days of the French Revolution. He lost faith in the revolution and returned to England in 1793, as the fight for equality and liberty turned to terror and bloodshed.

Wild genius

In 1798, Wordsworth and another poet, Samuel Taylor Coleridge, brought out a collection of their poems entitled *Lyrical Ballads*. In it, they set out a revolutionary manifesto for poetry. Imagination and emotions were more important to them than reason and order. They wanted to move away from the formal styles of previous generations, to write the way they spoke. A Scottish poet, Robert Burns, took this even further by writing many poems in his own local dialect.

Along with painters such as J.M.W. Turner and John Constable, many Romantic poets were inspired by nature and Britain's wild landscapes. For them, dramatic scenes of mountains, lakes and coastlines stirred powerful feelings, which they expressed in their work.

Some poets, particularly Lord Byron, Percy Shelley and John Keats, took their pursuit of sensations to extremes. They became notorious not only for their literary talents, but also for their wild antics. The rock stars of their day, they all died young.

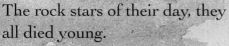

Gothic horror

In 1816, Byron invited Percy Shelley and Shelley's future wife Mary to stay with him near Lake Geneva in the Swiss Alps. It was a cold, wet summer, so they spent much of their time huddled indoors, and set themselves a challenge to see who could write the most frightening story.

Mary, aged only 19, wrote *Frankenstein*, a tale of a young medical student who builds a man from parts of dead bodies and then brings this monster to life.

Byron wrote only part of a vampire story. But this later led another guest, John Polidori, to write *The Vampyre*. His vampire character was based on Byron, and inspired Bram Stoker to create Count Dracula.

Regency style

This illustration shows stylish Georgians strolling in Brighton, with the Royal Pavilion in the background. The Prince Regent lived in Brighton until his father's death, and under his influence the town was transformed from a small seaside town to a fashionable resort.

Brighton Royal Pavilion was designed by John Nash for the Prince Regent. Its exotic facade was inspired by the Prince's love of Indian and oriental architecture.

In 1811, George III suffered another attack of the illness that had first struck him in 1788. Many experts now believe his symptoms were caused by a rare condition called porphyria. But at the time, the King's doctors believed he was insane. They subjected him to a series of humiliating treatments, including being force-fed and restrained in an iron chair.

Despite his doctors' efforts, the King never fully recovered. So, his son George became Prince Regent, ruling on behalf of his father. The regency period would last until the death of George III, in 1820.

The Prince Regent was a completely different character from his father. Intelligent, handsome and sociable, he was admired as a man of style with refined artistic tastes. But he also had extravagant tastes for heavy drinking, excessive eating and reckless gambling.

Out and about

In many ways, the Prince Regent set the trends for Britain's well-to-do. Balls, parties and lavish dinners were commonplace across the country, and even small towns had Assembly Rooms for public dances. Other popular pastimes included gambling at cards and horse races, and attending plays and concerts in the cities.

But there was also a serious purpose to much of this socializing. Being seen to be fashionable and rich was vital for making business contacts, and for young adults looking to marry someone from a respectable family.

Taking the waters

Another popular pastime was making trips to coastal or spa towns, to bathe in the water. Visitors flocked to stylish resorts such as Bath, Cheltenham and Brighton, the Prince Regent's own regular haunt. These towns were designed largely for pleasure, with rows of trees, romantic gardens, and many evening entertainments.

Witty writer

Jane Austen wrote six novels, set among the upper and middle classes of Regency society. The stories make witty observations of the manners and customs of the time, and give an insight into women's lives in particular. The Prince Regent was said to admire her books, which are still widely read today.

Greek goddesses and dashing dandies

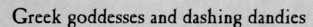

During the Regency period, fashions moved away from the powdered wigs, frills and embroidery of the 18th century, and became simpler and more sophisticated.

Instead of having tight bodices and full skirts, women began to wear 'empire line' dresses. These had high waists and loose, flowing skirts draped to look like the dresses of Greek statues.

Fashionable young men, or 'dandies' were influenced by the Prince Regent's friend George 'Beau' Brummell. They wore long breeches or trousers, tailored waistcoats, crisp linen shirts with cravats, and they didn't wear wigs.

Paper or silk parasols shaded women's fair skin from the sun.

Both women and men used fans to keep cool, and also for flirting at parties.

Coal, iron and rocket power

By the end of the 18th century, Britain's factories had found a new source of power: steam.

The very first steam engine had been built back in 1698 by an English engineer named Thomas Savery. It drove a pump to drain flooded coal mines. The engine broke down frequently, so a few years later, Thomas Newcomen improved on the design, making it more reliable.

Spanning the River Severn, in Shropshire this is the world's first iron bridge, built by Abraham Darby at Coalbrookdale in 1779.

Darby's grandfather, also named Abraham Darby, set up an ironworks at Coalbrookdale in 1709. He developed a process of producing iron goods on a much bigger scale than had been possible before.

As most steam engines and industrial machines were made from iron, Darby's work played a crucial role in the Industrial Revolution.

Watt's engine

Then, around 1764, James Watt, a Scottish engineer, was given a Newcomen engine to repair. He spent the next few years developing more efficient engines that had the power to run whole factories. By 1800 there were over 500 of Watt's engines in Britain's mines, ironworks, mills and factories and he retired, a wealthy man. A unit of power – the Watt – is named after him.

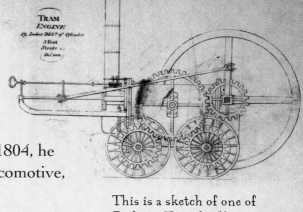

TRAM
ENGINE
1½ Inches DIAᵗ of Cylinder
3 Feet
Stroke
Del 1803

Locomotives

Soon, a mining engineer named Richard Trevithick realized that steam engines could replace horses for driving heavy vehicles. In 1804, he produced the first steam-powered train, or locomotive, to run on rails.

Trevithick's ideas were taken further by George Stephenson. He improved the designs of both locomotives and the rails they ran on. In 1825, he built the world's first public steam railway, which ran 40km (25 miles) from Stockton to Darlington. He also designed the engine that carried coal trucks and passenger wagons along the line.

With the help of these engines, and plentiful supplies of coal to fuel them, the railways expanded all over the country during the 19th century, and the Industrial Revolution rapidly gathered pace.

This is a sketch of one of Richard Trevithick's designs for a steam engine. His inventions helped many engineers after him, but didn't make him much money. Sadly, he died a pauper.

The Rocket

Stephenson's most famous engine, the *Rocket*, reached speeds of up to 50km (30 miles) an hour. Here's how it worked: Coal burned in an iron fire box heated water in the boiler to make steam. The steam drove pistons, which turned the large wheels at the front of the engine and pulled the train.

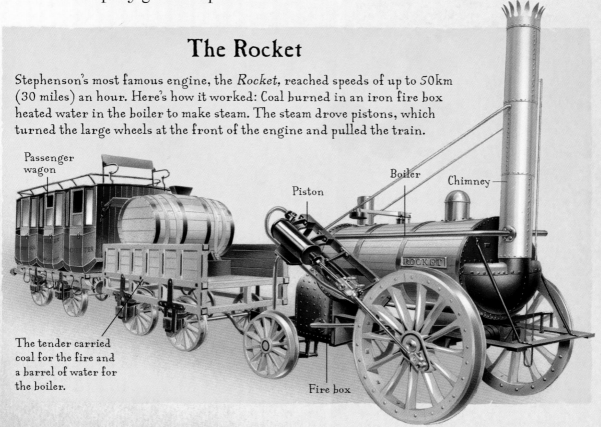

Passenger wagon

Piston

Boiler

Chimney

ROCKET

The tender carried coal for the fire and a barrel of water for the boiler.

Fire box

This cartoon shows the chaos and carnage of the Peterloo Massacre. The cavalry soldier on the left is saying, "chop 'em down my brave boys... the more you kill the less poor rates you'll have to pay."

Fancy dress

After ruling Britain for nearly nine years, the Prince Regent became King George IV in 1820. Despite the poverty of many of his subjects, he spent thousands of pounds on a lavish Tudor-style coronation.

Riots and reforms

While socialites lived it up, the gap between the lives of the rich and the poor was growing. Mostly, only rich landowners were allowed to vote in elections, so the needs of poor people, and even the middle classes, were often ignored in Parliament. The first decades of the 19th century saw much unrest, as many people began protesting against inequality and demanding change.

Since the outbreak of the French Revolution, it had been illegal for British workers to join trades unions. This meant they couldn't negotiate with their employers for better pay or conditions. In desperation, some took matters into their own hands.

In 1811, a group of stocking weavers in Nottingham began smashing up factory machinery that was putting them out of work. They became known as Luddites after their leader, Ned Ludd. Similar protests took place throughout the north of England.

Give us bread

During the war with France, wages had been frozen, but the price of many goods had tripled. A series of bad harvests led to a shortage of grain, and an even steeper rise in the price of bread. The answer was to import grain to keep bread cheap, but many landowners thought this would harm British farming. So in 1815, the government passed the Corn Law, banning the importing of cheap grain. Unable to afford the food they needed to survive, the hungry masses took to the streets.

In August 1819, tens of thousands of men, women and children gathered for a peaceful demonstration in St. Peter's Fields, in Manchester. Local magistrates feared the gathering could turn into a riot, so they sent in cavalry soldiers to arrest its leaders. They rode into the crowd with their swords drawn, causing mayhem: 11 people were killed and 400 were injured. Some of the soldiers had fought at Waterloo, so this tragic event was given the ironic nickname the 'Peterloo Massacre'.

Small steps and giant leaps

Under increasing pressure from protesters and reformers, the government began to take steps to make life easier for poor people. Gradually, new laws brought better working conditions in factories and improved the state of Britain's prisons.

The call for political reforms was growing louder too, but the ruling classes were reluctant to lose their grip on power. Not only were few people allowed to vote, but many of the new industrial towns had no Member of Parliament to represent them. Meanwhile, some MPs stood for areas, known as 'rotten boroughs', where only a handful of electors lived. Something had to change.

Getting better

Here are some of the key social reforms of the early 19th century:

1823 – The death penalty is removed from over a hundred crimes. Conditions in prisons are improved and wages for jailers are introduced.

1824 – The ban on trade union membership is lifted.

1829 – The Roman Catholic Relief Act allows Catholics to sit in Parliament. They had been given the vote in 1793.

1829 – The Metropolitan Police is set up in London.

1832 – The Great Reform Act improves the electoral system and gives more men the vote.

1833 – Factory Acts make it illegal to employ children under 9 in factories, and limits the hours children under 13 can be made to work.

289

The sailor and the actress

Before he became King, William had served in the Royal Navy for 47 years.

In 1789, he was made Duke of Clarence. He retired from the Navy a year later, and lived with his mistress, an actress named Dorothea Jordan.

Their children, known as the Fitzclarences, weren't seen as heirs to the throne as the couple weren't married.

Time for change

With the coming of the age of steam, and social reforms under way, there was a general sense that Britain was on the brink of a new era. This was reinforced in 1830, when George IV died, and his 64-year-old brother succeeded him as William IV. But a more significant change came later that year. The Tories, who had dominated government for decades, were voted out and a Whig, Earl Grey, became Prime Minister.

To prevent the revolution they feared was brewing, the Whigs set about bringing in electoral reforms Despite strong opposition, the Great Reform Act was passed in 1832. The vote was extended to more people, and rotten boroughs were abolished. The vast majority of the population still wasn't allowed to vote, but the act was a major landmark on the road to a more democratic government.

A new order

In October 1834, a fire ravaged the Palace of Westminster, the ancient seat of the Houses of Parliament and a powerful symbol of the old order. The fire was an accident, but many commentators believed this was just the fresh start the reformed Parliament needed, and the government launched a competition to design a new building.

On June 20, 1837, William IV died. His brother, Ernest Augustus, Duke of Cumberland, became Elector of Hanover, and his 18-year-old niece, Victoria, succeeded him to the British throne. With industry booming and a bright young monarch, the difficulties of the early 19th century seemed to be over. Many people looked forward to a better future.

Mother's pride

Princess Victoria turned 18 only a month before King William died. If he had died earlier, Victoria's mother, the ambitious Duchess of Kent – who William greatly disliked – would have taken over until Victoria was old enough to rule by herself.

People watch from boats on the Thames as the old Houses of Parliament are consumed in flames, in this painting by a Scottish artist, David Roberts.

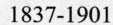

THE VICTORIANS

I n 1837, King William IV died, and his young niece Victoria was crowned Queen of Great Britain and Ireland. She was only 18 years old, but she would become Britain's longest reigning monarch so far.

During her 64 year rule, the Victorians built up a vast empire overseas, and achieved enormous social, economic and scientific progress at home. By the time Queen Victoria died, in 1901, Britain had become the wealthiest, most powerful nation in the world.

At four, Victoria, like all children of the time, was dressed as a miniature adult.

The young queen

People often picture Queen Victoria as she was in the last years of her reign – a grumpy, disapproving old lady. But this was far from true of the teenage girl who came to the throne. Although Victoria always took her royal duties very seriously, her diaries show that she was passionate and fun-loving too. As a girl, she enjoyed dressing in bright silks for the opera and attending lavish balls at Buckingham Palace.

Victoria was born in Kensington Palace, in London, in 1819 and christened Alexandrina Victoria. Her uncle, William IV, and his wife had no surviving children, so it soon became clear that Victoria would succeed him to the throne.

The young heiress had a strict, lonely upbringing, with little company apart from her over-protective mother and her governess. Despite her solitude, Victoria was a lively, playful child who enjoyed painting, riding, music, singing and dancing.

Learning to be a queen

As well as the usual school subjects, such as languages and mathematics, Princess Victoria felt it was her duty to study the kings and queens of Britain, in preparation for her future role. "A great queen but a bad woman," was how she described one of her predecessors, Queen Elizabeth I.

The princess also had to learn how to walk, talk and act like royalty. She was made to keep a special book, where she noted everything she did and how she behaved, especially when she was naughty. Entries that she made in this book, and in her personal diaries, showed that although she was anxious to be good, Victoria was often stubborn and quick-tempered too.

Walking tall

Victoria was taught to walk in a regal manner by balancing books on her head and having prickly holly leaves tied under her chin.

Public image

When Victoria became queen in 1837, public opinion of the monarchy was at an all time low. Her predecessors had been unpopular – George IV was seen as wasteful and sleazy and William IV was old and doddery. Their reigns had seen public protests and bloody riots, and some people even thought Britain might be on the brink of a revolution. Victoria was determined to restore the image of the monarchy. So it was vital that she made a good impression at her first major public event – her coronation.

It was a splendid, dignified affair. During the ceremony, an elderly lord tripped near the throne and Victoria helped him to his feet. This kind gesture won the people's hearts and convinced them that their new queen would be caring, humble and respectable. To them, she became known as England's rose.

This painting of the young Queen Victoria is by Franz Xavier Winterhalter, a German artist who painted more than 120 portraits of Victoria and her family.

Queen Victoria's family tree

GEORGE III
(1760-1820)

Frederick, Duke of York | Charlotte, Princess Royal | 10 others

GEORGE IV
(1820-1830)

WILLIAM IV
(1830-1837)

Edward, Duke of Kent

Charlotte
(died in childbirth, with no surviving children)

VICTORIA
(1837-1901)

The dates show the years of each monarch's reign.

Victoria and Albert

One of Victoria's main duties as Queen was to marry and produce an heir. Her German cousin Albert, Duke of Saxe-Coburg-Gotha, had been regarded by her family as a suitable match for her from early on. When they first met at 17, they didn't get along. Victoria could be hot-headed and rash, while Albert was cool and rational. But their differences brought out the best in each other and they grew to be a devoted couple.

Two years later, on October 15, 1839, Victoria asked Albert to marry her – it would have been improper for a prince to propose to the Queen – and he accepted. The following year, on February 10, hordes of cheering Londoners crowded outside Buckingham Palace to catch a glimpse of their Queen as her coach drove past. Victoria's dress was made of white satin and lace. In her hair were diamonds and orange blossoms. Over her heart she wore a diamond and sapphire brooch – a gift from Albert.

Prince Albert cuts a dashing figure in fashionable formal dress, including a top hat and tail coat.

Married life

Prince Albert was a quiet, clever man. He was happy for Victoria to take the limelight, but he was frustrated that he had no official title or duty. At first, his only job was to blot Victoria's signature on official papers. Gradually, Victoria relied more and more on his help and advice, until they were effectively ruling together. But parliament refused to make Albert King. So in 1857, Victoria gave him the title of Prince Consort, in recognition of his importance to her and the country.

The royal family

Victoria and Albert had nine children, and many Victorians saw them as the ideal happy family. For most of the year they lived in Windsor Castle, but they also had two country homes – Osborne House, on the Isle of Wight, and Balmoral Castle, in Scotland – where they could escape the formality of public life. The couple worked in the mornings and spent the rest of the day with their children, enjoying simple pastimes such as walking, riding and painting.

Victoria was anxious to see her children as happily married as she was and, when they grew up, she urged them to marry European royalty. When they began to have families of their own, she earned the nickname the Grandmama of Europe. Victoria hoped that their family ties would ensure future peace. But, sadly, when the First World War broke out in 1914, two of her grandsons, King George V and Kaiser Wilhelm II of Germany, were on opposing sides.

Festive fashions

Prince Albert was quite a trend-setter. He introduced the British people to the German traditions of decorating a Christmas tree...

...and of sending Christmas cards to each other.

Victoria and Albert pose for an informal family portrait with their children.

Politics and power

By Victorian times, Britain was a constitutional monarchy. This meant that political power rested with the government, not with the Queen. But she still held some influence, so ministers had to try to get along with her.

Ten prime ministers held office during Victoria's reign, and power swung between two main parties. The Whigs – later called the Liberals – supported political reform, while the Conservatives, or Tories, were usually against change. Victoria's first prime minister was the Whig, Lord Melbourne. He spent hours with her every day, teaching her about the business of government, and soon became like a father to her.

Victorian politicians wore long coats and top hats to Parliament. Etiquette dictated that they had to remove their hats when addressing the chamber.

The Houses of Parliament were designed by Charles Barry after the original buildings were destroyed in a fire in 1834. Queen Victoria opened the new parliament buildings in 1852.

Victoria grew so attached to Melbourne that when the Tories came to power in 1841 she almost refused to accept them. Eventually, Prince Albert persuaded her to remain above party politics and to cooperate with the new prime minister, Sir Robert Peel. In time, Victoria grew to admire him.

Political change

British politics had become more democratic during the late Georgian period, but it was still very different from today. At the start of Victoria's reign, only wealthy landowners could stand for Parliament, fewer than one in seven men could vote, and women weren't allowed to take part in elections at all.

In 1838, a group of workers published a people's charter demanding electoral reforms. The government rejected the charter, and after a decade of campaigning the movement declined. But, by the end of Victoria's reign many of the Chartists' reforms had been introduced.

Chartist demands

The Chartists made six demands, which they hoped would help to improve the lives of working people, by giving them a say in how the country was run.

PEOPLE'S CHARTER

1. Votes for all men over the age of 21

2. Votes to be secret

3. Candidates to stand for election regardless of their wealth

4. A salary for members of Parliament

5. All electoral districts to be of equal size

6. Elections to take place every year

The Chartists staged public rallies and strikes. They also took petitions to the government in 1839, 1842 and 1848.

The first petition was said to contain 11 million signatures and was three miles long.

A few parents couldn't afford to look after their children. Dr. Barnardo's charity took care of homeless children, like these, and gave them shelter and education.

What's cooking?

Alexis Soyer was a chef at a top London restaurant, where he cooked lavish meals for wealthy celebrities.

But he also set up soup kitchens in London and across Ireland to feed starving paupers.

Hard times

Life in the Houses of Parliament and Buckingham Palace was full of pomp and ceremony, but for ordinary people it was a very different story. Many Victorians faced a daily struggle against poverty and hardship, and had little chance of making things better.

In the late 18th century, most British people lived a rural life, working as farmers or as craftsmen producing handmade goods. Then, new machines were invented that could do the work in a fraction of the time. This left thousands unemployed, so they flocked to the towns in search of new jobs. This radical change in the way people lived and worked became known as the Industrial Revolution.

Daily bread

The Industrial Revolution made a small number of people incredibly wealthy, but for most, the 1830s and 40s were tough. Jobs remained scarce and wages were pitifully low. To make matters worse, bread became so expensive that many couldn't afford it. This was because of a new law called the Corn Law, which prevented the importing of cheap grain. It was supposed to protect the incomes of British farmers, but it also pushed up the price of bread, especially in the years when there was a bad harvest. The situation became so dire that people were starving in the streets.

A group of politicians and industrialists got together to campaign for an end to the Corn Law, and for fairer wages. Other groups, including religious charities such as the Salvation Army and Dr. Barnardo's, took more direct action to relieve the distress of the starving. They ran soup kitchens and orphanages, and provided clothing and shelters for the needy.

Poor relief

For the very poorest people, the last resort was to go to places called workhouses. The government made sure that nobody saw the workhouse as an easy option. Once inside, families were split up, as men, women and children – and those who were too old or too sick to work – were made to live in separate quarters, which were often crowded and dirty.

Inmates had to work very long hours. Women were usually given domestic chores like cooking and cleaning, while men were given heavy work including breaking rocks and chopping wood. All this was done on a diet of potatoes, bread, cheese and soup, served in small portions that often left people still hungry. If a man left the workhouse, his family had to leave too. But if he didn't find a job, they'd soon end up back inside.

The Victorian author Charles Dickens wrote about the suffering of the poor in many of his books, which were often based on his own experiences. His family had been imprisoned for debt when he was 12.

This illustration from Dickens's novel, *Oliver Twist*, shows Oliver in the workhouse, daring to ask for more food.

Troubles in Ireland

"There never was a country in which poverty existed to the extent that it exists in Ireland."

Arthur Wellesley,
Duke of Wellington

This Victorian Irish family was forced to live in this hut after being evicted from their farm for failing to pay their rent.

Relations between Britain and Ireland had been uneasy for centuries. But since 1801 Ireland had been part of the United Kingdom, ruled by the British government in London. While a few Irish people prospered under British rule, most lived as farmers in dreadful poverty and many held the government to blame.

Most of Ireland's farmland belonged to wealthy landowners who employed agents to manage their estates for them. The agents then leased the land to local farmers. The more tenants they had, the more rent they collected, so they divided the land into the smallest farms possible. The poor farmers had barely enough land to grow what they needed to survive.

In 1845, disaster struck. The Irish potato crop became infected with a fungal disease, called blight, which turned the potatoes to an inedible black pulp. Potatoes were the staple diet and many farmers had almost no other crops to fall back on. The next two years also saw failed harvests. Unable to pay their rent, thousands were evicted, left starving and homeless. To reduce the price of bread and to feed the starving, Robert Peel ended the Corn Law. But it was too little, too late. By 1850, over a million people had died.

Home Rule

After the famine, many Irish people felt that the government hadn't done enough to help. Some wanted independence from Britain, and a few were even prepared to use violence to achieve it. But an Irish politician named Charles Stuart Parnell ran a peaceful campaign for 'Home Rule' – for the Irish to have their own parliament. He called for fairer rents and for farmers to be given the chance to buy their own farms.

By 1885, Parnell's Home Rule party had 86 members of Parliament in London. They convinced Prime Minister William Gladstone that Home Rule was the best way to make peace in Ireland. He tried twice to pass an Irish Home Rule Bill, but was defeated by politicians who feared that it might encourage other parts of the British empire to claim independence. In 1890, Parnell was involved in a divorce scandal and forced out of office in disgrace. Without him, the Home Rule cause was weakened and the Irish problem remained unresolved for the rest of Victoria's reign.

Setting sail

About two million people left Ireland, mostly going to America, in search of a better life. By 1850, the Irish made up a quarter of the populations of New York city and Boston.

Irish peasants waiting for a ship to take them to America

In this cartoon, Gladstone – shown as a kangaroo – is defending Ireland against his political rival, Lord Salisbury in a boxing match.

Coal, steam and steel

The Industrial Revolution rapidly gained pace as engineers developed steam engines with enough power to drive whole factories. This led to a massive increase in manufacturing in Britain and enabled the Victorians to dominate world trade. By the mid-19th century, industrial output was so high that Britain became known as the workshop of the world.

Raw power

The raw materials that made the Industrial Revolution possible were coal and iron. Coal fired the steam engines, and most machines were made from iron. In 1856, Henry Bessemer invented a method for converting iron into steel cheaply and in bulk. Steel is lighter, stronger and less brittle than iron, so this meant that engineers could build bigger and better ships, bridges, buildings and machinery than ever before.

The men in this Victorian painting are stoking the huge blast furnace of a Bessemer steel converter.

This photograph from 1865 shows a group of shipyard bosses wearing 'stovepipe' hats. Behind them, a large ship is being built and smoke belches out from the chimneys of dockside steelworks and factories.

Workshop of the world

By the 1850s, more than half the world's textile goods were made in the huge mills that sprang up across the north of England and Scotland. And in the major ports, shipbuilding grew at an even greater rate. By the 1890s, over three quarters of all the ships in the world were British-built. But all this came at a price.

Workers, including thousands of young children, were often expected to work for up to 12 hours a day in unhealthy and dangerous conditions. Over time, the government introduced laws, enforcing a minimum age for child workers, limiting the number of hours people should work and setting safety standards.

Child workers

Before the government brought in laws to protect child workers, many endured tough, dangerous jobs for very little pay.

'Putters' hauled coal up from the mines along passages that were too narrow for adults to squeeze through.

In textile factories, 'scavengers' had to crawl inside working machines to pick up loose threads. Many got caught in the machinery and were badly injured.

Urban sprawl

National statistics

In 1837, only around a fifth of the British population lived in towns. By the end of Victoria's reign in 1901, the population had more than doubled to 40 million people, and three quarters of them lived in the rapidly expanding towns and cities.

As industry grew, more and more people moved to the towns and cities to find work. In 1851, the government carried out a survey, called a census, to find out exactly how many people there were in Britain, where they lived and what they did for a living. It showed that, for the first time anywhere in the world, more of the population lived in the towns than in the countryside.

This scene shows a Victorian town from around 1851.

Factory smoke pollutes the air.

Suburbs

Houses are crammed back-to-back in rows called terraces.

Up to 20 people live in each tiny house.

Houses are heated by coal fires.

Gas lamp

Chimney sweep

Water comes from a shared pump.

Life in the slums

Most people lived in filthy, crowded parts of the town, known as slums. In some slums people lived in decrepit old buildings that were barely standing. Elsewhere, the slums were made up of rows and rows of cheap new houses built hastily by factory owners for their workers to live in. These houses didn't have toilets or running water. Instead, people shared a communal lavatory, which was usually just a hole in the ground in a shed. Water came from a pump in the street, or from a nearby river.

Most household waste was tipped out into the streets or into the rivers, so they became polluted. With so many people living in these appalling conditions, it's hardly surprising that diseases spread rapidly through the slums and life expectancy was extremely low.

Trading up

Since the end of the Corn Law, the government had relaxed the laws restricting the trade of other goods too. Business boomed under this new policy of free trade, new jobs were created and life gradually got better for many people.

Among those who profited most were factory owners, bankers and businessmen. A number of modern British department stores began in the 19th century as market stalls and small shops that expanded. Soon, anyone who could afford it moved to large houses in the suburbs, away from the dirt and noise of the slums.

Street life

Poor Victorians found all kinds of ways to make money on the busy city streets.

Young boys offered shoe shines for a few pennies.

Others cleared away horse manure.

Girls sold bunches of flowers or boxes of matches on street corners.

Costermongers sold fruit and vegetables from barrows...

...those who were really successful later opened their own shops.

307

Law and order

As Britain's towns and cities swelled, crime levels soared at an alarming rate. Sensational accounts of crimes were regularly published in the popular press, which raised people's fears. Something had to be done to deal with the problem. The Victorian solutions were police and prisons.

"Send him to jail now, and you make him a jail-bird for life."

Sherlock Holmes, in *The Adventure of the Blue Carbuncle*, suggests that prison isn't always the best solution to crime.

On the beat

In 1829, Robert Peel established the Metropolitan police in London. The policemen were soon nicknamed 'bobbies' or 'peelers' after Robert Peel. The police force gradually grew, and by 1856 it covered the whole country.

The main task of the police was to patrol the streets, to prevent crime and protect people and their property. But their duties also included lighting street lamps and calling out the time. Anyone caught committing a crime faced harsh punishment – including imprisonment, flogging or being shipped to penal colonies in Australia.

This cartoon shows a bobby on the beat. The uniform was designed so that the police didn't look like a miltary force.

Top hat

Blue tail coat

Policeman in uniform from the 1830s

Shifty youth

Police kit

As well as their uniforms, Victorian bobbies were issued with various tools.

They had a whistle, to raise the alarm...

...handcuffs to restrain suspects...

...and a wooden truncheon.

Behind bars

It didn't take much to get sent to prison. Police records show that children as young as eight were jailed for crimes as petty as stealing a loaf of bread. Most Victorians believed that prisons were for punishment, rather than rehabilitation. So they designed the prison experience to be as unpleasant as possible, to deter people from committing crimes. In some prisons, inmates were blindfolded and kept silent at all times so they couldn't communicate with one another.

This detail from a painting, by Willian Powell Frith, shows convicts trudging around the exercise yard of Millbank Prison.

Dr. Watson

Sherlock Holmes

Detective work

Despite these strict new measures, a number of particularly gruesome crimes hit the headlines. One of the most infamous was that of a serial killer nicknamed Jack the Ripper, who terrorized London's East End in the 1880s. It was one of the first cases in which police collected forensic, or scientific, evidence from the crime scenes. Jack the Ripper was never caught, but forensic science later became a vital part of detective work.

Forensic science was made popular by Arthur Conan Doyle's fictional detective, Sherlock Holmes. He is shown here testing some evidence.

All aboard

The first rail passengers had to travel in dirty open wagons.

But, as rail travel took off, it became more comfortable. Plush seating, dining cars and lavatories were added to passenger trains.

Queen Victoria made frequent rail journeys in her own luxurious royal carriage.

Rain, Steam and Speed – The Great Western Railway, painted in 1839-1844 by J.M.W. Turner

Railway mania

It wasn't only the growth of towns, cities, and factories that transformed Victorian Britain. The railways also grew rapidly during this period, making an enormous impact on people's working lives, their social lives and the landscape.

Trains pulled by steam engines – known as locomotives – provided a quick, efficient way to transport raw materials and finished goods in bulk, and helped British industries to grow. Soon, they became a popular way to get around, too.

Until Victorian times, most people in Britain had never been further than the next town. The first passenger train was launched in 1825, but it wasn't until the middle of the 19th century that passenger travel really took off. As the Victorians built up a vast network of local and national train lines, the trains made it quicker, easier and cheaper to travel across the country than ever before.

Making tracks

Rail travel became popular with everyone, and the railways grew at an astonishing rate. To meet the growing demand, train companies and travel agents sprang up, offering excursions to the seaside, to exhibitions and even to public executions. Between 1845 and 1900, the number of passengers on Britain's railways tripled. By the end of the 19th century, over 29,000km (18,000 miles) of steel track had been forged and laid, criss-crossing the entire country.

It's difficult to imagine now, but people around the country used to set their watches to different times, depending on where they lived. For example, Oxford was five minutes behind London. This caused chaos with train timetables – people missed connections and there were even a few crashes when trains from rail companies using different local times tried to stop at the same platform at the same time. Gradually, rail companies all switched to London time and in 1880 it was finally adopted by the whole country, by law.

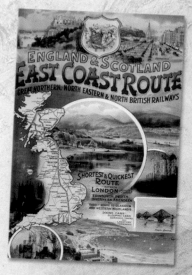

This Victorian railway poster advertises the route between England and Scotland. The map shows how the rail network extends across the country.

Great exhibitions

In 1851, the Victorians staged one of the most exciting and ambitious events of the age – the Great Exhibition. It was masterminded by Prince Albert to celebrate Britain's industry and its empire. It was an enormous show of arts, produce and manufactured goods housed in Crystal Palace, a gigantic structure of glass and steel, built specially for the event in Hyde Park, in the heart of London.

Crystal Palace was designed by Joseph Paxton, a former gardener who based the idea on a greenhouse. The building was the first of its kind, and a spectacular tribute to British engineering.

This is Joseph Paxton's first rough design for Crystal Palace. He drew it very sketchily, on blotting paper, and you can see where the ink has spattered and spread.

Queen Victoria opened the Great Exhibition on May 1, 1851. Over the next six months, millions of people from all over the country visited London to see it. Among the rare and exotic things on show were furs from Russia, an entire Turkish bazaar and a Tunisian nomads' tent covered in lion skins. But what excited people most was the machine hall. This housed an awesome display of new technology – from printing presses and threshing machines to steam engines. The Crystal Palace was like a crystal ball, offering its visitors a vision of the wider world and of the future.

Albert's legacy

The Great Exhibition ended in October 1851, having made a massive profit. Prince Albert used that money to set up the Royal Colleges of Music and Art, the Imperial College of Science and several museums. These included the Natural History Museum, the Science Museum and what is now called the Victoria and Albert Museum. Entry to the museums was free, so that everyone could enjoy them. Soon, museums and art galleries sprang up in towns all around Britain.

Show of numbers

2,700 men were employed to build the Crystal Palace in just six months.

It was made from 300,000 panes of hand-blown glass.

Crystal Palace covered an area the size of four soccer fields.

13,000 exhibits were put on display.

6,000,000 people visited the Great Exhibition.

Queen Victoria and her family visited the exhibition 13 times.

This painting shows the front entrance of Crystal Palace. Along the roof are the flags of all the nations that took part.

Natural history

The work of leading Victorian naturalists brought many new ideas about the natural world to the public. Some of these ideas sparked controversy, and revolutionized the way people thought about their place in the world.

Walking with dinosaurs

The dinosaur park at Crystal Palace in Sydenham (see below) became a fashionable place for Victorians to take a stroll.

The park included 15 different species of dinosaurs and extinct creatures.

Monsters from the past

For centuries, people had been digging up mysterious giant bones, but no one knew what they were. By the 1820s, most scientists believed that they were the fossilized remains of huge, ancient reptiles. In 1842, scientist Richard Owen studied these fossils and found that they belonged to a group that was quite distinct from reptiles. He named them dinosaurs, which means 'terrible lizard' in Greek.

The model dinosaurs were made from cast iron and painted to look as lifelike as possible.

Crystal Palace burned down in 1936, but the park and the dinosaurs are still there today.

Unfortunately, experts now consider Owen's model dinosaurs to be very inaccurate.

After the Great Exhibition, the Crystal Palace was taken down and rebuilt in the London suburb of Sydenham. There, Richard Owen oversaw the creation of one of its greatest attractions: a dinosaur park, where people could wander among life-size models of prehistoric creatures in supposedly natural settings among shrubs and ponds.

A cathedral to nature

In 1856, Richard Owen became the superintendant of the British Museum's natural history collection. He wanted to arrange specimens in groups by species to show their common features. But there wasn't enough room in the British Museum. So he persuaded the government that a new building was needed. What he called his grand 'cathedral to nature' in South Kensington, in London, is now known as the Natural History Museum.

Visitors to the Natural History Museum admired all kinds of exhibits, including a model of a dodo – a bird that has been extinct since the 1660s.

Survival of the fittest

In 1859, the English scientist Charles Darwin published his radical theory of evolution, suggesting that species of plants and animals had developed, or evolved, over millions of years. This allowed them to adapt as the environment changed, so that the species that adapted best survived and passed on their characteristics to their offspring.

Most Victorians believed that God had created all living things at the same time and so many were outraged at Darwin's theory. There was even a public debate between the scientist Thomas Henry Huxley, who supported Darwin, and Samuel Wilberforce, the Bishop of Oxford, who spoke against him. The argument caused such uproar that one shocked lady in the audience fainted and had to be carried out.

Despite the controversy at the time, Darwinian theory now forms the basis of much modern thinking about the natural sciences. But, more than a century later, Darwin's ideas continue to cause debate, as some people still object to them on religious grounds.

This Victorian cartoon of Charles Darwin pokes fun at his idea that people had evolved from apes.

The Crimean War

Sites of the Crimean War

RUSSIA

Black Sea

Sea of Azov

CRIMEA

Alma

Inkerman

Sevastopol   Balaklava

"Forward, the Light Brigade!
Charge for the guns!" he said:
Into the valley of Death
Rode the six hundred.

Lines from *The Charge of the Light Brigade*, by Alfred, Lord Tennyson

One of the bloodiest, most disorganized wars in European history took place in 1854-1856, in the Crimea, a region by the Black Sea between Russia and Turkey. It broke out when Russian forces attacked the Turkish fleet. The British and French governments were anxious to limit Russia's power in the area, so they joined forces with the Turks to fight against Russia.

The war became notorious for the huge numbers of soldiers who died on both sides. As many as half the 1,200,000 who went to fight lost their lives, often due to the incompetence of their officers.

The most disastrous battle took place at Balaklava, when a British cavalry unit, the Light Horse Brigade, was mistakenly ordered to charge at the enemy through a narrow valley. The Russians above the valley, simply bombarded the horsemen with cannon fire. Of 673 men in the charge, 118 were killed, 127 wounded, and over half of the men's horses died.

This is a scene from *The Charge of the Light Brigade*, a movie made in 1968, about the Battle of Balaklava.

Although many soldiers were killed in battle, thousands more died as a result of their appalling living conditions. The army camps and hospitals were crowded and insanitary, and soldiers didn't have enough food, clothing or medical supplies. Many fell prey to diseases such as cholera and malaria, while others died from infected wounds, exposure and starvation.

One thing was entirely new though: this was the first war ever to have journalists and photographers on the spot, recording events as they unfolded. Back at home, people could read the shocking horrors of the war in their daily copies of *The Times*. The news caused a public outcry and led two remarkable women to take decisive action.

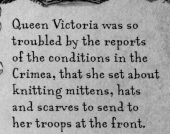

Queen Victoria was so troubled by the reports of the conditions in the Crimea, that she set about knitting mittens, hats and scarves to send to her troops at the front.

Florence Nightingale became known as the 'Lady with the lamp' because she made regular night rounds of her wards.

Angels of mercy

A British nurse named Florence Nightingale took 38 nurses from England to Turkey to work in the army hospitals. Within weeks, they had cut the number of soldiers dying in hospitals from 42% to 2% – mainly by improving hygiene.

Closer to the front, a Jamaican woman named Mary Seacole often treated men on the battlefield itself. To pay for medical supplies, she set up a guest house called the British Hotel, where she sold food and drink to soldiers and took care of the sick and wounded.

The war finally ended in the spring of 1856, when the Russian Emperor, Alexander II, signed a peace treaty at the Congress of Paris. But British generals and politicians argued for years over who was to blame for the charge of the Light Brigade.

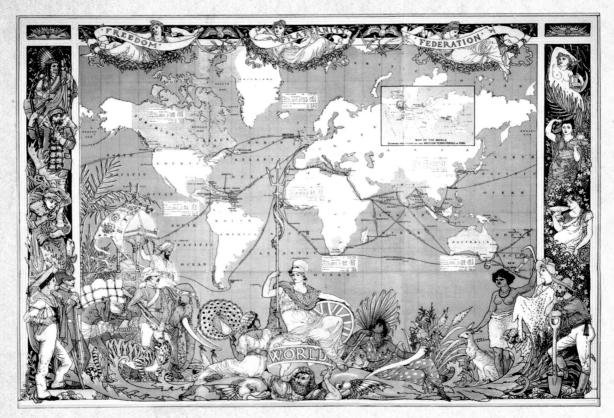

The pink areas on this Victorian world map show the extent of the British empire in 1886.

The lines across the oceans show the global trade routes. These were all under British control.

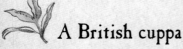

A British cuppa

Tea became a popular everyday drink in Britain in Victorian times, when it was imported in bulk from China, India and Sri Lanka.

The jewel in the crown

One of the reasons why the British got drawn into the Crimean War was to protect their trade shipping routes and their growing empire in Africa and Asia. People called it "the empire on which the sun never set" because it reached every corner of the globe. And India became one of Queen Victoria's most prized imperial possessions.

Since the 1600s, a British trading company called the East India Company had gained control of a number of Indian ports and settlements, where they set up colonies. Gradually, the Company took over more and more land and built up an army of British and local soldiers. By the start of Victoria's reign, large parts of India were technically in British hands, but not yet under British rule.

318

The Indian mutiny

Then, in 1856, something happened to change things dramatically. A story spread among the Indian soldiers in the East India Company's army that they had been issued with rifle cartridges smeared with cow and pig fat. This offended Hindu and Muslim soldiers, who mutinied, refusing to follow the orders of their officers. The mutiny soon led to violent clashes that spread across northern India and lasted 13 months. Thousands died, but eventually the British managed to restore their authority.

Sepoys

Indian foot soldiers in the British Army were known as sepoys. They came from all over India and included Sikhs, Muslims and Hindus.

This sepoy wears a turban with his uniform.

Empress Victoria

A year later, the British government decided that the only solution was to take direct control. India then became the keystone of the British empire, and the focus for rivalry with other European countries.

Extensive rail networks were built across the country and industries developed. As trade expanded, India became a source of great wealth and prosperity for Britain. In 1877, the British Prime Minister, Benjamin Disraeli, persuaded Victoria to take the exotic new title Empress of India and he described India as the "jewel" in her crown.

Lord Curzon, in the middle of this group, was Governor General and Viceroy of India in 1899-1904. Hunting tigers was a popular sport of princes in India, and the British rulers were no exception.

A widow queen

In 1861, the domestic bliss of the royal household was shattered when Prince Albert was diagnosed with typhoid and died, aged only 42. Queen Victoria was inconsolable with grief and went into deep mourning. She spent the next ten years away from the public eye, and wore widow's black for the rest of her life.

The Queen continued to read state papers, but refused to attend official functions, including the opening of parliament. After a while, people began to lose patience with her. Some newspapers complained that she was neglecting her duties and a few people began to suggest that the country might be better off without a monarchy at all.

In this photograph, taken not long after Albert's death, the grieving Queen is being comforted by her daughter, Princess Helena.

John Brown, in highland dress, takes the mourning Queen out on her horse.

Some people nicknamed Victoria 'Mrs. Brown' in mockery of her friendship with Brown. A few gossips even hinted that the pair had married in secret.

Rest cure

John Brown was a servant in charge of the stables at Balmoral Castle. At the height of Victoria's grief, her doctor suggested that exercise might help, so he encouraged Brown to take the Queen out riding. Victoria formed a close friendship with him, because he reminded her of Albert. But it caused a scandal among some people, who thought that a servant shouldn't be so familiar with the Queen.

In loving memory

Then, in 1871, Victoria's eldest son, Edward, Prince of Wales, fell seriously ill and nearly died. This finally shocked the Queen out of mourning and back to work. But she wasn't going to let anyone forget about Albert. Later that year, she opened the Royal Albert Hall and unveiled the Albert Memorial in London – the biggest and grandest of dozens of statues that she had built around the country in his memory.

Albert's hall

The Royal Albert Hall and the Albert Memorial were built in South Kensington, close to the site of Albert's greatest achievement: the Great Exhibition.

The whole area is something of a tribute to Prince Albert, as it is also the site of the museums and colleges that he set up after the exhibition.

321

Victorian women

Fashion slaves

For those who could afford it, keeping up with the latest fashions was often an uncomfortable experience.

Corsets were laced tightly to make the waist smaller.

As many as six petticoats were worn to add volume to skirts, and as much as 3-6kg (7-14lb) in weight.

From around 1850, women began to wear a hooped frame, called a crinoline, under their skirts to make them even wider.

Britain may have been ruled by a woman, but most Victorians believed that a woman's place was in the home, and that the only proper occupations for women were marriage and motherhood. The ideal Victorian woman was expected to be an "angel in the house" – beautiful, modest and virtuous, dutiful to her husband and devoted to her children. She was not supposed to express her own opinions and she certainly wasn't supposed to pursue her own career.

This ideal was reflected in Victorian fashions. Designed to make their hips look wider and their waists smaller, dresses made women look elegant and emphasized their femininity, but they would have been uncomfortable to move around in – and even more difficult to work in.

This Victorian woman needs a team of servants just to help her get dressed.

Women's work

In reality, few women could possibly live up to the Victorian ideal. Most were far too poor to afford the latest fashions and needed to take paid work to support their families. Some were able to combine this with cooking, cleaning and looking after their children, by working at home. They took on jobs including dressmaking, taking in other people's laundry and making things such as match boxes or brushes.

But most women had to find jobs outside the home. The majority were employed either as domestic servants, or in factories where they were usually paid much less than their male counterparts. The hours were long and when they got home they were still expected to do all the household chores.

This woman is a machine operator in a cotton mill. The majority of textile workers were women, but all the factory bosses were men.

Feminine professions

Life could be tough, even for women from wealthy families. Until 1882, a woman's income, and any property she inherited, legally belonged to her husband, even if the marriage broke down. Middle-class women only went out to work if they had no husband or parents to support them. But most careers, other than teaching or childcare, were considered unsuitable for them.

Gradually, in the late 19th century, people's attitudes began to change. In the 1870s, a few universities began to offer degrees to women for the first time, enabling them to qualify for careers such as medicine and law. But professional women were still very much in the minority and they often faced opposition from their families or employers.

Popular politics

British politics had changed little since the 1830s, but by the second half of Victoria's reign, the government began to bring in a number of reforms to improve the health, welfare and education of the population and to give more people a say in the way the country was run.

These changes were partly brought about by reformers within Parliament, but also as a result of pressure from outside organizations. This period was dominated by two charismatic political leaders: the Liberal, William Gladstone, and his Conservative rival, Benjamin Disraeli.

This illustration shows the Matchgirls' Union strike of 1888, when over 1,400 match factory workers protested against dangerous working conditions.

United front

As industry grew, more and more working people joined groups called trade unions. They challenged employers and the government, demanding better pay, shorter hours and safer places to work. When union members wanted to protest about something, they all agreed to stop working and go on strike. Until 1825, it had been illegal to belong to a union, but as the unions grew bigger and more powerful, the government had to take them more seriously.

In 1867, a Liberal MP, John Stuart Mill tried to get votes for women included in the Reform Act but he was defeated.

Several women's groups were disappointed that the reforms didn't go far enough, so they stepped up their campaigns for women's suffrage – the right to vote.

In 1897 the suffragettes, as they later became known, joined forces to form a national union.

They fought hard and gained massive support, but it wasn't until 1918 that women finally won the vote.

Casting votes

Gladstone's predecessor, John Russell, had been trying to introduce electoral reforms for years, but the issue split the party and toppled them from power. In a bid to gain popularity for his party, Disraeli pushed the new Conservative government to put through their own reforms. The resulting 1867 Reform Act gave more men the vote and almost doubled the electorate to around 2.5 million. Over the following years, more reforms were introduced, which made elections more democratic and extended the vote to one in three men.

A third way

Hardie caused an uproar when he arrived at Parliament wearing a cloth cap instead of a top hat.

As more people gained the vote, the old system of government was shaken up. In 1892, a former mining union leader named James Keir Hardie became the first working-class member of Parliament. A year later, he set up the Independent Labour Party to represent the interests of working people. This new third party later developed into the modern Labour Party.

A cholera victim
in the blue phase

King cholera

Cholera first appeared in
Britain in 1831. There
were two further major
outbreaks in 1848 and
1854, by which time it
had killed around
140,000 people.

The disease struck
suddenly, causing
dysentery, retching,
extreme thirst and pain
in the limbs and stomach.
If a patient's skin turned
blue, it was usually fatal.

This cartoon shows
Death as a skeleton,
spreading cholera
by giving people
polluted water.

Health and medicine

Public health improved enormously in the second half of
the 19th century. This was mostly due to the pioneering
work of Florence Nightingale and others, who made
new medical discoveries and convinced the government
to take responsibility for the nation's health.

Something in the water

During the 1830s and 40s a number of deadly diseases –
including influenza, typhoid, smallpox and cholera –
swept through Britain, killing hundreds of thousands of
people. The worst hit were the poor, in towns and cities.
A civil servant, named Edwin Chadwick, carried out a
study for the government to find out why. He argued
that the spread of diseases could be prevented by
cleaning up the slums.

Most Victorians believed that diseases were caused
by foul-smelling air, known as *miasma*, but a doctor
named John Snow disagreed. He proved that cholera
was carried in water polluted with sewage. In August
1854, an epidemic broke out in central London. By
marking all the cases of cholera onto a map, Snow
traced the source of the outbreak to a public water
pump. When he disabled the pump, the number
of new cases of cholera fell instantly.

Waterworks

Gradually, the government took note of the
work of men like Chadwick and Snow. It
began to build new sewerage systems,
improved water supplies and ensured
that local councils collected household
waste regularly.

Under the knife

Going to a hospital in Victorian times could be a frightening ordeal. Until the 1840s, there were no effective painkillers, and surgeons didn't use anaesthetics to put people to sleep during operations. Some patients were so traumatized by the pain of surgery, that they died of shock. Things improved radically in 1847, when chloroform gas was first introduced as a safe anaesthetic. Queen Victoria herself used it, during the birth of her three youngest children.

Compulsory vaccination for children against smallpox was introduced in 1853. After that, the number of cases dropped dramatically.

On the wards

When Florence Nightingale came back from the Crimean War, she was determined to raise the standards in British hospitals. She set up a nursing college in London and carried out an inspection of British hospitals. She found them so filthy that some patients were catching diseases on the wards, and others were dying from infections spread by doctors who didn't wash their hands or sterilize their instruments. Florence Nightingale campaigned with the government to improve hospital hygiene. Hospitals became even cleaner after 1869, when a doctor named Joseph Lister invented an antiseptic spray to kill the bacteria that spread infections.

This photograph was taken in a ward in the Royal Infirmary in Aberdeen in 1890. It's much cleaner than hospital wards were before Florence Nightingale's reforms.

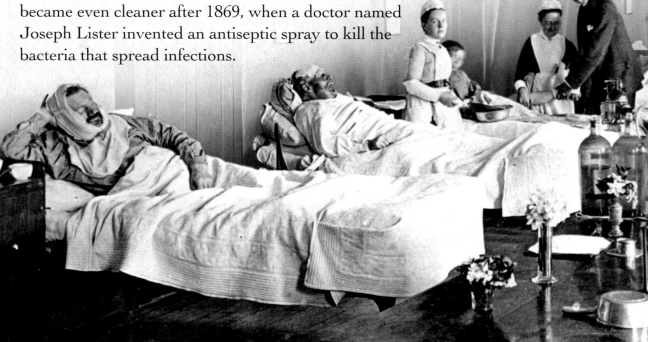

At school

The 19th century saw enormous changes in the way children were educated. At the start of Victoria's reign, around two-thirds of people in Britain were illiterate, meaning that they couldn't read or write. Schooling cost money, which most parents couldn't afford, so many children went without. For the children who did go to school, the sort of education that they received varied greatly.

Boys from wealthy families were mostly sent to elite private schools, where they learned Latin and Greek before going on to universities. Their sisters' schooling was often more limited. They took lessons at home, in subjects such as needlework and music.

For children from poorer families, there were schools run by charities and churches, and 'dame' schools, where unmarried women taught in their own homes. But even these schools charged a small fee, which was often too high for the poorest families.

Victorian children didn't do their work on paper. Instead, they used slates, which were like mini blackboards that could be used again.

Dame schools, like this one, provided only very basic education for the youngest children. They were often more like babysitting services than schools.

Learning to do the laundry (as you can see in this photograph from 1893) was considered a vital part of education for Victorian girls.

Education for all

Over the years, the government began to take more responsibility for children's education. From the 1870s, education was provided for everyone and hundreds of new schools were built. By the end of Victoria's reign, education was compulsory and free for all children up to 12 years old. The nation was now better educated than ever before.

The three Rs

Lessons focused on what the Victorians called the 'three Rs' – Reading, wRiting and aRithmetic. A lot of the work was dull, by today's standards. Pupils repeated what the teacher told them, again and again, until they knew it by heart. Talking in class was strictly forbidden and teachers often beat naughty or less able pupils. In addition to the three Rs and subjects such as history and geography, children were taught practical skills. To prepare them for work in trades, boys learned mathematics, woodwork and technical drawing. Girls were given lessons in cooking, sewing and housework.

Games

Victorians believed that healthy bodies made healthy minds, so all schools set aside a time for exercise.

Most schools had a small yard for drill classes – jogging on the spot, lifting weights and stretching in formation.

Boys at private schools played team sports including soccer, cricket and rugby.

Rugby was reputedly invented during a soccer match at Rugby School in 1823, when a boy named William Webb Ellis caught the ball and ran with it.

Books and the press

Education for all meant that more and more people were reading for pleasure, and demanding cheap forms of reading matter. The invention of steam-powered printing presses enabled publishers to print thousands of copies of books, papers or magazines at a time, and new techniques meant that books could be fully illustrated too.

Children's books

In early Victorian times, most people thought that children should only read the Bible, educational books, or stories with a moral to teach them right from wrong. All that changed in 1865, when Lewis Carroll published *Alice's Adventures in Wonderland*. It was written purely for entertainment, and was so popular that it started a whole new trend for children's books. Themes varied from exciting adventure stories set in distant countries, such as Robert Louis Stevenson's *Treasure Island* and Rudyard Kipling's *Jungle Book*, to the nonsense rhymes of Edward Lear.

This is one of Edward Lear's own drawings from his book of nonsense rhymes.

The Mad Hatter's tea party, from Lewis Carroll's *The Nursery Alice*, illustrated by John Tenniel

Books for the masses

One of the most popular Victorian authors, for young and old readers, was Charles Dickens. Most of his novels were first published in monthly parts, with each part ending on a cliff-hanger, to make sure the readers came back for the next issue. He was also a talented public speaker, who drew huge audiences of eager fans to his public readings, both at home and in America.

The Victorians loved trashy stories just as much as people do today. Cheaply produced paperback booklets, known as 'penny dreadfuls' – including romances, adventures, mysteries and detective stories – were particularly popular. They came in weekly parts that cost just a penny, so almost anyone could afford them. But they were looked down on because the writing wasn't very good and their subjects were often rather sensational.

From the 1850s, the first public libraries were opened in Britain, so that even people who couldn't afford to buy books could borrow them to read. Libraries began to spring up everywhere, and by 1900 there were 295 of them up and down the country.

Writing it out

Until the typewriter was invented in the late 1860s, Victorian authors wrote their work out by hand.

Goose feather quill pen

Ink bottle

Dickens wrote all his books with a quill pen, dipped in ink.

Read all about it!

There had been newspapers in Britain since the late 18th century. But, because paper was taxed, they were so expensive that not everyone could afford to buy them. When the tax was removed in 1855, papers began to circulate more widely and sales soared. A new type of printing press, using rolls of paper instead of sheets, also made printing quicker and cheaper. As a result, many new publications were launched, including illustrated newspapers, women's magazines, sporting journals and theatrical papers.

Newsboys competed to sell their papers to people in the streets.

On the move

By the second half of the 19th century, the Victorians were getting around more than ever before. But in London the streets had become so congested that engineers had to come up with a new solution – going underground. In 1863, the world's first underground railway opened in London. At first, passengers sat in open wagons pulled by steam locomotives. Imagine being covered in soot in the smoky, narrow tunnels!

Outside London, the best way of getting around town was on the buses or trams (buses that run on tracks set into the roads) that were pulled by horses. But, by the 1890s, horse power was beginning to give way to new driving forces, as buses became motorized for the first time and trams switched to electric power. Underground trains went electric too, which made travel below street level much cleaner.

Travel on the underground might have been quicker, but it was certainly dirtier than going by road.

This double-decker horse-drawn bus is covered in advertisements. Passengers on the top deck paid half fares.

Pedal power

Remarkably, bicycles were invented long after the steam train. The 'ordinary bicycle' was the first design to catch on. It was difficult to mount and very unstable because the back wheel was smaller than the front one. In the 1880s, 'safety bicycles' were invented. They were more like modern bikes, with wheels of equal size, gears and brakes. From then on, cycling was all the rage. During the weekends, parks and lanes were filled with eager cyclists, dressed in the latest cycling fashions.

Ordinary bicycles were nicknamed 'penny farthings' because the wheels were rather like two coins: a penny and a farthing.

Need for speed

In around 1885, the earliest cars, known as horseless carriages, appeared. But they were mostly imported from Germany and France, at a price most people could only dream of.

At first, motorists were forced to drive at frustratingly low speeds. This was because a law, known as the Red Flag Act, required all self-powered road vehicles to be driven behind a man walking with a red flag. The law was lifted in 1896, but it wasn't until cars began to be mass-produced in the early 20th century that people enthusiastically took up the idea of travel by car.

The first cyclists often fell off their wobbly bikes.

Safety bicycles had hard wheels, which must have made a bumpy ride.

Motorists were frustrated by the Red Flag Act.

One of the most popular Victorian pastimes was going to the music halls to see shows like the cabaret announced on this poster.

This cartoon shows a typical Victorian seaside scene. Many Victorians went to the beach fully clothed and rented huts, so they could change into their bathing suits in private.

Time out

Until Victorian times, very few people could afford any time out for leisure activities. But by the second half of Victoria's reign, industry was booming and the country was more prosperous. The government introduced new public holidays and limited the number of hours people could be made to work. All this meant that, for the first time, many people had time to spend on having fun.

Day trippers

The trains made it possible for working people to escape the grime of the cities cheaply and quickly, for a revitalizing trip to the seaside. As more and more people flocked to the beaches, Victorian seaside resorts grew rapidly. Hotels, piers, concert halls and shopping arcades sprang up to meet the increasing demand. An entrepreneur, named Thomas Cook, started to run excursions to the sea, with the travel, entertainment and food included in the price. With that, he became the first ever travel agent and his business boomed.

Stage shows

Without television or radio to entertain them, many Victorians amused themselves by going to plays or concerts. Bandstands were built in parks for people to listen to string quartets or brass bands. The rich went to operas or classical concerts in plush, elegant playhouses and concert halls. For poorer people, there were music halls, where you could pay a penny to watch comedy shows, acrobats or cabaret acts.

Healthy competition

For hundreds of years, people had been playing many of the sports we play today, but without proper rules. Different versions of the same games were played in different parts of the country. Now people had more time to play sports, and could travel to compete, sports had to become more organized. Players formed organizations to enforce rules and set up local teams and large competitions. For the first time, watching sports became as big a pastime as playing them.

Sporting dates

1863 – Football Association (F.A.) formed

1866 – Amateur Athletic Club established

 1871 – Rugby Football Union set up

1872 – First F.A. Cup competition held

1877 – First international cricket Test Match

1877 – First Wimbledon tennis championship

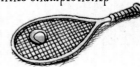

1888 – Lawn Tennis Association established

Building the nation

> "When we build,
> let us think that we
> build for ever."
>
> John Ruskin, *The
> Seven Lamps of
> Architecture* (1849)

Victorian architects and designers believed it was their duty to leave their mark on the country for future generations. And they certainly succeeded. Many of the grandest, most ornate public buildings you can see in Britain today were built during the 19th century.

They may have been building for the future, but Victorian architects were also fascinated by the past. The designs of several buildings were influenced by archaeological discoveries taking place in Europe at the time. Buildings like the British Museum in London were built in a Neo Classical style to look like the temples and arcades of Ancient Greece and Rome.

London's St. Pancras Hotel and St. Pancras Station (built in 1868-74) were designed by Sir George Gilbert Scott.

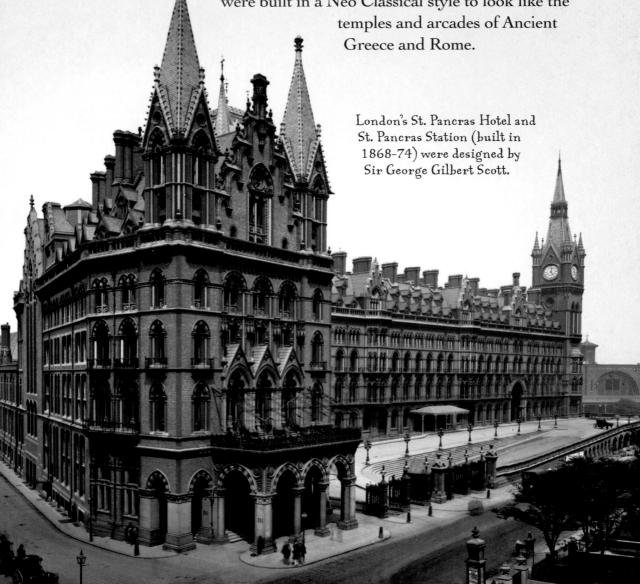

Attention to detail

Victorian houses were often given decorative features. Many of them are still standing today, so it's easy to spot them. These drawings show you some details to look out for.

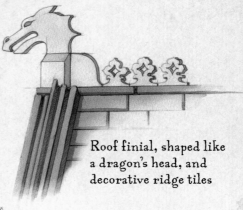

Roof finial, shaped like a dragon's head, and decorative ridge tiles

Front door with glass panels and an ornate porch

Carved, pointed gables, topped with finials and ridge tiles

Fancy terracotta chimneys

Divine inspiration

But Victorian architects were probably even more inspired by the religion and romance of the Middle Ages. Many Victorian buildings, such as St. Pancras Station and the Houses of Parliament in London, or the town halls in Manchester and Birmingham, were designed to look like medieval cathedrals. This style is known as Victorian Gothic, and you can recognize it by its pointed arches, decorative carvings and high, vaulted ceilings.

When it came to grand designs, the Victorians didn't stop at public buildings. Even very functional buildings, such as factories and sewage stations, were built on a monumental scale, to reflect Britain's great industrial wealth and progress. And many ordinary houses were given some extraordinary features, such as gothic arches, decorative brickwork and even gargoyles.

Gothic style arched windows surrounded by patterned brickwork

Engineering landmarks

Some of the greatest Victorian building projects were carried out by engineers. They laid thousands of miles of train tracks, canals and sewers, and constructed huge bridges, changing the face of Britain. Many of these ambitious projects were made possible by the use of new building techniques and materials, such as steel.

Isambard Kingdom Brunel

One of the leading lights of Victorian engineering was Isambard Kingdom Brunel. His first major project was the Clifton Suspension Bridge, which crosses the Avon Gorge at Clifton, providing a vital link to the city of Bristol from the east. While it was being built, Brunel also designed and oversaw the construction of the Great Western Railway line between London and Bristol. This involved building viaducts, a bridge and a 1.5km (2 miles) tunnel through Box Hill.

Brunel worked ceaselessly throughout his prolific career. His many other achievements included docks and iron steamships. Like his friend – and sometimes professional rival – the train engineer Robert Stephenson, he died in 1859 from overwork.

Brunel stands next to the giant landing chain of his steamship, the *Great Eastern*.

This photograph of the Clifton Suspension Bridge was taken shortly after it was completed, in 1864. At 215m (700ft) long, it was the world's longest bridge at that time.

Digging deep

Another impressive feat of Victorian engineering was Joseph Bazalgette's construction of a vast network of sewers under London, which set the standard for cities all over the country. At first, sewers were usually built by a 'cut and cover' method. This involved digging out a deep trench, building a roof and then covering it again. Later, new machinery made it possible to bore far deeper tunnels, without disrupting life up above.

Under and over the sea

In the 1880s, British and French engineers used the latest machines to begin digging a rail tunnel under the English Channel. But the project was abandoned in 1883 because British army generals feared that the French might use the tunnel to invade Britain.

It wasn't just in Britain that British engineers and builders left their mark. They exported their talents all around the world, laying train lines in South America and India and advising on sewerage systems for cities as far apart as Budapest, in Hungary, and Port Louis, in Mauritius.

Building big

The largest structure built during the 19th century was the massive Forth Railway Bridge, in Scotland.

It has a span of 2.5km (1.5 miles) and is still the second longest of its kind today.

The building work took 54,000 tons of steel, 21,000 tons of cement and seven million rivets.

At the peak of the work, 4,600 men were employed to build the bridge and 57 died during its construction.

This is a photographic portrait taken by Julia Margaret Cameron in 1872. The sitter is Alice Liddell, for whom Lewis Carroll wrote *Alice in Wonderland* when she was a young girl.

Victorian art

The Industrial Revolution had a dramatic effect on the British landscape and the way people lived. This gave many artists new subjects and caused others to think again about what art was for and how it should be produced. In the 1830s and 40s, early methods of photography were invented. These provided a new artistic medium and had a huge impact on the way painters worked. Photography also meant that works of art could be easily reproduced, for all to admire, in magazines or as prints to be hung in people's homes.

Pre-Raphaelites

In 1848, a group of artists, including John Everett Millais, Dante Gabriel Rossetti and William Holman Hunt, formed a society called the Pre-Raphaelite Brotherhood. They were influenced by art critic John Ruskin, who felt that industrial life was unspiritual and impersonal. The Pre-Raphaelites believed paintings should convey a moral message – something they thought art had lost since the time of Renaissance artist Raphael. They often took their subjects from the Bible, Shakespeare, and Arthurian legends, painting in fresh tones, with an almost photographic attention to detail.

This is a detail from *Ophelia*, by Millais. It depicts the heroine's death scene from Shakespeare's *Hamlet*.

Arts and crafts

William Morris, another Pre-Raphaelite, was concerned that, in an age of machines, the work of skilled craftsmen was no longer valued. He believed that even useful things should be hand-crafted, beautiful and unique.

In the 1860s, Morris founded the Arts and Crafts movement. He and his followers used traditional crafts and designs inspired by art from the Middle Ages to produce wallpaper, pottery, textiles and furniture as well as paintings. Soon, homes throughout Britain were decorated and furnished in the Arts and Crafts style.

Still lives

One of the first and most influential art photographers was Julia Margaret Cameron, who was given her first camera at the age of 48. She created dramatic compositions by using strong lighting and stage props, and by dressing her models in theatrical costumes. She also took powerful portraits of many leading Victorians from the arts and the sciences. Among her most eminent sitters were the poet Alfred, Lord Tennyson and the astronomer Sir John Herschel.

Art for art's sake

By the end of Victoria's reign another new style was emerging. As a reaction against the Victorian taste for moral messages, artists such as James Abbott McNeil Whistler, Aubrey Beardsley and Walter Crane believed that the only purpose of art was to be beautiful. These artists painted in a highly decorative style, influenced by Japanese art, French writers and artists and authors and playwrights such as Oscar Wilde.

This is part of William Morris's sketch for Rose wallpaper. He designed the pattern to be repeated over and over, when it was printed onto a roll of wallpaper.

"The only excuse for making a useless thing is that one admires it intensely. All art is quite useless."

Oscar Wilde, *The Picture of Dorian Gray*

341

In the home

Home life improved dramatically for the new middle classes, especially in the late 19th century. Mass-production gave people a greater choice of home furnishings and household goods, and at lower prices. Better transportation also increased the range of foods available in the shops, and new technology allowed gas and water to be piped into people's houses, providing better lighting and sanitation.

Housework

Most housework had to be done by hand, so it's hardly surprising that many Victorians hired servants to do it for them.

Carpets were beaten to remove dirt and dust.

Entire days were devoted just to doing the laundry.

Before hanging out the washing, maids squeezed out the water by passing the laundry through a mangle.

Hired help

Most middle-class families employed at least one servant, usually a maid, who visited the house every day to help with the household chores. Richer families might employ several live-in servants, including a butler to answer the door and wait on the family, a cook, footmen to serve food and numerous maids to help cook, serve food, and clean. The hours were long, and there was little time off, but for many people, it was the best way to escape life in the slums.

Mrs. Beeton

Every Victorian housewife tried to run her home efficiently and economically, and there were lots of books on how to do this. One of the most famous was Isabella Beeton's *Book of Household Management*, which gave her readers advice on how to furnish a house, how to save money and what to do in medical emergencies. It also contained over two thousand recipes, and pictures of how different dishes should be served.

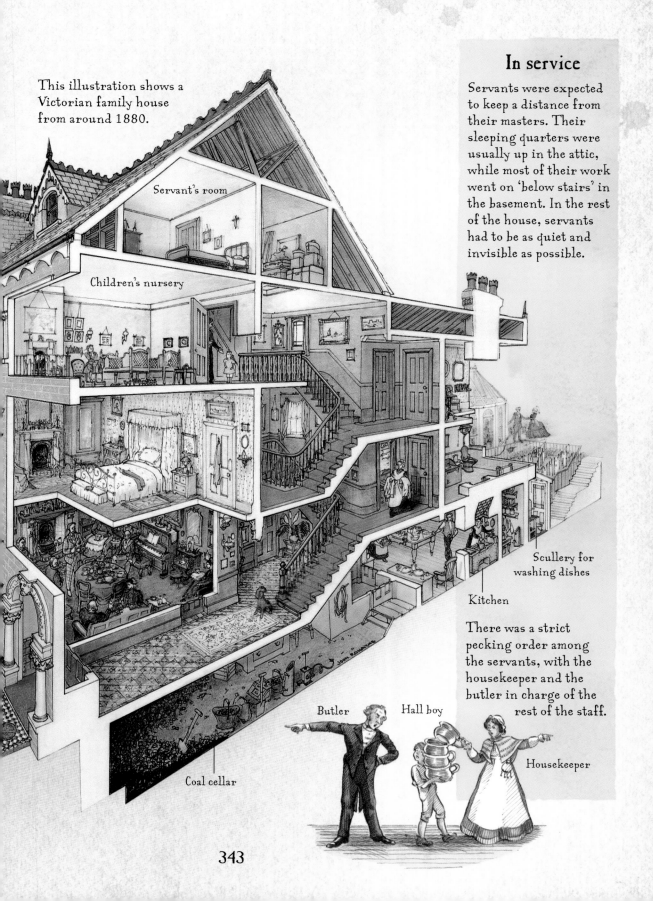

This illustration shows a Victorian family house from around 1880.

Servant's room

Children's nursery

In service

Servants were expected to keep a distance from their masters. Their sleeping quarters were usually up in the attic, while most of their work went on 'below stairs' in the basement. In the rest of the house, servants had to be as quiet and invisible as possible.

Scullery for washing dishes

Kitchen

There was a strict pecking order among the servants, with the housekeeper and the butler in charge of the rest of the staff.

Coal cellar

Butler

Hall boy

Housekeeper

343

Bright sparks

The Victorian age saw an astonishing number of new inventions, which accelerated the rapid pace of change. Some brought modern conveniences to people's lives at home and at work, or helped to improve their health. Others provided new systems of global communication and ways of recording sounds and images, which gave people new art forms and transformed the way they ran businesses, fought wars and broadcast news.

Not all of these inventions were British, but they all had an enormous impact on life in Britain.

1837
The Victorian age begins.

1837
Two British inventors – William Cooke and Charles Wheatstone – invent the first electric telegraph machine.

1837
Isambard Kingdom Brunel launches the first transatlantic steamship.

1839
William Fox Talbot demonstrates to the British Royal Society his method of developing photographs on light sensitive paper.

1847
Chloroform gas introduced as a safe anaesthetic in British hospitals.

1878 & 1879
Joseph Swan in Britain and Thomas Edison in America both independently invent electric lightbulbs, within months of one another.

1877
America's most prolific inventor, Thomas Edison, invents the phonograph, a machine that can record sounds and play them back.

1876
To settle a bet, photographer Eadweard Muybridge takes a series of photographs, each a fraction of a second apart. It's the first step in the development of moving pictures.

1881
Emile Berliner, a German scientist working in America, invents the gramophone, a device which plays sounds recorded onto discs, which can be mass-produced.

1895
Guglielmo Marconi, an Italian physicist, invents the wireless, to transmit telegram signals on radio waves.

1885
German Karl Benz builds the first motor car.

1886
Linotype machines enable the text for newspapers and books to be printed quicker than ever.

1888
George Eastman, in America, produces the Kodak no. 1 camera and develops customers' films.

344

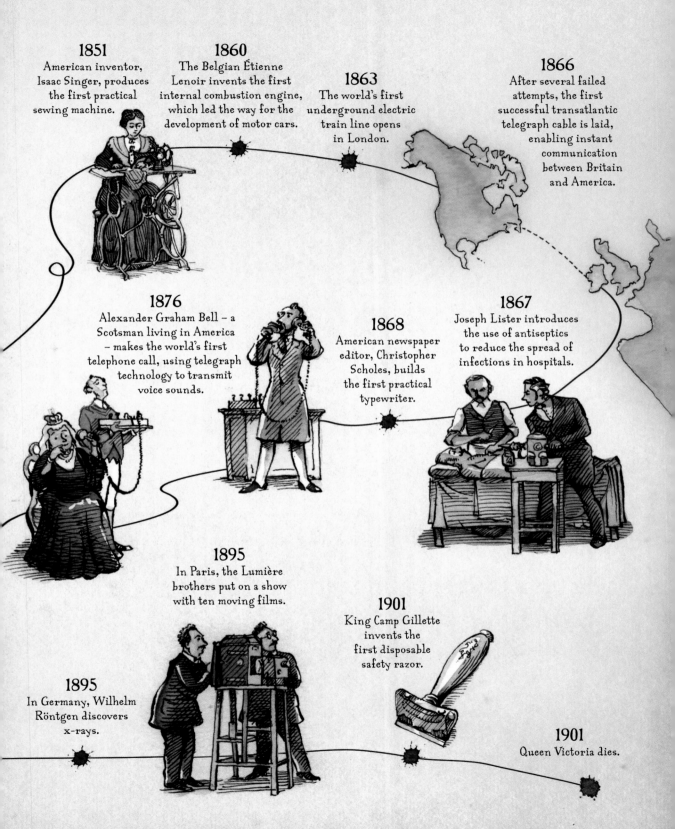

1851
American inventor, Isaac Singer, produces the first practical sewing machine.

1860
The Belgian Étienne Lenoir invents the first internal combustion engine, which led the way for the development of motor cars.

1863
The world's first underground electric train line opens in London.

1866
After several failed attempts, the first successful transatlantic telegraph cable is laid, enabling instant communication between Britain and America.

1876
Alexander Graham Bell – a Scotsman living in America – makes the world's first telephone call, using telegraph technology to transmit voice sounds.

1868
American newspaper editor, Christopher Scholes, builds the first practical typewriter.

1867
Joseph Lister introduces the use of antiseptics to reduce the spread of infections in hospitals.

1895
In Paris, the Lumière brothers put on a show with ten moving films.

1901
King Camp Gillette invents the first disposable safety razor.

1895
In Germany, Wilhelm Röntgen discovers x-rays.

1901
Queen Victoria dies.

345

On a mission

One of the first missionaries in Africa was David Livingstone. He explored and mapped large parts of Africa, and publicized the horrors of the African slave trade.

In 1855, he became the first European to see the great waterfall on the Zambezi River. He named it Victoria Falls.

Livingstone vanished while he was tracing the source of the Nile. In 1869, Henry Stanley, an explorer and journalist, set out to find him. Two years later, they finally met near Lake Tanganyika.

Livingstone continued his journey, but a fever left him in poor health and he died in 1873. He was buried in Westminster Abbey.

This illustration shows Livingstone and Stanley on Lake Tanganyika.

The Scramble for Africa

In the late 19th century, the industrialized European nations began what became known as the 'Scramble for Africa' as they competed for territory in Africa. Industries in Europe were expanding and there was a demand for new sources of raw materials. Many Europeans saw Africa as the last great unexplored land, and some Victorians also went there as missionaries, setting up churches, schools and hospitals.

African resistance

In many parts of Africa, the British established colonies relatively easily. But against the Zulus of southern Africa, it appeared they had met their match. Armed only with spears and shields, the Zulus inflicted a crushing victory on the better-equipped British soldiers at the Battle of Isandhlwana in 1879.

The British faced another blow in 1884-85 in Sudan. A religious leader, known as the Mahdi, led an uprising against British and Egyptian colonists there. The rebels killed the British commander, General Gordon, and held out for four years. Sudan finally came under Anglo-Egyptian control in 1899.

The British in Africa

The pink areas on this map show African countries under British control by the end of the 19th century.

By 1914 most of the continent was in European hands.

GAMBIA
SIERRA LEONE
GOLD COAST
NIGERIA
Suez Canal—
EGYPT
ANGLO-EGYPTIAN SUDAN
BRITISH SOMALILAND
UGANDA
KENYA
Lake Victoria—
—Lake Tanganyika
N. RHODESIA
NYASALAND
Victoria Falls ●
S. RHODESIA
BECHUANALAND—
ORANGE FREE STATE —
—TRANSVAAL
—NATAL
CAPE COLONY
Battle of Isandhlwana

Passage to India

The opening of the Suez Canal, in Egypt in 1869, created a new shipping route between Europe and Asia, which halved the journey between Britain and India. To secure this vital passage, the British government bought majority shares in the canal. But, by 1882, Egypt was close to civil war. British troops occupied the country and brought it under British rule.

The Anglo-Boer Wars

The British and the Boers (Dutch settlers) both held territory in Southern Africa, where fighting over land led to two wars. In 1877, Britain, who already held Cape Colony and Natal, took over Transvaal from the Boers. But the Boers rebelled and won it back after the first war, in 1880-1881.

The discovery of gold in Transvaal led to a second bitter war in 1899-1902. The Boers adopted guerilla tactics, sending small units of men to capture supplies and attack when least expected. In response, the British burned down their farms and imprisoned their families in concentration camps, where thousands died of disease. The Boers were forced to surrender, and their land in the Transvaal and Orange Free State became part of Britain's empire.

The Boy Scout movement was set up in 1908 by Major-General (later Lord) Robert Baden-Powell, a British hero of the Boer War. Today, it is an international youth organization for boys and girls.

This brooch was made in 1897, as a memento of Victoria's diamond jubilee.

Crowds gather in London to watch Queen Victoria's funeral procession.

End of an era

On New Year's Day, 1900, people weren't sure whether it was the start of a new century, or the end of the old one. But to many, January 22, 1901 was more significant still. That was the day Victoria died and the Victorian era came to an end. Many people looked back over her reign, amazed at the progress that had been made, but they also looked forward to the new century with trepidation.

Despite great progress in health and education, a third of the population still lived in poverty. The country was at war in Africa and the Irish question was unresolved. Britain had led the world into the Industrial Revolution, but now the United States and Germany were beginning to catch up. Britain no longer had the power and influence it had held in 1837.

A celebrated life

Queen Victoria's popularity had soared during her last years. Her golden and diamond jubilees marked 50 and 60 years on the throne with street parties all over the country. But her funeral was a more solemn affair. London's streets were packed with mourners from every corner of the empire. Victoria, who had spent her last 40 years in black, ordered a white funeral. Her coffin was decked in white flowers, and it was taken to Windsor to be buried beside her beloved Albert.

In with the new

Victoria's eldest son Edward succeeded her to the throne. He was very different from his mother, who had considered him frivolous and irresponsible. Edward was 59 when he became King. He was popular and energetic, but he had a lot to live up to.

Family album

Queen Victoria died aged 82 – old enough to see three generations of future monarchs.

Her son, Edward VII, was known as "Bertie" to his family.

Her grandson, George V, was king in 1914, when the First World War broke out.

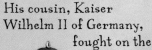

His cousin, Kaiser Wilhelm II of Germany, fought on the other side.

Victoria's great-grandson became Edward VIII in 1936, but stood down later that year so that he could marry an American divorcée named Wallis Simpson.

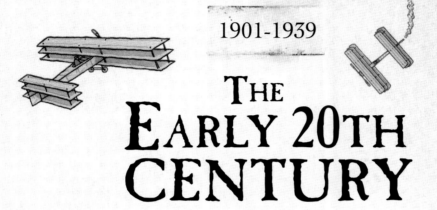

1901-1939

The Early 20th Century

With its vast empire and far-ranging fleet, Britain was at the peak of its powers at the opening of the new century. British explorers, scientists and sportsmen were world leaders, and many people thought the country was entering a golden age of boundless wealth and global influence.

But while the rich celebrated, millions of poor British families were slaves to poverty or the grinding routines of life in the industrial age. They watched nervously as European nations jostled for supremacy, threatening to drag the world into an unprecedented and all-consuming war.

Hope and glory

In 1901, Edward VII succeeded his mother, Queen Victoria, to the throne. The new King had a great passion for all things modern – from electricity to motor cars and aviation – and he seemed to embody the excitement and optimism of the new century. Protected by a powerful navy, Britain's empire was the largest in the world and a source of enormous wealth and pride for the country. To many, it seemed Britain really was a land of hope and glory.

The playboy statesman

As a fun-loving prince, Edward was a disappointment to his parents. Queen Victoria refused to involve him in matters of government, so he threw all his energy into the pursuit of pleasure – especially horse racing, gambling, women and, later, fast cars. Despite his often scandalous lifestyle, Edward was popular with the public, and when he became King, at the age of 59, he took his role more seriously.

Because he was related to most European monarchs, Edward made frequent state visits to Europe, to build peaceful relations. In 1903, he met the French government in Paris and paved the way for an agreement between Britain and France, which became known as the *Entente Cordiale* – French for friendly understanding.

This is a photograph of Edward as a young man. He was a heavy smoker and enjoyed rich foods and fine wines, so he gained a lot of weight later in life.

352

Peter Pan and Wendy fly across the night sky in this picture from the poster for the 1904 stage play.

A golden age

The Edwardian era was a golden age for many children. As well as their formal schooling, they were encouraged to learn through play, and a number of books were published to excite their imaginations. These included many that are seen as classics today, such as J.M. Barrie's *Peter Pan*, Kenneth Grahame's *Wind in the Willows*, *The Tale of Peter Rabbit* by Beatrix Potter, *Kim* and the *Just So Stories* by Rudyard Kipling and E. Nesbit's *Five Children and It*.

Sporting times

Like Edward, Britain's rich and famous enjoyed a hectic social calendar. They usually spent the winter in the countryside, hunting, shooting and playing golf, or relaxing in the south of France. The summer months were spent in London, attending shows, dinners and parties, as well as the horse racing at Ascot, the regatta at Henley and the sailing at Cowes.

   One of the most exciting sporting events of Edward's reign took place in 1908, when London hosted the Olympic Games in a stadium built specially for the event. More than 2,000 athletes, from 22 countries, took part in the competition.

Conspicuous consumption

Meals were an elaborate affair for wealthy Edwardians. Edward VII treated his dinner guests to ten-course meals that each would have cost more than his butler earned in a year.

Even breakfasts were huge. They included porridge, omelette, curried eggs, cutlets, kippers, toast and jam, all washed down with tea, coffee or even claret.

It also became fashionable to be seen taking tea and cake in the stylish and sumptuous surroundings of the Ritz Hotel, which first opened in 1906.

Shopping list

Seebohm Rowntree found that almost a third of people in York were too poor to afford these basic items in their weekly shopping:

Milk

Bread

Porridge

Coffee or cocoa

Margarine

Pease pudding

Tea

Cheese

Bacon

Vegetable broth

War on want

While a few Edwardians were taking tea at the Ritz and buying exotic foods in new shops like Selfridges, many more were living below the 'breadline' – meaning they were too poor to afford even the most basic necessities.

A number of social reformers – including Seebohm Rowntree, in York, and Charles Booth, in London – carried out surveys into the way working people lived. Their shocking reports revealed that, for thousands, life was a constant struggle just to make ends meet. Without regular jobs or decent wages, they suffered squalid housing conditions, malnutrition and illness. And it was children and old people who suffered the most.

These ragged children are from a such a poor family that most of them don't even have shoes.

Liberal attitudes

In the 19th century, most politicians believed that if people were poor, it was because they were lazy, or they wasted their money on alcohol. Now, social reformers began to persuade them that the main causes of poverty were unemployment, low wages and sickness. As attitudes changed, reformers demanded that the government do more to help people out of poverty.

In 1906, the Liberal Party took power from the Conservatives, after winning a massive 'landslide' victory in the General Election. Driven by two particularly energetic and ambitious young politicians, David Lloyd George and Winston Churchill, the Liberals brought in measures to fight poverty. These included free school meals and medical checks for children, pensions for people over 70, and Labour Exchanges, where people who were out of work could go to find jobs.

"This is a war budget. It is for raising money to wage implacable warfare against poverty and squalidness."

David Lloyd George announces his 'People's Budget' in 1909.

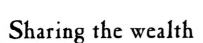

Sharing the wealth

All these reforms didn't come cheap. In 1909, David Lloyd George proposed new taxes to pay for them. The so-called 'People's Budget' caused an outcry, and the House of Lords refused to pass it. So, Prime Minister Herbert Asquith called a General Election, which he won, forcing the Lords to back down. The budget was passed, and in 1911, a National Insurance scheme was set up. Workers had to pay a weekly sum to the scheme, topped up by employers and the government. In return, they would receive benefit payments if they lost their jobs or fell sick. This was the beginnings of what is now known as the Welfare State.

This cartoon shows David Lloyd George 'putting the screw' on a rich Edwardian by imposing new taxes on him.

It wasn't just wealthy people who opposed the new taxes. The National Association of Domestic Servants protested against National Insurance too, though they eventually saw the benefits.

These people have taken to the streets to demand votes for women. As this photograph shows, the suffragists had many male supporters.

VOTES FOR WOMEN
1D

WANTED EVERYWHERE!

The suffragists put up posters and distributed newsletters, like this one to promote their cause and gain new members.

Votes for women

The poor were not the only disadvantaged social group in Britain at the start of the 20th century. Women had been campaigning for political reform for decades, but still could neither stand for Parliament, nor vote in elections. Many women felt that the laws relating to marriage, health and working conditions didn't give them enough protection against abuse. They believed that if they had the vote they could get laws passed to improve women's rights. Others simply believed that women should be given the vote on the same terms as men.

In 1897, a number of groups campaigning for women's suffrage (the vote) got together to form the National Union of Women's Suffrage Societies. The suffragists, as they were known, held rallies to gain support, gathered petitions and published pamphlets. Already backed by a handful of politicians, they believed it was only a matter of time before they could persuade the government to grant women the vote.

"Deeds not words"

But some women grew impatient, believing that they would only achieve their aim by taking more direct action. So, in 1903, Emmeline Pankhurst started a breakaway group, known as the suffrag*ettes*. "Deeds not words" was their motto, and some of them used increasingly militant acts to get their message across. They chained themselves to railings in public places, set fire to buildings, set off bombs and cut telegraph wires.

Many were arrested, then went on hunger strike until they were released. Not everyone approved of these tactics, but the suffrage groups gained hundreds of new members and the support of many politicians. Despite this, women still hadn't won the vote by 1914, when Mrs. Pankhurst called a truce, as Britain went to war.

Militant martyr

The most infamous militant suffragette was Emily Davison, who died after throwing herself under the King's racehorse, during the 1913 Epsom Derby.

Explorers and pioneers

The advances of the Victorian era brought a new age of exploration and engineering to the early 20th century. As trains, boats and planes grew more sophisticated, people were able to travel to more distant and dangerous lands.

Scott of the Antarctic

In 1910, Captain Robert Falcon Scott set sail for Antarctica, hoping to be the first man to reach the South Pole. But when Scott and his team of four men set out on the 2841km (1766 miles) trek to the Pole, they were plagued by unusually bad weather.

Nearly three months later, they reached the Pole, but they were devastated to find the flag of a rival Norwegian expedition already flying. Their morale plummeted and they became increasingly weak. None survived the journey back. Scott was considered a hero by many – but others believed the tragedy happened because he hadn't planned the trip properly.

This photograph shows members of Captain Scott's team pulling all their equipment and supplies as they struggle towards the South Pole.

Flying into history

Since the turn of the century, engineers from all over the world had been competing to invent the perfect powered flying machine.

In 1903, the Wright brothers from America became the first to get off the ground. Soon after, lots of people were taking to the skies.

The first Briton was an engineer named Edwin Alliott Verdon Roe. One of his later designs was used extensively by the military in the First World War.

The *Endurance* is trapped in the frozen sea in this incredible photograph by Frank Hurley.

Feat of endurance

Sir Ernest Shackleton set out in 1914 in an attempt to become the first to walk all the way across Antarctica, through the South Pole. But it soon became a matter of survival when his ship, the *Endurance*, became frozen in pack ice off the Antarctic coast. Shackleton and his crew watched in horror as the ship was crushed to pieces, leaving them marooned on a huge island of ice with only limited rations. Nearly five months passed before the ice broke up enough for the men to launch the lifeboats and reach the nearest island – but they found it deserted.

Shackleton picked a small team to sail with him to the island of South Georgia to get help. As they battled the treacherous waves of the South Atlantic Ocean, precise navigation was crucial, but bad weather meant they were only able to take readings from the stars four times on the 1290km (800 miles) journey.

They made it to South Georgia unharmed and set out with supplies to rescue the rest of the crew. Four months later, Shackleton saved them all.

Tragedy at sea

At the start of the 20th century, the British were world leaders in ship design.

In April 1912, the White Star Line's new ocean liner, RMS *Titanic*, set out on its first, or maiden, voyage across the Atlantic.

The *Titanic* was the world's largest and most luxurious passenger steamship. It was also considered to be unsinkable.

But the unthinkable happened. The *Titanic* hit an iceberg and sank.

There weren't enough lifeboats for all the passengers, and about 1,500 people died. It was one of the worst ever disasters at sea during peacetime.

Ruling the waves

Public image

Amid anti-German feeling in Britain, George V changed his family name from the German-sounding Saxe-Coburg-Gotha to Windsor, in 1917.

This painting, from 1911, shows George V in his naval uniform.

In 1910, Edward VII died and his son was proclaimed King George V. Newspaper reports hailed Edward's funeral a 'parade of kings' because seven European kings and several princes took part in the procession. And yet, beneath the pomp and pageantry, there was a sense of unease. Already, the optimism of the start of the 20th century was beginning to wane, and some people had even begun to believe that war was on the horizon.

Among those in the parade was George's cousin, Kaiser Wilhelm II of Germany, who was a cause of much anxiety to the British King and his government. Not only was Germany beginning to outstrip Britain's industrial power, but the Kaiser had imperial ambitions, too. In order to conquer an empire to rival that of Britain, he had been steadily expanding his armed forces and building a new fleet of warships. It looked to many as though Wilhelm was preparing for war.

Arms race

The British Royal Navy responded to Germany's naval expansion by launching a new battleship: HMS *Dreadnought*. It was bigger, faster and had greater firepower than any battleship before and gave its name to all similar warships built after that. It wasn't long before the Germans began to build dreadnought-style ships of their own. Soon a fierce arms race grew up between the two countries, as each tried to build more dreadnoughts than the other.

While Britain and Germany competed for mastery of the seas, other European governments began to modernize their armed forces and made plans for what to do if war did break out. Relations between countries in Europe became more and more tense, but few people really believed this would lead to war.

In this photograph, you can see two generations of British warship together, as HMS *Dreadnought* steams past HMS *Victory*, which led the British fleet to victory at the Battle of Trafalgar, in 1805.

British sea power

HMS *Dreadnought* was launched in 1906.

The battleship was mounted with ten big guns, each with a 10km (6 miles) firing range.

It also had five tubes for launching torpedoes – self-propelled underwater missiles.

Powered by steam turbines, *Dreadnought* could reach speeds of 40kmph (25mph) – faster than any other battleship at the time.

The body of the ship was protected from enemy fire by steel plates 28cm (11inches) thick.

By 1914, the Royal Navy had 30 dreadnoughts and the Germans had 20.

Police in Sarajevo seize one of Archduke Franz Ferdinand's assassins.

Europe at war

Princip was 19 when he was arrested. He received a 20-year sentence, but he was already suffering from tuberculosis, which eventually killed him. He died in prison on April 28, 1918.

On Sunday, June 28, 1914, in the Bosnian capital of Sarajevo, the opening shots were fired that would bring tensions in Europe to a head. The man who pulled the trigger was Gavrilo Princip, a member of a Serbian terrorist group. He shot and killed the heir to the Austro-Hungarian throne, Archduke Franz Ferdinand, sparking a crisis in the Balkans.

As people in Britain read reports of the assassination in the newspapers, few of them could have imagined the impact it would have on their lives. But, when the Austro-Hungarian government declared war on Serbia, a terrible chain of events was set off that soon dragged Britain into the most destructive war the world had ever seen.

Taking sides

This map shows the European alliances during the First World War.

- Allies
- Central Powers
- Neutral countries

1. MONTENEGRO
2. ALBANIA
3. GREECE
4. TURKISH EMPIRE

UNITED KINGDOM

BELGIUM

GERMANY

RUSSIA

FRANCE

AUSTRIA-HUNGARY

ITALY

BOSNIA

SERBIA

RUMANIA

BULGARIA

PORTUGAL

1.

2.

3.

4.

Since the late 19th century, the most powerful countries in Europe had gradually split into two rival groups. On one side, Germany, Austria-Hungary and Italy formed the Central Powers. On the other side were Britain, France and Russia, who later became known as the Allies. As fighting broke out in the Balkans, Germany backed Austria-Hungary and the Russians supported the Serbs. So, on August 1, Germany declared war on Russia. When the French rallied their troops in support of Russia, the Germans declared war on them too.

The Germans now faced fighting on two fronts – against France to the west and Russia to the east. To avoid this they hoped to crush France on the Western Front, before dealing with Russia on the Eastern Front. On August 4, they invaded neutral Belgium, heading for Paris by the shortest, flattest route. Eleven hours after the invasion, the British, bound by a promise to protect Belgium, declared war on Germany. Europe was at war.

Not all of these countries joined the war right from the start.

The Turkish Empire joined the Central Powers in November 1914. Italy (now on the side of the Allies) and Bulgaria entered the war in 1915. The following year, Rumania and Portugal also joined the fighting, and Greece entered in 1917.

Royal Artillery soldiers of the BEF disembark at the French port of Rouen, August, 1914.

The Western Front

In early August 1914, a British Expeditionary Force (BEF) of around 100,000 soldiers crossed the English Channel to help defend Belgium and France. Before the month was out, the BEF was locked in battle with German troops near the city of Mons. Britain's soldiers were tough veterans of other wars, but the massive German army punched holes in the Allied line and the BEF was soon retreating with the French army to Paris.

Tommies

The men of the BEF were professional soldiers, many of whom had been recruited from India. They were nicknamed Tommies, from the name Tommy Atkins.

Some people think Atkins was a brave soldier in the 1800s, but the name was also used as an example name on sample military forms.

Saving the city of love

While the citizens of Paris prepared for an invasion, French generals organized a desperate counter-strike. With the Germans only 50km (30 miles) from the capital, French soldiers forced a gap in the German lines along the River Marne. Allied troops swept into the gap, forcing the Germans back to a ridge of high ground. Paris was saved.

Carving the line

The Germans were stalled and began digging trenches to protect their territorial gains. Meanwhile, the Allies decided to rush their soldiers around the northern edge of the battlefield and attack the enemy from the rear. But the Germans had the same idea, and both sides scrambled north, digging trenches along the way to defend themselves. This 'Race to the Sea' ended in a dead heat in the sand dunes bordering the North Sea. In its wake lay hundreds of miles of trenches slashing across France, all the way to the borders of neutral Switzerland. The trench war had begun.

A last stab

German commanders thought they could smash the Allied line in the Belgian region of Flanders. In October, they attacked BEF troops guarding the city of Ypres, hoping to push through and capture the vital Channel ports.

The BEF held their ground, but at the cost of tens of thousands of dead and wounded. These losses broke the back of Britain's old, professional army and were a taste of the pitiless fighting to come. The battle rumbled on at Ypres until the winter weather arrived and soldiers dug in along what their generals now called the Western Front.

Battle lines

This map shows the sites of some of the key battles fought along the Western Front.

1. Mons (Aug. 1914)
2. Marne (Sept. 1914)
3. First Ypres (Oct. 1914)
4. Arras (Oct.1914)
5. Neuve Chapelle (March 1915)
6. Second Ypres (April 1915)
7. Loos (Sept. 1915)
8. Verdun (Feb. 1916)
9. Somme (July 1916)
10. Passchendaele (July 1917)
11. Cambrai (Nov. 1917)
12. Belleau Wood (June 1918)
13. Second Marne (July 1918)

Six feet under

Mud and rain meant that the trenches were easily flooded and needed constant maintenance.

These British soldiers are taking a break from repairing a trench. They are wrapped up in a variety of scarves and furs to keep as warm and dry as possible.

When the war started, men scratched holes in the earth to protect themselves from exploding shells and bullets. But, as the rival armies of Europe became bogged down along the Western Front, they used all their manpower and industrial might to build a vast maze of trenches and tunnels. Few soldiers could have imagined that they would be living and fighting below ground for years.

By the end of the war, there were over 32,200km (20,000 miles) of trenches dug into the mud of the Western Front.

Heads down

Trenches were usually twisting and narrow, to make it harder for enemy raiders to rush through them. They were just deep enough to protect the average-sized man from any watching snipers, but thousands still died from head wounds.

The most dangerous times of day were at dawn and dusk, when the changing light made it difficult to spot attacks. Every man had to be on full alert, peering into the stretch of shell-scarred land that stretched to the enemy's front line. This ghostly strip of churned-up mud and tangled barbed wire was known as no-man's land. It was scattered with dead bodies, and crawled with rats and other vermin attracted to the stench of the battlefield.

Creature comforts

Soldiers died every day in the trenches – from falling shells, bullets and disease – but they enjoyed some 'luxuries' too. Letters and parcels from home arrived quickly, and men read newspapers and books in quiet moments. British troops received a daily tot of rum in harsh weather and the Germans drank beer and brandy.

Stalemate

In 1915, the British and French launched a series of huge attacks along the Western Front. The raids were disastrous, as troops marched across no-man's land into an impenetrable curtain of German machine-gun fire.

Army generals needed new tactics to break the enemy line, but instead they began talking of a 'war of attrition' – they planned to keep fighting, grinding down the Germans until they had no more resources or fighting men. This master plan claimed the lives of millions.

Combat zone

This diagram shows a typical layout of trenches on the Western Front.

Reserve trenches

Communication trenches

Front trench

Barbed wire

No-man's land

Front trench

British soldiers spent around eight days in the front trench before moving back to safer reserve areas for a week's rest and other duties.

Christmas truce

On the morning of Christmas Day, 1914, curious British and German soldiers put down their weapons and wandered into no-man's land.

For several hours they chatted with each other, shaking hands, trading goods and collecting their dead.

367

New recruits like these learned basic rifle skills in training camps before being sent to fight.

Shrinking soldiers

Early in the war, new recruits to the army were required to be at least 167cm (5ft 6 inches) tall.

As the army became desperate for more men, the limit was reduced. Special battalions were even formed for shorter men.

By February, 1916, height no longer mattered. Now, all single men aged 18 to 41 were made to join the British army.

Your country needs you

By spring 1915, two things had become obvious to the government: the war would not be won quickly, and the army needed more soldiers. Lord Kitchener, Secretary of State for War, quickly appealed for volunteers. Propaganda posters, leaflets and newspaper articles appeared around Britain, designed to build patriotic feelings and public enthusiasm for the war.

"Go! Fight!"

Often, propaganda campaigns were targeted at women, suggesting that they should persuade, or shame, their menfolk into enlisting. Some men, known as conscientious objectors, refused to fight because it was against their moral or religious beliefs. But the pressure to sign up was immense – anyone not in uniform was branded a coward. The recruitment drive was a huge success. By the end of 1915, around two million men had enlisted in the British army. By 1916, the figure had risen to over three million.

368

War on words

As the government encouraged men to sign up, they also acted to silence voices criticizing the war campaign. From the start of the war, it became illegal for the members of the public to write anything that might be useful to the enemy. Soldiers had their letters censored, and newspaper reporters were banned from the Western Front. At first, only one official journalist was allowed to report on the war, although others were later given permission. Even then, the government had to approve everything they published.

Defending the realm

Censorship was just one way the government controlled people's behaviour during the war. The 1914 Defence of the Realm Act banned all sorts of activities:

NO GOSSIPING
about the army in public places.

NO FLYING KITES or LIGHTING BONFIRES
– both of which could attract enemy airships.

NO FEEDING BREAD
to horses and chickens – it's a waste of food.

Posters like this were plastered all over Britain, encouraging men to join the army.

Lord Kitchener, in this 1914 recruitment poster, urges men to sign up.

John Singer Sargent's painting *Gassed* shows British soldiers injured and blinded after a gas attack.

Deadly weapons

The First World War was fought on an industrial scale, with scientists developing terrifying new weapons to kill and maim. From explosive shells to clouds of poison gas, there were a thousand different ways to die.

Fighting for air

In April 1915, Allied soldiers at Ypres noticed a yellow-green mist drifting over their lines. The Germans had opened hundreds of canisters of deadly chlorine gas, defying an international treaty that banned the use of chemical weapons. French colonial troops panicked when the gas filled their trenches, burning their eyes, throats and lungs. They fled, leaving the way open for a German raid, but the gas soon rolled away and Canadian soldiers moved in to close the gap.

Within a few months the British army retaliated by using gas in their attacks. It was an unreliable weapon, often changing direction on the wind, but it struck terror in soldiers' hearts. After Ypres, men had to carry masks and breathing equipment at all times, dreading the warning signal that a gas attack was coming.

First Aid

British women weren't allowed to fight, but many got close to the action, working as nurses and ambulance drivers, taking care of wounded soldiers. Some risked their lives by giving First Aid on the battlefield, often under enemy fire.

Steel rain

Artillery shells killed more men in the war than any other weapon. Hidden miles behind the front line, field guns fired a barrage of millions of shells into enemy trenches before big battles. One soldier compared the explosion of an artillery shell to the force of an express train slamming into the earth. The noise and violence of a barrage drove some men mad. They shook and trembled with fear, in a condition known as shellshock.

Take cover

Soldiers hurled exploding grenades and carried shotguns for close-quarter fighting. The Germans were the first to develop portable flamethrowers – spurting jets of burning fuel – and the Allies soon copied them. But none of these weapons could match the power of the newly invented machine guns, as they spat out hundreds of bullets. A single machine gun could defend long sections of trench, cutting down attacking infantry, and trapping Europe's armies in a long, gruelling war.

The shell scandal

In the opening years of war, British factories struggled to produce enough guns and shells. Quality control was a problem too. In May 1915, the 'shell scandal' revealed that many of the shells produced were 'duds' that failed to explode.

So the government created the Ministry of Munitions, which enlisted thousands of women to work in the factories. This improved the quality and quantity of munitions sent to the front.

In this photograph from June 1916, British troops are using massive field guns, called howitzers, to pound the enemy front line with shells.

Zeppelins, like this one, cruised at high altitudes, but were still easy targets for anti-aircraft guns on the ground. Several were shot down over Britain.

This government poster shows people how to tell the difference between British and German aircraft and warns them to take shelter if they spot an enemy aircraft.

Home under fire

The war affected the lives of British civilians more than any previous war because, for the first time, they were expected to help in the war effort. Workers had to step up production to keep their troops armed, clothed and fed. This meant they became targets for enemy attacks.

On January 13, 1915, two huge German airships, known as zeppelins, appeared over the east coast of England. Bombs fell from them, killing four people below. This was the first of over fifty air raids over Britain that year, including several on London.

The Germans hoped the attacks would dampen the British spirit. In fact, it had the opposite effect. Now, people were determined to 'do their bit' on what became known as the Home Front.

Working girls

Before the war, the jobs available to women were limited. But, as more and more men left for the front, women had to take their places at work, and many of them relished this new opportunity. They operated telephone exchanges, drove buses, worked in agriculture and even took on dangerous jobs such as mining, shipbuilding, and packing explosive shells.

War and want

Even with women replacing male farm workers, Britain still experienced food shortages. The situation became worse early in 1917, when German submarines began attacking ships bringing supplies to Britain. Goods such as sugar and fresh meat became scarce, and prices rose faster than people's wages. Many struggled to afford even the basics. In January 1918, the government fixed food prices, and introduced rationing to restrict how much people could buy.

This munitions factory worker is checking and packing shells to send to the front. This was a hazardous job, as accidental explosions were a constant danger.

A painful duty

Each morning, people on the Home Front scoured casualty lists printed in newspapers, anxious to find out whether anyone they knew had died in action.

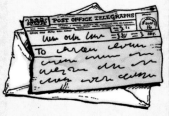

Official notices that men had been killed were sent to the soldiers' relatives by telegram. The message opened with the words, "It is my painful duty to inform you…"

War and empire

> "Our duty is quite clear – to gird up our loins and remember that we are Britons."
>
> Andrew Fisher,
> Australian Prime Minister,
> August 1914

At the start of the war, Britain, as well as Germany, Italy and France, ruled several colonies beyond Europe. The war quickly spread around the world as each side launched attacks on the other's overseas territories, hoping to divert their enemy's attention away from the Western Front.

Britain's colonies were also a source of new soldiers. Troops from India fought alongside the British on the Western Front as well in East Africa and the Middle East. Australians, New Zealanders and Canadians also joined the war in France, and even more soldiers were recruited from British colonies in Africa and the West Indies.

Tackling the Turks

In April 1915, Britain called on 17,000 soldiers from the Australian and New Zealand Army Corps (Anzacs) to join an Allied invasion of northern Turkey. The Turks had joined the war in November 1914, on the side of the Central Powers. The Allies hoped to capture the Gallipoli Peninsula so that naval forces could then push through to the Turkish capital, Constantinople, forcing the Turks to surrender.

The Gallipoli Peninsula, in northern Turkey

Constantinople (now Istanbul)

Gallipoli Peninsula

TURKISH EMPIRE

Aegean Sea

Bayonets at the ready, Anzac troops scramble uphill to attack the Turkish front line.

Misery in Gallipoli

On April 25, Allied troops landed along the Gallipoli coast, amid a barrage of enemy machine-gun fire. Thousands died before even reaching the shore. Unable to advance, the Allies dug in for nine terrible months of trench warfare.

Spring turned to summer, and the heat at Gallipoli became unbearable. Flies contaminated the soldiers' food, spreading disease. Then winter set in, with men suffering from both frostbite and pneumonia. In November, the Allies admitted defeat. They had lost nearly 50,000 men, and had very little to show for it.

Anzac Day

Gallipoli was the Anzacs' first major action of the war. Many Anzacs were British-born, but they returned home with a strong sense of their own distinct national identities. Each year they remember their war dead on April 25, which is named Anzac Day.

The man with the donkey

Among the Anzac heroes of Gallipoli were Australian soldier John Simpson Kirkpatrick, and his donkey Murphy. Each day, Kirkpatrick rode Murphy around hills dotted with enemy snipers, searching for wounded troops to carry back to the army hospital.

Kirkpatrick rescued over 300 men, before he was killed by a sniper. No one knows what happened to Murphy.

Brave youth

Boy seaman John Cornwell was only 16 years old when he fought at the Battle of Jutland.

He was a member of a gun team onboard the HMS *Chester*. An explosion killed the rest of the team and wounded him, but he kept on fighting.

The ship returned safely to port and Cornwell was rushed to hospital. But he died the next day.

Cornwell was awarded the highest medal for bravery – the Victoria Cross – and the public turned out in droves for his funeral procession.

War at sea

As soon as war broke out, the Royal Navy set about using their ships to cut off all sea routes to Germany. British sailors searched merchant vessels and confiscated their cargos, hoping to starve the enemy into surrender. This tactic is known as a blockade.

German admirals were desperate to smash the blockade, but the Royal Navy was the strongest in the world, and most of the German fleet was trapped inside the North Sea by British warships.

North Sea raids

Warships were extremely expensive to build, so neither side wanted to risk losing them in a big sea battle. But there were raids and skirmishes. At the Battle of the Heligoland Bight, in 1914, the British sank four enemy ships. The Germans hit back, shelling British coastal towns. The next year, the Royal Navy ambushed some enemy ships at Dogger Bank, sinking another warship.

The Battle of Jutland

In January 1916, Admiral Reinhard Scheer took charge of the German High Seas Fleet. He thought his navy had been too timid, so he took the whole fleet out to sea, hunting for British patrols.

On May 31, near Jutland in Denmark, Scheer's fleet came face to face with a huge British fleet, commanded by Admiral John Jellicoe. It was the biggest naval engagement of the war. The British lost 15 ships, including three battle cruisers, while the Germans lost a single battle cruiser, and 10 other ships.

But, despite sinking more ships, Scheer knew his fleet was no match for Jellicoe's, and fled back to base.

Submarine warfare

The Germans claimed victory, but the British had seen off Scheer's fleet, and shown that they ruled the North Sea. After the Battle of Jutland, there were no more big naval battles for the rest of the war. Instead, the Germans relied more and more on their submarines – known as U-boats – to slip past the enemy blockades and sink supply ships heading for Britain.

In 1917 the Germans announced 'unrestricted submarine warfare' on the Allies. Their U-boats aimed to sink any ships bound for an Allied port – even civilian vessels. A number of US civilians died in U-boat attacks, which angered the US President Woodrow Wilson. He had vowed to keep his country out of the war, but now many Americans began to urge their government to join the fight against Germany.

The Lusitania

In 1915, a German U-boat sank a British passenger liner, the *Lusitania*, killing nearly 2,000 civilians and causing an international uproar. For a while after this, the Germans had to scale back their U-boat attacks.

Admiral John Jellicoe's British fleet on their way to the Battle of Jutland.

This painting, from 1919, shows a battle in the sky between British and German aircraft. Following the Red Baron's example, some German pilots decorated their planes with bright paints. This led Allied pilots to nickname them the 'Flying Circus'.

Dogfights

Most air fights came down to one-on-one shootouts known as dogfights. Planes sometimes broke apart as the pilots dived and climbed, blasting each other with machine guns.

French and German pilots were equipped with parachutes, but British flyers weren't. Parachutes were considered too bulky, and some generals thought pilots would be tempted to jump at the first sign of danger.

Air aces

Aircraft design was still in its early stages when war flashed across Europe. At first, both sides sent unarmed scout planes to spy on enemy positions. When two rival pilots met in the sky, they simply waved or took pot shots at each other with their pistols. Designers soon realized that a plane fitted with machine guns could win battles in the sky. Aircraft could also be used to launch bombing raids on enemy trenches.

Early fighter planes were not very effective. Machine gun bullets often hit their own aircraft's propellers, and bombs were released by the pilot, who simply tossed them over the side of his cockpit. But technology quickly developed, turning planes into agile fighters.

Throughout the winter of 1915, the Allies were losing two or three planes a day to superior German flyers. Allied casualties were so great, British pilots jokingly described their Royal Flying Corps (RFC) as the Suicide Club. But, as the war went on, the Allies improved their tactics, and won control of the skies.

Knights of the air

The most successful pilots of each nation became known as 'aces', and were presented as dashing daredevils in the popular press. The RFC's most successful ace was Major 'Mick' Mannock. He was almost blind in one eye, but he still managed to shoot down 73 German planes.

Victory in the sky

Early in 1917, new machines once again gave the Germans the upper hand. In April alone, the RFC lost 245 planes to German pilots. But, by the winter, the tide turned again, as German factories struggled to produce enough aircraft. New Allied planes, such as the British Sopwith Camel, combined power with agility, enabling the Allies to become the masters of the sky.

The Red Baron

The war's greatest flying ace was the German pilot Manfred Baron von Richtofen – better known as the Red Baron. Richtofen destroyed 80 Allied aircraft, before he was shot down and killed, in early 1918.

The Red Baron earned his nickname after painting his plane blood red. The sight of it approaching terrified inexperienced pilots.

379

Tragedy at the Somme

By 1916 the British army had been swelled by young recruits from all walks of life. These new soldiers formed the main thrust of an Allied attack at the River Somme, designed to draw German troops away from the Battle of Verdun, where a French army was fighting for its life. The commander of the British forces, Sir Douglas Haig, ordered his artillery to shell the enemy for a full week. On July 1, Haig's men stepped into no-man's land, expecting an easy walk to victory.

Deep shelter

Haig and his generals thought nothing could have survived their ferocious barrage, but they were wrong. The Germans had constructed deep dugouts below their trenches, safe from even the largest artillery shells. As soon as the explosions stopped, they dragged their machine guns to the surface. Even the fields of barbed wire surrounding their positions were still intact. British shells had simply lifted the wire into the air and dropped it back down in a knotted mess.

A new weapon

One of the most powerful symbols of modern warfare is the tank, crushing everything in its path.

A year before the Somme, the British were secretly testing the first tanks. They called them 'water tanks' to trick enemy spies, and the tank name stuck.

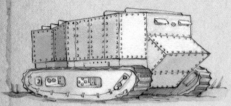

Although they offered a solution to the deadlock of trench fighting, early tanks broke down and got stuck too often to be effective weapons.

The British used tanks at the Somme, but their first major victory was at the Battle of Cambrai, in November 1917.

Walk, don't run

The British troops were ordered to walk across no-man's land in waves. Their officers were worried that inexperienced soldiers might scatter, panic or stumble if they broke into a run. Some stretches of no-man's land were only a few hundred yards wide, but the German machine guns began firing before the men could get across. They scythed through the British ranks, slaughtering thousands.

The worst day

By the end of the first day at the Somme, 20,000 British soldiers were dead and many more were injured or missing. It was the bloodiest day in the army's history. Some men broke through the German line, but they were driven back by fierce counter-attacks. Fighting went on until November, and the Germans retreated to a new, stronger defensive line. The British had gained a few miles of muddy ground and a million German and Allied soldiers were dead or wounded.

Friends and brothers

To encourage men to join the army, Kitchener had set up so-called Pals Battalions, in 1914. These were units made up of friends and brothers from the same town, village or workplace, who trained and fought together.

Many of the Pals Battalions saw their first action at the Somme, and they suffered heavy casualties. As a result, many local communities across the country were decimated at a stroke.

British infantry advance through the barbed wire into no-man's land. This photograph is a still taken from the *Battle of the Somme*, a movie made in 1916 combining real footage of the battle with re-enactment scenes.

Russian surrender

Even as the British awaited the arrival of their new allies from the United States, they were losing their Russian allies on the Eastern Front.

Facing food shortages at home and carnage on the battlefield, the Russians reached a crisis point. In March 1917, they overthrew their ruler, the Tsar. They struggled on with the war until November, when another revolution swept across the country, and its new leaders negotiated a peace with Germany.

Australian soldiers walk across a wooden track over the flooded battlefield of Passchendaele, in this photograph, taken by Frank Hurley.

To the bitter end

After years of resisting all calls to fight, German spying and submarine attacks on their shipping finally goaded the US into joining the war in the spring of 1917. While the Americans raised an army to send to Europe, Sir Douglas Haig launched a new battle at Ypres that quickly descended into chaos.

A familiar plan

Haig wanted to break out of Ypres and seize the high ground held by the enemy around the village of Passchendaele. From there, his soldiers could attack and destroy the German Navy's submarine bases along the Belgian coast. Haig thought that the Germans' strength and morale had been broken at the Somme. He ordered a barrage of their front line, lasting for ten days, and sent his troops into battle at the end of July.

The barrage didn't break the enemy line, but it churned up all the fields around Passchendaele. Heavy rains turned them into a nightmarish swamp of thick mud, broken roads and flooded shell holes.

A hollow victory

Thousands of men drowned in the quagmire of the battlefield. After months of terrible carnage, Canadian soldiers finally occupied Passchendaele village in November. But the Allies couldn't advance to the submarine bases and German troops soon recaptured all their lost ground.

Breaking through

In the Spring of 1918, the Germans broke through the Allied line at several places with a massive force of new troops. These men had been released from fighting on the Eastern Front when the Russians pulled out of the war. German generals saw a last, desperate chance to win the war before American troops could arrive in strength. They made spectacular gains, but their men ran out of food and ammunition. Exhausted by years of war, the Germans began to retreat.

While the Germans fell back, thousands of US troops were streaming into France. They fought bravely, joining the Allies on the march to Germany and victory.

A final cease-fire

As the Germans were retreating from the Western Front, their allies collapsed. Although German soldiers were still battling, their country was in ruins and close to revolution. In October, Germany's leaders approached the Allies to ask for peace. The warring nations signed an agreement to end the fighting – an Armistice – on November 11, 1918.

Coming to terms

With the fighting over, European leaders met to set out the terms needed for a lasting peace.

The League of Nations was set up, as a peacekeeping organization.

Germany was blamed for starting the war, and given harsh punishments.

Country boundaries were redrawn in Europe and the Middle East.

Sadly, the peace treaties caused much resentment that would later lead to further conflicts.

From left to right, this photograph shows Prime Minister Lloyd George, French President Clemenceau and US President Wilson at the peace talks.

Remembrance

> "Look up, and swear by the green of the spring that you'll never forget."
>
> From *Aftermath*, by Siegfried Sassoon

This is Tyne Cot military cemetery, in Belgium. It is the largest of several cemeteries built for British soldiers who died on the Western Front.

Even as people in Britain celebrated the end of the war, many were grieving for those they had lost. Around 900,000 soldiers from Britain and its empire had died, and 190,000 were still missing. Surviving soldiers returned home, unable to forget the horrors they had witnessed.

During the war, the Imperial (later Commonwealth) War Graves Commission was set up to build and maintain cemeteries near the battlefields. So that no grave looked more important than another, each was marked by a simple headstone recording a name and a date.

Back in Britain, many communities, as well as schools and workplaces, set up their own war memorials, carved with the names of those who had died.

In the years following the war, November 11, the anniversary of the Armistice, was set aside as a day of remembrance. Now, on that day every year, people all around the world wear poppies and lay wreaths at war memorials to remember those who have died in every war, not just the First World War.

Lest we forget...

Many soldiers were struck by the beauty of the poppies that grew on the battlefields after the fighting had stopped.

Later, the poppy became a symbol of remembrance of those who had died.

The roaring twenties

> "Are we really trying for a better world, or are we going to slip back to the same old world before 1914?"
>
> Lady Nancy Astor, MP

David Lloyd George had promised Britain's troops that they would return to a "land fit for heroes". But life wasn't going to be easy – the war had cost nearly a million lives, and left the government with huge debts. Even so, as the painful memories of the war faded, young people were determined to enjoy themselves.

Bright young things

Lady Astor became the first female Member of Parliament in 1919, one year after women over the age of 30 had been given the vote. It wasn't until 1928 that all women were granted the same voting rights as men.

As businesses began to grow again and living standards improved, people found they had more time and more money to spend on having fun. A fitness craze swept the country, as people wanted to look good in the new sporty fashions, and were convinced it was their national duty to stay fighting fit and healthy.

Movies, dance halls and jazz music were all the rage. Jazz was fast, lively and liberating, and by the 1920s it had gained a bad reputation. Jazz clubs became the haunts of young men and women, whose wild antics filled the gossip columns. Their carefree attitudes shocked their more conservative elders, who worried that Britain was becoming an immoral nation.

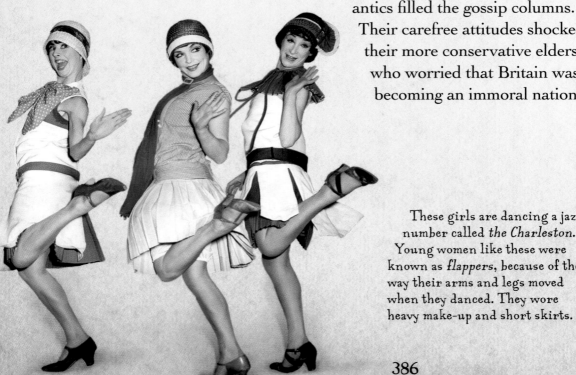

These girls are dancing a jazz number called *the Charleston*. Young women like these were known as *flappers*, because of the way their arms and legs moved when they danced. They wore heavy make-up and short skirts.

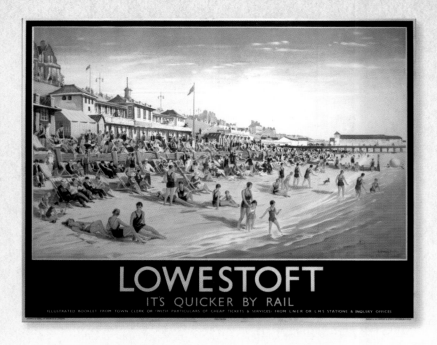

LOWESTOFT

IT'S QUICKER BY RAIL

ILLUSTRATED BOOKLET FROM TOWN CLERK OR (WITH PARTICULARS OF CHEAP TICKETS & SERVICES) FROM L.N.E.R. OR L.M.S STATIONS & INQUIRY OFFICES

This railway poster is advertising a popular seaside resort on the east coast. Holidaymakers flocked to places like this to take in the sea air, enjoy the sunshine and to swim. Trains were cheap and people from all classes could afford to get away.

Outdoor pursuits

While some were dancing in smoky jazz clubs, many were also spending more time in the fresh air. Dozens of open-air public swimming pools, called lidos, were built across Britain. Thousands of young people joined the Youth Hostel Association and the Ramblers Association, and membership of the Girl Guides and Boy Scouts hit one million for the first time.

Although only one family in ten could afford a car, attending motor races was a very popular pastime and the first British Grand Prix was held in 1926.

Radio times

In 1922 the BBC was set up to transmit radio broadcasts that would 'educate, inform and entertain' the nation. People all over the country bought radio sets so that they could listen to the BBC's output of music, drama, news, sports and children's shows. During the 1930s, the BBC extended its radio service across the British empire and broadcast Britain's first television shows.

British troops barricade a street in Dublin during the Easter Rising.

"MacDonagh and MacBride
And Connolly and Pearse
Now and in time to be,
Wherever green is worn,
Are changed, changed utterly:
A terrible beauty is born."

From *Easter, 1916*, a poem about the leaders of the Easter Rising, by William Butler Yeats.

Yeats admires the "terrible beauty" of their sacrifice, which stirred the Irish to fight for their freedom.

A rebel leader is shot by a British firing squad.

A terrible beauty

Ireland had been part of the UK since 1801, but many Irish people wanted more control over their own affairs. In 1914, the British government had agreed that Ireland could set up its own parliament. But plans were put on hold when the First World War broke out.

Meanwhile, some Irish nationalists saw the war as a chance to win total independence. At Easter, 1916, a group of them took control of the city of Dublin and declared independence. But after five days of fierce street fighting, they were defeated by British forces, and 15 rebel leaders were executed by firing squad.

Sinn Féin

In the 1918 General Election, the leading Irish political party, Sinn Féin, won 73 seats in Parliament. They refused to take them up, and set up a parliament of their own, called the *Dáil*, in Dublin. Then they began organizing the Irish Republican Army (IRA) to drive the British out of their country.

The Irish War of Independence

The IRA carried out a fierce campaign of guerilla attacks on police and government buildings. So, in 1920, the British sent in ex-soldiers known as 'Black and Tans' (because of their uniforms) to keep order. Both the IRA and the Black and Tans gained a reputation for appalling brutality, carrying out bombings and shootings, in which many innocent people were killed.

Stopping the bloodshed

The British government was desperate to stop the bloodshed, particularly as the terrible violence of their own forces was drawing condemnation from all over the world. But there was no easy solution. Most Irish people were Catholic and nationalist, but in Northern Ireland, most people were Protestant, and wanted to remain part of the UK.

Ireland divided

In 1921, Sinn Féin and the British government reached an agreement, and signed the Anglo-Irish Treaty. Northern Ireland stayed in the UK, while southern Ireland became the independent Irish Free State, although it remained part of Britain's empire.

The Treaty split the nationalists. Some of them were happy with it, but others were angry that Northern Ireland was still part of Britain. This led to a bloody civil war between the two factions, which ended in victory for those who supported the Treaty. But many people were still unhappy that their country had been partitioned. The struggle for control of Ireland was far from over.

Michael Collins

Michael Collins led the IRA during the Irish War of Independence, and helped to set up the Irish Free State.

He was shot dead during the civil war that followed the signing of the Anglo-Irish Treaty.

Many Irish nationalists remember him as a hero, who forced the British to negotiate with Sinn Féin.

This map shows how Ireland was partitioned in 1921.

389

These men from Jarrow are marching to London with their MP, Ellen Wilkinson.

The hungry thirties

The 1920s had been exciting and dynamic as Britain celebrated the end of the war, but by the 1930s people were suffering – unemployment and poverty gripped the country, and radical political movements in Europe meant that war loomed once again.

The Great Depression

Britain's economy was still recovering from the cost of the war when the New York Stock Exchange crashed. International trade was devastated and demand for British products collapsed. The country had depended on traditional industries in the north, such as shipbuilding and coal mining, but with nobody to buy the products, there was no money to pay any wages. Millions of people were made redundant and lived in terrible poverty for most of the 30s.

This period of international economic crisis is known as the Great Depression.

The Wall Street Crash

The US economy – and that of the world – suffered a severe blow when the New York Stock Exchange (on Wall Street) crashed in October 1929.

As share prices fell, people panicked and sold their shares, causing share values to plummet until they were almost worthless. Jobs were lost, businesses failed, and many countries were plunged into poverty.

Marching in protest

Industrial communities struggled, as shipyards and mines closed. People felt that the Prime Minister, Stanley Baldwin, didn't understand the hardship they faced. Many towns organized marches to London in protest against the poor financial support he offered.

The most famous of these hunger marches was the Jarrow Crusade. On October 5, 1936, 200 men set off on the 480km (300 miles) journey from Jarrow, in north-east England, to London, to present a petition before Parliament. They walked for 25 days, but Baldwin refused to meet them. However, they won much public support and, gradually, conditions began to improve.

Political extremes

The 1920s and 30s saw the rise of an extreme form of politics, known as fascism. The war and the depression had left many Europeans desperately poor, and fascist leaders seemed to offer easy solutions.

Mussolini and his Fascist Party had swept to power in Italy in the 1920s, promising wealth and stability. But his regime soon turned violent. When Hitler gained control of Germany in 1933, he pledged to rebuild the country's strength. He blamed high unemployment on Jews, and vowed to do whatever it took to get rid of them.

In Britain, Oswald Mosley was inspired by Hitler's ideas. He founded the British Union of Fascists, and in 1936, thousands of its members descended on Cable Street, a Jewish area of East London, to intimidate people there. But they were met with 300,000 protesters and a riot swiftly broke out. Mosley was forced to cancel the rally. But although the protesters celebrated, the sense of victory would be short-lived. There would soon be a much greater and much more sinister battle to be fought.

Talkies

By the 1930s, almost every British town had its own cinema. Silent movies had made way for *talkies*, movies with sound, and people were hooked.

Charlie Chaplin was one of the biggest stars of the 1930s. Raised in the wings of London's music halls, he was on the stage from the age of five.

Chaplin often used his comic skills to make a serious point. *Modern Times* criticizes the inhumanity of factory life, and in *The Great Dictator*, he stars as a crazed tyrant, based on Hitler.

THE SECOND WORLD WAR

Barely twenty years after the horrors of the First World War, German tanks stormed across Europe and started the bloodiest and most pitiless conflict ever seen. The Second World War was a global battle for survival — for most nations, their citizens and their way of life.

Britain's Prime Minister, Winston Churchill, called on every man, woman and child to join the fight. After six years of terrible fighting alongside their allies, the British won victory and the chance to help shape the modern world.

Hitler's Germany

Adolf Hitler and his extreme racist Nazi Party came to power in 1933.

The Nazis believed that people of pure Germanic blood were a 'master race' – superior to other races. They built up the German army so that they could conquer a new empire in Europe.

Hitler blamed the Jews living in Germany for the country's economic problems. As a result, they faced increasing persecution and violence, and many were driven from their jobs and their homes.

No choice but war

The 1930s had been desperate years in Britain and across Europe. Economic depression forced millions into poverty, while ruthless politicians preached hate and violence to angry crowds looking for someone to blame. But war might have been avoided, if it hadn't been for the rage of a single, terrifying man – Adolf Hitler.

Hitler felt betrayed by the German surrender after the First World War. Using cunning and brute force, he seized political control in Germany and built up a powerful army. World leaders looked on in despair as Hitler sent troops to the French border and into Austria. When he threatened to invade a region of Czechoslovakia, it became clear to Germany's old enemies, Britain and France, that they would have to take action to maintain peace in Europe.

Appeasement and betrayal

To most people in Britain, the political problems in Europe seemed a long way away. They had problems of their own, and were in no mood to fight. Desperate to avoid war, the British Prime Minister, Neville Chamberlain, met Hitler at Munich in September 1938. They were joined by Edouard Daladier and Benito Mussolini, the French and Italian heads of government.

The four agreed that Hitler could take Sudetenland – part of Czechoslovakia with a large German population. In return, Hitler promised not to invade any more territories.

Hitler gave rousing speeches about the 'master race' at massive rallies.

A broken promise

But Chamberlain had been tricked. Hitler's tanks swarmed into the rest of Czechoslovakia too, and on September 1, 1939, they crashed across Poland. Applying speed and overwhelming firepower, in a new style of attack known as *Blitzkrieg* or lightning war, Hitler's generals smashed the Polish army in less than a month. The time for making peace was over.

On September 3, Chamberlain made a radio speech telling the British people that they were at war with Germany. Only minutes later, air raid sirens sounded across London.

"My good friends, for the second time in our history, a British Prime Minister has returned from Germany bringing peace with honour. I believe it is peace for our time."

Neville Chamberlain announces the Munich Peace Agreement to the people of Britain.

A jubilant Chamberlain returns from Munich, waving a signed peace agreement between Britain and Germany. Just six months later, Hitler would disregard it.

Action stations

The first air raid warning over London was a false alarm. But, even so, there was an atmosphere of fear across the city. Britain's Royal Navy was strong, but the country was badly prepared for war.

Thousands of men and women throughout Britain decided that now was the time to 'do their bit' to defend their country. Many joined the ARP – Air Raid Precautions – as wardens. Most ARP wardens were unpaid volunteers, and their chief task was to make sure everybody knew what to do during an air raid. They sounded sirens to warn of an imminent raid and looked after public shelters.

At dusk, every city light was put out or covered up, to stop bomber crews from spotting targets. This was called the blackout, and the wardens made sure it was strictly enforced.

> "Always have your gas mask with you – day and night. Learn to put it on quickly."
>
> This advice, from the Ministry of Home Security to the people of Britain, was published in the Sunday newspapers.

Gas masks

The government was so worried that the Germans might use poison gas in an air attack that it issued 38 million gas masks by September 1938.

People had to carry their gas masks with them at all times.

Special gas masks were designed for babies...

...elderly people...

...and even some animals.

Preparing for war

The country was finally gearing up for war. Young men were conscripted (called up for compulsory service) into the armed forces and Chamberlain ordered his generals to send a force to France. He also appointed Winston Churchill, a tough veteran of the First World War, to take charge of the Royal Navy.

Two days before Chamberlain's radio speech, a massive evacuation project was set in motion, as millions of children from Britain's cities were moved to the countryside, to try to escape the bombers. Most went by train, moving across a landscape that was rapidly changing in the face of war.

All over the country, the nation waited anxiously, wondering when the first air raids would strike – but nothing happened.

There were lots of accidents during the blackout. This poster warns people to let their eyes adjust before going out in the dark.

This ARP warden (with W for warden marked on his helmet) is directing a family to the nearest air raid shelter during a drill.

Lightning war

The Germans first used *Blitzkrieg* against Poland. This is how the tactic worked:

First, bombers attacked enemy air bases, military headquarters, ammunition depots and train stations.

Next, Stuka dive bombers swooped in machine-gunning and bombing enemy front line troops...

...and paratroopers made surprise raids.

Then, tanks broke through, calling in dive bombers to help clear any obstacles.

Enemy groups were then surrounded and crushed, while the main attack force advanced.

The fall of western Europe

After Hitler's whirlwind success in Poland, the fighting came to a standstill, during the winter months. Hitler's army was sitting tight inside Poland, no bombs had fallen on Britain, and by January 1940, most of the children who had been evacuated from the cities had returned home.

The phoney war

As the months went by, people began talking about a "phoney" war and some British politicians thought it might still be possible to arrange a peace. But, although no shots were fired on land, there was savage fighting at sea. A German U-boat submarine sank the battleship, *Royal Oak*, and almost a thousand British sailors drowned. Two months later, off the coast South America, the German warship, *Admiral Graf Spee*, was hunted down by the British and scuttled by its own crew, to prevent it from being captured.

Lightning strikes

On April 9, Hitler put an end to all talk of peace by launching *Blitzkrieg* against Denmark and Norway. Next, his tanks broke through at a weak point in France's northern frontier. The Germans kept advancing, using paratrooper landings and Stuka raids to spread panic before them. In six weeks they had overwhelmed the French, and pushed the British army onto the beaches around Dunkirk. The seven-month phoney war was over, and the British had suffered what would turn out to be one of the greatest military disasters of the war.

398

German Stukas sweep across the sky in formation. These black, gull-shaped dive bombers had sirens fitted under the wings. They made a terrifying screech as they dived, causing panic, even among experienced soldiers.

This map shows Europe in summer 1940, by which time much of Western Europe and Scandinavia was under Nazi occupation.

NORWAY

DENMARK

SOVIET UNION (formerly Russia)

UK

Dunkirk•

NETHERLANDS

BELGIUM

POLAND

GERMANY

CZECHOSLOVAKIA

FRANCE

AUSTRIA

ITALY

Friends and enemies

■ Allies:
Britain and its empire, France and Poland, were joined, in December 1941, by the United States.

■ Axis Powers:
Germany, Italy and Japan

■ Areas under Axis control by summer 1940

■ Neutral countries
The Soviet Union announced its neutrality before the war and agreed not to attack Germany in return for a share of land in Poland. Later, Hitler attacked the Soviets, who then joined the Allies.

ʃ Maginot Line
The French built this line of fortified trenches along the German border to prevent an invasion. The plan failed when Hitler's tanks simply stormed around it.

Warrior Winston

As *Blitzkrieg* blazed across France, many people wondered if the war was lost already. Chamberlain was blamed for the crisis and was forced to resign, opening the way for the old soldier and statesman, Winston Churchill, to become Prime Minister on May 10, 1940.

In a typically defiant pose, Winston Churchill inspects a Thompson submachine gun, or 'Tommy' gun, during a tour of England's northeastern coast, August, 1940.

No surrender

Churchill was already in his mid-sixties when he became Prime Minister, and he had had his share of adventures. He came from an aristocratic family, inheriting an upper-class lifestyle, but without the money to go with it. Before going into politics, he'd served in the army, supporting himself mainly by writing war reports. He was involved in the Anglo-Boer War, and the First World War, and witnessed battles across four continents. Gruff and tough, Churchill brushed aside any talk of making peace with Germany. In an astonishing speech to the House of Commons, he promised to lead the country in a fight to the death, rather than surrender.

"You ask, what is our aim? I can answer in one word: it is victory... for without victory, there is no survival... no survival for the British Empire, no survival for all that the British Empire has stood for..."

Winston Churchill, May 13, 1940

400

ALL BEHIND YOU, WINSTON

This picture was drawn by the cartoonist David Low, the week Churchill became Prime Minister. It shows him as a man of action who has inspired the support of the entire nation.

Tough talk

For years, Churchill had been warning of the dangers posed by Hitler and his Nazi political party – and now that German tanks were pushing the army back towards the English Channel, the dangers seemed all too real. In a speech on becoming Prime Minister, he laid out what people could expect in the coming months: "I have nothing to offer but blood, toil, tears and sweat. We have before us an ordeal of the most grievous kind."

But despite this gloomy prediction, Churchill was confident of final victory. He believed the Royal Navy could defend his island nation from attack and was convinced that America and Russia would eventually join the fight against Hitler.

In a series of electrifying speeches, Churchill won over the British public with his boldness and defiance, bracing them for the greatest struggle of their lives.

About Churchill

Flamboyant and daring, Churchill was a charismatic and inspiring politician.

He often wore a 'siren suit' during the war. This was an all-in-one, designed to be put on quickly – sometimes over pyjamas – during air raids. Although it was a very practical garment, he also had one made from red velvet.

His favourite drinks were very old brandy and cold champagne, on which he is said to have quoted Napoleon: "In defeat I need it, in victory I deserve it."

He was prone to bouts of depression, which he called Black Dog.

A talented painter and writer, in 1953 Churchill won the Nobel Prize for Literature for his historical writings.

A miracle at Dunkirk

On May 24, 1940, the British army and thousands of their French and Belgian allies were trapped at Dunkirk, facing capture or annihilation. Hitler sent the German airforce, the *Luftwaffe*, to destroy the crowded port. In response, Churchill ordered an emergency evacuation, codenamed Operation Dynamo. He expected the Royal Navy to bring back only one tenth of his army. But, against all odds, the Dunkirk rescue turned into a breathtaking triumph.

Up to their necks in water, these British soldiers are wading out from the beach at Dunkirk to reach a waiting rescue ship.

Hot water

British, French and Belgian troops were still streaming into Dunkirk when the rescue began. They were greeted by a shocking vision of tens of thousands of men scattered across the beaches, waiting to be rescued.

Thick smoke from the burning city gave them some protection from German planes, but the sea was still full of wrecked ships and drowned soldiers. The water by the beach was too shallow for big ships to sail close to the shore, so the men had to wait in line to reach a long pier. Others waded out to waiting rescue ships, or rowed out on small boats. Shells and bullets exploded around them, and they risked being attacked by Stukas as they moved slowly out to sea.

The little ships

To speed things up, the Royal Navy needed a huge number of smaller ships to collect soldiers directly from the beach. Over 700 river boats, pleasure cruisers and fishing boats made the journey across the English Channel. Most were crewed by navy sailors, but some civilian boat owners came along as volunteers. They risked their lives, picking men out of the waves and ferrying them to larger ships.

These are just a few of the 'little ships' that took part in the Dunkirk evacuation.

Fight another day

In nine days, the Royal Navy's rescue fleet carried almost 340,000 soldiers to safety. German generals were furious that an enemy army had slipped through their fingers, while in Britain people celebrated the return of their husbands, sons and friends. Every fighting man would be needed, if Hitler gave the order to invade.

"Wars are not won by evacuations."

Winston Churchill warns people that the war is not over yet.

Enemy occupation

Churchill's army had escaped, but the Germans still managed to snatch a piece of Britain. Just weeks after the evacuation of Dunkirk, German troops occupied the Channel Islands.

Churchill had already evacuated thousands of islanders, having decided that the islands couldn't be defended without heavy loss of life. Those who stayed behind now had to adjust to life under the Nazis.

Islanders were issued with identity cards and German money.

Their radios were seized, but some hid them and continued to listen to the BBC in secret.

The Germans fortified Jersey and Guernsey with gun emplacements and lookout posts that still stare out to sea today.

The Battle of Britain

Just three weeks after Dunkirk, France surrendered and Hitler's conquering army began drawing up plans to invade England. Protected by its moat of stormy sea and the mighty Royal Navy, the British Isles had fought off invaders for almost 900 years. But, if the Germans won control of the skies, they could bomb the British out of the water, clearing the way for their landing craft. Through a blazing hot summer, Britain's fighter pilots struggled desperately to save their country.

On July 10, 1940, the 'Battle of Britain' started, with *Luftwaffe* bombers attacking ships and airbases along the southern coast of England. Their plan was simple: to lure Britain's RAF – Royal Air Force – fighter planes into the sky and shoot them down. They thought the RAF could be destroyed within a week.

These are replicas of British fighter planes from the Second World War. The Spitfire was a dazzling aircraft and pilots fell in love with it. It had a top speed of around 580kmph (360mph) and was amazingly agile in the sky.

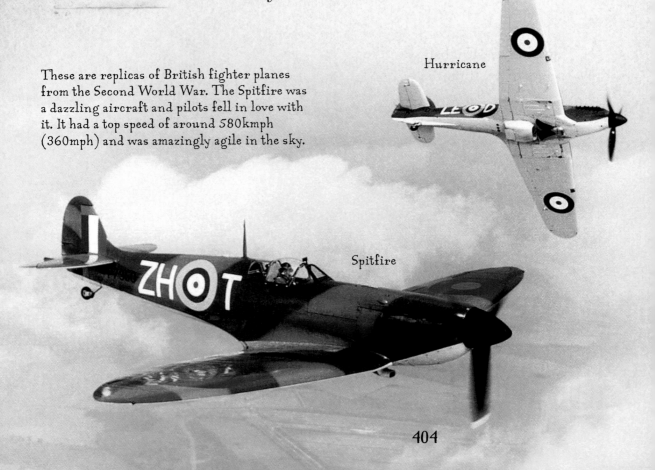

Hurricane

Spitfire

404

This Messerschmitt Me 109 was the *Luftwaffe's* principal fighter plane during the Battle of Britain.

Tracking the enemy

The *Luftwaffe* had over 2,000 planes and skilled pilots to fly them, but they had underestimated the RAF. In the build-up to war, RAF scientists had built a network of radar stations to guard their coast. Using powerful radio signals, radar equipment spotted and tracked any planes crossing the English Channel. This helped RAF commanders to position their fighters carefully and block enemy raids.

Home ground

British Hurricane and Spitfire fighter planes could hold their own against German aircraft and, because they were flying over home turf, RAF pilots could quickly land to refuel and re-arm their machines. If they were attacked and had to parachute to safety, they came down among friends and might be flying another plane within hours.

But the RAF's greatest strength had nothing to do with radar or flying machines – it was the fighting spirit of its airmen.

Off duty

Airmen from other Allied countries fought with the RAF. It was a multinational air force and some of its best flyers came from Poland and Czechoslovakia.

RAF pilots led something of a double-life during the battle. In the daytime they were out blasting at enemy planes and trying to stay alive. But at night, they came back to base and could pop into a local bar for a glass of beer and a game of darts.

Saving the palace

RAF pilot Ray Holmes became an overnight hero when he was involved in a dramatic fight above London.

Holmes spotted a German Dornier bomber heading for Buckingham Palace. He tried to shoot the plane down, but found he had run out of ammunition.

Determined to save the palace, he rammed the bomber, slicing through its tail and ripping its wings off.

The German plane crashed just outside Victoria train station.

Holmes jumped from his broken plane and made a parachute landing in someone's back yard.

Miraculously, no civilians were hurt, and Holmes was soon back in action.

A few good men

When the Battle of Britain began, the RAF had just over 600 fighter planes to defend the country against the *Luftwaffe*'s 2,000. The British pilots – who became known as 'The Few' – were often young, fresh out of school, and many had never flown into battle before. But they had good reasons to fight hard. While *Luftwaffe* pilots were just doing their job, RAF flyers were struggling to save their homes and families from destruction.

Spitfire summer

The Battle of Britain raged through a searing July and August, as *Luftwaffe* bombers pounded Britain's airports, radar stations and landing strips. Between sorties, RAF pilots lounged in the grass, trying to keep cool and rest until a siren or bell sent them sprinting to their planes again. They were only given minutes to take off and climb high into the clouds before intercepting the enemy raiders.

No mercy

People on the ground stopped to watch the clash in the skies, but they had no idea of the speed and ferocity of the fighting. Enemy planes passed in a dizzying blur, as pilots tried to fire short bursts at each other from machine guns set into the wings of their fighters. It was a savage and bloody contest, with little mercy shown on either side. Almost one in five of the 3,000 RAF airmen who took part in the Battle of Britain was killed in the struggle.

A first victory

But, by late September, the *Luftwaffe* accepted that their mission to crush the RAF had failed. Despite taking a terrible battering, the British pilots had always managed to keep fighting. It was Britain's first victory in the war, and it sent a message of hope around the country.

"Never, in the field of human conflict, was so much owed by so many to so few."

Churchill describes the sacrifice and bravery of the RAF's airmen.

This photograph of RAF pilots appeared on a poster produced to celebrate the achievements of the Air Force in the Battle of Britain.

Hell came to London

On September 7, 1940, a black cloud of almost 1,000 German warplanes attacked London. By nightfall, the docklands and some of the eastern districts were ablaze and the sky glowed red. At dawn, Londoners saw a great cloud of thick smoke looming over their city. Having failed to crush the RAF, the German Luftwaffe had changed tactics. They began pounding the British capital with high explosive bombs, trying to force Churchill and his government to beg for peace. Months of deadly night raids followed and people quickly named this new ordeal *the Blitz.*

Going underground

In areas that were under threat from air raids, people were given 'Anderson shelters' to build in their back yards.

Anderson shelters were designed to sleep six people. They were made from curved sheets of corrugated iron, half buried, with earth piled on top.

But many more people ended up taking refuge in public shelters, including ones in underground stations.

Taking shelter

After the first raid, thousands of civilians streamed out of the city, looking for safety in the countryside or with relatives in distant towns. But most stayed behind, reluctant to abandon their friends, families and jobs. The attacks began with sirens wailing across the rooftops to warn of raiders approaching. Wardens helped people into public shelters – brick and concrete huts that offered some protection from the bombs. But, as the planes circled overhead, everyone on the ground knew there was little chance of surviving a direct hit.

Desperate to escape the noise and danger of the raids, up to 177,000 Londoners took to sleeping on the platforms of the city's underground railway stations. As the Blitz continued, local councils organized beds, medical care, and even mobile libraries and entertainers, to make life more bearable in these subterranean shelters.

Business as usual

Despite all the dangers and disruption, most Londoners managed to get on with their lives. People went to work – walking, if necessary – along the shattered roads. Shops and restaurants stayed open, even when all their windows had been blown out. "More open than usual" was the cheeky sign left outside some blitzed shops.

The fighting spirit of London was never broken, something Churchill and the national newspapers were quick to point out. But in diaries and private conversations, many people confessed their worries. How long would the Blitz last, and how much more could London take?

St. Paul's Cathedral stands alone in an ocean of fire, in this photo taken from the rooftops at the height of an air raid on December 29, 1940.

Still ticking

Another threat came from unexploded bombs, known as UXBs. Some 10% of the German bombs were either faulty or had been set to explode after impact with the ground. Streets had to be closed while UXBs were made safe by army engineers.

It took engineers three days to disarm a 1000kg (2210lb) UXB lodged under St Paul's Cathedral. When they finally unearthed the monster, they had to load it onto a truck and drive through deserted streets to detonate it in open fields.

Protection

With no fighters to protect them at night, blitzed cities relied on spotlights to trace the skies for enemy bombers, and anti-aircraft, or 'ack-ack' guns, to shoot them down.

Barrage balloons floated on heavy steel cables. These cables were designed to snag any low-flying enemy aircraft. London had a protective canopy of over 400 balloons.

Later in the war, the RAF fitted radar sets to their fighter planes to track night bombers. Desperate to keep their invention a secret, they told journalists that British pilots ate lots of carrots, and this helped them to see in the dark.

The Coventry inferno

Although London bore the brunt of the Blitz, the shadow of German bombers fell across dozens of other British towns and cities. Ports and industrial zones were raided, from Edinburgh and Belfast to Portsmouth, and thousands of civilians living close to military targets were killed or maimed. But the air war took a new and horrific turn in November 1940, when the *Luftwaffe* raided Coventry and burned it to the ground.

Coventry was a major target because its factories were vital to the British war effort. But RAF fighters couldn't protect the city from a night attack. At this stage in the war, pilots still relied on their eyesight to find and intercept enemy planes. Flying at high altitudes and hiding in the dark, enemy bombers were almost impossible to spot.

Firestorm

The first wave of *Luftwaffe* raiders arrived directly over Coventry and dropped thousands of small incendiary bombs – metal tubes packed with burning chemicals. As the main force of 400 bombers approached their target, the Germans could see the city from 240km (150 miles) away, covered in giant flames.

High explosive bombs demolished buildings and spread burning materials across the city. The fires grew so hot they melted bricks and sucked the air out of underground shelters. Over 500 people were killed, cremated or buried alive in the firestorm.

The next morning, the 'All Clear' sirens sounded at last. The survivors clambered out of their air raid shelters into a smoking, hellish landscape of twisted steel and rubble. Even their stately cathedral had been reduced to a charred ruin.

Recovery and retaliation

Such was the extent of the destruction in the city, that a new term was coined: 'coventrated' – meaning flattened by bombing. But, amazingly, Coventry recovered from the attack. Although the *Luftwaffe* claimed the raid a success, many factories reopened within six weeks, and people built new homes. Later in the war, as a reprisal for Coventry and other cities blitzed in 1940 and 41, the RAF launched a series of devastating air raids on German towns and cities, killing a shocking estimated total of 650,000 civilians.

Peace beacon

In recent years, Coventry – with its new cathedral – has become a symbol for the suffering experienced by civilians in wartime. The city hosts an annual conference devoted to peace and understanding between nations.

Winston Churchill walks through the devastated ruins of Coventry Cathedral.

A pack of seven German U-boats sets out to sea to hunt down and destroy Allied convoys.

The Germans called the U-boat tactic of hunting merchant ships in large groups *Rudeltaktik*, or pack tactic, so these gangs of U-boats were nicknamed 'wolf packs'.

Posters, such as this one, warned people not to say anything in public that might give away the routes of convoy ships to German spies.

Beating the wolf packs

Britain's vast fleet of cargo ships was its lifeline to the outside world. The merchant navy supplied two thirds of the country's food and brought precious guns, fuel and steel from America. But German submarines, or U-boats, lurked in the wastes of the sea, sinking hundreds of ships with their torpedoes. The British had to keep the ocean highways open, or they would quickly lose the war.

Sea hunters

The Royal Navy had beaten the U-boats in the First World War by using the "convoy" system. Cargo ships crossed the Atlantic Ocean in large groups, or convoys, protected by armed merchant ships. Royal Navy warships only joined them when they entered the dangerous waters close to home. But in 1940, from their new bases in occupied France, U-boats could hunt deep in the heart of the Atlantic, for convoys that had no warship escorts.

After spotting a convoy, U-boat captains tracked it for days, sending radio messages to other submarines. They waited until a 'wolf pack' of six or more U-boats assembled, before surfacing and attacking under cover of darkness. Raids could stretch over several nights and some convoys lost as many as half of their ships.

The longest battle

The Battle of the Atlantic, as Churchill named it, turned into a desperate struggle which lasted until the end of the war – although the worst was over by May 1943. Although merchant sailors were civilians, they took the same risks as soldiers. Around 30,000 of them died at sea, while the U-boats and Allied navies wrestled for control of the waves.

Search and destroy

Churchill understood that his first task was to protect the convoys. In September 1940, he signed an agreement with the United States, who gave him 50 old destroyer warships. The Royal Navy had also been busy building a new fleet of small escort vessels. Soon every convoy had a warship escort right across the Atlantic.

These new escorts were fitted with special weapons for detecting and destroying U-boats. Radar picked them up on the surface, and sonar equipment used sound waves to locate them underwater. Destroyers and other vessels chased after any U-boats, attacking them with drums of explosives called depth charges.

Britain was fighting back, but the Battle of the Atlantic was far from over. It intensified in 1941, when the Germans sent their most powerful warship, *Bismarck*, to help their U-boats smash the convoys.

Chasing echoes

Sonar was used to hunt submarines. It works in a similar way to radar, except it uses sound instead of radio waves.

The submarine hunter sends out pulses of sound, in a cone shape, under the water.

When sound bounces off the submarine, the hunter hears an echo in his headphones. He follows the echo to locate the submarine.

As the hunter passes over the submarine, it attacks, dropping depth charges.

Home Front fighters

Bombed in their cities and under siege at sea, the British people quickly adapted to life in a war zone. Getting about, shopping and working became a daily struggle, and old habits and attitudes had to change. As men were drafted into the army, millions of women took up new jobs to keep the country fighting.

Tightening the belt

To make the best use of Britain's food supplies, the government brought in rationing in January 1940. Everyone received a ration book that listed how much sugar, bacon and butter they were allowed to buy each week. Shopkeepers had to check and stamp these books before selling any goods.

Even with rationing in force there were shortages. Shoppers had to wait in long lines outside each store, hoping the shelves wouldn't be empty when they got inside. Not everyone played by the rules. Small time crooks, known as spivs, supplied luxuries like chocolate and silk stockings to anyone who could afford them.

A ration book contained coupons to be exchanged for rations. One person's rations for a week were:

· A few slices of bacon or ham and one portion of other meat

· A tub of butter, a small piece of cheese, one egg and two or three pints of milk

Making do

By 1943 most foods were either rationed or difficult to find in the shops, and fuel, paper, soap and clothing had been added to the list. But, despite the shortages, people found ways of 'making do' with what they had.

The government issued recipe books to help people to make the most of their rations. These included cake mixtures made with powdered eggs...

...and fudge made with carrots.

People were urged to repair and recycle their old clothes.

With nylon stockings in short supply, some girls painted fake seams onto their legs.

414

The stronger sex

Many women had little time for food shopping. They were just too busy working long shifts in Britain's growing armaments industry. At the height of the war, a third of all factory workers were female. Young mothers helped build planes and tanks, as other women set up nurseries to care for their children. Every woman aged between 18 and 50 was 'called up' for some kind of war service. Thousands worked as wardens, ambulance drivers and fire spotters. Others joined the armed forces, where they were expected to do everything a man would do, except go into combat.

On the farm

Even in the quiet of the countryside, the old way of life was changing. By 1944, tens of thousands of women toiled in the fields as part of the Women's Land Army, helping farmers plant and harvest their crops. They were known as 'Land Girls' – although many of them had never been out of the city before.

Grow your own

To supplement food rations, the Ministry of Food launched a 'Dig For Victory' campaign, to get people gardening.

Parks, tennis courts and flowerbeds were dug up and planted over with vegetables, as everyone tried to grow extra food for the table.

The government also encouraged clubs of friends or co-workers to keep pigs and chickens.

By the end of the war, Britain had halved the amount of food it imported by sea.

These Land Girls are making hay while the sun shines.

The Home Guard

Lots of British men were too young or too old to serve in the regular forces, but they still wanted to fight if there was an invasion. In May 1940, the government asked for male volunteers to join a new defence force. Over a million signed up – from teenage boys to retired generals. This became known as the Home Guard.

But the British army was struggling to rearm itself after Dunkirk and there were no spare weapons for Home Guard units. So volunteers carried pitchforks, old shotguns and swords until they received better equipment. Almost half the men were veteran fighters from the First World War and what they lacked in equipment they made up for in enthusiasm. They were a reassuring sight for the public, patrolling the countryside and capturing crashed German airmen.

This teenage Home Guard volunteer is being trained to use a 'Tommy' gun.

These Bevin Boys are on their way to work down the coal mines in Pontefract, Yorkshire.

In the pits

Call-up papers arrived in the post, ordering men to report to their local barracks for training. But some young recruits were handed a shovel instead of a gun – and sent to dig coal in Britain's mines. Too many coal miners had enlisted and the Minister of Labour, Ernest Bevin, needed almost 50,000 extra men to strengthen the workforce. Many of these new recruits, who became known as Bevin Boys, were shocked by the miner's hard, dangerous life underground.

Coal was in short supply for years after the war, and some Bevin Boys weren't released from duty in the mines until 1948.

Mixing and mingling

Rationing, war work and the blackout made life a struggle on the Home Front, but most people pulled together and shared the hardships. As young men and women went into new jobs in new places, they had a chance to see how others lived. Some were surprised by the poverty and poor living conditions they came across. In the grip of war, Britain was discovering itself, and learning lessons for the future.

Even members of the Royal Family had to 'do their bit' – Princess Elizabeth, the future Queen, trained as a mechanic.

Children in Liverpool station, waiting to be evacuated to the countryside

War kids

The war years were the best and worst of times for Britain's children. Of the millions evacuated to the country, some loved their new homes, while others were homesick and miserable. In the cities, children lived in fear of air raids, but it was exciting to be in the thick of the action. Despite all its terrors and upheavals, growing up during the war was an incredible adventure.

Choose me

Children who were being evacuated usually went by train, leaving in small groups from their schools. Each child had a name label pinned to their clothes, and the lucky ones received a ration of chocolate for the journey. After arriving in country villages and towns, the evacuees met local people who had offered to take them in. Some children were herded together, while adults looked them up and down as though they were choosing a new pet. Waiting to be chosen was a heartbreaking experience for many evacuees.

Evacuees

People taking evacuees received cash from the government and could shop with their ration books. So some foster parents may have been more interested in the extra rations than in the children.

Some evacuees had never left their cities before and were amazed when they saw cows and sheep for the first time.

418

Hard times

Country people were often shocked to discover lice and other vermin living on their new guests. Lots of the evacuees came from slum areas in the cities, where poverty and housing conditions were far worse than they are today. Houses with bathrooms and running hot water were rare, and most city kids had only one good clean a week – in council wash houses or public baths.

Sandbag scholars

Even in the worst days of the Blitz there was no escape from school. When the air raid sirens began to howl, children rushed to public shelters or to schoolrooms that had been strengthened with sandbags and steel girders. Pupils who lived nearby and had an Anderson shelter in the garden were allowed to run home.

Dangerous games

Air raids provided the material for a new kind of treasure hunting – collecting shrapnel. Children scoured bomb sites for bits of twisted steel from exploded bombs, and then traded them in the playground.

Aircraft spotting was another pastime, and city kids soon learned how to identify enemy planes from the noise of their engines.

Later in the war, American soldiers arrived with exciting treats – chewing gum, chocolate and comics.

Playing in the rubble of their bombed city street, these boys have rigged up a makeshift swing from a broken lamp post.

The secret war

While Britain's armed forces licked their wounds after Dunkirk, Churchill assembled a secret army of spies, scientists and elite soldiers. His special agents and intelligence experts launched raids into occupied Europe and helped make one of the most important breakthroughs of the war – cracking the top-secret code that the Germans used to send their radio messages.

Special forces

Churchill told his commanders he wanted to "set Europe ablaze" with sudden attacks and sabotage missions. The army asked its best soldiers to volunteer for a new fighting unit to carry out these raids, known as the Commandos. Volunteers had to undergo a gruelling training course in special combat skills, deep in the forests of the Scottish Highlands.

Commando troops learned how to use small boats and parachute drops to strike into enemy territory. Their missions were secret – and often fatal – as German soldiers had orders to shoot any commandos they captured.

X-men

Despite the dangers, there were still lots of volunteers, including hundreds of Jewish refugees from Nazi-occupied Europe. Some of these men were wanted by the German secret police, the *Gestapo*, and their unit was so secret, it was known only as X-troop.

This photograph shows a commando abseiling down a sheer cliff, during a training exercise.

Commando training also included long hikes through snow and rain, after which commandos had to drag themselves over a forest assault course of rope swings, ditches and high fences, while grenades and machine guns went off all around them.

420

Double-dealings

Britain used its spies inside Europe to watch German troop movements and smuggle crashed Allied airmen back to safety. Other agents pretended to be working for the enemy, but passed them false information. These 'double agents' wasted the German's time and resources, and tricked them about the true locations of planned operations.

The British army didn't send women into combat, but Churchill decided that an exception should be made with its special agents. Dozens of women parachuted into occupied France to help local Resistance groups fighting the Germans. It was dangerous work: many agents of both sexes were caught by the *Gestapo* and murdered or sent to prison camps.

Cracking the code

The war's most amazing spying success took place far from any battlefield, in a quiet country house in southern England. A group of British and Allied scientists, maths experts and spies had gathered at Bletchley Park, to make sense of the German military's radio messages. The Germans had devised a typewriter-sized machine called Enigma to scramble their messages into an unreadable code.

Building on the work already done by Polish mathematicians, the Bletchley Park team began to unpick Enigma. They built a machine that could quickly run through millions of calculations – an early version of a computer – and by 1940 they were decoding the German messages. The Enigma triumph saved thousands of lives and helped the Allies win the war.

Spy gadgets

Agents needed special equipment for missions into enemy territory. They carried forged identity papers, portable radios and explosives.

British scientists made fake logs, hollowed out to hide weapons in. They designed special toothpaste tubes for sneaking in coded messages and they even developed a 'dead rat' bomb!

An Enigma machine

Hunting Bismarck

Big guns

Bismarck's guns fired shells as big as a man, weighing as much as a car. They had a long range, too. The shell that sank the *Hood* was fired at a distance of 14.5km (9 miles) away.

This photograph shows the German battleship *Bismarck* in 1941, shortly before the ship was sent into combat.

Towering over the waves, warships displayed the raw power of fighting nations. The massive HMS *Hood* was a floating fortress and the pride of the British fleet. When Germany's fearsome battleship, *Bismarck*, set out to raid the Atlantic convoys, the Royal Navy sent a task force led by *Hood* to stop her.

Launched in 1918, *Hood* was old for a warship, but still packed a deadly punch with eight huge guns. The ship was longer than two soccer pitches, and was famed and feared around the world. But *Hood* had a fatal flaw: the steel plates protecting her decks were vulnerable to shells falling from above. In contrast, *Bismarck* was a state-of-the-art killing machine, with better gun accuracy and defensive protection. Even so, most British sailors thought *Hood* was unbeatable.

Bismarck and a smaller warship, *Prinz Eugen*, tried to sneak into the Atlantic Ocean through the Denmark Straits – the channel between Greenland and Iceland. But, early in the morning of May 24, 1941, *Hood* and another Royal Navy battleship, HMS *Prince of Wales* intercepted them. The British fired first, heading towards the enemy at top speed.

An unlucky shot

Only minutes later, a plunging shell from *Bismarck* smashed through *Hood's* deck and exploded inside the magazine, where all the ship's munitions are stored. Sailors on the *Prince of Wales* stared in horror, as *Hood* was torn apart by a huge blast. The Royal Navy's strongest ship lurched into the air and vanished below the sea. *Hood* sank so quickly, that only three of the 1,418 crew survived.

Alone, outgunned and badly damaged, the *Prince of Wales* broke off the attack, granting victory to the Germans. The battle shocked the Allies, and was a triumph for Hitler. But celebrations on board the *Bismarck* were short-lived. A British shell had flooded the ship's fuel tanks, and her captain decided to run for a safe port in France to make repairs. He never made it.

Out for revenge

Desperate to avenge the loss of *Hood*, the Royal Navy sent every ship it could muster to chase the *Bismarck*. An attack by Swordfish planes dropping torpedoes struck the first blow, wrecking the German battleship's rudder. Unable to steer, the *Bismarck* wheeled around in a huge circle, while British warships closed in for the kill. After two hours of heavy shelling and torpedo attacks, *Bismarck* joined *Hood* on the bottom of the sea.

Lumbering through the air with its heavy torpedo attached underneath, the Fairey Swordfish was comical to look at. But these planes could sink ships and became essential to the war at sea.

Fight to the last

Under British fire, a German admiral on the *Bismarck* knew he was beaten, but sent a message saying, "Ship incapable of manoeuvring. Will fight to the last shell. Long live the Fuhrer!"

It is said that he stood, saluting, on the deck of the ship as it went down.

New players

The dramatic events of 1941 brought two very different world leaders to stand alongside Winston Churchill.

Stalin had taken power in Russia in 1927, after assassinating his political rivals. His secret police imprisoned and murdered anyone who criticized him.

Roosevelt was re-elected US President on the promise that he would keep America out of the war, but he had been supplying Britain with weapons and ships since 1940.

New allies, new enemies

By May 1941, the Blitz was over. German bombs had killed more than 40,000 civilians and pulverized towns, factories and homes, but Britain was still unbeaten. For almost a year, the country had been under siege and fighting alone. Now the war was spreading, and the most powerful nations on earth would be forced to take sides.

Uncle Joe

The *Luftwaffe* broke off their attacks on Britain to support a new invasion – into the Soviet Union. For years, Hitler had dreamed of capturing its fertile lands and oil fields. In June he unleashed an army of three million men to bring the country to its knees. Many of these soldiers never came home.

Hitler was a ruthless tyrant with a passion for war, but he had met his match in Stalin. A cunning, brutal man, Stalin expected his soldiers to fight to the death. Over the coming years, 24 million Russians (military and civilians) died, as Stalin steadily annihilated Hitler's army. Although Churchill was deeply suspicious of Stalin and his intentions in Europe, he welcomed him as a vital ally.

A day of terror

Many Americans wanted no part in the war. But, on December 7, 1941, a new enemy stunned the United States with a sneak attack on American battleships in the Pacific. Japan had entered the war.

Like Germany, Japan was hungry for new territories and the two countries were already political allies. But Japanese naval commanders feared the power of the American fleet moored at Pearl Harbor, Hawaii. In a dawn attack, hundreds of Japanese dive bombers and torpedo planes mauled the US fleet, sinking several battleships and killing more than 2,000 sailors.

The Americans were outraged, and US congress declared war on Japan the following day. But even as the British celebrated gaining a strong new ally, Japanese troops were storming Britain's colonies in the Far East.

Posters like this one persuaded thousands of American men to join the armed forces to defend their nation.

A US warship explodes during the Japanese raid on Pearl Harbor, December 7, 1941. US President Roosevelt described it as "a date which will live in infamy."

Japanese troops march in to occupy the British colonial city of Singapore.

Disaster in the East

The military base at Singapore was a cornerstone of the British empire, standing guard over Britain's territories across South East Asia. With almost 100,000 troops and two large warships at his disposal, the base commander, General Percival, thought he could smash any enemy attack. But he was soon proved wrong.

Gunboat diplomacy

Japan had been at war with China since 1937, and desperately needed the rich reserves of rubber, metals and oil found in Britain's eastern colonies and the Dutch East Indies. Within hours of the Pearl Harbor raid on Decmber 7, 1941, Japanese troops landed in Malaya, 800km (500 miles) north of Singapore. The British sent their two warships to intercept the enemy's fleet. But the Japanese, using dive bombers and torpedo planes, sank both British ships on December 10.

South East Asia

The red shading on this map shows areas under Japanese occupation by 1942.

CHINA

BURMA

Hong Kong

THAILAND

FRENCH INDOCHINA

MALAYA

Singapore

BORNEO

SUMATRA

DUTCH EAST INDIES

Singapore falls

Many British officers thought their men – including troops from New Zealand, Australia, and India – were fitter and braver than their attackers. But Japan's soldiers were battle-hard after years of savage combat in China and fought their way down to Singapore by the end of January. On February 15, the British were forced to surrender the base. It was a humiliating defeat. Churchill's forces were broken in the East, and countries as far away as India, New Zealand and Australia were now under threat of invasion.

A green hell

After the surrender, Percival and over 80,000 of his men became POWs – prisoners of war – and many were sent to camps in the jungle. The Japanese treatment of their prisoners was one of the worst atrocities of the war. POWs were beaten, starved and worked to death building roads and train lines for their captors. Their ordeal would last until the war ended, three long years later.

This is a sketch by Ronald Searle, a British artist who was a Japanese POW.

It shows emaciated prisoners cutting into a mountain with hammers and chisels, and hauling rocks to make way for a new train line from Thailand to Burma.

Bicycle blitzkrieg

Many of Japan's soldiers advanced through Malaya using bicycles to speed their progress along narrow jungle tracks.

The savagery of the Japanese soldiers horrified the British. Thousands of local civilians, especially those of Chinese origin, were murdered.

As well as the military prisoners, the Japanese rounded up and imprisoned some 130,000 Allied civilians who had been living in the region.

'The Full Monty'

Montgomery liked to stand out from the crowd. He always wore his trademark black beret for photographers. More at ease in the company of ordinary soldiers than generals, his men adored him.

 Some people think the term 'the Full Monty' came from Monty's habit of always eating huge, cooked breakfasts with all the trimmings – even in the desert.

Duel in the desert

Some of Britain's earliest, and most spectacular victories of the Second World War were won in the deserts of North Africa. The stakes were high. Churchill's army in Egypt had to protect the Suez Canal and the oilfields in Iraq and Iran that powered Britain's tanks and factories. After a series of breathtaking tank battles, the British commander, Bernard Montgomery, emerged as a national hero.

The fox arrives

The British had been fighting in the desert since 1940, when they had smashed the Italian forces in Libya. Italy was Hitler's major ally – alongside Japan – among the Axis Powers. Hitler sent a daredevil tank commander, Erwin Rommel, to help the Italians. A brilliant and cunning general, Rommel soon earned himself the nickname, the Desert Fox. His *Afrika Korps* soldiers quickly outfought and outflanked the British army, pushing it back into Egypt.

A British tank raises clouds of dust and sand as the Allies storm through the desert during the Battle of El Alamein.

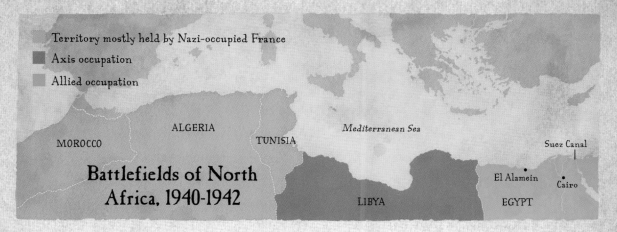

Territory mostly held by Nazi-occupied France
Axis occupation
Allied occupation

ALGERIA

TUNISIA

Mediterranean Sea

MOROCCO

Suez Canal

Battlefields of North Africa, 1940-1942

El Alamein

Cairo

LIBYA

EGYPT

Under a burning sun

Allied soldiers rested in Cairo, drinking and socializing, before setting out into the pitiless heat of the desert battlefields. Water, food and ammunition were always in short supply, and sudden sandstorms could blow up, trapping men inside their vehicles for days.

By July 1942, Rommel's men were within striking distance of Cairo. The British dug in at the coastal town of El Alamein, blocking the approaches to Cairo with trenches and minefields. In August, a new commander took charge – Montgomery, or "Monty" as soldiers called him. Monty had studied Rommel's tactics and secretly stockpiled huge numbers of guns and vehicles. In October he pierced Rommel's line, using air strikes and artillery to clear the way for his tanks.

Monty's triumph

Rommel's army scrambled back to Libya, losing thousands of men, tanks and trucks. Monty had beaten one of Germany's best generals and became a celebrity across the Allied nations. The Axis troops in North Africa surrendered in May 1943, and the Desert Fox slipped away to Germany. Only a year later, he would face Monty in the battlefields of Normandy.

Time out

At rest in Cairo, Allied soldiers had a chance to see the pyramids or catch a movie. There were also shows by entertainers, such as George Formby, who went out to keep up the morale of the troops.

Lots of soldiers who fought in the desert described it as a gentlemanly war. In some battles, soldiers arranged an afternoon truce, so that the British could 'brew-up' – make tea – and let the Germans drink coffee.

Boffins and bouncing bombs

Barnes Wallis (on the left) and four British officials watch as his bouncing bomb – codenamed 'Upkeep' – bounces along the water during a trial run.

Britain's scientists and designers were world class and they worked feverishly to develop winning tools for the armed forces. Their radar and code-breaking computer were dazzling achievements, but perhaps the most ingenious British invention of the war was a bomb that could bounce across water.

'Boffin' was a cheeky term for the brilliant – but absent-minded – scientists who assisted the British military.

A boffin known only as 'Q' features in the James Bond stories by Ian Fleming. The writer had served with the Royal Naval Intelligence Division services during the war.

Thirsty work

Some of Hitler's most important weapons factories were located in the Ruhr region of Germany. These factories relied on several, massive dams in the area for power and water. RAF commanders wanted to blast the dams and wreck the factories, but bombs dropped from above didn't have enough explosive power to break the thick dam walls. The Germans had even hung underwater nets across the reservoirs to stop torpedo plane attacks.

It was a British aircraft designer, Barnes Wallis, who came up with the breathtaking solution for blowing up the dams. Wallis believed that an underwater bomb, placed next to the dam wall, would have enough power to breach it.

Marbles

Instead of dropping the bomb from above, Wallis suggested *bouncing* it across the reservoir like a spinning stone. The bomb would hit the dam and sink, hugging the wall before exploding. The RAF thought Wallis was crazy.

But instead of giving up, Wallis decided to prove that his idea was possible. With the help of his children, he conducted experiments with a bucket of water, some marbles and a catapult. These tests helped Wallis to calculate the exact height and speed of the bombing attack. He then persuaded the RAF to build a dummy bomb and drop it from one of their planes. The bomb bounced, and the RAF began planning a raid.

Not all wartime science was destructive. In 1944, Allied chemists helped to save the lives of thousands of soldiers and civilians by developing a new infection-killing drug – penicillin.

The Dambusters

In May 1943, 19 Lancaster bombers flew deep into Germany. Their bouncing bombs destroyed two dams, flooding miles of open country and disrupting the work going on in the Hitler's factories. The raid was a success, but it came at a terrible price. Wallis wept when he learned that eight of the bomber crews – who became known as the 'Dambusters' – had been killed or shot down during the attack.

Water floods through the breach in the Mohne Dam, four hours after the Dambusters' raid in May 1943.

431

The road to Rome

American commanders had always believed that the quickest way to defeat Hitler was to strike at him through France. After victory in North Africa, they wanted to invade as soon as possible, but Churchill persuaded Roosevelt that the Allies should first attack the weak underbelly of the Axis – in Italy.

Major Martin

The island of Sicily was only a short sea crossing from Allied bases in Tunisia. From Sicily, Allied soldiers could stream into southern Italy and capture Rome. Italian and German troops were expecting an attack. But British secret agents came up with an amazing bluff to put them off their guard.

In April 1943, German spies got hold of the body of a British man, Major Martin, found floating at sea. With him were plans for an invasion of Greece and Sardinia. Hitler moved guns and troops to these locations, instead of Sicily. But the mystery major was a decoy and the plans were fakes.

Snail's pace

This German poster pokes fun at the slow progress the Allies made from Sicily, at the southern tip of Italy, to Rome.

Italy is a narrow, mountainous country, which made it easy to defend, but difficult for the Allies to attack.

The sinking ship

In July, Allied troops made a landing on Sicily. With enemy troops inside his country's borders, the Italian king decided it was foolish to support Hitler. So he sacked Mussolini and surrendered to the Allies. Hitler sent paratroopers to rescue his old friend, but by then, Mussolini was a broken man. Germany's main ally in Europe was out of the war.

Bomb proof

Allied troops celebrated when they heard that the Italians had put down their weapons, but the fighting in Italy dragged on. By the spring of 1944, they were locked in a ferocious struggle with German defenders south of Rome. The Germans occupied a mountain monastery – Monte Cassino – which blocked the Allied advance. Even after a massive bombing raid, the monastery's foundations stood firm. It took the Allies four months of vicious fighting to capture this cliff top fortress. But on June 4, they finally reached Rome and freed the city from the Germans.

Sunny Italy

The Italian campaign never received the same newspaper attention as the invasion of France (D-Day) and many British soldiers thought they were mocked at home for taking a holiday in sunny Italy.

We're the D-Day Dodgers, way out in Italy, Always on the vino, always on the spree...

Veterans of Monte Cassino made up this song after a joke went around that they were D-Day Dodgers.

After heavy fighting in the mountains, these are the shattered remains of the grand, historic monastery at Monte Cassino.

This is a poster for a 1942 movie, written by and starring Noël Coward. The movie told the heroic story of a ship's crew that took part in the Dunkirk evacuation. It was a big hit, and won an Academy Award.

In this photograph, British sailors are crowded on the deck of HMS *Nelson* to watch Phyllis Stanley perform.

Tonic for the troops

The war was a strange and unsettling experience for millions of Allied soldiers, scattered around the globe. Most of them had never been away from their friends and families before, and when they weren't fighting they suffered from boredom and homesickness. A visit from a movie star or famous singer was a welcome relief from the terrors of war.

Home entertainment

Soldiers decorated their quarters with postcards or pin-up photographs of movie starlets taken from magazines. There were no televisions, but the troops had radios and movie projectors and could watch news bulletins and cartoons. British units formed their own concert parties made up of any singers, comedians and musicians from among their ranks. They staged shows and sketches and many of them, like Peter Sellers and Spike Milligan, went on to become stars after the war.

Forces' Sweetheart Vera Lynn receives a grand welcome from some of her sailor fans as she arrives to put on a show for British troops.

In addition to her concert performances, Vera Lynn also had her own radio show in which she sang and read out messages from those separated by the conflict.

Sweethearts and swingers

Visiting starlets were more popular than amateur entertainers. Probably the most popular was a British singer, Vera Lynn, known as the Forces' Sweetheart. She performed concerts for Allied troops across Egypt, India and Burma. Lynn wanted British soldiers to know that the people at home had not forgotten them. Her 1939 song, 'We'll Meet Again' became an anthem for troops and civilians all around the world.

American troops introduced their own brand of entertainment to the Brits. Among the most popular American performers were a cheeky British-born comedian named Bob Hope, and Major Glenn Miller, a musician. Miller had joined the US forces in 1942, to set up a touring band playing swing jazz. In 1944, he brought his band to England to play for the thousands of American soldiers in training there.

But, entertaining in a war zone could be a dangerous business. In December 1944, Miller's plane disappeared without a trace during a flight to Paris.

Wartime anthems

Here are some of the most popular songs of the war:

'(There'll be Bluebirds Over) The White Cliffs of Dover' was one of Vera Lynn's best-loved recordings.

'We'll Meet Again' gave its name to a movie made in 1942 starring Vera Lynn.

'Boogie Woogie Bugle Boy' was a massive hit for the Andrews Sisters.

'Lili Marleen' was a German love song that became popular with troops on both sides.

'Run Rabbit Run' featured in Noël Coward's movie 'In Which We Serve'.

A day to remember

On June 6, 1944, British and Allied forces launched the largest sea invasion the world had ever seen. Against all odds, they landed an army on the beaches of Normandy, France and began a long and bloody advance on Germany that would end the war.

Swimming tanks

Allied engineers developed a number of unusual tanks to take part in Operation Overlord. These tanks were known as 'funnies' by the troops.

The 'Crocodile' carried a powerful flamethrower.

The 'Crab' cleared minefields by lashing at the ground with long chains.

One of the strangest innovations was the floating tank. The British fixed waterproof screens to Sherman tanks, to hold them up in the water. In calm seas, the tanks could swim to shore and clear a path for Allied soldiers.

Breaking the wall

The Germans were expecting the Allies and had been busy fortifying the European coast from Norway to Spain with minefields, machine gun posts and concrete watchtowers. Hitler called this defensive line his Atlantic Wall and gave Field Marshal Rommel the job of holding it against all attacks. Rommel was a bold commander, and promised Hitler that his tanks would push any invading army back into the sea.

Operation Overlord

The Atlantic Wall was a tough nut to crack, but the Allies were desperate to open a new battlefront in France. This was the most direct route into Germany, and for months Stalin had been demanding that Allied troops take the pressure off his exhausted army, fighting in the East. Using the codename *Overlord*, British and American officers began planning a massive military strike into occupied France.

This is a photograph of the Sherman floating tank. In the water, the screen around the tank was raised to make it float and propellers at the rear drove it forward.

Normandy landings

This map shows the five beaches – each given a codename – where the Allies planned to land their troops.

Utah (USA)

Omaha (USA)

Gold (UK)

Normandy

Juno (Canada)

Sword (UK)

FRANCE

ENGLAND

Calais

FRANCE

Landing places

While they prepared for the attack, the Allies assembled a fake invasion force on the English coast across from Calais. This convinced Rommel that they were heading there instead.

Most troops would get to Normandy by sea, on flat-bottomed landing craft, but others would arrive by parachute or glider.

Plan of attack

Overlord called for an armada of ships to carry more than one million fighting men – and all their equipment – across the English Channel to Normandy. Arriving at dawn, Allied warships would pound the coast with massive shells, while a fleet of small landing craft ferried the troops to shore. Crack soldiers and special tanks would smash through any German opposition, pushing miles inland before stopping for the night.

There were no safe ports in Normandy – so the Allies built their own floating concrete docks, called Mulberries. These would be towed across the English Channel to receive supplies.

Storm warning

America's General Dwight Eisenhower was the Allies' overall commander of the operation, with Montgomery in charge of the ground troops. Both agreed that June 5 was the best date for D-Day – the day of the attack – because of good weather and tide forecasts. But, on the evening of June 4, a storm was brewing. Thousands of men had already boarded their ships, weighed down with weapons and supplies. They waited in port until a British weather expert predicted clear skies for the morning of June 6 and Eisenhower gave the order to go.

Red devils

The Germans called British paratroopers 'Red devils' – in a tribute to their courage and the maroon beret they wore into battle.

On the beaches

The first Allied soldiers to land in France were British and American paratroopers, with orders to capture vital bridges and roads ahead of the main attack. Although some paratroopers dropped miles from their targets, they soon spread panic and confusion among the German defenders.

The beach landings began just after dawn. Hundreds of Allied troops drowned in the surf, or were machine-gunned as they struggled on the sand. The most savage fighting was at Omaha Beach, where the Americans landed. At one stage it looked as though the attackers might be beaten back, but the Americans rallied and broke through the German lines. By nightfall, all five beaches were under Allied control.

British commandos rush off their flat-bottomed landing craft onto the beach at Normandy on D-Day.

A new front

Despite the hard fighting, D-Day ended in a total victory for the Allies. By the end of June, they had landed 850,000 men and 150,000 vehicles. Allied planes ruled the skies over Normandy, their bombers blasting German tanks and trucks with rockets, miles behind enemy lines. British commandos and paratroopers had fought deep into German occupied territory, and all Rommel's efforts to counter-attack with his elite tank divisions were defeated.

Since 1940, Churchill had supported the French General Charles de Gaulle in building French forces outside France. Known as the Free French, they played a key role in driving out the Germans from France. Fighting was tough, but by the end of August, the Allies had liberated Paris and begun their long march to Berlin.

Bravery beyond the call of duty

It was the courage of ordinary soldiers, like Stanley Hollis, that gave the Allies victory on D-Day. Arriving on Gold beach, Hollis rushed two enemy machine guns and captured dozens of Germans.

Later in the day, he risked his life again when he rescued some friends under fire.

Hollis won the Victoria Cross – Britain's highest award for bravery.

This is a German V-1 flying bomb being launched. Powered in the sky by a jet engine, the bomb was usually launched from a ramp, using a catapult.

'Bomber' Harris

The Germans weren't the only ones to blitz enemy cities. Under the command of Sir Arthur Harris – nicknamed 'Bomber' Harris– the RAF, along with the US Air Force, carried out a number of bombing raids on German cities.

Cologne, May 1942: 469 killed and 450,000 left homeless

Hamburg, July 1943: 42,000 civilians killed

Dresden, February 1945: hundreds of historic buildings destroyed, and an estimated 25,000-35,000 people killed

Rocket blitz

The triumph of D-Day gave the British public their first real hopes for a quick end to the war. For almost four years they had endured air raids, hunger and hard work, and the misery of the blackout. But while they celebrated, a nightmarish new weapon was aimed against them – the German rocket bomb.

Flying bombs

In mid-June 1944, small, pilotless planes with explosive warheads began crashing into London and the south coast of England. These were the first of Hitler's vengeance weapons – known as V-1s – designed to slaughter civilians. Powered by crude jet engines, V-1s were launched from bases across Nazi occupied France and Holland and more than 2,000 crashed into the British capital.

Watching and waiting

The flying bombs had a terrifying impact on Londoners. Many V-1s arrived in the daytime, when everyone was out of the shelters and the streets were busy. Their engines made a rumbling growl as they sliced across the sky, but when the noise suddenly stopped, people ran for their lives. This was the signal that the bomb would dive to earth, and hundreds might die.

Closing the gap

In the early attacks, most V-1s reached London and southern England. But the RAF soon developed tactics for destroying the flying bombs. Radar stations tracked them as they crossed the English Channel, sending radio warnings to fighter pilots who intercepted the bombs. By late August, the RAF was stopping almost every V-1. Just weeks later the raids ended, when Allied troops captured the launching sites.

Silent killer

The next vengeance weapon seemed unstoppable. In September, a massive blast ripped through West London and the city was soon hit by dozens of mystery explosions. German scientists had unleashed a new weapon – the V-2. It was an early version of the space rocket that flew faster than the speed of sound. Hitler boasted that the V-2 would win him the war, but his rocket was so expensive and difficult to make, only a few thousand were launched before Germany lay in ruins.

Tipping point

RAF pilots discovered a dangerous trick for destroying V-1s – even when their guns had run out of ammunition.

They flew next to the weapon and slowly raised their wingtip, until it was only inches from the bomb's wing. The turbulence from the fighter's wing flipped the V-1 over and it crashed to the ground, safely away from any highly-populated areas.

A V-2 rocket is launched by British scientists, after it was abandoned by retreating Nazis.

Horror at Belsen

Seeking refuge

Some Jews escaped the terrors of the death camps. Thousands tried to leave Germany before the war, but foreign governments were often reluctant to give them sanctuary.

In November 1938, Nazi thugs ransacked Jewish homes and businesses. The violence spurred Britain's government into action. They offered shelter to any Jewish children under the age of seventeen. Around 10,000 girls and boys made the desperate journey across Europe by train and boat, as part of the *Kindertransport* – moving the children.

Hitler closed Germany's borders when the war started and most of the newcomers never saw their parents again.

Many joined Britain's armed forces as soon as they were old enough, and fought bravely to defeat the evil that had driven them from their homes.

Many soldiers have moments of panic on the battlefield, when they question their reasons for risking their lives. But in April 1945, British troops came across something that made it crystal clear why they were fighting. In a lonely forest, hidden from the world, the Germans had built a death camp full of unimaginable horrors.

When British soldiers entered the camp at Bergen-Belsen, in Germany, they found 60,000 men, women and children, trapped behind barbed-wire fences. Most of the prisoners were on the point of dying – from hunger, exhaustion or disease. Thousands had already collapsed and their bodies lay piled around the camp. The other prisoners were too weak to dig graves, and barely had the strength to eat, speak or stand as British medics struggled to help them.

Killing machine

Belsen was a concentration camp, one of hundreds the Nazis had set up across occupied Europe. Their chilling purpose was to imprison or murder anyone who didn't conform to the Nazis' insane vision of the world. Millions of Jews died in the camps, victims of the Nazi's racial prejudice. They were shot, gassed or worked to death by guards who had been taught that camp inmates were no better than wild animals.

On arrival at the camps, young children and old people were often gassed, because the guards considered them unfit for work. The rest of the prisoners were quickly stripped of their possessions and their identities, as other inmates shaved their heads and gave them ragged uniforms to wear. They lived on scraps of food, in constant fear for their lives. Few prisoners survived more than six months.

Ashes and dust

British medics worked day and night at Belsen, but thousands of the prisoners were too sick to be saved. Typhus fever was raging through the camp, so doctors evacuated the inmates to a local army base and burned the reeking prison to the ground. All that remained of Belsen was a smoking scar on the earth – a permanent reminder of the German Nazi party's mad and murderous hate.

At least six million Jews died in the concentration camps or were shot by Nazi killing squads. Their mass-murder is now known as the Holocaust.

Young victim

Anne Frank was a young Jewish German girl who kept an amazing diary of the years she spent hiding in Nazi-occupied Holland. She was betrayed and caught in 1944, and died at Belsen shortly before the British arrived.

Older than their years, these children are former inmates of Bergen-Belsen. They are waiting to receive soup from British troops. Some still wear their striped camp uniforms.

Defeating Germany

People walk past the once-triumphal Brandenburg Gate, which stands amid rubble and wreckage in the blasted German capital, Berlin.

While the Allies were advancing through France, Russian forces pressed in from the East – Germany had lost the war. But, like a trapped beast snarling and raging until the terrible end, Hitler ordered his soldiers to keep fighting. British troops had to battle harder than ever before they could finally celebrate a victory.

The bridge too far

While Hitler's armies kept on fighting, many German civilians struggled to survive. Left homeless and hungry by the war, this woman in Berlin is cooking for her family by the roadside.

In the summer of 1944, Allied commanders were hoping they could finish the war by Christmas. But the Allies stalled before the German's 'Siegfried Line' – a defensive belt of bunkers, minefields and barbed wire snaking along Germany's western border.

Montgomery came up with a plan to sidestep the Siegfried Line, by grabbing a series of vital bridges across the River Rhine, and then advancing into Germany. He sent paratroopers to capture bridges at Eindhoven, Nijmegen and Arnhem and keep them open for a column of his tanks. But the Germans stopped the column before it could reach the last bridge at Arnhem. After this disaster, the Allies advanced more cautiously, planning new attacks for spring 1945.

444

A last gasp

While the Allies settled in for a miserable Christmas, the battered remnants of the German army were gathering in the Ardennes forest. On December 16, they launched what became known as the Battle of the Bulge. It was a massive tank assault into Belgium, to try to break the Allied front and reach the sea. Almost 20,000 American soldiers died in the battle before the German attack was smashed.

To the bitter end

In March 1945, the Americans captured a bridge across the Rhine at Remagen. Montgomery's troops forced a crossing further north and the Allies raced into Germany. Realizing he was defeated, Hitler shot himself in his Berlin bunker, as Russian troops seized the city. On May 7, 1945, the head of the German armed forces ordered his men to surrender.

After over five years of struggle and suffering, the war in Europe was over. But Britain and the Allies still had to brace themselves for one last challenge – the battle with Japan.

Victory in Europe

Churchill declared May 8, Victory in Europe (VE) Day. He joined the Royal Family as they waved to the crowds from the balcony of Buckingham Palace.

In every town and village people hung out flags and drank toasts to their fighting men. Young and old, people celebrated with dances and street parties.

In this photograph, jubilant Londoners and British sailors celebrate VE Day with an impromptu street party.

The sun goes down on Japan

While millions of people celebrated peace in Europe, British troops were still fighting for their lives in Burma. The country's remote, impenetrable jungles were a terrifying battleground. Men struggled against disease, pounding heat, tropical storms and Japanese soldiers who would fight to the death rather than surrender.

Pulling back

After capturing Singapore, in 1942, Japanese forces had invaded nearby Burma and seized the capital, Rangoon. Burma's mountain ridges and rainforests protected the borders of India, Britain's most important colonial territory. But the Japanese advanced quickly, forcing the British to abandon most of their heavy equipment and retreat across almost a thousand miles of wild country.

British troops stopped the Japanese at the Indian frontier, but they had been badly mauled in the jungle, and were low on supplies. In contrast, Japanese soldiers had adapted well to the jungle, eating rodents, snakes and plants growing around them.

Rumble in the jungle

A maverick British commander, General Orde Wingate, formed a special jungle force to hit back at the enemy. Taking their name from a mythical beast, Wingate's *Chindits* marched deep into Burma and were supplied by mules and parachute airdrops.

After *Chindit* raids in 1943 and 1944, the British swept across Burma, overwhelming Japan's jungle troops. The Allies recaptured Rangoon in May, 1945, and made plans to invade Malaya. Allied armies were poised to attack Japan, but the country's leaders still refused to give in.

A final blow

On August 6, 1945, the Americans exploded a new and unimaginably destructive weapon over the Japanese city of Hiroshima – the atomic bomb. The city was reduced to dust, and over 80,000 civilians were killed. Only three days later, another bomb destroyed the city of Nagasaki. Japan's generals agreed to surrender on August 15. This date is remembered as VJ Day – victory in Japan.

At last, the Second World War was over.

Little Boy

The bomb that blasted Hiroshima was codenamed *Little Boy*.

The explosion caused a massive fireball that burned up everything within an area of 13 square km (5 square miles) and sent up a huge mushroom cloud of radioactive smoke.

A further 80,000 civilians died later of radiation poisoning, and many more people suffered sickness and disability as a result.

This photograph of Hiroshima was taken a few weeks after the city was almost completely flattened by an atomic bomb.

Out of the ashes

Counting the cost

At least sixty million soldiers and civilians died in the Second World War, more than in any other conflict.

Almost 400,000 British people lost their lives – including 60,000 civilians.

After more than five years of brutal war, the British people were exhausted. Thousands had died in air raids, in sinking ships and on lonely battlefields, and a million fathers and sons in uniform were still scattered around the world. It was time for the nation to heal its wounds and prepare for the future.

Some of Britain's soldiers had to wait months before their units stood down and they were shipped home. This process was known demobilization, or demob. But adjusting to civilian life after the war wasn't easy for everyone. Many returned to ruined homes and families they hadn't seen for a year or more.

A British soldier is cheered by local children, as he returns home.

The 1930s had been a time of unemployment and hardship for many people, but Britain's servicemen and women had risked their lives fighting for a better world. Now, they demanded jobs and more help from the government – and people across the country supported them.

In it together

The British had learned a lot about themselves and their nation's problems since 1939. Men and women from all classes and backgrounds had trained, worked and struggled together to win the war. This national effort gave people a sense of unity and the confidence to make Britain a better place.

Wartime evacuations of children from city slums had opened people's eyes to the plight of the poor. Millions were living in squalor, with no chance of finding good schools or jobs and no health care if they became sick. People wanted to clear the slums and build a fairer society. They expected great things from their leaders.

A new team

In July, 1945, Churchill called an election. The man who had saved Britain from Hitler expected an easy victory for his Conservative Party. But Clement Attlee's Labour Party won the election by a landslide. Churchill was astonished. The voters would always respect their pugnacious war leader, but he moved into the shadows of history as the country prepared for the challenges of a new era.

Britain had helped win the war, but now the country had to face the new challenges of peacetime.

Nazis in the dock

Like Hitler himself, many Nazi leaders committed suicide before they could be caught by the Allies.

Those who survived were arrested and put on trial in the German city of Nuremberg. Most were found guilty of war crimes and sentenced to death.

This is one of the posters that helped the Labour Party to win the 1945 General Election.

POST-WAR BRITAIN

After the Second World War, Britain lost much of the power and influence that it had during the 19th century. The government struggled to find a new role for the country in a world that was rapidly changing. Many heavy industries fell into decline, but over time daily life became more comfortable for most people.

British society was changing too. The empire was dismantled, and many people from the former colonies came to live in Britain, bringing greater diversity to the nation's culture than ever before.

From cradle to grave

The people of Britain made weekly payments to cover the costs of Attlee's new Welfare State.

A new act made it compulsory to attend school up to the age of 15. This education was free for everyone.

The government made benefit payments to the unemployed, and to sick people who could not work.

The National Health Service was set up in 1948, offering free health care for everyone. The state even paid for funerals.

Rebuilding Britain

With the horrors of the Second World War behind them, the people of Britain wanted a fresh start. In 1945, they voted in a Labour government, with Clement Attlee, a quiet, serious statesman, as their new Prime Minister. Attlee promised social and economic reform, and pledged to rebuild the nation, which was exhausted by war.

The new government faced an uphill struggle. Britain was more than £3,000 million in debt. Homes, roads and factories lay in ruins. Nearly 500,000 lives had been lost. Nevertheless, the war had brought people together, and now that there was peace, Attlee was determined not to let everyone down.

In 1947, a family brings home coal in a pram, during a national fuel crisis. People stored up as much fuel as possible, to help them last through the cold winter.

Welfare State

Back in 1942, the economist Sir William Beveridge had identified five 'evil giants' in British society: poverty, ill-health, unemployment, poor education, and inadequate housing. Attlee brought in laws to solve these problems. Together, the laws created a 'Welfare State' – in which it was the state's responsibility to look after people 'from cradle to grave.' He also nationalized large industries, including electricity, coal, and the rail network. This meant they came under the control of the state, instead of being owned by private companies.

Hard times

Life was hard in the first few years after the war. Basic goods, such as clothing, meat and sugar, had to be rationed long after the fighting had ended, and few luxuries were available. But under Attlee's supervision, things slowly began to look up. With the help of large loans from the USA, thousands of houses were built for people whose homes had been bombed. In 1948, London hosted the first Olympic Games in 12 years.

Cold War

Meanwhile, the Soviet Union was extending its influence across eastern Europe. Many people in the West (western Europe and the USA) felt threatened by this – especially as the Russians were armed with powerful nuclear weapons. In Britain, government scientists developed nuclear weapons too. This was the start of the Cold War, a period of distrust and hostility between the Soviet Union and the West, which would last for the next 40 years.

A lasting peace?

Attlee's government worked with other nations to try to prevent another war.

In 1945, Britain became a founding member of the United Nations, a new international peacekeeping body.

In 1949, Britain helped form the North Atlantic Treaty Organization (NATO) with the USA and several European countries. NATO members agreed to protect each other in case of war.

This map shows the Soviet Union and European members of NATO during the Cold War.

- Neutral countries
- Soviet Union
- NATO

End of an empire

After the war, the government realized that it could no longer afford to keep running its overseas colonies. Many people in the colonies were also pushing for the right to rule themselves independently. It was the beginning of the end for the British empire.

India and Pakistan

In India, resistance to British rule had been growing for decades, and it was clear that something had to be done. But many Indian Muslims were worried that an independent India would be mainly Hindu. They called for a separate Muslim state.

In 1947, India was granted independence, and divided in two. Part of it kept the name of India, and became an independent Hindu state. The other part became a separate Muslim country, called Pakistan. Within a matter of weeks, millions had to leave their homes and travel to join their religious communities. There were riots and mass murders along the way, and thousands of people lost their lives.

Wind of change

With India's independence, Britain lost the 'jewel in the crown' of its empire, and the floodgates opened for other colonies wanting to be free. In 1957, the Gold Coast became the first African colony to be given independence, renaming itself Ghana. Others swiftly followed. In 1960, the Prime Minister Harold Macmillan declared that "the wind of change is blowing through this continent." Many countries kept a link to Britain by joining the Commonwealth of Nations, a free association of ex-colonies.

Gandhi

In the early 1900s, the charismatic Indian Mohandas Gandhi became a national hero by organizing peaceful protests against British rule.

He is sometimes known as *Mahatma* – meaning 'great soul' – and in India, he is considered to be the father of the nation.

In 1948 Gandhi was shot dead by a Hindu man, who hated the leader's tolerance of Muslims.

"You must be the change you want to see in the world."

Mohandas Gandhi

Multicultural Britain

The British government encouraged people from the colonies to move to Britain, as workers were needed to replace those killed in the war. On June 22, 1948, the ship *Empire Windrush* arrived at Tilbury docks in London, bringing nearly 500 Jamaicans to a new life in Britain. Immigrants later flowed in from the rest of the Caribbean, Africa and Asia.

Although in the 1950s, immigrants still made up only a tiny proportion of the population, it was the beginning of a more 'multicultural' Britain.

Prejudice

But many people were prejudiced against the immigrants. Some were suspicious of people of a different race, while others feared they would lose their jobs to the newcomers. Many immigrants were skilled workers, such as doctors or scientists, but they often had trouble finding work because of prejudice against them.

In 1965, Parliament set up the Race Relations Board to protect people from racial prejudice, so everyone would be treated equally, regardless of race.

A young woman from the West Indies arrives in Britain.

Carnival

The immigrants introduced new foods, music and clothing to Britain.

In the 1960s, the first Notting Hill Carnival was held. It takes place every year in London, celebrating Caribbean culture in Britain.

Elizabeth II greets her subjects from the balcony of Buckingham Palace, on the day of her coronation.

In 1951, the Festival of Britain was held throughout the country. It was a huge celebration of British achievements in industry and design.

Never had it so good

In 1951 the Conservatives won the General Election, and Winston Churchill was back in charge. The next year, King George VI died, leaving his daughter to become Queen Elizabeth II. Just like Elizabeth I, the new Queen was 25 years old when she came to the throne. After the hard times of the 1940s, people were hoping for a second Elizabethan Golden Age.

The Queen's splendid coronation certainly seemed like the start of a new era. Joyful parties were held in the streets, while many families watched the ceremony on television sets. Television was still quite a recent invention, and many people bought a set specially for the occasion. That same day, news reached London that members of a British expedition had been the first to climb Mount Everest, the world's highest mountain. The future seemed bright with possibility.

All mod cons

For many, the 1950s truly was a golden age. Britain had recovered from the war, and began to prosper. The population was booming, so the government built smart new homes, with the latest 'mod cons' (modern conveniences) – gas, electricity and indoor toilets. People could afford to buy new gadgets such as vacuum cleaners, washing machines and televisions. This created jobs and boosted industries.

In 1954, rationing ended for good, and the first supermarkets appeared, selling frozen foods. Exotic ingredients, such as olive oil and garlic, arrived from the continent, and plates of tough meat, boiled potatoes and cabbage were replaced with exciting foods such as pizza – or 'Italian Welsh rarebit' as it was called at first. At the end of the 1950s, Harold Macmillan declared proudly that "most of our people have never had it so good."

The Suez Crisis

But while life at home was better than ever, Britain was no longer the great world power it had once been. In 1956, Egypt took control of the British and French-owned Suez Canal. The canal was invaluable to Britain, as it was the gateway to the Middle East, the source of most of the country's oil. The British and French governments decided to invade Egypt and take back the canal. But the UN condemned the action, and they had to withdraw, humiliated.

The days of the British empire were truly over, and politicians realized that they could no longer go to war if the rest of the world disapproved. Britain had lost its place alongside the USA and the USSR as one of the 'Big Three' world powers.

Rock 'n' roll

In the 50s, young people had more money and free time than ever before. Many began listening and dancing to a new kind of music from America – rock 'n' roll. The music was fast and loud. Most adults hated it.

CND

The Campaign for Nuclear Disarmament (CND) was founded in 1958. It held protests against the government developing nuclear weapons.

The CND held marches to Aldermaston in Berkshire, where the weapons were built.

Mods and rockers

The word 'teenager' began to be used to describe 13-19 year-olds. Some teenagers formed groups, or gangs, with their own style of clothing and music.

In the mid 1950s, the Teddy Boys appeared. They wore expensive clothes influenced by Edwardian dress, greased their hair into quiffs, and listened to rock 'n' roll.

In the 1960s, two new teenage gangs appeared – the Mods and the Rockers. They often fought each other.

Mods wore smart clothes, rode scooters, and listened to modern pop music.

Rockers wore black leather jackets, rode motorbikes, and liked rock 'n' roll music.

The swinging sixties

By the 1960s, British society was changing rapidly. Most young people had good jobs and money to spend, and for the first time music and clothing were being made just for them. They felt little connection with the older generation who had lived through the war, and they rebelled against their elders' way of life, which they saw as old fashioned. Many were critical of the government – especially after several politicians were involved in scandals over their private lives.

Social reform

But it wasn't just teenagers who were changing. The 1960s heralded a new dawn of tolerance and open-mindedness. The magazine *Private Eye* and the BBC television show *That Was The Week That Was* openly made fun of politicians. In turn, the government introduced new laws to keep up with the changing times. In 1965, the death penalty was abolished. In 1967, a law was passed to allow women to have abortions, and in 1969, the Divorce Reform Act made it easier for people to end their marriages.

Britain is number one

Some people worried that the reforms were going too far, turning Britain into a 'permissive society' in which moral standards were declining. For most, though, it was the 'swinging sixties' – and British culture was number one. In 1963, the Beatles, a pop group from Liverpool, released their first hit single. It was the start of Beatlemania, a craze which swept the world, making four boys from Liverpool into the most successful group in history.

Fabulous fashions

At the same time, London became the capital of fashion, and British designers opened up busy shops on Carnaby Street and on the King's Road. Older people were shocked to see girls wearing mini-skirts, and boys letting their hair grow long.

In the late 1960s, many young people thought that life would keep getting better, and some believed that a new age of peace and harmony was dawning. Little did they know that difficult times lay ahead.

World Cup

In 1966, the England soccer team beat West Germany 4-2 at Wembley Stadium to win the World Cup for the first time ever.

This is a photo of Mary Quant, one of the leading fashion designers of the 1960s. She named her mini-skirts after the popular small British car, the Mini.

Lots of young people wanted to look like the Beatles. In the early 1960s, the band sparked a trend for the 'mop-top' hairstyle shown on the cover of this magazine.

459

Women's Lib

The Women's Liberation movement formed in the late 1960s. It campaigned for men and women to be treated equally.

In 1970 they protested at the 'Miss World' beauty pageant. Some threw bags of flour at the stage.

That year, the government passed the Equal Pay Act, to make sure that women were paid the same as men. In 1975, the Sex Discrimination Act made it illegal to treat women differently from men in the workplace.

In 1979, the British people elected their first ever female Prime Minister – Margaret Thatcher.

Troubled times

The 1970s was a stormy time, with strikes, protests and riots. Many women were angry that they still didn't have the same opportunities as men. In Northern Ireland, there were violent clashes between Protestants and Catholics. Worst of all, the prices of housing, food and other goods were rocketing, while wages remained low. Employers simply couldn't afford to pay any more, since most industries had been in decline since the 1950s. Workers became more and more unhappy.

The coal miners' strike

In 1972, the coal miners asked for a pay rise. When the government refused, miners across the nation went on strike, refusing to work. This was devastating for Britain's power supply, which depended on coal. Schools, factories and offices were forced to close down, and the desperate Prime Minister, Edward Heath, had to reduce the working week to three days, to save electricity. In the end, after seven weeks, the government gave in. The miners won their pay rise. But more trouble was to come.

Industries in trouble

In 1973, Britain joined the European Economic Community, or EEC, a group of European states which traded freely with each other. Suddenly, people could buy cheap European goods instead of the more expensive British ones – and many British industries, such as car and clothing manufacturers, could not sell their products. To make matters worse, a war in the Middle East stopped oil from reaching Britain, reducing the nation's fuel supply.

The Winter of Discontent

In 1974, the miners went on strike once again, and won another pay rise. But prices continued to climb. During the winter of 1978-9, many more workers went on strike, demanding higher wages. Lorry drivers, waste collectors and even ambulance drivers refused to work. As vast piles of household waste built up on the streets, and emergency calls were ignored, the government could do nothing to control the situation. It became known as the Winter of Discontent.

Piles of rubbish build up in Leicester Square, central London, in 1979.

Glam, disco and punk

The troubled times of the 70s inspired new kinds of music, that offered people an escape from everyday life.

Glam rock appeared at the beginning of the decade. Glam rockers, such as T. Rex and David Bowie, wore bright, space-age costumes and makeup.

Disco became popular in the late 70s. It was upbeat dance music with a strong rhythm. Young people flocked to discotheques to dance to the latest songs.

Punk rockers played angry, fast music which criticized the establishment, and tried to shock people as much as possible.

Margaret Thatcher worked as a chemist before going into politics. As an MP, she became known as 'Margaret Thatcher, Milk Snatcher' when she abolished free milk in schools.

Falklands War

The Falkland Islands, lying off the coast of Argentina, were among the last remaining British colonies. When Argentina invaded, the islanders appealed to Britain for help. Thatcher sent a force by sea to retake the islands.

HMS *Sheffield*, a British ship, is hit by a missile.

The Iron Lady

After the Winter of Discontent, the nation was in turmoil. People were terrified of further strikes, industry was still struggling, and there weren't enough jobs. People had begun to call Britain the 'Sick Man of Europe.' In May 1979, the Conservatives, led by Margaret Thatcher, won the General Election. It was up to them to save the nation from disaster.

Thatcher was nicknamed the 'Iron Lady' because of her strong leadership. Believing Britain had become a nanny state – one in which people relied on the government to look after them – she wanted people to work hard to make a profit for themselves. She was determined to revive the economy, and stop the strikes.

Thatcherism

Thatcher sold off the big industries that Clement Attlee had nationalized. Without the government's support, many of them went bankrupt, and millions lost their jobs. She changed taxation to make it easier for the rich, but harder for the poor, hoping that this would force people to find better jobs. She allowed people to buy their council houses, so that they could own their homes, instead of renting them.

Slowly but surely, the economy improved. Fuel prices dropped, thanks to cheap oil from the North Sea. Many 'yuppies' (young urban professionals) became rich – but unemployment and poverty got worse, making 'Thatcherism' unpopular. Nevertheless, in 1981 the wedding of the Queen's son, Prince Charles, to Lady Diana Spencer lifted the nation's spirits, and the next year Thatcher led Britain to victory over Argentina in the Falklands War. To many, she was a national hero.

462

Thatcher vs. the miners

In 1984, Thatcher faced up to a mass miners' strike. The miners had heard that the government planned to close down 20 coal mines, which would cause huge job losses. The government, meanwhile, had stored up plenty of coal and oil, so the strike wouldn't cut off Britain's power. After a year, the miners couldn't afford to live any longer without wages, and had to go back to work. Thatcher had won.

Poll tax

But the victory was not to last. In 1989, Thatcher tried to introduce a 'community charge' – which became known as the 'poll tax' – to pay for local government. Most people were furious, because everyone had to pay the same amount of money, no matter how rich they were. There were riots in the streets, and soon Thatcher's own party refused to support her. After eleven turbulent years, the Iron Lady stood down.

When the strikers tried to stop other miners from working, the police were called in. There were bloody clashes between strikers and police officers.

Live Aid

In 1985, a worldwide music event was held to raise money to fight famine in Ethiopia. 'Live Aid' was a concert that took place in different places all over the world. In Wembley Stadium in London, more than 70,000 people gathered to watch British bands such as Queen and Status Quo.

BAND AID presents

LIVE AID

SAT 13th JULY 1985

WEMBLEY STADIUM

ALL DAY

ARTIST

463

Northern Ireland

Ever since Ireland was partitioned in 1921, many Catholics in Northern Ireland had felt that the Protestant authorities discriminated against them when it came to jobs, housing and voting. In the late 1960s, some began campaigning for civil rights by holding peaceful marches and protests. But Protestant groups began counter-demonstrations, and violence flared up between Catholic Nationalists – who wanted all of Ireland to be independent – and Protestant Unionists – who wanted to remain part of the UK. In 1969, the British government sent in troops to restore order.

Bloody Sunday

Most locals welcomed the troops at first, hoping that they would bring peace to Northern Ireland. But on 'Bloody Sunday' – January 30, 1972 – British soldiers shot dead 13 unarmed men at a demonstration in Derry. After this, British troops were viewed with distrust and hatred, and the violence grew worse.

Orangemen

In Northern Ireland, Catholics and Protestants hold regular marches to celebrate important events in their history.

A Protestant group called the Orange Order holds marches every year on July 12. This is in memory of the victory of the Protestant William of Orange over the Catholic James II in 1690.

The march often leads to protests and riots.

The IRA

One Nationalist group, the Irish Republican Army – or IRA – hoped to force the British to leave by carrying out bombings, murders and shootings of British soldiers and Unionists. Meanwhile, on the other side, the Ulster Volunteer Force – or UVF – used the same brutal tactics against Nationalists. This time of terrible bloodshed became known as the Troubles.

Brighton bomb

Soon, the IRA began a bombing campaign in English cities, injuring and killing civilians. In 1984, they bombed a hotel in Brighton, where Margaret Thatcher was staying. Five people died, but Thatcher herself was unharmed. The IRA sent a chilling message: "Today we were unlucky. But remember we only have to be lucky once. You will have to be lucky always."

Meanwhile, the British government held talks with Nationalists and Unionists, to try to find a peaceful solution to the Troubles.

Writing on the wall

On the streets of Northern Ireland, many houses were painted with murals that show support for the Nationalists or Unionists. This IRA mural is titled 'The Easter Rising' in Gaelic. This was an unsuccessful rising against British rule, that took place in Dublin in 1916.

Police officers, armed with riot shields and batons, face rioters in Bogside, a Catholic area of Derry, Northern Ireland, in 1969.

Genetics

Some of the most exciting discoveries of the 20th century have been in the field of genetics – the study of genes.

Genes exist in every cell in a person's body. They contain instructions that affect how that person looks and behaves – from whether their eyes are blue or brown, to whether they are good at sports. Genes are made up of a chemical called DNA.

The science of life

In the 20th century, medical breakthroughs came thick and fast. During the two world wars, doctors had to work quickly to come up with new treatments for battlefield wounds, and for diseases that spread rapidly among the soldiers. Antibiotics had been discovered back in 1928, but it was only during the Second World War that they were first used to kill germs and treat illness.

After the war, the breakthroughs continued. In 1900, the average life expectancy had been less than 50 years, since many babies died in infancy. But by 1980, far fewer babies died, and people lived longer. Meanwhile, discoveries about genetics led to strange experiments, such as cloning – creating an exact replica of a plant or animal – and genetically modifying food crops, such as rice or tomatoes, to make them grow bigger or to give them resistance to diseases.

1967

In South Africa, Dr Christiaan Barnard performs the first successful heart transplant. Barnard's own brother had died of heart problems, at the age of five. The following year, surgeons perform the first heart transplant in Britain.

1950s

Scientists develop contraceptive pills to prevent pregnancy, for women who don't want to have a baby. The pills become available to the public in the 1960s.

1953

Two scientists, the American James Watson and the British Francis Crick, discover the spiral structure of DNA – the chemical which makes up people's genes. They later receive a Nobel prize for their work.

1954

Doctors successfully test a vaccine for polio. Polio is an infectious disease which attacks muscles and often leads to death.

466

1970s

Medical lasers are used for the first time, in eye surgery. The lasers are much more precise than scalpels, which had been used before.

1970s

A vaccine is developed to protect people from measles, mumps and rubella (MMR) with a single injection. In 1988 it is introduced in Britain.

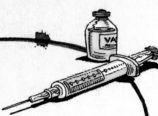

The environment

Since the 1970s, people have become increasingly worried about the damage that humans cause to the environment.

Deforestation is driving many species to extinction.

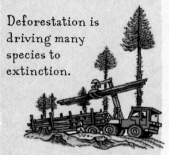

Some substances, such as the gases in aerosol cans, damage the ozone layer. This is the layer of protective gases that surrounds the planet.

Burning fossil fuels, such as coal and oil, causes global warming. This is a slow rise in air temperature which could have a serious impact on the world's climate.

1981

A terrifying new disease, called AIDS, is reported. It is caused by a virus known as HIV, which attacks the immune system. The disease has spread across the world, and to date, no vaccine has been found.

1978

Louise Brown is born in Manchester. She is the world's first 'test-tube baby' – conceived in a laboratory instead of inside her mother's body.

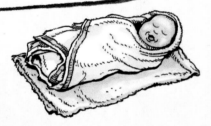

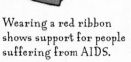

Wearing a red ribbon shows support for people suffering from AIDS.

1990s

Scientists modify the genes of crops to produce genetically modified (GM) foods. But there are debates over how safe GM crops are, and whether they damage the environment.

1990s

Deadly BSE, or mad cow disease, infects thousands of British cattle. It also spreads to humans, through beef. Millions of cows are killed to try to stamp out the disease.

1997

Scientists use genes from one sheep to produce another, which they call Dolly. She is the first ever clone, and is genetically identical to the sheep from which she was produced.

Global village

By the 1990s, many big businesses had become multinational, while new technology such as cell phones and the internet enabled people to contact each other with ease, wherever they were. Countries, peoples and cultures were becoming closely connected, and some people began to refer to the world as a 'global village' – as it seemed to be getting smaller and smaller.

The end of the Cold War

In 1985, Mikhail Gorbachev became leader of the Soviet Union.

He formed good relationships with Margaret Thatcher and US President Reagan, and the Cold War began to thaw.

In 1989, the Berlin Wall was pulled down. A symbol of the Cold War, it had split the city into West and East Berlin since 1961.

At the end of the 1980s, the Soviet Union collapsed, and the Cold War finally ended.

Closer to Europe

In 1994, the Channel Tunnel opened. It ran under the English Channel, and linked Britain to France. A joint project between the two nations, the Tunnel had taken more than seven years to build, but it brought Britain closer to Europe than ever before. Now people could travel from London to Paris by train, in three hours.

In the same year, the European Economic Community changed its name, and became the European Union. The EU drew its members together into a political union, with its own laws and policies.

British or European?

But British people were divided over whether they wanted to be part of a unified Europe or not. Some thought that the EU was the first step on the road to a European 'superstate' – much like the USA – and they worried that Britain might lose its independence.

When the EU intoduced a new European currency, the Euro, Britain stuck with the pound. At the same time, the British government strengthened relations with the USA. Some Europeans were angry that the British seemed more committed to this 'special relationship' with the US, than to Europe.

Peacekeeping

Meanwhile, the government believed that as a member of the global community, Britain had an important role to play in international affairs – especially when it came to keeping the peace, and protecting the world's most vulnerable people.

In 1990, UN spy satellites showed that President Saddam Hussein of Iraq was gathering troops to attack nearby Kuwait. On August 2, they invaded, and British troops went in as part of the UN forces to help drive the Iraqis out. The Gulf War, as it became known, was over within a month. It was a decisive victory for the UN and its allies, although Saddam Hussein remained in power.

As a member of both the UN and NATO, Britain sent its forces to help in several other peacekeeping operations during the 1990s. Many of these took place in the Balkans in eastern Europe, where communities were torn apart by civil war.

Hong Kong

At midnight on July 1st, 1997, the British handed over their last great colony, Hong Kong, to China.

The British flag was lowered for the last time, and the Chinese flag raised in its place.

Albanians living in Kosovo, in the Balkans, welcome British soldiers in 1999. This was part of a NATO mission to protect the Albanians from attacks by the Serbs.

Cool Britannia

Late-1990s Britain was sometimes described as 'Cool Britannia' because of the global success of young British artists, musicians and designers. The artist Damian Hirst caused a stir with bold works, such as a shark in a tank of formaldehyde.

New Labour

In 1994, the Labour Party leader, John Smith, died suddenly of a heart attack, and a young MP, Tony Blair, took his place. Blair decided that the only way to win power from the Conservatives was to reform his party. 'New Labour' – as it came to be known – abandoned one of the Labour Party's oldest beliefs, that the state should own and run the big industries. Blair hoped to win over people who normally voted for the Conservatives, even if it meant upsetting traditional Labour supporters.

In the 1997 General Election, New Labour swept to power, promising a new life for Britain. Blair was extremely popular, and many people saw his leadership as a breath of fresh air after almost 20 years of Conservative government.

Tony Blair greets his supporters after winning the 1997 election.

Devolution

Blair allowed the Welsh and the Scots to vote on whether they wanted to run their own day-to-day affairs, instead of having decisions made for them by Parliament in London. In both countries, people voted to have their own assemblies, and make their own decisions.

Some people worried that this meant the end of a unified Britain. Others welcomed the change. Nevertheless, in 1999, the Welsh Assembly and the Scottish Parliament were created. This handover of power was known as devolution.

The Royal Family

The Royal Family suffered a series of blows throughout the 1990s. In 1992, it was announced that Prince Charles and Diana would separate. That same year, there was a huge fire at Windsor Castle. Queen Elizabeth called it her *"annus horribilis"* – horrible year. But worse was to come. In 1997, Diana was killed in a car crash in Paris. When the Queen didn't join in the public mourning, many accused her of being cold and unfeeling. It was a rare low point in her popularity.

Peace in Northern Ireland

Meanwhile, in Northern Ireland, there was finally some cause for hope. On Good Friday, April 10, 1998, the government's talks with Unionists and Nationalists ended with an agreement. Just as in Wales and Scotland, an assembly was created, to run daily affairs. The Good Friday Agreement didn't solve all the problems, but at last, peace seemed like a possibility.

Prince Charles and his sons, William and Harry, look at the flowers left outside Kensington Palace, Diana's home.

The People's Princess

After Diana's death, Tony Blair gave a speech in which he called her the People's Princess.

Her death caused a tide of grief, and more than a million people went to her funeral.

Millennium

Millennium buildings

Monuments were built all over Britain to mark the Millennium.

The Gateshead Bridge in Newcastle spans the River Tyne. It can tilt to allow ships to pass underneath.

The Glasgow Science Centre stands beside the River Clyde. Its smooth, shiny surface is coated with titanium plates.

The Millennium Dome is a vast tent on the banks of the Thames in London. It is the biggest dome in the world.

As the clock ticked down to midnight on December 31, 1999, the people of Britain celebrated the end of a century, and the dawn of a new millennium. Some people stayed at home with their families, while others held parties, or gathered in city streets to see in the New Year. At the stroke of twelve, Big Ben began to toll, as cheers went up and rockets were launched into the dark sky.

Wrapped up warm against the chilly night, the people of Britain gazed up at fireworks bursting high above them. The 20th century had brought two world wars, the loss of an empire, and more rapid changes in science, culture and medicine than ever before. But who could say what challenges the new millennium would bring?

In London, crowds line the banks of the Thames and Westminster Bridge, to watch the New Year fireworks display.

FACTFILE

R ead on to find out more about exploring the history of Britain, on the internet, in books and movies, and by visiting buildings, battlefields and other historic sites.

You'll also find a timeline of British history and a glossary to explain any difficult or unusual words.

Exploring British history

There are lots of different ways to find out more about Britain's history. Buildings, monuments and even the names of places all give clues about who lived there and what went on in times gone by.

The history of a place is not always so easy to spot, as many ancient remains all over Britain are now buried under fields and buildings. Sometimes they are discovered by accident, shedding new light on the mysteries of the past.

Many things, such as ancient jewels, maps and legal documents, have been carefully preserved. You can see some of them displayed in museums. People have a history too, in their memories of the past, or in stories of their families that have been passed down through the generations.

This is a detail from a picture map of Great Yarmouth in Norfolk that was made around 1585. It gives lots of clues about the history of the town, as it shows the 16th century streets and buildings in great detail. It also includes things like windmills that are no longer there.

Internet links

If you visit the Usborne Quicklinks Website, you'll find links to some exciting websites that are packed with activities and information to help you to find out more about Britain's past.

- click on a timeline of British history to find out more about different periods and events

- investigate the history of the royal families who have ruled Britain over the centuries

- learn more about famous Britons through the ages

- discover what people's houses were like in the past

- watch computer animations of some of Britain's most famous battles

- explore famous museums and historical sites across Britain and find out how to visit them

For links to these sites, go to the Usborne Quicklinks Website at www.usborne-quicklinks.com and enter the keywords "history of britain".

When using the internet, please follow the internet safety guidelines shown on the Usborne Quicklinks Website. The links at Usborne Quicklinks are regularly reviewed and updated, but Usborne Publishing is not responsible and does not accept liability for the content on any website other than its own. We recommend that children are supervised while using the internet.

Investigate the families of Britain's many kings and queens.

Explore the history of Britain's armed forces.

Find out more about fashions of ages past.

Places to visit

There are historic sites to visit all across the British Isles, from castles and battlefields to old factories and mines. A nation-wide network of museums also displays artefacts from ancient weapons to clothes, transport, and even human remains. Here are just a few of them. For more information, visit the Usborne Quicklinks Website at www.usborne-quicklinks.com

General

The Geffrye Museum (London)
Each room in this museum is furnished to show how a British family would have lived at different times.

British Museum (London)
Collection of historical objects from Britain and the rest of the world.

Museum of London (London)
See how London has changed, from 450 million years ago to the present.

National Museum of Scotland (Edinburgh)
Explore the history and the origins of the Scottish people.

National Museum Wales (Cardiff)
Learn all about the history and culture of Wales.

Victoria and Albert Museum (London)
A fantastic collection of costumes, furnishings and decorative arts from across the centuries.

The National Trust
A charity that maintains hundreds of sites across England, Wales and Northern Ireland, including castles, houses and gardens.

Historic Scotland
A body that cares for historic sites in Scotland.

Cadw: Welsh Historic Monuments
Maintains and protects Welsh historic sites.

English Heritage
An organization that protects historical buildings and sites throughout England.

Prehistoric Britain

Creswell Crags (Nottinghamshire)
Take a tour around ancient caves, and come face-to-face with art carved by their Ice Age residents.

Grime's Graves (Norfolk)
One of the oldest mines opened to the public in Britain, where flint was mined 5,000 years ago.

Stonehenge (Wiltshire)
Take a walk around this massive, beautifully preserved ancient stone circle.

Great Orme Mines (Conwy)
One of the largest known prehistoric mines, with tunnels and shafts made over 4,000 years ago.

Jarlshof (Shetland Islands)
Ancient buildings dating as far back as the Iron and Bronze Ages.

Maiden Castle (Dorset)
A huge hillfort first built in the Iron Age to protect its inhabitants from attacks.

Skara Brae (Orkney Islands)
A village of stone houses that were built over 4,000 years ago.

Butser Ancient Farm (Hampshire)
Discover how the early Britons lived at this working reconstruction of an ancient farm.

Roman Britain

Housesteads (Northumberland)
One of the finest remaining Roman forts, positioned along the remains of Hadrian's Wall.

Caerleon (near Newport)
A massive Roman fortress and army base, with barracks, baths and an amphitheatre.

Roman Baths (Bath)
Explore these superbly preserved Roman baths, then visit the pump room and taste the spa water.

Dover Lighthouse (Kent)
A 2,000 year old lighthouse, built by the Romans to guide ships and watch out for raiders.

Portchester Castle (Hampshire)
This towering Roman castle was built to defend the coastline against Saxon invaders.

Hull and East Riding Museum (Hull)
Exhibits include Roman mosaics taken from the nearby villa at Rudston.

The Early Middle Ages

Sutton Hoo (Suffolk)
Visit a recreation of the famous Anglo-Saxon ship burial, and explore the area where it was found.

Tintagel Castle (Cornwall)
Many myths link the site on which this 13th century castle stands with King Arthur.

Lindisfarne Priory (Northumberland)
Explore the ruins of the ancient church on the island of Lindisfarne.

Iona Abbey (Isle of Iona)
This abbey was founded in the 6th century by St. Columba. Early Scottish kings are buried nearby.

Offa's Dyke Centre (Powys)
Exhibition about the ditch built in the 9th century to separate England from Wales, and how it looks today.

Ashmolean Museum (Oxford)
Among this museum's many exhibits are Anglo-Saxon coins, and the famous Alfred Jewel.

Jorvik Viking Centre (York)
Experience the sights and smells of life in Viking York in these recreated Viking streets.

Westminster Abbey (London)
A magnificient church founded by Edward the Confessor, in the heart of London.

The Middle Ages

Durham Cathedral (Durham)
Beautiful 11th century cathedral, with much of its original Norman architecture preserved.

Tower of London (London)
Fortress built by William the Conqueror and now home to the Crown Jewels.

Windsor Castle (London)
This is the largest castle in England, and has been a royal residence for over 900 years.

Caernarfon Castle (Gwynedd)
Edward I built this castle on the Welsh shoreline to protect the country from invaders.

Canterbury Cathedral (Canterbury)
Pilgrims flocked to this cathedral for centuries after Thomas Becket was murdered here.

Edinburgh Castle (Edinburgh)
Imposing medieval castle perched on an extinct volcano in the heart of the Scottish capital.

Kenilworth Castle (Warwickshire)
A huge ruined castle dating from the 12th century.

York Minster (York)
It took 250 years to build this cathedral. Go inside to look at the beautiful stained glass windows.

Stirling Castle (Stirling)
Stirling Castle overlooks the site of the Battle of Bannockburn, and also Stirling Bridge.

Royal Armouries Museum (Leeds)
An exhibition showing a range of objects used in battles, dating back to medieval times and earlier.

Chepstow Castle (Monmouthshire)
One of the oldest surviving stone castles in Britain, this fort played a vital role in medieval politics.

Caernarfon Castle in Wales

Tudors and Stuarts

Hampton Court (Surrey)
Henry VIII's magnificent red brick palace. Visit the Tudor kitchens and get lost in the maze.

Deal Castle (Kent)
This coastal fort was built on Henry VIII's orders to protect against possible naval attacks.

Holyrood House (Edinburgh)
This Scottish palace was home to Mary, Queen of Scots in the 16th century.

St. Paul's Cathedral (London)
A magnificent church, designed by Sir Christopher Wren after the original burned down.

Globe Theatre (London)
Watch Shakespeare's plays in a reconstruction of his famous open air theatre.

Kentwell (Suffolk)
Volunteer to live as a Tudor for a weekend, and learn how a Tudor house was run.

Mary Rose (Portsmouth)
Learn about life on board a Tudor warship, with exhibits including tools, clothes and weapons.

National Maritime Museum (London)
Find out about the history of exploration, and the explorers whose travels have become famous.

Cromwell Museum (Cambridgeshire)
Learn more about Oliver Cromwell in this museum, housed in what was once his old school.

Hardwick House (Derbyshire)
This magnificent mansion was built for one of the richest ladies of the era, and is surrounded by parks and gardens.

The Georgians

Buckingham Palace (London)
Explore the magnificent state rooms, learn about the kings and queens who lived here and find out how the monarchy works today.

Jane Austen's House Museum (Hampshire)
The house where Jane Austen wrote several of her novels is now a museum dedicated to her life.

Maritime Museum (Liverpool)
This museum has a section on the slave trade that developed in the 18th century.

HMS Victory (Portsmouth)
Take a tour around this historic warship that played a key role in the Battle of Trafalgar.

The Royal Pavilion (Brighton)
Built for George IV when he was Prince Regent, this palace is filled with exotic decorations.

Trafalgar Square (London)
In this famous square, a huge column raises a statue of Lord Nelson into the air.

Culloden (near Inverness)
Walk on the land where the Jacobites took their final stand, and learn more about the battle in the nearby museum.

Burn's National Heritage Park (Ayr)
See the cottage where Robert Burns was born, and see the first copies of some of his poems.

Dr. Johnson's House (London)
Samuel Johnson wrote the first proper English dictionary in this house.

Fashion Museum (Bath)
Discover more about Georgian fashions with this collection of clothing.

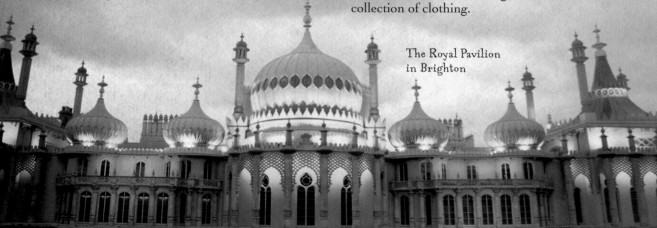

The Royal Pavilion
in Brighton

The Victorians

Darlington Railway Museum (County Durham)
This museum stands on the site of the world's first public steam railway.

Ironbridge Gorge Museums (Shropshire)
A collection of museums dedicated to the Industrial Revolution, based around the world's first iron bridge.

Ragged School Museum (London)
Find out what it was like to be a pupil at an East End school in Victoria's reign.

Ulster Folk and Transport Museum (County Down)
Learn about the history of Irish railways and everyday life in 19th century Ireland.

York Castle Museum (York)
Walk down a reconstructed Victorian street, lined with shop window displays.

The National Motor Museum (Hampshire)
This museum houses antique cars, including some of the first cars to be built.

Osborne House (Isle of Wight)
See the house where Victoria and Albert spent time relaxing with their children.

Beamish Open Air Museum (County Durham)
Discover the practical effects of the Industrial Revolution on life in 19th and 20th century northern England.

Balmoral Castle (Aberdeenshire)
A royal estate, first purchased by Queen Victoria, set in the midst of the Highlands.

Crystal Palace Park (London)
Come face-to-face with lifesize models of dinosaurs made during the Victorian era.

Brunel's SS Great Britain (Bristol)
Explore the first iron-hulled steamship, designed and built by Isambard Kingdom Brunel.

The Sherlock Holmes Museum (London)
Visit the recreated Baker Street house of one of the best-loved fictional detectives ever created.

The 20th century

Cadbury World (Birmingham)
Discover the history behind one of the major UK chocolate manufacturers.

Discovery Point (Dundee)
Tour the RRS *Discovery*, the ship on which Captain Scott and Ernest Shackleton first voyaged to Antarctica.

The National Media Museum (Bradford)
Learn about the origins of cinematography, and view some of the earliest cameras and projectors.

Imperial War Museum (London, Manchester, Cambridgeshire)
Museum with branches around the country, packed with information on 20th and 21st century wars involving Britain.

HMS Belfast (London)
A ship which took part in the D-Day landings.

National Army Museum (London)
Explore the history of the British army, from the Norman invasion to the present day.

Fleet Air Arm Museum (Somerset)
See a wide range of aircraft, including fighter aircraft and the first British Concorde.

Bletchley Park (Buckinghamshire)
Find out about the work of British code-breakers during the Second World War.

Beatles Story (Liverpool)
Learn about one of the most successful bands in history, and what life was like in the 1960s.

National Coal Mining Museum (Wakefield)
A museum about the history of coal mining in Britain, built around the oldest mine shaft still in daily use in Britain.

The Big Pit (Torfaen)
Take an underground tour of a coal mine, and learn more about mining in the adjacent museum.

Glasgow Science Centre (Glasgow)
See exhibits on science and technology in this futuristic centre, built for the Millenium.

Stories from history

Novels often give a great sense of how things used to be. Here is a selection of books set – and written – in different periods of British history.

Prehistoric Britain

Chronicles of Ancient Darkness by Michelle Paver

Historical fantasy series about the adventures of Torak, a young boy who grows up in an isolated forest and can communicate with wolves.

Roman Britain

The Eagle of the Ninth by Rosemary Sutcliff

A young Roman seeks to find out the truth about the disappearance of his father's legion.

The Early Middle Ages

Feasting the Wolf by Susan Price

Two farm boys join the Viking army in search of adventure. But their experiences fighting the Saxons threaten their friendship and their lives.

The Middle Ages

Strongbow by Morgan Llywelyn

The Normans are invading Ireland, but one of their knights, Strongbow, has fallen in love with Aoife, an Irish princess.

Crusade by Elizabeth Laird

Adam, a young serf from England, sets out on the 3rd Crusade. He befriends a Muslim boy, and starts to question what he is fighting for.

Fire Bed and Bone by Henrietta Branford

The story of a peasant family set during the Peasants' Revolt of 1381.

Tudors and Stuarts

Raven Queen by Pauline Francis

Gentle Jane Grey is mistreated by her ambitious parents, and becomes Queen against her will.

The Children of the New Forest by Frederick Marryat

A Cavalier officer's orphaned children hide from the Roundheads in a kind gamekeeper's cottage.

The Georgians

Coram Boy by Jamila Gavin

Atmospheric novel about orphans and a child murderer set in 18th century London.

Smith by Leon Garfield

A young thief gains possession of a mysterious document that is being sought by murderers.

Powder Monkey by Paul Dowswell

Adventurous Sam Witchall is drawn into the war at sea between England, France and Spain.

Kidnapped by Robert Louis Stevenson

Set soon after the Jacobites' defeat, this novel describes David Balfour's travels across the Scottish Highlands to reclaim his inheritance.

The Victorians

Oliver Twist by Charles Dickens

Orphaned Oliver gets drawn into a life of crime in Victorian London.

Black Beauty by Anna Sewell

Told from the perspective of a horse, this novel highlights animal cruelty in Victorian Britain.

Set in Stone by Linda Newbery

Two servants to a wealthy family living in a grand house narrate this thrilling tale.

The 20th century

The Railway Children by E. Nesbit

A mother and her children fall on hard times, and move to a small country house. There the children make friends at the local railway station.

Goodnight Mister Tom by Michelle Magorian

During the Second World War, a young evacuee forms a bond with the gruff man that he's placed with. But his sad life in London isn't far away.

The Machine Gunners by Robert Westall

A boy finds a machine gun in a crashed German aircraft. With his friends, he sets about defending their wartorn town.

Across the Barricades by Joan Lingard

In 1970s Belfast, a Catholic and a Protestant fall in love but must keep their relationship secret.

Using an early
movie projector

History on screen

Movies, television dramas and documentaries can help bring the past to life, but beware: they're not always historically accurate! Many of these films may not be suitable for younger viewers, especially those marked with an asterisk *.

Roman Britain

Gladiator* (2000)
Atmospheric film about a Roman general who is betrayed and is forced to become a gladiator.

The Early Middle Ages

Beowulf* (2007)
Animated tale loosely based on the ancient Anglo-Saxon legend.

King Arthur* (2004)
This film portrays Arthur as a Roman general defending the Britons against Saxon raids.

The Middle Ages

Braveheart* (1995)
Mel Gibson stars as William Wallace in this violent but moving film.

Blackadder* (1983)
This television comedy imagines a very different outcome to the Wars of the Roses. Later series are set in Elizabeth I's reign and the Regency.

Tudors and Stuarts

Elizabeth* (1998) and Elizabeth: the Golden Age* (2007)
Cate Blanchett stars as Elizabeth I, in these two films depicting her transformation from struggling young monarch to powerful queen.

Shakespeare in Love* (1998)
Tudor London is brought to life in this romantic comedy based on Shakespeare's life and work.

Lady Jane (1986)
A film showing the short reign and fate of Lady Jane Grey, and her husband Lord Dudley.

The Georgians

The Madness of King George (1994)
Moving film about the later years of George III.

Pride and Prejudice (1995)
Faithful television adaptation of Jane Austen's most famous novel.

Amazing Grace (2006)
William Wilberforce struggles to abolish slavery in 19th century Britain.

The Victorians

An Ideal Husband (1999)
Oscar Wilde's witty social comedy about finding a husband in 19th century London.

Mrs. Brown (1997)
Story of the relationship between Queen Victoria and her servant John Brown.

The 20th century

Blackadder Goes Forth* (1989)
The end finally comes for Blackadder when he goes 'over the top' during the First World War.

The Battle of Britain (1969)
Classic film about the 1940 battle to control British air space.

The World at War (1973)
Television series about the Second World War.

Empire of the Sun (1987)
An English boy struggles to survive under Japanese occupation of Shanghai in the 1940s.

The Queen* (2006)
This film shows the aftermath of the death of Diana, Princess of Wales from the perspective of Queen Elizabeth II.

Timeline of British history

This timeline charts some of the most significant events in Britain's history, and some of the most influential monarchs and leaders. The dates given for rulers indicate the length of their reigns. Where 'c' appears next to a date, it means the exact date is not certain. It stands for *circa*, which means 'about' in Latin.

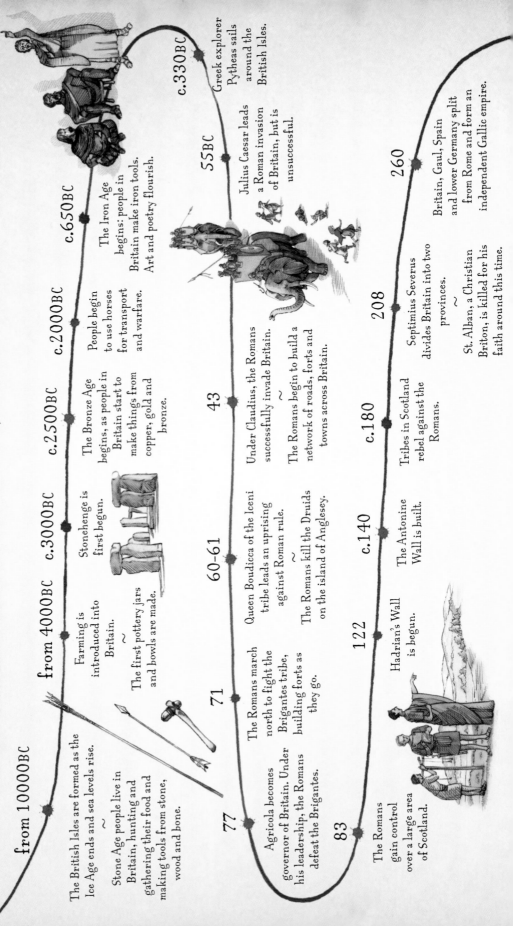

from 10000BC

The British Isles are formed as the Ice Age ends and sea levels rise.

~

Stone Age people live in Britain, hunting and gathering their food, and making tools from stone, wood and bone.

from 4000BC

Farming is introduced into Britain.

~

The first pottery jars and bowls are made.

c.3000BC

Stonehenge is first begun.

c.2500BC

The Bronze Age begins, as people in Britain start to make things from copper, gold and bronze.

c.2000BC

People begin to use horses for transport and warfare.

c.650BC

The Iron Age begins: people in Britain make iron tools. Art and poetry flourish.

c.330BC

Greek explorer Pytheas sails around the British Isles.

55BC

Julius Caesar leads a Roman invasion of Britain, but is unsuccessful.

43

Under Claudius, the Romans successfully invade Britain.

~

The Romans begin to build a network of roads, forts and towns across Britain.

60-61

Queen Boudicca of the Iceni tribe leads an uprising against Roman rule.

~

The Romans kill the Druids on the island of Anglesey.

71

The Romans march north to fight the Brigantes tribe, building forts as they go.

77

Agricola becomes governor of Britain. Under his leadership, the Romans defeat the Brigantes.

83

The Romans gain control over a large area of Scotland.

122

Hadrian's Wall is begun.

c.140

The Antonine Wall is built.

c.180

Tribes in Scotland rebel against the Romans.

208

Septimius Severus divides Britain into two provinces.

~

St. Alban, a Christian Briton, is killed for his faith around this time.

260

Britain, Gaul, Spain and lower Germany split from Rome and form an independent Gallic empire.

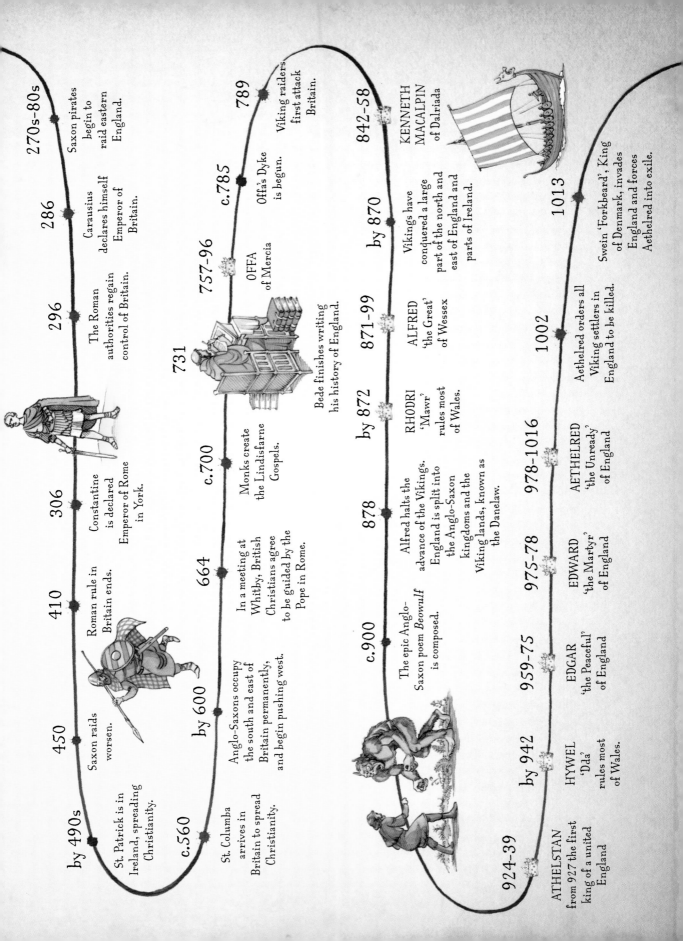

270s-80s Saxon pirates begin to raid eastern England.

286 Carausius declares himself Emperor of Britain.

296 The Roman authorities regain control of Britain.

306 Constantine is declared Emperor of Rome in York.

410 Roman rule in Britain ends.

450 Saxon raids worsen.

by 490s St. Patrick is in Ireland, spreading Christianity.

c.560 St. Columba arrives in Britain to spread Christianity.

by 600 Anglo-Saxons occupy the south and east of Britain permanently, and begin pushing west.

664 In a meeting at Whitby, British Christians agree to be guided by the Pope in Rome.

c.700 Monks create the Lindisfarne Gospels.

731 Bede finishes writing his history of England.

757-96 OFFA of Mercia

c.785 Offa's Dyke is begun.

789 Viking raiders first attack Britain.

842-58 KENNETH MACALPIN of Dalriada

by 870 Vikings have conquered a large part of the north and east of England and parts of Ireland.

871-99 ALFRED 'the Great' of Wessex

by 872 RHODRI 'Mawr' rules most of Wales.

878 Alfred halts the advance of the Vikings. England is split into the Anglo-Saxon kingdoms and the Viking lands, known as the Danelaw.

c.900 The epic Anglo-Saxon poem *Beowulf* is composed.

924-39 ATHELSTAN from 927 the first king of a united England

by 942 HYWEL 'Dda' rules most of Wales.

959-75 EDGAR 'the Peaceful' of England

975-78 EDWARD 'the Martyr' of England

978-1016 AETHELRED 'the Unready' of England

1002 Aethelred orders all Viking settlers in England to be killed.

1013 Swein 'Forkbeard', King of Denmark, invades England and forces Aethelred into exile.

1014
Aethelred returns from exile.

1016
EDMUND 'Ironside' of England

1016-35
CANUTE of England, also King of Denmark 1018-35

1035-7
Struggle for the English throne.

1037-40
HAROLD I of England

1040-42
HARTHACANUTE of England

1042-66
EDWARD 'the Confessor'

1066-87
MALCOLM III 'Canmore' of Scotland

1066
Battle of Hastings
The Normans conquer England and begin to build castles.

1066-87
WILLIAM 'The Conqueror'

1069-70
The Harrying of the North – William crushes resistance in the north of England.

1072
William forces Malcom III of Scotland to swear allegiance to him. The border between England and Scotland is set.

1086
Domesday survey is completed

1087-1100
WILLIAM II 'Rufus'

1095
The Pope calls for western knights to capture Jerusalem from its Muslim rulers, starting the First Crusade.

1100-35
HENRY I

1124-53
DAVID I of Scotland

1135-54
STEPHEN
The Anarchy – civil war in England, as Matilda fights Stephen for the crown.

1145
The Pope calls for a Second Crusade.

1153-65
MALCOLM IV of Scotland

1154-89
HENRY II 'Castle Breaker'

1163
Henry II invades Wales to force its princes to recognize him, but is defeated.

c.1169-70
English settlers colonize part of Ireland, known as the Pale.

1170
Archbishop Thomas Becket is murdered in Canterbury Cathedral.

1189-90
Angry mobs attack Jewish people in York and London.

1189–99
RICHARD I
'The Lionheart'

1189–92
The Pope calls for a Third Crusade, to recapture Jerusalem from Muslim forces led by Saladin.

1290
Edward expels all Jews from England.

1292–6
JOHN BALLIOL
of Scotland

1284
Wales officially becomes part of England.

1282
Dafydd ap Gruffydd leads a Welsh rebellion; Edward I invades and conquers Wales.

1295
Edward I summons the Model Parliament – the first English parliament.

~
The Scots make a treaty with France against England.

1296
England invades Scotland. John Balliol is taken prisoner.

1337–1453
The Hundred Years War between France and England.

1333
Edward III invades Scotland and defeats David II.

1199–1216
JOHN

1215
King John signs the Magna Carta

1277
Edward I invades North Wales and forces Llywelyn ap Gruffydd to sign a peace treaty.

1272–1307
EDWARD I

1297
William Wallace leads the Scots to victory against Edward I's forces at the Battle of Stirling Bridge.

1329–71
DAVID II
of Scotland

1216–72
HENRY III

1249–86
ALEXANDER III
of Scotland

1264–5
Civil war breaks out as powerful lords fight Henry III for power. Henry is imprisoned briefly, then returns to the throne.

1304
Edward I defeats the Scots. William Wallace is executed.

1306–29
ROBERT BRUCE
of Scotland

Robert leads attacks on the English.

1307–27
EDWARD II

1327–77
EDWARD III

1328
England officially recognizes Scottish independence.

1327
Edward II's wife, Queen Isabella, has him killed and puts their son on the throne.

1314
Robert Bruce defeats the English at the Battle of Bannockburn.

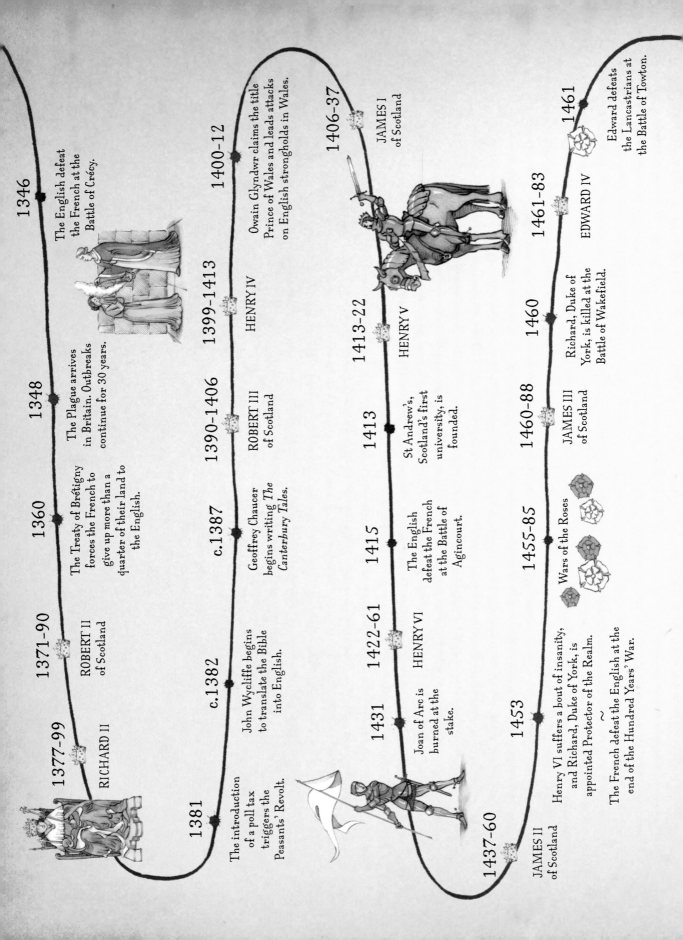

1346
The English defeat the French at the Battle of Crécy.

1348
The Plague arrives in Britain. Outbreaks continue for 30 years.

1360
The Treaty of Brétigny forces the French to give up more than a quarter of their land to the English.

1371–90
ROBERT II of Scotland

1377–99
RICHARD II

1381
The introduction of a poll tax triggers the Peasants' Revolt.

c.1382
John Wycliffe begins to translate the Bible into English.

c.1387
Geoffrey Chaucer begins writing *The Canterbury Tales*.

1390–1406
ROBERT III of Scotland

1399–1413
HENRY IV

1400–12
Owain Glyndwr claims the title Prince of Wales and leads attacks on English strongholds in Wales.

1406–37
JAMES I of Scotland

1413
St Andrew's, Scotland's first university, is founded.

1413–22
HENRY V

1415
The English defeat the French at the Battle of Agincourt.

1422–61
HENRY VI

1431
Joan of Arc is burned at the stake.

1437–60
JAMES II of Scotland

1453
The French defeat the English at the end of the Hundred Years' War.

1455–85
Wars of the Roses

1460
Richard, Duke of York, is killed at the Battle of Wakefield.

1460–88
JAMES III of Scotland

Henry VI suffers a bout of insanity, and Richard, Duke of York, is appointed Protector of the Realm.

1461
Edward defeats the Lancastrians at the Battle of Towton.

1461–83
EDWARD IV

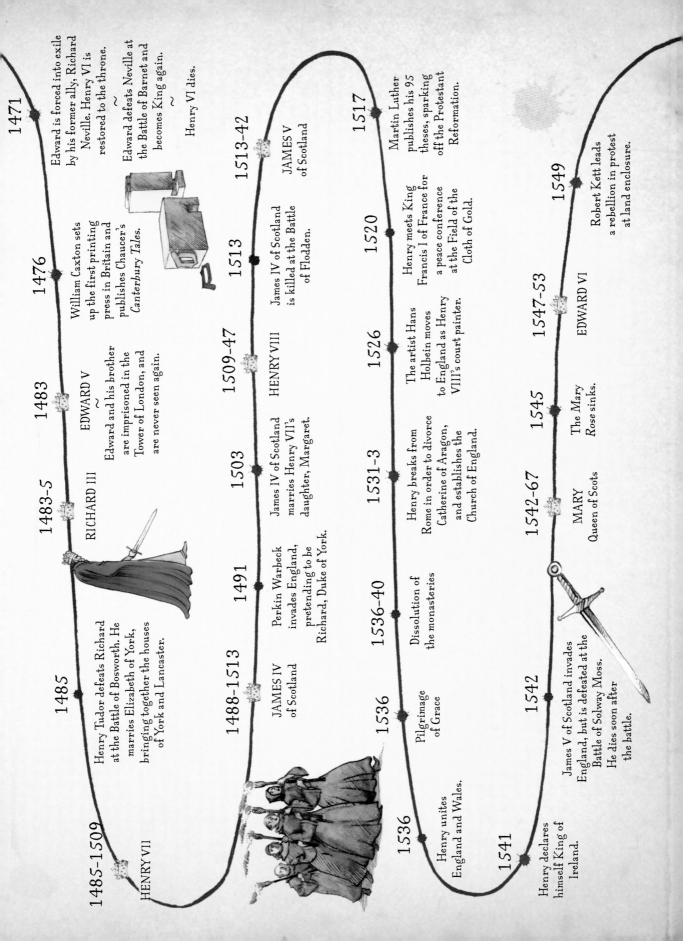

1471
Edward is forced into exile by his former ally, Richard Neville. Henry VI is restored to the throne.

Edward defeats Neville at the Battle of Barnet and becomes King again.

Henry VI dies.

1476
William Caxton sets up the first printing press in Britain and publishes Chaucer's *Canterbury Tales*.

1483
EDWARD V
Edward and his brother are imprisoned in the Tower of London, and are never seen again.

1483–5
RICHARD III

1485
Henry Tudor defeats Richard at the Battle of Bosworth. He marries Elizabeth of York, bringing together the houses of York and Lancaster.

1485–1509
HENRY VII

1491
Perkin Warbeck invades England, pretending to be Richard, Duke of York.

1488–1513
JAMES IV
of Scotland

1503
James IV of Scotland marries Henry VII's daughter, Margaret.

1509–47
HENRY VIII

1513
James IV of Scotland is killed at the Battle of Flodden.

1513–42
JAMES V
of Scotland

1517
Martin Luther publishes his 95 theses, sparking off the Protestant Reformation.

1520
Henry meets King Francis I of France for a peace conference at the Field of the Cloth of Gold.

1526
The artist Hans Holbein moves to England as Henry VIII's court painter.

1531–3
Henry breaks from Rome in order to divorce Catherine of Aragon, and establishes the Church of England.

1536
Pilgrimage of Grace

1536
Henry unites England and Wales.

1536–40
Dissolution of the monasteries

1541
Henry declares himself King of Ireland.

1542
James V of Scotland invades England, but is defeated at the Battle of Solway Moss. He dies soon after the battle.

1542–67
MARY
Queen of Scots

1545
The *Mary Rose* sinks.

1547–53
EDWARD VI

1549
Robert Kett leads a rebellion in protest at land enclosure.

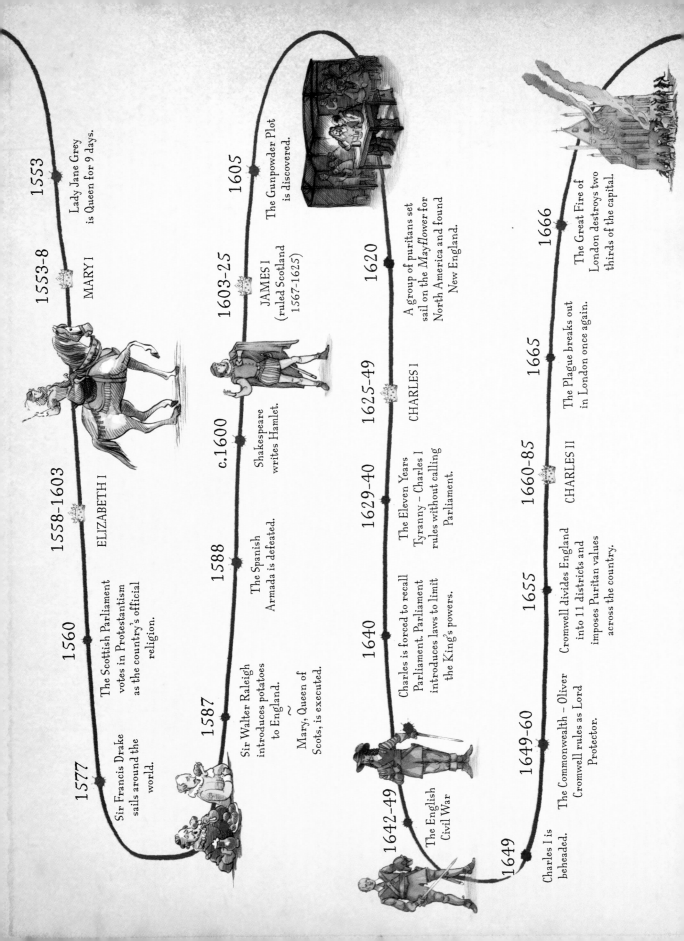

1553
Lady Jane Grey is Queen for 9 days.

1553-8
MARY I

1558-1603
ELIZABETH I

1560
The Scottish Parliament votes in Protestantism as the country's official religion.

1577
Sir Francis Drake sails around the world.

1587
Sir Walter Raleigh introduces potatoes to England.

Mary, Queen of Scots, is executed.

1588
The Spanish Armada is defeated.

c.1600
Shakespeare writes Hamlet.

1603-25
JAMES I (ruled Scotland 1567-1625)

1605
The Gunpowder Plot is discovered.

1620
A group of puritans set sail on the Mayflower for North America and found New England.

1625-49
CHARLES I

1629-40
The Eleven Years Tyranny – Charles I rules without calling Parliament.

1640
Charles is forced to recall Parliament. Parliament introduces laws to limit the King's powers.

1642-49
The English Civil War

1649
Charles I is beheaded.

1649-60
The Commonwealth – Oliver Cromwell rules as Lord Protector.

1655
Cromwell divides England into 11 districts and imposes Puritan values across the country.

1660-85
CHARLES II

1665
The Plague breaks out in London once again.

1666
The Great Fire of London destroys two thirds of the capital.

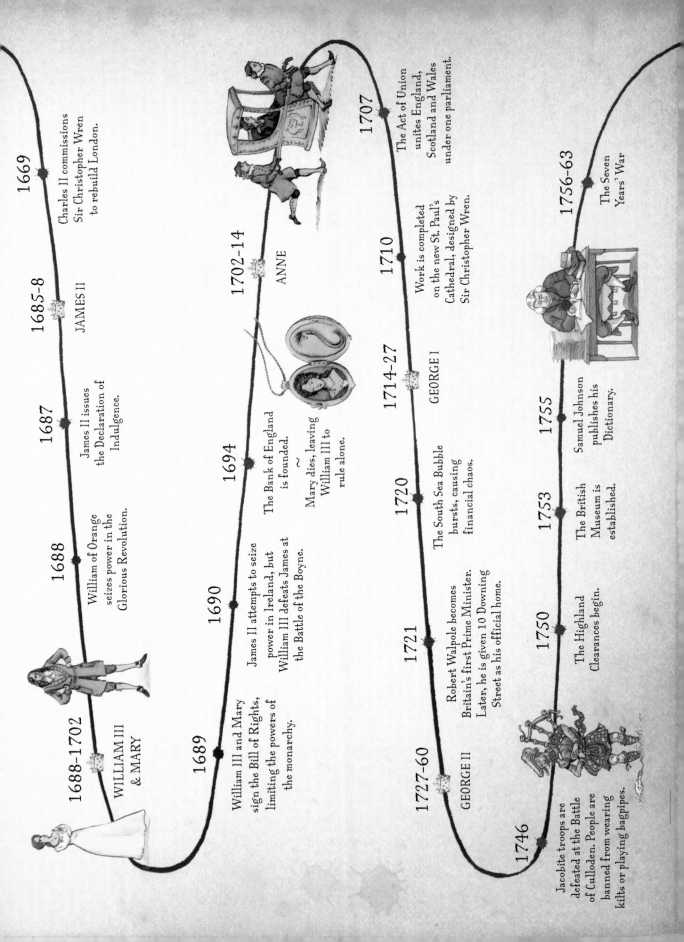

1669
Charles II commissions Sir Christopher Wren to rebuild London.

1685-8
JAMES II

1687
James II issues the Declaration of Indulgence.

1688
William of Orange seizes power in the Glorious Revolution.

1688-1702
WILLIAM III & MARY

1689
William III and Mary sign the Bill of Rights, limiting the powers of the monarchy.

1690
James II attempts to seize power in Ireland, but William III defeats James at the Battle of the Boyne.

1694
The Bank of England is founded.
~
Mary dies, leaving William III to rule alone.

1702-14
ANNE

1707
The Act of Union unites England, Scotland and Wales under one parliament.

1710
Work is completed on the new St. Paul's Cathedral, designed by Sir Christopher Wren.

1714-27
GEORGE I

1720
The South Sea Bubble bursts, causing financial chaos.

1721
Robert Walpole becomes Britain's first Prime Minister. Later, he is given 10 Downing Street as his official home.

1727-60
GEORGE II

1746
Jacobite troops are defeated at the Battle of Culloden. People are banned from wearing kilts or playing bagpipes.

1750
The Highland Clearances begin.

1753
The British Museum is established.

1755
Samuel Johnson publishes his Dictionary.

1756-63
The Seven Years' War

1760–1820

GEORGE III

1768

James Cook sets sail on his first voyage to explore the South Pacific.

1771

Richard Arkwright opens Britain's first cotton mill in Derbyshire. The factory age begins.

1773

The Boston Tea Party

1775

The American War of Independence begins.

1776

Britain's 13 colonies in America sign the Declaration of Independence.

1780

The Gordon Riots

1787

The first fleet of convicts sails from Britain to Australia.

1789

George Washington becomes the first President of America.

~

The French Revolution begins.

1793

Britain goes to war with France

1798

Wolfe Tone leads a rebellion against British rule in Ireland.

1801

The Act of Union creates the United Kingdom.

1805

Nelson defeats the French at Trafalgar.

1807

The slave trade is abolished in Britain.

AM I NOT A MAN AND A BROTHER?

1811–20

The Regency

1815

Wellington defeats Napoleon at the Battle of Waterloo.

1820–30

GEORGE IV

1825

The world's first passenger train line opens between Stockton and Darlington.

1829

Robert Peel sets up the Metropolitan Police.

1830–37

WILLIAM IV

1832

The Great Reform Act is introduced.

1833

Slavery is outlawed in all British colonies.

1834

The Tolpuddle Martyrs are transported to Australia.

1837

Dickens writes *Oliver Twist*.

~

Isambard Kingdom Brunel launches the first ever transatlantic steamship.

1837–1901

VICTORIA

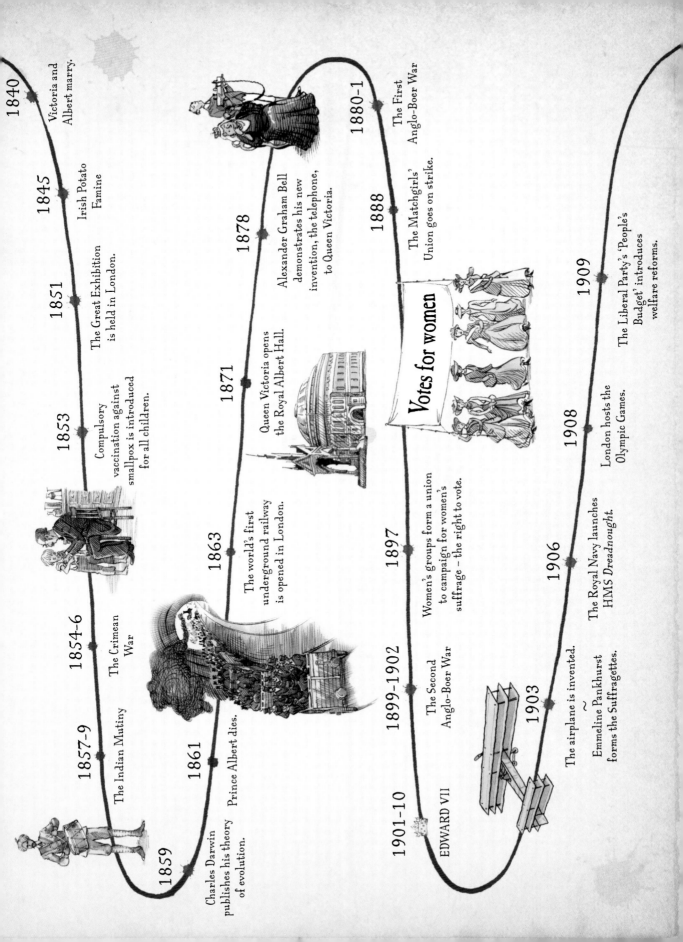

1840
Victoria and Albert marry.

1845
Irish Potato Famine

1851
The Great Exhibition is held in London.

1853
Compulsory vaccination against smallpox is introduced for all children.

1854–6
The Crimean War

1857–9
The Indian Mutiny

1859
Charles Darwin publishes his theory of evolution.

1861
Prince Albert dies.

1863
The world's first underground railway is opened in London.

1871
Queen Victoria opens the Royal Albert Hall.

1878
Alexander Graham Bell demonstrates his new invention, the telephone, to Queen Victoria.

1880–1
The First Anglo–Boer War

1888
The Matchgirls' Union goes on strike.

Votes for women

1897
Women's groups form a union to campaign for women's suffrage – the right to vote.

1899–1902
The Second Anglo–Boer War

1901–10
EDWARD VII

1903
Emmeline Pankhurst forms the Suffragettes.

The airplane is invented.

1906
The Royal Navy launches HMS *Dreadnought*.

1908
London hosts the Olympic Games.

1909
The Liberal Party's 'People's Budget' introduces welfare reforms.

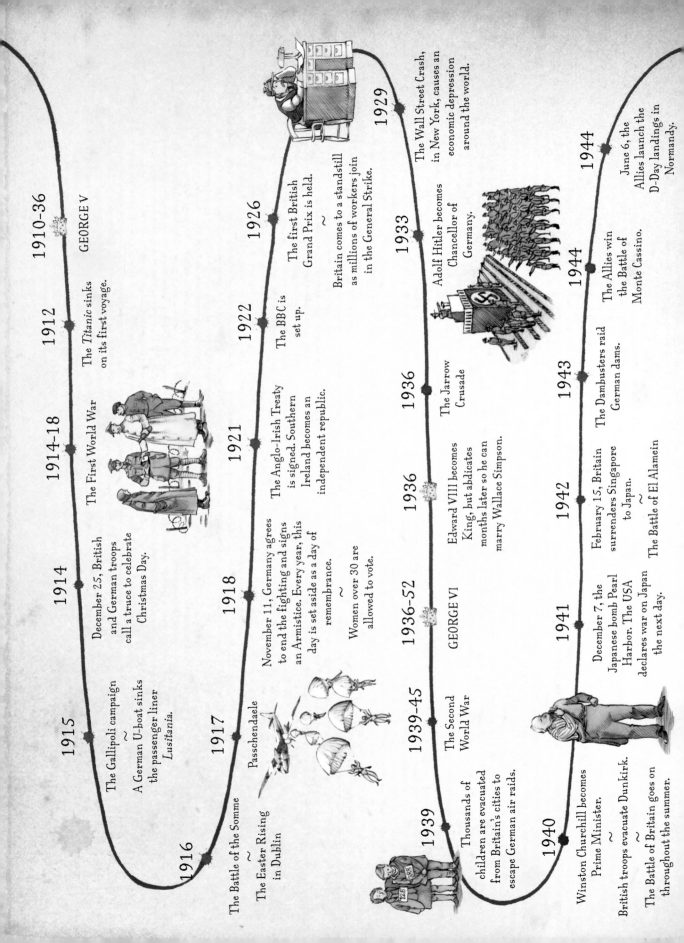

1910-36
GEORGE V

1912
The *Titanic* sinks on its first voyage.

1915
The Gallipoli campaign
~
A German U-boat sinks the passenger liner *Lusitania*.

1914
December 25, British and German troops call a truce to celebrate Christmas Day.

1914-18
The First World War

1916

1917
The Battle of the Somme
~
The Easter Rising in Dublin

Passchendaele

1918
November 11, Germany agrees to end the fighting and signs an Armistice. Every year, this day is set aside as a day of remembrance.
~
Women over 30 are allowed to vote.

1921
The Anglo-Irish Treaty is signed. Southern Ireland becomes an independent republic.

1922
The BBC is set up.

1926
The first British Grand Prix is held.
~
Britain comes to a standstill as millions of workers join in the General Strike.

1929
The Wall Street Crash, in New York, causes an economic depression around the world.

1933
Adolf Hitler becomes Chancellor of Germany.

1936
The Jarrow Crusade

1936
Edward VIII becomes King, but abdicates months later so he can marry Wallace Simpson.

1936-52
GEORGE VI

1939-45
The Second World War

1939
Thousands of children are evacuated from Britain's cities to escape German air raids.

1940
Winston Churchill becomes Prime Minister.
~
British troops evacuate Dunkirk.
~
The Battle of Britain goes on throughout the summer.

1941
December 7, the Japanese bomb Pearl Harbor. The USA declares war on Japan the next day.

1942
February 15, Britain surrenders Singapore to Japan.
~
The Battle of El Alamein

1943
The Dambusters raid German dams.

1944
The Allies win the Battle of Monte Cassino.

1944
June 6, the Allies launch the D-Day landings in Normandy.

1945 — May 8, VE Day, marks the end of the war in Europe.

After the Americans drop atomic bombs on Hiroshima and Nagasaki in Japan, the Japanese surrender and the Second World War is over.

1947 — India is divided into two new independent states: India and Pakistan.

1948 — The National Health Service is set up.

The *Empire Windrush* arrives, bringing 500 Jamaican immigrants to Britain.

1949 — Britain becomes a founding member of the North Atlantic Treaty Organization (NATO).

1951 — The Festival of Britain

1952 — ELIZABETH II

1953 — James Watson and Francis Crick discover the structure of DNA.

1956 — The Suez Crisis

1957 — The Gold Coast becomes the first African colony to achieve independence, renaming itself Ghana.

1958 — The Campaign for Nuclear Disarmament (CND) is founded.

1963 — The Beatles release *Please please me* – their first hit single.

1965 — The Race Relations Board is set up.

The death penalty is abolished.

1966 — England wins the soccer World Cup.

1972 — January 30, British soldiers shoot dead 13 unarmed men at a demonstration in Derry. This becomes known as Bloody Sunday.

1973 — Britain joins the European Economic Community (EEC).

1975 — The Sex Discrimination Act is passed.

1978-9 — The Winter of Discontent

1979 — Margaret Thatcher becomes Prime Minister.

1981 — Prince Charles marries Lady Diana Spencer.

1982 — The Falklands War

1985 — Live Aid concerts

1989 — The Berlin Wall is pulled down.

The Soviet Union collapses, ending the Cold War.

1990-1 — The First Gulf War

1994 — The Channel Tunnel opens, linking Britain to France.

The EEC becomes the European Union (EU).

1997 — Tony Blair becomes Prime Minister.

Britain hands over Hong Kong to China.

Diana, Princess of Wales, dies in a car crash in Paris.

1998 — April 10, the Good Friday Agreement gives hope for peace in Northern Ireland.

1999 — The Welsh Assembly and the Scottish Parliament are established.

December 31, people celebrate the dawn of the new millennium.

Glossary

This glossary explains some of the words you may come across when reading the History of Britain. If a word used in an entry has an entry of its own, it is shown in *italic* type.

Agricultural Revolution A period of rapid development of farming methods in the 18th century, bringing great changes to rural life.

air raid An attack on a town or city by bombs dropped from enemy planes.

Allied Powers The countries that fought against the *Central Powers* in the First World War. The main Allied nations were Britain, France, Russia, Italy and the United States of America.

allies 1. People who fight on the same side in a war. **2.** The countries that fought on the same side as Britain in the Second World War were called the **Allies**. The main Allies were Britain, the Soviet Union, the United States and France.

archaeology The study of historic or *prehistoric* humankind, by examining remains and artefacts which are often hidden underground.

archbishop A senior Christian priest, in charge of the Church over a large area. Priests in the rank below this are called **bishops**.

assassinate To murder a leader or politician.

atomic bomb An explosive weapon that releases enormous energy by splitting elements such as uranium or plutonium.

Axis Powers The countries that fought on the same side as Germany in the Second World War.

bard A person who composes and recites poetry.

the Blitz A period of intensive *air raids* on British cities during the Second World War.

Blitzkrieg A swift attack, using tanks, troops and aircraft, used to great effect by the German army at the beginning of the Second World War. The word means 'lightning war' in German.

cabinet A group of high-ranking members of *Parliament* who assist the Prime Minister.

Catholicism A branch of the Christian Church which is led by the *Pope* in Rome.

Celts A group of people who lived in Europe over 2,000 years ago.

censorship The control, often by a *government*, of information that may threaten its security.

Central Powers The nations that fought against the *Allied Powers* in the First World War. The Central Powers were Germany, Austria-Hungary, the Turkish Empire and Bulgaria.

civil war A war in which armies from the same country fight each other.

civilian Anyone who is not a member of the armed forces.

civilization An advanced way of life, where people live in towns and have a system of laws and a way of writing.

climate The average weather conditions for an area, usually based on temperature and rainfall.

Cold War The struggle for power between the United States and the Soviet Union, which was at its height during the 1950s and 1960s.

colony A *settlement* created in a foreign land, by people who have moved away from their homeland.

Commonwealth 1. The *government* led by Oliver Cromwell after the *execution* of Charles I at the end of the English *Civil War*. **2.** The association of countries which were formerly members of the British *empire*.

concentration camp A prison camp where *civilians* and political prisoners are held during wartime, usually under harsh conditions.

conscription Compulsory recruitment of *civilians* into the armed forces.

constitution A set of laws used to rule an organization or country.

constitutional monarchy A form of *government* in which a *monarch* is the head of *state*, but a *parliament* holds political power.

convict A person who has been found guilty of a crime and put in prison.

coronation A ceremony in which a new *monarch* is crowned.

cremation The ceremonial burning of a dead body.

culture The shared ideas, beliefs and values of a group of people.

democracy A political system in which citizens can freely elect people to represent them in *government*.

dictator A ruler who imposes his rule by force.

diplomacy Negotiations between *government* officials of different nations.

Divine Right of Kings The belief that a *monarch* is chosen by God to rule.

dynasty A series of rulers from the same family.

economy The financial system of a country.

EU (formerly EEC) A growing body of European member *states* which creates its own common laws and policies.

election Selecting, by vote, a person or party to a position of power.

empire A group of countries or *territories* under the control of another country.

emigrate To leave one's native country and settle in another.

Enlightenment An 18th century philosophical movement based on the idea that science could explain everything in nature.

evacuation Removing people from a threatened area, for safety. During the Second World War, many *civilians* were evacuated from cities to rural areas.

evolve To change or develop gradually.

execute To kill a person who has been sentenced to death by law.

famine A serious shortage of food which causes many people to die.

Fascism The form of military *government* in Italy from 1922 to 1943, led by the *dictator* Benito Mussolini. Fascism is also used to describe similar forms of *government* in other countries, such as Hitler's Nazi Germany.

fortress A group of buildings surrounded by a wall so that they can be easily defended.

general A soldier who leads an army.

General Election An election to determine the ruling political party in the United Kingdom.

global warming The slow warming of the Earth's *climate*, which is caused by harmful gases from power stations, factories and car exhausts.

government The group of people who run a country.

Great Depression The period of worldwide unemployment and poverty, which began after the Wall Street Crash of 1929.

guerrilla warfare Fighting by launching surprise attacks, usually used against a larger, more professional army.

guild An organization for craftsmen or traders.

heir The person who will inherit, by law, the property or titles of someone when they die.

heretic Someone whose beliefs differ from the main teachings of their religion.

hillfort A fortified hilltop *settlement*.

Hindu A person who follows the Hindu faith, the main religion of India.

Holocaust The term given to the Nazis' systematic slaughter of European *Jews* and other groups during the Second World War.

home front Anyone or anything in the home country during a foreign war.

immigration The arrival of people coming to live in a country from elsewhere.

Industrial Revolution The rapid growth of mechanical, factory-based industries in the 18th and 19th centuries.

inheritance The passing on of property to an *heir* after death.

intelligence Secret military information about an enemy, often gathered by the *Secret Service*.

invasion Entering an area with the intention of taking control of it.

Jew a person who belongs to the race of people who are descended from the ancient tribes of Israel. The Jewish religion is based on the teachings of the Old Testament of the Bible.

kingdom An area that is ruled or reigned over by a king or queen.

knight A man in the Middle Ages who was trained to fight on horseback.

Latin The language spoken by the people of ancient Rome and the Roman *empire*. It was also used by *scholars* in *medieval* Europe.

mass production The manufacture of products on a large scale, usually by the use of machines.

medieval Anything relating to the Middle Ages.

Methodism A branch of *Protestantism* founded by John Wesley in the 18th century.

missionary A person who travels to a foreign country and tries to persuade the people living there to follow a different religion.

monarchy A system of *government* in which a country is ruled by a **monarch** – a king or queen.

munitions Military equipment including weapons and ammunition.

Muslim A person who follows the Islamic faith.

nationalism **1.** A feeling of pride in one's nation. **2.** The shared feeling by people who live in the same region and who have the same language, *culture* or religion, that they would benefit from forming their own nation.

NATO The North Atlantic Treaty Organization: an international organization which was set up in 1949 to defend Western countries against the Soviet Union. The USA, Canada and Britain are members of NATO.

neutral country A country that takes no side in a war between other countries, in the hope that it will not be attacked.

noble A member of a family that belongs to the ruling class, or **nobility**, of a country.

occupy To seize and take control of an area.

officer A senior member of the armed forces.

pagan A person who believes in many gods.

parliament A group of people who meet to make decisions and create laws for their country.

partition The division of a country into two or more separate nations.

peasant A person who works on the land.

pension A regular payment made to someone who no longer works.

petition A written document signed by a number of people, requesting some form of action from a *government* or other authority.

pilgrimage A journey to a holy place, undertaken by **pilgrims**.

plague A disease which spreads fast and kills many people.

Pope The head of the *Catholic* Church, who resides in Rome.

prehistory The period of time before the development of the written word.

press gang A group who force *civilians* to serve in the army or navy.

propaganda Information that is systematically spread to promote or damage a political cause.

Protestantism A branch of the Christian Church that does not have the *Pope* as its leader.

Protestant Reformation An attempt in the 16th century to reform the *Catholic* Church, which resulted in *Protestantism*.

province An area within an *empire*. Britain was a province in the Roman *empire*.

Puritanism A strict branch of *Protestantism*.

Quakerism A Christian sect founded by George Fox around 1650. It is also known as the Society of Friends.

rationing A fixed allowance of food and goods. Usually applied during times of war or shortage.

rebellion An organized resistance to a *government* or other authority.

refugee A person who is forced to leave their homeland, usually fleeing dangers such as war, *famine* or persecution.

regent A person who rules a country in the absence of a *monarch*.

Renaissance A movement that began in Italy around 1350, which was based on a revival of classical *culture*.

republic A country without a king or queen, whose leaders rule on behalf of the people.

Restoration The re-establishment of the *monarchy* in 1660, with reign of Charles II.

revolt A *rebellion* against authority.

revolution The overthrowing of a leader or *government* by the people.

royalty A *monarch* and his or her family.

sacrifice A ritual killing of a person or an animal to please a god or gods.

scholar A person who studies, teaches, and writes books.

scribe A person in ancient or *medieval* times whose job was to read and write for everyone else.

secret service A *government* agency engaged in *intelligence*-gathering activities.

settlement A group of dwellings, that form a community.

shareholder A person who invests money by buying a portion, or share, of the value of a company, hoping to make a profit.

state An area with its own laws. A state can be independent, or part of a larger country.

strike A protest in which workers demand better pay or fairer conditions by refusing to work.

submarine A ship that can travel under the water for long periods, widely used for the first time in the First World War.

suffrage The right to vote. In the late 19th and early 20th centuries, women who campaigned for the right to vote were known as **Suffragists** or **Suffragettes**.

taxes Money collected from the people by a *government* or a ruler.

territory An area of land under the control of a particular group or *government*.

trade union An organization of workers who campaign together for better pay and fairer working conditions.

transportation Sending *convicts* overseas to a penal colony.

treason An act seen as a betrayal of a country or leader, such as trying to overthrow a *government*.

treaty An agreement between two or more countries.

tribe A group of people, usually one that has not developed a written language, who share common ancestry, *cultural*, religious and regional origins.

U-boat A German *submarine*. The name comes from *Unterseeboot*, which means 'undersea boat' in German.

UN The United Nations, an international peacekeeping organization that was set up in 1945, after the failure of the **League of Nations**, which was set up following the First World War.

Index

Index of British monarchs

Aethelbald, King of Mercia, 100, 101
Aethelbert, 99
Aethelred the Unready, 112, 113, 114, 116
Aethelred, King of Wessex, 108
Alexander III, King of Scotland, 149, 152
Alfred the Great, 108-109
Anne, 231, 232-233, 235, 236, 237
Arthur, 90-91, 175
Athelstan, 111

Canute, 114-115, 116
Charles I, 208-213
Charles II, 214, 216-217, 221, 222-223, 226

David, King of Scotland, 136, 138
David II, King of Scotland, 154

Edgar the Peaceful, 111, 112, 116
Edmund II, Ironside, 114, 115, 116
Edward the Confessor, 116, 117, 120, 129
Edward the Martyr, 112, 116
Edward I, 149-153

Edward II, 153, 154
Edward III, 91, 154, 155, 157, 158, 168, 170, 172, 175
Edward IV, 173, 174
Edward V, 173, 174
Edward VI, 181, 190
Edward VII, 349, 352, 360
Edward VIII, 349
Elizabeth I, 191, 192-193, 194, 196, 200, 202-205, 294
Elizabeth II, 456, 471

George I, 233, 235, 236-237, 238, 239
George II, 236, 238, 239, 244, 256
George III, 256-257, 258, 259, 260, 272, 273, 274, 277, 284, 295
George IV, 257, 288, 290, 295
George V, 349, 297, 360
George VI, 456

Harold II, Godwinson, 117, 120, 121, 122-123
Harold I, 116
Harthacanute, 116, 117
Henry I, 136
Henry II, 136, 137, 138-139, 140, 141, 142
Henry III, 148, 149, 167
Henry IV, 168-169, 170
Henry V, 170-171

Henry VI, 171, 172, 173
Henry VII, Henry Tudor, 91, 174-175, 178-179
Henry VIII, 180-185, 189
Hywel Dda, the Good, 111

James I, 206-207, 236, 277
James I, King of Scotland, 168
James II, 216, 217, 228-229, 231, 464
James III, the Old Pretender, 233
James IV, King of Scotland, 179, 189, 277
James V, King of Scotland, 183
James VI, King of Scotland, see James I
John, 142, 143, 148
John Balliol, King of Scotland, 152

MacAlpin, Kenneth, 110
Malcolm III, Canmore, King of Scotland, 128, 129
Malcolm IV, King of Scotland, 138
Mary I, 181, 190-191
Mary I, Queen of Scots, 183, 191, 202-203, 206
Mary II, 229, 230-231
Matilda, 136-137

Offa, King of Mercia, 100, 101, 102

Rhodri the Great, King of Gwynedd, 111
Richard I, the Lionheart, 142-143, 148
Richard II, 158-159, 160, 168, 170
Richard III, 174-175, 178-179
Robert III, King of Scotland, 168
Robert Bruce, King of Scotland, 152, 153

Stephen, 136-137
Swein Forkbeard, 113, 114

Victoria, 9, 293-299, 303, 306, 310, 313, 317, 318, 319, 320, 321, 324, 327, 328, 329, 345, 348, 349, 352

William I, the Conqueror, 117, 120, 121, 122-3, 125, 126, 128-129, 130, 134, 136
William II, 136
William III, of Orange, 229, 230-231, 464
William IV, 257, 290, 291, 293, 294, 295

Index of wars and battles

American War of Independence, 272-273
    Yorktown, 273
Bannockburn, 153
Boer War, 347, 400
Boyne, 231, 276
Cold War, 453, 468
Crimean War, 316-317, 318, 327
    Balaklava, 316
Culloden, 244, 245, 246
Dettingen, 239
English Civil War, 210-213
    Edgehill, 210-211
    Marston Moor, 211, 212
    Naseby, 212
    Preston, 213
    Worcester, 214
Falklands War, 462
First World War, 9, 297, 351,

357, 358, 362-385, 388, 400
    Arras, 365
    Belleau Wood, 365
    Cambrai, 365, 380
    Dogger Bank, 376
    Heligoland Bight, 376
    Jutland, 376-377
    Loos, 365
    Marne, 365
    Mons, 365
    Passchendaele, 365, 382-383
    Somme, 365, 380-381, 382
    Verdun, 365, 380
    Ypres, First Battle, 365
    Ypres, Second Battle, 365, 370
Flodden, 179
Gravelines, 205

Gulf War, 469
Hastings, 6, 8, 120, 121, 122-123
Hundred Years War, 154-155, 158, 170-171
    Agincourt, 170, 171
    Castillon, 171
    Crécy, 155, 170
    Poitiers, 155, 170
    Sluys, 154
Irish War of Independence, 389
Isandhlwana, 346, 347
Maldon, 113
Nile, 278
Plassey, 251
Second World War, 9, 393-449, 452, 453
    Atlantic, 413
    Britain, 404-407

    Bulge, the, 445
    El Alamein, 429
    Monte Cassino, 433
Seven Years' War, 248-251
    Quebec, 249
Sheriffmuir, 237
Shrewsbury, 169
Solway Moss, 183
Stamford Bridge, 121
Stirling Bridge, 152
Trafalgar, 278-279, 361
Vinegar Hill, 277
Wars of the Roses, 172-175
    Barnet, 173
    Bosworth, 175, 178
    Evesham, 149
    Lewes, 148
    Towton, 173
    Wakefield, 173
Waterloo, 280-281, 289

General Index

abbeys,
  Battle, 123
  Dunfermline, 129
  Fountains, 182
  Westminster, 117, 152
  Whitby, 99
Aboriginals, 261
Act of Settlement, 231, 233
Acts of Union, 233, 277
Adam, James, 265
Adam, Robert, 240, 241, 265
Aelfthryth, 112
Africa, 58, 60, 80, 106, 200,
  201, 223, 248, 270, 271,
  346-347, 348, 374, 428-429,
  454, 455
Afrika Korps, 428
Age of Reason, *see*
  Enlightenment
Agricola, Julius, 52-53, 57
Agricultural Revolution,
  246-247
agriculture, *see* farming
AIDS, 467
Air Raid Precautions (ARP),
  396, 397
air raids, 372, 395, 396, 397,
  401, 408, 409, 410-411, 418,
  419, 440-441
aircraft, 372, 378-379
  airships, 369, 372
  British, 404-407, 410, 423,
  439
  Fairey Swordfish, 423
  fighter planes, 378, 410
  German, 398, 399, 404,
  405, 406, 407, 408, 410
  Hurricanes, 404, 405
  Japanese, 425, 426
  Lancaster bombers, 431
  Messerschmitts, 405
  Sopwith camels, 379
  Spitfires, 404, 405, 406
  Stukas, 398, 399
Alba, 110
Albanians, 469
Albanus, 69
Albert Memorial, 321
Albert, Prince Consort, 296,
  297, 299, 312, 313, 320,
  321, 349
alchemy, 147
Alcuin, 102
Aldermaston, 457
Alexander II, Emperor of
  Russia, 317
Alice in Wonderland, 330,
  340

Allies,
  First World War, 363, 364,
  365, 370, 371, 374, 375,
  377-381, 383
  Second World War, 399,
  405, 413, 429, 43-439
America, *see also* United
  States of America, 106,
  200, 201, 233, 235, 246,
  248-249, 270, 272-273, 274
American Revolution,
  272-273, 276, 282
Amesbury, 19
Anarchy, the, 81, 136-137
Anderson shelters, 408
Angles, 84, 89, 90, 91, 92
Anglesey, 67, 85
Anglo-Irish Treaty, 389
Anglo-Saxon Chronicle, 113,
  130, 137
Anglo-Saxons, 92, 93, 94-97,
  98, 99, 100, 101, 102, 103,
  105, 107, 109
Anne Boleyn, 181
Anne of Cleves, 181
Antarctica, 358, 359
anti-aircraft guns, 410
antibiotics, 466
antiseptics, 345
Antonine Wall, 55, 85
Antoninus Pius, 55
Anzac Day, 375
Anzacs, 374, 375
Aquae Sulis, see Bath
aqueducts, 48, 49
Archbishop of Canterbury,
  99, 140, 158, 181, 190
architecture,
  Baroque, 222
  Georgian, 264-265
  Palladian, 240-241
  Perpendicular, 157
  Regency, 284-285
  Roman, 48-49
  Victorian, 336-337
Aragon, Catherine of, 181
Argentina, 462
Arkwright, Richard, 253
armed forces,
  American, 382, 383, 445,
  447
  Australian, 374, 375, 382,
  427
  British, 364, 365, 368, 369,
  370, 371, 380, 381, 397,
  415, 427, 429, 444, 446
  Canadian, 370, 374, 383
  European, 361, 366, 371

  Free French, 439
  French, 280, 281, 378, 380
  German, 281, 360, 361, 364,
  367, 370, 371, 378, 379,
  383, 398, 445
  Indian, 250-251, 319, 364
  Japanese, 426, 427, 446,
  447
  New Zealand, 374-375, 427
  Russian, 382, 444, 445
Armistice, 383, 385
Arnhem, Netherlands, 444
art, 12, 78-79, 98, 99, 160,
  162, 188-189, 196, 282, 283,
  262-263, 340-341, 470
Arts and Crafts movement,
  341
Asquith, Herbert, 355
Astor, Lady Nancy, 386
Atkins, Tommy, 364
Atlantic Ocean, 359, 412
Atlantic Wall, 436
Atlee, Clement, 449, 452,
  453, 462
Atrebates tribe, 33
Augustine, 99
auld alliance, 152
Aurelian, 81
Austen, Jane, 285
Australia, 260-261, 308, 427
Austria, 232, 248
Austria-Hungary, 362, 363
aviation, 352, 358
Axis Powers, 399, 428, 429,
  432

Babington plot, 203
Bacon, Roger, 147
Baden-Powell, Robert, 347
Bakewell, Robert, 247
Baldwin, Stanley, 391
Balkans, 362, 363, 469
Balliol, John, 152
ballista, 34
Balmoral Castle, 297
Bank of England, 223
Banks, Joseph, 260-261
barges, 255
Barnard, Dr. Christiaan, 466
Barnardo's Charity, 300
Baroque style, 222
barrage balloons, 410
Barrie, J.M., 353
Barry, Charles, 298
basilica, 44, 50, 51
Bath, 46-47, 67, 85, 264, 285
bathhouses, 40, 46-47, 48, 49
battles, *see* Index of battles

Bayeux Tapestry, 117,
  120-121, 123
Bazalgette, Joseph, 339
BBC, 387, 403
bear baiting, 196, 214, 242
Beardsley, Aubrey, 341
Beatles, The, 458, 459
Beaufort, Joan, 168
Becket, St. Thomas, 140-141,
  161
Beaumaris Castle, 150-151
Bede, 6, 102
Beeton, Isabella, 342
Beggar's Opera, 242
Belgium, 280, 281, 363, 364,
  365, 382, 384, 445
Bell, Alexander Graham, 345
Benz, Karl, 344
Beowulf, 103
Bergen-Belsen, 442-443
Berlin, 439, 444, 445, 468
Berlin Wall, 468
Berliner, Emile, 344
Bessemer, Henry, 304
Beveridge, Sir William, 453
Bevin Boys, 417
Bevin, Ernest, 417
bicycles, invention of, 333
Bignor Roman Villa, 78, 85
Bill of Rights (1689), 230
Birmingham, 337
Bismarck, 413, 422, 423
Black and Tans, 389
Black Death, *see also* plague,
  218-219, 221
Black Hole of Calcutta, 250
Black, Joseph, 259
Black Prince, 155, 158,
Black Sea, 316,
Blackbeard, Edward Teach,
  233
blackout, 396, 397, 440
Blair, Tony, 470, 471
Blake, William, 282
Blenheim Palace, 232
Bletchley Park, 421
Blitz, 408-411, 419
Blitzkrieg, 395, 398, 400
blockades, naval, 376, 377
Blood, Colonel, 216
Bloody Assizes, 228
Bloody Sunday, 464
Bludworth, Thomas, Lord
  Mayor of London, 220, 221
Blücher, Field Marshal, 281
Boers, 347
Boleyn, Anne, 181
Bombay, India, 250

bombing, 357, 372, 378, 389, 404, 408-411, 425, 433, 465

bombs, 430-431
  atomic, 447
  bouncing, 430
  'dead rat', 421
  incendiary, 410
  Little Boy, 447
  unexploded, 409
  V-1s and V-2s, 440, 441

Bonnie Prince Charlie, see Stuart, Charles Edward

Book of Martyrs, 191

Booth, Charles, 354

Bosnia, 362

Boston Tea Party, 272

Botany Bay, 260, 261

Boudicca, 36-37, 51, 52, 66, 74

Boy Scouts, 347, 387

Bradshaw, John, 213

Braganza, Catherine of, 216

Brancaster Roman Fort, 82, 85

Brigantes tribe, 52-53, 85

Brighton, 284, 285, 465

Brindley, James, 255

Bristol, 198, 248, 264, 270, 338

British
  colonies, 9, 248-249, 270, 271, 272, 273, 308, 318-319, 346, 347, 374, 451, 454-455
  East India Company, 250-251
  empire, 9, 251, 293, 303, 312, 318, 319, 351, 352, 360, 374-375, 387, 389, 400, 426, 451, 454-5, 457
  Expeditionary Force, 364, 365
  government, 238, 239, 244, 245, 251, 256, 261, 272, 274, 276, 277, 289, 290, 291, 298-299, 301, 302, 305, 307, 316, 319, 324-325, 326, 329, 334, 347, 355, 356, 360, 369, 388, 389, 391, 396, 414, 416, 449, 451, 452, 454, 455, 457, 458, 460-461, 462-463, 468, 469, 470
  Hotel, 317
  Museum, 259, 315, 336
  Royal Society, 226, 227, 344
  Union of Fascists, 391

Britons, 56-57, 67, 77, 92, 93, 96, 98, 105

Bronze Age, 18-24

Brown, John, 321

Brown, Lancelot 'Capability', 241

Bruce, Robert, 153, 154

Brummell, George 'Beau', 285

Brunel, Isambard Kingdom, 338, 344

BSE, 467

Buckingham Palace, 294, 296, 300, 456

Bulgaria, 363

burials, 17, 19, 93, 106

Burma, 446, 447

Burns, Robert, 153, 283

Bute, Earl of, see Stuart, John, Earl of Bute

Butser Ancient Farm, 32

Byron, Lord, 282, 283

Cable Street Riot, 391

Caerleon, 40, 64, 85

Caernarfon, 52, 85

Caesar, see Julius Caesar

Cairo, Egypt, 429

Calcutta, India, 250

Calgacus, 57

Caledonia, see also Scotland, 30, 52, 57, 84

Caligula, 31, 34

Cambridge University, 147, 157

Cameron, Julia Margaret, 340, 341

Campaign for Nuclear Disarmament (CND), 457

Canada, 248-249

canals, 255

Canterbury Cathedral, 141, 161

Canterbury Tales, The, 161

Caracalla, 81

Caratacus, 33, 35, 85

Carausius, 82

Caribbean, see also West Indies, 9, 204, 248, 270, 271, 455

Carisbrooke Castle, 213

Carnaby Street, 459

Carroll, Lewis, 330, 340

cars, invention of, 333, 344

Cartwright, Edmund, 253

castles, 126-127, 128, 129, 137, 138, 297
  Balmoral, 297
  Beaumaris, 150
  Chepstow, 128, 129
  Carisbrooke, 213
  Colchester, 66
  Corfe, 112

Edinburgh, 152

Fotheringhay, 203

Maiden, 24

motte and bailey, 127

Nottingham, 211

Portchester, 82, 85

Windsor, 297, 471

cat-o-nine-tails, 261

Catesby, Robert, 207

Catherine of Aragon, 181

Catherine of Braganza, 216

Catholicism/Catholics, 140, 144, 177, 181, 183, 189, 190-191, 192, 202, 203, 206, 207, 208, 210, 214, 217, 228-229, 231, 237, 276, 277, 389 460, 464

Catuvellauni tribe, 33, 35, 85

Cavaliers, 211

cavalry, 39, 210, 211, 289, 316

Cavendish, Henry, 259

Caxton, William, 161

Celtic languages, 25, 33, 77, 92, 96

Celts, 26, 92, 93

cemeteries, First World War, 384

censorship, 369

census, 306

Central Powers, 363, 374

ceorls, 96

Chadwick, Edwin, 326

chain mail, 124

Chamberlain, Neville, 394, 395, 397

Channel Islands, 403

Channel Tunnel, 339, 468

chantries, 145

Chaplin, Charlie, 391

chariots, 31, 37, 64, 65

Charlemagne, King of the Franks, 102

Charles, Prince of Wales, 90, 462, 471

Charleston, 386

Charlotte, Queen, 256, 257, 274

Chartists, 299

Chaucer, Geoffrey, 161

Chedworth Roman Villa, 71, 85

Chepstow Castle, 128, 129

Chester, 40, 85

Chester, HMS, 376

children, 74-75, 76-77, 269, 328, 329, 353, 354, 355, 387, 418-419

child workers, 269, 289, 301, 305

China, 248, 426, 469

Chindits, 447

Chippendale, Thomas, 266

chloroform gas, 327, 344

cholera, 317, 326

Christianity, see also Catholicism, the Church, Methodism, Presbyterianism, Protestantism, Puritanism, 68-69, 93, 96, 98-99, 107, 109, 134, 142, 143, 166, 184, 189,

Christina of Markyate, 163

Christmas, 108, 123, 144, 166, 215, 297, 367

chronometer, 260

Church, the, 98, 140, 144, 146, 157, 161, 163, 166, 181, 182, 189, 190-191, 199, 227, 268

churches, 144-145, 215, 268
  Battle Abbey, 123
  Canterbury Cathedral, 141, 161
  Coventry Cathedral, 411
  Dunfermline Abbey, 129
  Fountains Abbey, 182
  Lincoln Cathedral, 137
  St. Paul's Cathedral, 220, 222, 409
  Westminster Abbey, 117
  Whitby Abbey, 99

Churchill, John, Duke of Marlborough, 232

Churchill, Winston, 232, 355, 397, 400-401, 402, 403, 404, 407, 409, 411, 413, 420, 427, 428, 432, 439, 445, 449, 456

Chysauster, 56

Cirencester, 83

civil war, 80, 81
  English Civil War, 209, 210-213
  in Ireland, 389
  Wars of the Roses, 172-173

civitates, 45, 85

Clarkson, Thomas, 271

Claudius, 34, 35, 50, 66

Clemenceau, Georges, 383

Clifton Suspension Bridge, 338

Clive, Robert, 250, 251

Clodius, Albinus, 80

clothing, 15, 25, 26, 41, 60, 62-63, 97, 193, 194-195, 222, 285, 294, 298, 322, 323, 386, 455, 458, 459

Coalbrookdale, 286

coal mining, see miners' strike, mining

Cobham's Cubs, 241, 249
Cobham, Viscount, 241
cock fighting, 196, 242
coffee, 223, 354
    coffee houses, 223, 242
coins, 27, 58, 101
Coke, Thomas, 247
Colchester, 35, 36, 41, 45, 51,
    66, 85
Colchester Castle, 66
Cold War, 453, 468
Coleridge, Samuel Taylor,
    283
Collins, Michael, 389
coloniae, 45, 51, 85
colonies, see British colonies
Columba, 98
Columbus, Christopher, 200
Commandos, 420, 439
Commodus, 80, 83
Commonwealth
    of Nations, 454
    period, 213, 214-215
Conan Doyle, Arthur, 309
concentration camps, 442, 443
confraternities, 135
Congress of Paris, 317
Congress of Philadelphia, 272
conscientious objectors, 368
conscripts, 397
Conservative Party, see also
    Tories, 298, 299, 324, 325,
    355, 449, 456, 462, 470
Constable, John, 282, 283
Constantine, 69, 80, 83
Constantinople, Turkey, 80,
    374
Constantius, 83
constitutional monarchy, 298
Cook, Captain James,
    260-261
Cook, Thomas, 334
Cooke, William, 344
Coram, Thomas, 268, 269
Corfe Castle, 112
Corn Law, 289, 300, 303, 307
Cornwall, 56
Cornwell, John, 376
coronations,
    Elizabeth II, 456
    George IV, 288
    Victoria, 295
    William and Mary, 230
    William the Conqueror, 123
corsets, 322
cottars, 131
courtiers, 180, 193, 195, 206
courts of law, 125, 131, 135,
    140, 170
Coventry, 410-411

Coward, Noël, 434
Craig, James, 265
Crane, Walter, 341
Cranmer, Thomas, 181, 190
Creswell Crags, 12
cricket, 256, 335
Crick, Francis, 466
crime, 61, 96, 199, 242-243,
    261, 308-309
Crimea, 316
crinolines, 322
Cromwell, Oliver, 212-215
Cromwell, Richard, 215
Cromwell, Thomas, 182
crop rotation, 70, 247
Crusades, 142-143
Crystal Palace, 312, 313, 314
Curzon, Lord, 319
Czechoslovakia, 394, 395, 405

Dafydd ap Gruffydd, 151
Da Gama, Vasco, 200
Dáil, 388
Daladier, Edouard, 394
Dalriada, 92, 110, 111
Dambusters, 431
dandies, 285
Danes, see also Vikings,
    104-105, 106-107, 108-109,
    111, 112-113, 114-115, 116
Danelaw, 109, 111
Darby, Abraham, 227, 286
Dark Ages, 88-89
Darnley, Lord, 202-203
Darwin, Charles, 315
Davy, Humphrey, 259
David, St., 98
Davison, Emily, 357
D-Day, 433, 436-439, 440
de Beauharnais, Josephine,
    278
de Gaulle, General Charles,
    439
de Grey, Reginald, 168
de Montfort, Simon, Earl of
    Leicester, 148, 149
de Troyes, Chrétien, 91
Declaration of
    Independence, American,
    272
Declaration of Indulgence,
    228
decolonization, 451, 454, 457,
    469
Defence of the Realm Act,
    369
deforestation, 467
demobilization, Second
    World War, 448
Denmark, 6, 104, 108, 114,

115, 116, 376, 398
destroyers, 413
devolution, 470
Dewidd, St., 98
Diana, Princess of Wales, 471
Dickens, Charles, 301, 331
dinosaurs, 314
Diocletian, 69
disco, 461
diseases, see also plague, 170,
    198, 261, 307, 317, 326, 327,
    354, 355, 367, 375, 466, 467
Disraeli, Benjamin, 319, 324,
    325
dissolution of the
    monasteries, 182
Divine Right of Kings, 206,
    208
Divorce Reform Act, 458
DNA, 466
dogfights, 378
Dolly the Sheep, 467
Domesday Book, 130
Domitian, 53
Domna, Julia, 81
Donne, John, 196
Doré, Gustav, 91
Dover, 49, 85
Downing Street, 239
Drake, Sir Francis, 200, 201,
    204
Dreadnought, HMS, 361
Druids, 27, 37, 67, 76
Dryden, John, 91
Dublin, Ireland, 6, 107, 111,
    265, 277, 388
Dudley, Robert, Earl of
    Leicester, 193
Dumnonii tribe, 56
Dunkirk, France, 398, 399,
    402-403, 404, 416, 434
Dutch East Indies, 426
Dutch, see Netherlands

Eadric, Streona, 114
East Africa, 374
East Anglia, 89, 105
East Indies, 200, 201
Easter Rising, 388, 465
Eastern Front, 363, 382, 383
Eastman, George, 344
Eboracum, see York
Edinburgh, Scotland, 152,
    244, 259, 264, 265, 410
Edison, Thomas, 344
education, see also schools,
    146-147, 224, 269, 300,
    328-329, 330, 348, 452
Edward, Prince of Wales, see
    also Edward VII, 321

Egypt, 51, 60, 67, 347, 428,
    457
Eisenhower, General Dwight,
    437
Elba, 280, 281
Eleanor of Aquitaine, 139
El Draque, see Drake, Sir
    Francis
elections, 288, 355, 356, 388,
    462
electoral reform, 290, 324,
    325, 356
electric
    light bulb, 344
    power, 332
    telegraph, 344
elephants, war, 34
Eleven Years' Tyranny,
    208-209
Elgar, Edward, 352
Elizabeth of York, 175, 178
Elizabeth, Princess, see also
    Elizabeth II, 417
Emmet, Robert, 276
enclosures, 187, 246, 253
Emma of Normandy, 113,
    115, 116
Empire Windrush, 455
Encyclopaedia Britannica,
    259
Endeavour, HMS, 260-261
Endurance, HMS, 359
English Channel, 82, 121,
    139, 154, 204, 279, 339, 364,
    401, 403, 405, 437, 441, 468
English Common Law, 140
Enigma, 421
Enlightenment, 258-259, 274,
    282
Entente Cordiale, 352
environmental damage, 466
Equal Pay Act, 460
Equiano, Olaudah, 270, 271
Erasmus, 189
Ernest Augustus, Duke of
    Cumberland, 291
Erskine, John, Earl of Mar,
    237
Essex, 89, 98, 99, 113
Euro, 468
European
    Economic Community
        (EEC), 460, 468
    Union, 468
evacuation, 397, 398, 418,
    449
Evelyn, John, 220, 230
Everest, Mount, 456
exploration, 200-201,
    260-261, 351, 358-359

factories, 252-253, 289, 323, 324, 371, 373, 379, 415
Factory Acts, 289
fairs, 135
Fairey Swordfish, 428
Falklands War, 462
family life, 74-75, 76-77, 79, 96, 186, 224-225, 342-343, 354, 387
farming, 16-17, 20, 21, 22, 56, 57, 70-71, 94, 97, 131, 132-133, 186-187, 235, 246-247, 253, 261, 300, 302-303, 372, 373, 415
fashion, see also clothing, 62-63, 97, 193, 194-195, 222, 228, 238, 285, 322-323, 386, 458, 459
Fawkes, Guy, 207
Festival of Britain, 456
Field of the Cloth of Gold, 184-185
fighter planes, see aircraft
fire ships, 204-205
First World War, see Index of wars and battles
Fisher, Andrew, 374
Fitzclarence family, 290
Fitzgerald family, 183
Fitz Osbern, William, Earl of Hereford, 128
Flanders, Belgium, 365
flappers, 386
Fleming, Ian, 430
Flying Circus, 378
flying shuttle, 252
football, see also soccer, 166, 335
Formby, George, 429
Forth Railway Bridge, 339
forts, 184
    French, 248, 249
    Roman, 40-41, 42, 48, 49, 50, 52, 53, 55, 70, 82, 85
forum, 44, 50, 51
Fotheringhay Castle, 203
Foundling Hospital, 268, 269
Foxe, John, 191
France, 25, 30, 31, 51, 61, 102, 113, 119, 120, 135, 137, 138, 139, 140, 143, 148, 152, 154-155, 158, 170-171, 174, 179, 184, 191, 202, 208, 214, 217, 229, 230, 231, 232, 237, 239, 244, 245, 248-249, 250-251, 273, 274, 275, 276, 278, 279, 280, 281, 316, 333, 339, 352, 353, 363, 364, 365, 367, 370, 374, 383, 397, 398, 399, 404, 436,

438, 457, 468
Francis I, King of France, 184
Frank, Anne, 443
Franz Ferdinand, Archduke of Austria, 362
Frederick, Duke of York, 295
Frederick, Prince of Wales, 256
Free French, 439
Freetown, Sierra Leone, 271
French Revolution, 274, 275, 276, 282, 288
Frith, William Powell, 309
Fry, Elizabeth, 269
funerals,
    Diana, Princess of Wales, 471
    Edward VII, 360
    John Cornwell, 376
    Roman, 75, 79
    Victoria, 348-349

Gaelic, 129, 139, 465
Gainsborough, Thomas, 263
Gallipoli Peninsula, 374-375
gambling, 242, 284, 285, 352
Gandhi, Mohandas (Mahatma), 454
gas masks, 370, 396
gas, poison, 370
Gateshead Bridge, 472
Gaul, 30, 31, 33, 60, 61, 81
Gay, John, 242
general elections, see elections
genetics, 466
Geoffrey of Anjou, 136, 138
Geoffrey of Monmouth, 91
George, Prince of Denmark, 232
George, Prince Regent, see also George IV, 284-285, 288
Germany, 18, 51, 60, 81, 82, 84, 89, 92, 102, 103, 236, 333, 345, 348, 360, 361, 363, 364, 365, 367, 374, 376, 377, 391, 394, 395, 399, 400, 420, 431, 436, 444, 445
Gestapo, 420, 421
Ghana, 454
Gildas, 91
Gillette, King Camp, 345
Gillray, James, 247, 274
Gin Act, 243
Girl Guides, 387
gladiators, 64-65
Gladstone, William, 303, 324
glam rock, 461
Glasgow, Scotland, 248
    Science Centre, 472

Glencoe, 231
Globe Playhouse, 196-197
Glorious Revolution, 229, 230-231
Gloucester, 41, 45, 85
Glyndwr, Owain, or Glendower, 168-169, 170
GM foods, 467
gods and goddesses, 25, 26, 27, 47, 66-67, 68-69, 75, 78, 79, 96, 107
Gold Beach, 437
Gold Coast, see Ghana
Golden Hinde, 200, 201
Good Friday Agreement, 471
Gorbachev, Mikhail, 468
Gordon, General, 346
Grahame, Kenneth, 353
gramophone, invention of, 344
Grand Prix, 387
Grand Tour, 240
graves, see burials
Great
    Council, 148-149
    Depression, 390
    Eastern, 338
    Exhibition, 312-313, 321
    Fire of London, 220-221, 226
    Reform Act, 289, 290
    Western Railway, 338
Greece, 363
Greeks, ancient, 27, 60, 66, 69, 76, 77
Gregory VIII, Pope, 142
Grey, Earl, 280
Grey, Lady Jane, 190
Guernsey, 403
guilds, 135, 163, 167
Gulf War, 469
Gunpowder Plot, 206-207
Gurkhas, 446
Gutenberg, Johannes, 161, 189
Guthrum, 108, 109
Gwynedd, 111

Hadrian, 54-55, 63
Hadrian's Wall 6, 54-55, 56, 57, 61, 80, 84, 85
ha-has, 241
Haig, Field Marshal Sir Douglas, 380, 382
Handel, 236, 268
Hanover, Germany, 235, 236, 238, 239, 248, 256
Hanoverians, 235-291, 293-349
Hardie, James Keir, 325

Hardrada, Harald, 117, 120, 121
Hargreaves, James, 253
Harris, Sir Arthur, 440
Harrison, John, 260
Harry, Prince, 471
Harrying of the North, 126, 129
Harvey, William, 227
Hawkins, John, 200
Hayman, Francis, 251
heart transplant, first, 466
Heath, Edward, 460
Helena, Princess, 320
Henri Grâce à Dieu, 185
Henrietta Maria, Queen Consort, 208
heraldry, 154, 164
Herschel, Sir John, 341
Hibernia, 30
Highland Clearances, 246
Highlands, Scottish, 31, 53, 231, 237, 244, 245, 420
High Seas Fleet, German, 376, 377
highwaymen, 243
Hild, 99
hillforts, 24-25, 32, 34, 35, 93
Hiroshima, 446-447
Hirst, Damien, 470
Hitler, Adolf, 391, 394, 398, 401, 402, 403, 423, 424, 428, 432, 433, 436, 445, 449
HIV, 467
Hogarth, William, 242, 243, 257
Holbein, Hans, 180, 188, 189
Hollis, Stanley, 439
Holmes, Ray, 406
Holmes, Sherlock, 308, 309
Holocaust, 443
Home
    Front, 372-373, 414-419
    Guard, 416-417
    Rule, Irish, 303
Hong Kong, 469
Honorius, 84
Hood, HMS, 422, 423
Hope, Bob, 435
Hopkins, Matthew, 227
horses, 22, 23, 26, 122, 123, 124, 125, 255, 287, 316
    horse racing, 352, 353, 357
hospitals, 135, 317, 327, 375
Hotspur, Henry Percy, 169
Houghton Hall, 240
Houses of Parliament, see also Parliament,
    building, 291, 298, 337
    House of Commons, 149,

209, 213, 271, 275, 400
House of Lords, 149, 355
Housesteads Roman Fort, 40, 55, 85
housing, types of, 15, 32, 45, 56, 68, 70-71, 95, 132-133, 186, 224-225, 240-241, 265, 266-267, 307, 342-343
Howard, Catherine, 181
Howard, Lord of Effingham, 204
howitzers, 371
Hume, David, 258
Hundred Days, the, 280
hunger marches, 391
hunger strikes, 357
Hunt, William Holman, 340
hunting, 12-13, 14-15, 16, 59, 71, 97, 165, 187, 319, 353
Hurley, Frank, 359, 382
Hurricanes, 404, 405
Hussein, Saddam, 469
Huxley, Thomas Henry, 315
Hyde Park, 312

Ice Age, 12-14
Iceni tribe, 36-37, 85
immigration, 9, 455
Imperial College of Science, 313
Imperial (later Commonwealth) War Graves Commission, 384
Independent Labour Party, 325
India, 9, 235, 248, 250-251, 318-319, 364, 374, 427, 454
Indian Mutiny, 319
Industrial Revolution, 235, 252-253, 286, 287, 300, 304, 348, 351
industries, 254, 255, 268, 291, 310, 312, 325, 360, 366, 390, 391, 451, 460, 462
  textiles, 252-253, 305
influenza, 326
insulae, 44, 45
intelligence, see spying
internal combustion engine, 345
International Gothic, 160
invasions, 6, 7, 18, 19, 29, 30-31, 33, 34-35, 80, 83, 89, 92, 104-105, 112-113, 114, 119, 120-123, 138, 152, 153, 154
Invisible College, see Royal Society
Iona, 98, 105, 110, 111
Ipswich, 102

Iran, 428
Iraq, 106, 428, 469
Ireland, see also Hibernia, 6, 8, 17, 25, 53, 68, 84, 87, 92, 98, 103, 105, 111, 119, 138, 139, 177, 183, 205, 206, 214, 231, 276-277, 293, 302-303, 348, 388-389, 464-465
Irish
  Free State, 389
  Home Rule Bill, 303
  nationalism, 388-389, 460, 464, 465, 471
  Parliament, 276, 277, 388
  potato famine, 303
  Republican Army (IRA), 388-389, 465
  War of Independence, 389
iron, 24, 88, 198, 227, 255, 286, 304
Iron Age, 24-27, 32, 93
Isabella, Queen, 154
Isle of Wight, 89, 213, 297
Italy, 31, 51, 98, 363, 374, 391, 399, 432-433

Jack the Ripper, 309
Jacobites, 237, 238, 244-245
Japan, 399, 425, 426, 427, 428, 446-447
Jarrow, 105, 390, 391
jazz, 386, 435
Jefferson, Thomas, 273
Jellicoe, Admiral John, 376-377
Jenner, Edward, 259
Jersey, 403
Jews, 68, 134, 142, 150, 391, 394, 420, 442-443
Joan of Arc, 171
John of Gaunt, 158, 168
Johnson, Dr. Samuel, 259
Jonson, Ben, 197
Jordan, Dorothea, 290
Jorvik, see also York, 107
journalists, 259, 317, 369
jousting, 164, 165
Julius Caesar, 30, 31, 33, 34, 61
Juno Beach, 437
Jutes, 84, 89

Kay, John, 252
Keats, John, 283
Kempe, Margery, 163
Kensington Palace, 294, 471
Kent, Duchess of, 291
Kett, Robert, 187
Kindertransport, 442

King's Friends, 256
kings, see Index of monarchs
Kipling, Rudyard, 330, 353
Kirkpatrick, John Simpson, 375
Kitchener, Lord, 368, 369, 381
knights, 123, 124-125, 126, 127, 139, 140, 149, 153, 154, 155, 164-165, 169, 170, 171
Knox, John, 191
Kodak camera, 344
Kosovo, 469

Labour Party, 325, 449, 452, 470-471
Lancaster bombers, 431
Lancastrians, 172-173, 174, 175, 178
landed gentry, 240-241, 264
Land Girls, see Women's Land Army
landowners, 71, 94, 101, 187, 240, 246, 288, 289, 299, 302
landscape gardening, 241
languages,
  Anglo-Saxon, 92, 96, 103
  Celtic, 77, 93, 103
  French, 139
  Gaelic, 129, 139, 465
  Latin, 30, 41, 77, 96, 99, 102, 103, 144, 147, 161, 189
Laud, William, Archbishop of Canterbury, 208, 209
laughing gas, 259
laws, 111, 115, 148, 150, 183, 289, 305, 453, 458
  Anglo-Saxon, 94, 96
  English Common Law, 140
  Equal Pay Act, 460
  Factory Acts, 289
  Gin Act, 243
  Great Reform Act, 289, 290
  Poor Law, 198
  Roman, 30, 40, 45, 52, 77
  Roman Catholic Relief Act, 289
  Sex Discrimination Act, 460
  Statute of Labourers, 157
  sumptuary laws, 194
League of Nations, 383
Lear, Edward, 330
Leicester, 41, 85
Leopold, Duke of Austria, 143
Lenoir, Étienne, 345
Liberal Party, see also Whigs, 298, 324, 355

Libya, 428, 429
Light Horse Brigade, 316, 317
Ligny, Belgium, 281
Lincoln, 45, 83, 85, 137
Lindisfarne, 98, 105
Lister, Joseph, 327, 345
Live Aid, 463
Liverpool, 248, 264, 270, 418
Livingstone, David, 346, 458
Llewelyn ap Gruffydd, Prince of Wales, 149, 150-151, 169
Lloyd George, David, 355, 383, 386
locomotives, 287, 310
Lollards, 161
Londinium, see also London 36, 50-51, 85
London, 36, 47, 50-51, 55, 60, 61, 80, 85, 99, 100, 102, 105, 123, 139, 140, 142, 148, 158, 166, 190, 197, 198, 205, 210, 211, 212, 217, 218, 220-221, 222, 244, 248, 254, 255, 262, 264, 265, 269, 270, 272, 294, 302, 309, 311, 312, 314, 315, 321, 326, 345, 348-349, 353, 354, 372, 390, 391, 406, 408-409, 410, 440, 441, 453, 455, 456, 459, 461, 463, 468, 470, 472-473
Lord Protector, see also Cromwell, Oliver, 214-215
lords, medieval, see nobles
Louis
  VII, King of France, 139
  XIV, King of France, 217
  XVI, King of France, 275
Low, David, 401
Ludd, Ned, 288
Luddites, 288
Luftwaffe, 402, 404, 405, 406, 407, 408, 410, 411, 424
Lullingstone Roman Villa, 68, 85
Lumière brothers, 345
Lusitania, RMS, 377
Luther, Martin, 189
Lynn, Vera, 435

Macadam, Robert, 255
MacDonald clan, 231
MacDonald, Flora, 245
MacFergus, Constantin, 110
Macmillan, Harold, 454, 457
Maginot Line, 399
Magna Carta, 148, 149
Mahdi, the, 346
Maiden Castle, 24

malaria, 317, 326
Malaya, 426-427
Malory, Sir Thomas, 91
Manchester, 41, 289, 255, 337
Mannock, Major 'Mick', 379
manuscripts, illuminated, 98, 102, 115, 116, 141, 143, 146, 149, 151
marcher lords, 128, 129, 168, 183
Marconi, Guglielmo, 344
Margaret of Anjou, 172
Margaret, St., of Scotland, 129
markets, 44, 52, 58, 61, 79, 133, 134-135, 187, 198, 199, 307
Marlowe, Christopher, 197
Marne, River, 364, 365
Martin, Major, 432
Mary of Modena, 229
Mary Rose, 185
Matchgirls' Union strike, 324
medicine, 75, 147, 227, 259, 317, 323, 326, 327, 355, 431, 466, 467
medicinal plants, 75, 147, 224
Melbourne, Lord, 298, 299
mêlée, 164
Mercia, 98, 100-101, 105, 108, 111
Merton College, Oxford, 146
metalwork, 23, 32, 45, 59, bronze, 18, 23, 24, 26, 27
copper, 18, 19
gold, 18, 19, 23, 26, 30, 103
iron, 24, 27
metalworkers, 18, 20, 23, 26, 93, 103
silver, 103
Methodism, 268
miasma, 326
Middle East, 16, 51, 68, 142-143, 374, 383, 457, 460, 467
Mildenhall treasure, 79
milecastles, 55
milestones, 43
Mill, John Stuart, 325
Millais, John Everett, 340
Millbank Prison, 309
millennium, 472-473
Millennium Dome, 472
Miller, Glenn, 435
mills, 132, 133, 252-253, 270, 286, 305, 323, 390, 391
miners' strike, 460-461, 463
mining, 27, 56, 59, 286, 287, 288, 289, 305, 390, 391, 417, 452, 453, 460-461, 463

mini skirts, 459
Mir Jafar, 251
missionaries, 68, 98, 346,
MMR, 467
Mods, 458
monasteries, 89, 98, 99, 104, 105, 115, 129, 146, 182-183
money, *see also* coins, 58, 81, 101, 102, 223, 468
monks, 89, 98, 99, 100, 102, 105, 137, 146-147, 182, 189
Monmouth, Duke of, 228
Monmouth Rebellion, 228
Monteagle, Lord, 207
Montgomery, Field Marshal Bernard, 428, 429, 437, 444
More, Hannah, 269
Morris, William, 91, 341
mosaics, 65, 69, 71, 78, 84
Mosley, Oswald, 391
motte and bailey castles, 127
mounds, prehistoric, 20
Munich Peace Agreement, 394, 395
munitions factories, 371, 373
music, 65, 67, 72, 73, 75, 145, 189, 236, 263, 386, 391, 434-435, 455, 457, 458, 459, 461, 463, 470
musketeers, 210, 211
Muslims, 142, 143, 454
Mussolini, Benito, 394, 433
Muybridge, Eadweard, 344

Nagasaki, 447
Napoleon Bonaparte, 278-279, 280-281
Nash, John, 265, 284
National
Association of Domestic Servants, 355
Covenant, 209
Health Service, 452
Insurance, 355
Union of Women's Suffrage Societies, 325, 356
NATO, 453, 469
Natural History Museum, 313
Nawab of Bengal, 250, 251
Navy,
French, 278, 279
German, 360, 361, 376, 377, 382
Merchant, 412
Royal, 185, 210, 260, 261, 278-279, 290, 352, 367-377, 396, 401, 402, 403, 404, 412, 422-423
Nazis, 391, 394, 399, 401,

403, 442, 443, 449
Nelson, Horatio, 278-279
Nelson's Column, 279
Nennius, 91
Neo-classical style, 336
Nesbit, E., 353
Netherlands, 18, 204, 205, 217, 229, 232, 273, 281
Neville, Richard, Earl of Warwick, 173
New Labour, 470
New Lanark, 252
New Model Army, 212-214
New World, *see also* America, 200, 223
New York Stock Exchange, 390
New Zealand, 261, 374, 375, 427
Newcomen, Thomas, 227, 286
Newgate Prison, 269
newspapers, 331, 356, 360, 362, 367, 368, 369, 373
Newton, Sir Isaac, 226
Nightingale, Florence, 317, 326, 327
Nithsdale, Lord, 237
nobles, 112, 114, 115, 116, 117, 125, 126, 129, 131, 136, 139, 148, 149, 162, 164-165, 166, 167, 168, 172, 173, 178, 179, 180, 183, 186, 187, 194, 199
no-man's land, 367, 380, 381
Normandy, France, 113, 170, 436-439
Normandy landings, 437-439
Normans, 6, 8, 119, 120-137
North Atlantic Treaty Organisation (NATO), 453, 469
North, Lord, 257, 273
North Sea, 82, 365, 376-377
Northern Ireland, 231, 389, 460, 464-465, 471
Northumbria, 98, 101, 102, 105, 111, 136
Norway, 6, 104, 105, 115, 120, 121, 358, 398
Nottingham Castle, 211
Notting Hill Carnival, 455
nuclear weapons, 447, 453
nuns, 99, 162, 163, 182
Nuremberg trials, 449
nurses, 317, 327, 370

oil, 428, 457, 460, 463, 467
Olympic Games, 353, 453
Omaha Beach, 437, 438

Operation Dynamo, 402-403
Operation Overlord, 436
Orange Order, 464
orphanages, 269, 300
Osborne House, 297
Owen, Richard, 314, 315
Oxford University, 146, 147, 161

paganism, 23, 25, 26, 27, 66-67, 92, 96, 98, 166
Paine, Thomas, 274-275, 282
Pakistan, 454
Palace of Westminster, 291
Pale, the, 139
Palladian style, 240-241
Pals Battalions, 381
Parnell, Charles Stuart, 303
Pankhurst, Emmeline, 357
parachutes, 378, 437, 438
paratroopers, 398, 438, 439
Paris, 281, 352, 363, 364, 439, 468
Parliament, 148-149, 150, 168, 181, 206-207, 208, 209, 210, 211, 212-213, 214, 217, 228, 230, 231, 233, 237, 238, 239, 256, 257, 271, 272, 277, 288, 289, 291, 296, 298-299, 303, 324-325, 356, 386, 388, 391, 470
Parliamentarians, 209, 210-214
Parr, Catherine, 181
Paston, Margaret, 163
Patrick, St., 68
Pax Romana, 52-53
Paxton, Joseph, 312
Pearl Harbor, 425, 426
peasants, 71, 131, 132-133, 157, 158-159, 166, 167, 170
Peasants' Revolt, 158-159, 168
Peel, Sir Robert, 299, 303, 308
penal colonies, 245, 261, 308
penicillin, 431
pensions, 355
People's Budget, 355
People's Charter, 299
Pepys, Samuel, 219, 221, 226
Percival, General, 426, 427
Perpendicular style, 157
Persia, 67
Peterloo Massacre, 288, 289
Philip II, King of Spain, 191, 193, 204-205
phoney war, 398
phonographs, 344
photography, 317, 340-341, 344

pickpockets, 199, 243
Picts, 57, 84, 85, 92, 98, 110
pilgrims, 144, 161, 163, 182
Pilgrims, 208
pirates, 49, 58, 82, 168, 201, 233, 243
Pitt, William, the Elder, 249, 256, 274
Pitt, William, the Younger, 274, 275
plague, 119, 156-7, 159, 218-219, 221
Plantagenets, 138-175
plantations, 248, 270
Plautius, Aulus, 35
plays, 64, 65, 167, 196-197, 214, 216, 242, 335, 353
poetry, 26, 103, 164, 193, 282-283, 330
Poland, 395, 398, 399, 405
police, 243, 308, 463, 465,
    Metropolitan, 289, 308
Polidori, John, 283
pollution, 307,
poll tax, 158, 463
Poor Law, 198
Pope, the, 99, 140, 141, 142, 148, 181, 189, 191
Pope, Alexander, 242
poppies, 385
porphyria, 284
Portchester Castle, 82, 85
Portugal, 280, 363
Potter, Beatrix, 353
pottery,
    prehistoric, 16, 20, 27
    Roman, 45, 51, 59, 75, 76, 77, 78
poverty, 198, 242, 268-269, 288, 289, 300-301, 302-303, 306-307, 326, 348, 351, 354-355, 390, 391, 394, 417, 419, 462
Prasutagas, 36
Pre-Raphaelites, 340
Presbyterianism, 208, 211
press gangs, 261
Priestley, Joseph, 259
priests,
    Christian, 69, 99, 144-145, 147, 157
    Druid, 67, 76
    Roman, 66, 67
Prince Eugen, 422
Prince of Wales, HMS, 422, 423
Princip, Gavrilo, 362
printing press, 161, 189, 313, 330, 331
prisoners of war, in Asia, 427

prisons, 289, 308, 309
Private Eye, 458
Privy Council, 193
propaganda, 368-369
Protestantism/Protestants, 177, 189-190, 191, 192, 202, 204, 205, 206, 207, 208, 217, 228, 229, 230-231, 236, 276, 277, 389, 460, 464
Protestant Reformation, 189, 190, 191
Protestant Unionists, 464, 465, 471
Prussia, 248, 281
Prynne, William, 208
punk rock, 461
Purcell, Henry, 91
Puritanism, 207-212, 214-215
Pym, John, 209, 211
Pytheas, 27

Quant, Mary, 459
Quebec, 249
Queen Anne's Revenge, 233
queens, see Index of monarchs

racial prejudice, 455
radar, 405, 410, 413, 430, 441
radio, 344, 387
railways, 255, 287, 310-311, 319, 334, 338, 339, 387, 453
    underground railways, 332, 345, 408
Raleigh, Sir Walter, 200
Ramblers Association, 387
rationing, 373, 414, 418, 457
razor, 345
Reagan, Ronald, 468
rebellions, 30, 36-37, 45, 52-53, 55, 80, 83, 114, 126, 139, 143, 152, 158-159, 168, 183, 187, 228, 270, 271, 272-273, 276-277, 346, 388-389
Red Baron, 378, 379
redcoats, 245, 249
Red Flag Act, 333
Redwald, 93
Reform Act, 325
Reformation, 189, 191
reforms,
    electoral, 298, 290, 324-325, 356-357
    social, 268, 289, 290, 354, 355
Regency style, 284-285
Reign of Terror, 275
religion, see also Christianity, paganism, 52, 64, 66-67,

68-69, 92, 93, 107, 140, 142, 144-145, 146,147, 157, 162, 177, 181-183, 189-191, 202, 226, 228, 268, 269, 315, 368, 454
Rembrandt, 227
Remembrance, day of, 384-385
Renaissance, 188-189
Restoration, 215, 216-217
revolutions, 274, 382, 383
    Agricultural, 246-247
    American, 272-273, 282
    French, 274, 275, 282, 288
    Glorious, 229, 230-231
    Industrial, 235, 252-253, 286, 287, 300, 304, 348, 351
Reynolds, Joshua, 262
Ribchester Roman Fort, 40
Richard, Duke of York, 179
Richtofen, Baron Manfred von, see Red Baron
Rizzio, David, 203
Roberts, David, 291
Rockers, 458
Rocket, Stephenson's, 287
rock 'n' roll, 457
Roe, Edwin Alliott Verdon, 358
Roman/Romans, 6, 8, 27, 29, 87, 88, 92, 99
    army, 29, 30-31, 34, 35, 38-43, 45, 52-53, 54-55, 60, 80
    empire, 29, 32, 34, 41, 42, 50, 51, 52, 53, 55, 56, 58, 60, 61, 63, 66, 67, 68, 69, 73, 80, 83
    emperors, 31, 34, 36, 51, 63 64, 66, 68, 79, 80, 81, 82, 83
        Antoninus Pius, 55
        Aurelian, 81
        Caligula, 31, 34
        Caracalla, 81
        Claudius, 34, 35, 50, 66
        Commodus, 80, 83
        Constantine, 69, 80, 83
        Constantius, 83
        Diocletian, 69
        Domitian, 53
        Hadrian, 54-55, 63
        Honorius, 84
        Septimius Severus, 80, 81, 83
        Theodosius, 69
        Vespasian, 35
    games, 64-65
    government, 36, 45, 51, 61, 72, 77, 79, 80
    roads, 42-43, 48, 56, 58, 70

Roman Catholic Relief Act, 289
Romanticism, 282-283
Rome, 29, 33, 35, 39, 42, 53, 54, 60, 61, 80, 83, 432, 433
Rommel, Erwin, the Desert Fox, 428, 429, 436, 437, 439
Röntgen, Wilhelm, 345
Roosevelt, Theodore, 424, 425, 432
Rossetti, Dante Gabriel, 340
rotten boroughs, 289, 290
Rouen, France, 364, 365
round houses, 32, 56, 71
Roundheads, 211
Rousseau, Jean Jacques, 274
Rowlandson, Thomas, 242
Rowntree, Seebohm, 354
Royal
    Academy, 262-263, 282
    Air Force (RAF), 404-408, 430-431, 440, 441
    Albert Hall, 321
    Artillery, 364
    Botanic Gardens, Kew, 260
    Colleges of Music and Art, 313
    Flying Corps, 378-379
    Naval Intelligence Division, 430
    Navy, 185, 210, 260, 261, 278-279, 290, 352, 367-377, 396, 401, 402, 403, 404, 412, 422-423
    Oak, HMS, 398
    Observatory, Greenwich, 226
    Pavilion, Brighton, 284
    Society, 226, 227, 344
Royalists, 209-214
Rudeltaktik, 412
Rudston Roman Villa, 65, 85
rugby, 329, 335
Rumania, 363
Rupert, Prince of the Rhine, 211
Ruskin, John, 336, 340
Russell, John, 325
Rus tribe, 106
Russia, see also Soviet Union, 106, 248, 280, 316 363, 382, 383, 401

sacrifices, sacred, 27, 67
Salah al-Din, or Saladin, 142-143
Salisbury, Lord, 303
Salvation Army, 300
sanitation, 342

Sarajevo, Bosnia, 362
Sargent, John Singer, 370
Sassoon, Siegfried, 384
Savery, Thomas, 286
Saxe-Coburg-Gotha, 296, 360
Saxons, 6, 8, 82, 84, 89-92
Scheer, Admiral Reinhard, 376-377
Scholes, Christopher, 345
schools, 76-77, 144, 146-147, 269, 328, 329, 353, 355, 385, 419, 452, 460
science, 147, 188, 226-227, 258-259, 260, 313, 314-315, 351, 370, 421, 430-431, 453, 466-467
Scotland, see also Caledonia, 8, 25, 52, 53, 54, 56, 57, 80, 84, 87, 92, 98, 103, 110, 119, 128, 129, 136, 138, 147, 152-153, 154, 168, 177, 179, 183, 189, 191, 202, 205, 206, 208, 209, 211, 213, 214, 231, 233, 237, 244-245, 246, 297, 305, 311, 470
Scott, Captain Robert Falcon, 358
Scott, Sir George Gilbert, 336
Scottish Parliament, 470
Seacole, Mary, 317
Searle, Ronald, 427
seaside resorts, 284, 311, 334, 387
Second World War, see Index of wars and battles
secret agents, see also special agents, spying, 432
seed drill, 227, 247
Segontium Roman Fort, 52, 85
sepoys, 250, 319
Septimius Severus, 80, 81, 83
Serbs/Serbia, 362, 363, 469
serfs, 131
Seven Years' War, see Index of wars and battles
Severn, River, 286
sewers, 48, 326, 339
Sex Discrimination Act, 460
Seymour, Jane, 181
Shackleton, Sir Ernest, 359
Shakespeare, William, 169, 174, 196-197, 340
Sharp, Granville, 271
Sharpe, Sam, 271
Sheffield, HMS, 462
shell scandal, 371
shellshock, 371
Shelley, Mary, 283

Shelley, Percy, 283
Shepherd, Jack, 243
shipbuilding, 304, 305, 372, 390, 391
ships, 31, 49, 51, 53, 58, 82, 373, 376-377, 382
    Anglo-Saxon, 109
    battleships, 360-361, 376, 398, 412, 413, 422, 423, 426, 437
    Bismarck, 413, 422, 423
    Chester, HMS, 376
    destroyers, 413
    Dreadnought, HMS, 361
    Empire Windrush, 455
    Endeavour, HMS, 260-261
    Endurance, HMS, 359
    Golden Hinde, 200, 201
    Great Eastern, 338
    Henri Grâce à Dieu, 185
    Hood, HMS, 422, 423
    knorrs, 106
    longships, 106, 113
    Lusitania, 377
    Mary Rose, 185
    Prince Eugen, 422
    Prince of Wales, HMS, 422, 423
    Queen Anne's Revenge, 233
    Royal Oak, HMS, 398
    Sheffield, HMS, 462
    slave ships, 248
    steamships, 344, 359
    submarines, 373, 377, 382, 383, 398, 412, 413
    Titanic, RMS, 359
    U-boats, see submarines
    Victory, HMS, 361
    Viking, 106, 112
    Zong, 271
Sicily, 432, 433
Siegfried Line, 444
Silbury Hill, 20
Simnel, Lambert, 179
Simpson, Wallis, 349
Singapore, 426, 427
Singer, Isaac, 345
Sinn Féin, 388-389
slavery/slave trade, 27, 46, 60-61, 62, 63, 64, 72, 73, 76, 96, 97, 99, 131, 200, 215, 223, 228, 248, 270-271, 346
Sloane, Sir Hans, 259
slums, 268, 307, 419
small pox, 259, 326
Smellie, William, 259
Smith, John, 470
smuggling, 243

Snow, John, 326
soccer, 459
Society for the Abolition of the Slave Trade, 271
Solway, River, 55
Somerset, Duke of, 190
Somerset, James, 271
sonar, 413
Sophia, Princess of Hanover, 233
soup kitchens, 300
South Georgia, 359
South Pole, 358, 359
South Sea Bubble, 239
South Shields, 61, 85
Soviet Union, see also Russia, 399, 424, 453, 457, 468
Soyer, Alexis, 300
Spain, 51, 56, 60, 81, 158, 184, 191, 200, 201, 204-205, 232, 239, 248, 273, 280
Spanish Armada, 204-205
special agents, 420, 421
Spencer, Lady Diana, see also Diana, Princess of Wales, 462
Spenser, Edmund, 196
Spinning Jenny, 253
Spitfires, 404, 405, 406
sports, 64-65, 166, 329, 335, 351, 353, 387
spying, 203, 382, 420-421
St. Albans, 36, 69, 85
St. Andrew's University, 147
St. Helena, 281
St. Pancras Station, 336, 337
St. Paul's Cathedral, 220, 222, 409
Stalin, Joseph, 424, 436
Stanley, Henry, 346
Stanley, Phyllis, 434
Star Chamber, 178
stately homes, 240-241
Statute of Labourers, 157
steam engines, 227, 286-287, 304, 310, 313, 332
Stephenson, George, 287
Stephenson, Robert, 338
Stevenson, Robert Louis, 330
Stoker, Bram, 283
Stone Age, 14-15, 20, 21,
Stone of Destiny, 110, 152
Stonehenge, 6, 19, 20-21, 264
Stowe House, 240, 241
Strafford, Earl of, 209
Streona, Eadric, 114
strikes, 324, 460, 461, 462, 463
Stuart, Charles Edward, 244-245

Stuart, James, 237, 244
Stuart, John, Earl of Bute, 256, 257
submarines, 375, 377, 382, 383, 398, 412, 413
Sudan, 346,
Suez Canal, 347, 428, 457
Suez Crisis, 457
suffragettes, 325, 356, 357
suffragists, 356
Sulis-Minerva, 67
Sussex, 89
Sutton Hoo, 93
Swan, Joseph, 344
Sweden, 104, 115, 248
Swift, Jonathan, 242
Switzerland, 365
Sword Beach, 437
Syria, 58

Tacitus, 35, 53, 57, 60
Tacky, 271
Talbot, William Fox, 344
Tanganyika, 346
tanks, 380
    British, 415, 428, 436
    German, 398, 399, 439
taxes, 30, 33, 45, 51, 57, 81, 130, 131, 148, 150, 168, 178, 230, 239, 243, 272, 355, 462, 463
tea, 272, 318, 353, 354
Teddy Boys, 458
teenagers, 458
telegrams, 373
telegraph, 344, 357
telephones, 344, 345, 372
television, 387, 456, 457, 458
Telford, Thomas, 255
temples, Roman, 45, 47, 66-67, 69, 85, 240
tennis, 166, 335
Tennyson, Alfred, Lord, 91, 316, 341
Thames, River, 36, 50, 51, 60, 216, 236, 291, 298-299, 472-473
Thatcher, Margaret, 460, 462-463, 465, 468
thegns, 94, 95, 96
Theodosius, 69
Times, The, 327
Titanic, RMS, 359
tithes, 131, 133, 144
toilets, public, 41, 48, 307
Tommies, 364
Tommy Atkins, 364
Tone, Theobald Wolfe, 276, 277

Tories, see also Conservative Party, 217, 238, 257, 290, 298, 299
tournaments, 164,
Tower of London, 173, 179, 190, 207, 221, 237
Townsend, Viscount, 247
trade, 6, 8, 9, 18, 19, 22, 25, 27, 32, 41, 45, 50, 51, 57, 58-59, 60, 61, 77, 102, 107, 134-135, 198, 215, 223, 248, 252, 253, 255, 260, 264, 272, 307, 318, 319, 390, 460
trades unions, 288, 289, 324, 325
Trafalgar Square, 279
trains, see railways
transportation, 23, 42-43, 49, 50, 51, 58, 254-255, 332-333, 344, 358, 387
Transvaal, South Africa, 347
trenches, 365, 366, 367, 370, 371, 375, 378, 380
Trevithick, Richard, 287
tribes,
    British, 25, 26, 32-33, 40, 52-53, 54, 55, 56, 57, 71, 84, 85, 93
    Germanic, 82
    Irish, 84
    Scottish, 56, 57, 80, 84, 85
Troubles, Ireland, 465
Tull, Jethro, 227, 247
Turkey, 67, 316, 317, 374, 375
Turner, J.M.W., 283, 310
turnpikes, 254-255
Turpin, Dick, 243
Twain, Mark, 91
Tyler, Wat, 158-159
Tyne Cot Cemetery, 384
Tyne, River, 55, 472
typewriters, 345
typhoid, 326
typhus, 443

U-boats, 377, 412
Ulster Volunteer Force (UVF), 465
underground railways, 332, 345, 408
unemployment, 198-199, 355, 390, 391
Union Jack, 206, 277
Union of Wales and England, 151, 183
United Irishmen, 276-277
United Nations (UN), 453, 457, 469
United States of America (USA), see also America,

272-273, 303, 344, 345, 348, 358, 377, 382, 399, 401, 413, 425, 453, 457, 468
universities, see also St. Andrew's, Cambridge, Oxford, 323
Urban II, Pope, 142
Utah Beach, 437
UXBs, 409

V1s and V2s, 440, 441
VE Day, 445
Verica, 33, 34
Verulamium, 36, 69
Vespasian, 35
Viceroy of India, Lord Curzon, 319
Victoria and Albert Museum, 313
Victoria Cross, 376, 439
Victorian architecture, 336-337
Victory, HMS, 361
Vikings, 6, 8, 104-117
villas, Roman, 65, 68, 69, 70-71, 72, 78, 84, 85
villeins, 131
Vindolanda Roman Fort, 41, 72, 85
VJ Day, 447
Voltaire, 274
voting, 276, 288, 289, 299, 356-357, 386

Wales, 8, 25, 37, 43, 52, 53, 56, 64, 71, 87, 90, 91, 98, 100, 101, 103, 111, 119, 128, 129, 136, 138, 139, 150-151, 168, 169, 177, 183, 206, 233, 470
Wall Street Crash, 390
Wallace, William, 152-153
Wallis, Barnes, 430, 431
Walpole, Horace, 241
Walpole, Robert, 238, 239, 240, 241, 242, 243
Walsingham, Sir Francis, 203
Warbeck, Perkin, 179
war memorials, 385
wars, see Index of wars
Warwick, Earl of, 179, 187
Washington, George, 272-273
Watson, James, 466
Watt, James, 286
weapons, 24, 25, 34-35, 36-37, 39, 52, 56, 57, 65, 88, 95, 97, 105, 124-125, 164, 165, 197, 370-371, 380
    anti-aircraft guns, 372, 410
    armaments, 415
    artillery, 281, 371, 380

atomic, see nuclear
axes, 15, 16, 23, 97, 124, 175
bows and arrows, 15, 34, 122, 123 155
cannons, 171, 185, 197, 281, 316
catapults, 34, 35
chemical, 370, 396
crossbows, 155
daggers, 65
flamethrowers, 371, 436
harpoons, 15
hatchets, 15
howitzers, 371
knives, 19, 446
lances, 124
longbows, 155, 170
maces, 124
machine guns, 371, 367, 375, 378, 380, 381
muskets, 210
nuclear, 446-447, 453, 457
pikes, 210, 211
pistols, 210
rifles, 319, 368
seax, 82
shields, 25, 26, 39, 65, 124
spears, 13, 15, 23, 25, 88, 124
swords, 23, 25, 27, 39, 52, 65, 97, 124, 210, 289
tommy guns, 416
torpedoes, 361
Webb Ellis, William, 329
Wedgwood, Josiah, 266, 271
Welfare State, 355, 452, 453
Wellesley, Arthur, Duke of Wellington, 280-281, 302
Welsh Assembly, 470
Wesley, John, 268, 269, 271
Wessex, 89, 98, 101, 104, 105, 108, 109, 111, 116
West Indies, see also Caribbean, 200, 201, 215, 253, 374, 455
Western Front, 363-369, 374, 383, 384
Westminster Abbey, 117
Wheatstone, Charles, 344
Whigs, see also Liberal Party, 217, 238, 239, 241, 256, 298
Whistler, James Abbott McNeil, 341
Whitby Abbey, 99
White Star Line, 359
wics, 102
Wilberforce, Samuel, Bishop of Oxford, 315
Wilberforce, William, 271

Wild, Jonathan, 242, 243
Wilde, Oscar, 341
Wilhelm II, Kaiser of Germany, 297, 349, 360
Wilkes, John, 257
Wilkinson, Ellen, 390
William, Prince, 90, 91, 471
Wilson, Woodrow, 377, 383
Winchester, 109, 115
Windsor, 349
    Castle, 297, 471
    family, 360
Wingate, General Orde, 447
Winter of Discontent, 461, 462
Winterhalter, Franz Xavier, 295
Witan, 120
witch hunts, 227
Wolfe, General James, 249
Wolsey, Cardinal Thomas, 181
Women's Land Army, 415
Women's Liberation, 460
women's lives, 25, 96, 97, 162-163, 164, 299, 322-323, 414, 421, 458, 460, 466
women's rights, 299, 356-357, 386, 460
Wood, John, 264
Woodville, Elizabeth, 173, 174
Wordsworth, William, 282, 283
workhouses, 301
World Cup, 459
Wren, Christopher, 222, 226
Wright brothers, 358
Wright, Joseph, 258
Wulfstan, Archbishop of York, 114
Wycliffe, John, 161

X-rays, 345
X-troop, 420

Yeats, William Butler, 388
yeomen farmers, 179
York, 40, 45, 80, 83, 85, 102, 105, 107, 142, 172, 173, 354
Yorkists, 172-173, 174, 175, 178-179
Youth Hostel Association, 387
Ypres, 365, 370, 382
yuppies, 462

zeppelins, 372
Zong, 271
Zulus, 346

Acknowledgements

Every effort has been made to trace and acknowledge ownership of copyright. If any rights have been omitted, the publishers offer to rectify this in any future editions following notification. The publishers are grateful to the following individuals and organizations for their permission to reproduce material on the following pages: (t=top, b=bottom, l=left, r=right)

Cover: Detail from the Bayeux Tapestry – 11th century. By special permission of the City of Bayeux; p1 © Hulton-Deutsch Collection/Corbis; p2-3 © Historical Picture Archive/Corbis.

Prehistoric Britain

p16(c) © Salisbury & South Wiltshire Museum; p17 (b) © David Lyons/Alamy; p18 (c) © Wessex Archaeology 2007; p20 (tl) © Bjanka Kadic/Alamy; p20-21 (b) © Adam Woolfitt/Corbis; p23 (t) © The Trustees of the British Museum; p24 (l) © Skyscan/ Corbis; p26 (b) © The Trustees of the British Museum; p27 (tr) © The Trustees of the British Museum.

Roman Britain

p32 (tl) © British Museum/HIP/Topfoto; p32-33 (b) © Butser Ancient Farm, www.butser.org; p38-39 © Charles and Josette Lenars/Corbis; p40-41 © Skyscan/Corbis; p40 (tl) © British Museum/HIP/Topfoto; p41 (br) © Philippa Walton, Courtesy The Portable Antiquities Scheme, with thanks to Bob Middlemass and Rolf Mitchenson; p43 (br) © The Trustees of the British Museum; p44-45 © National Museum of Wales; p46-47 (b) © Jon Eisberg/Getty Images; p47 (tr) © Museum of London/ HIP/Topfoto; p49 Ronald Sheridan@Ancient Art & Architecture Collection Ltd.; p50-51 (b) © Museum of London; p52 (t) © Ellice Milton/2006 Topfoto, (bl) © Gwynedd County Council; p54-55 (b) © Adam Woolfitt/Corbis; p55 (tr) © The Trustees of The British Museum; p56 © English Heritage Photo Library. Illustrator; Judith Dobie; p57 (br) © C.M.Dixon/Ancient Art & Architecture Collection Ltd; p60 © Museum of London; 61 (t) The Manchester Museum, The University of Manchester; p62 (tl) © British Museum /HIP/Topfoto, (bl) © The Trustees of The British Museum, (tm) © Museum of London/Bridgeman; p63 (r) © Museum of London/HIP/Topfoto; p65 (tr) © Hull and East Riding Museum, Humberside/Bridgeman; p67 (tr) © R. Sheridan/ Ancient Art and Architecture Collection; p68 © Peter Dunn/English Heritage; p69 (t) © The Trustees of The British Museum, (br) © Crown copyright. NMR; p71 (tr) © Topfoto; p75 (r) © National Museum of Wales; p77 (br) © The British Museum/HIP/ Topfoto; p78 © Ancient Art and Architecture Collection; p79 (t) © The British Museum/HIP/Topfoto, (br) © The Trustees of The British Museum; p81 (t) © Staatliche Museen, Berlin/ Bridgeman, (br) © The Trustees of The British Museum; p82 (b) © Skyscan/Corbis; p84 (b) © Museum of London/HIP/Topfoto.

The Early Middle Ages

p88 (tl) © Museum of London/HIP/TopFoto; p90 (b) © British Library Board. All rights reserved, Add. 10292 f.101; p93 (b) © Trustees of the British Museum; p94 (tl) © British Library Board. All Rights Reserved/Bridgeman; p96 (b) © Trustees of the British Museum; p97 (tr) © Trustees of the British Museum; 98 (t) © British Library Board. All rights reserved, Cotton Nero D. IV, f.29; p99 (b) © Mark Sykes/Alamy; p100 ©TopFoto; p101 (tr) Fitzwilliam Museum, University of Cambridge, UK/Bridgeman, (mr) © Trustees of the British Museum, (br) © Trustees of the British Museum; p102 (tl) © British Library Board. All rights reserved, Cotton Tiberius C. II, f.5v; p103 (br) © National Museums of Scotland: Licensor www.scran.ac.uk; p105 (br) © Museum of London, UK/Bridgeman; p106 (tl) Viking Ship Museum, Oslo, Norway/Bridgeman; p108(tl) ©Ashmolean Museum, University of Oxford, UK/Bridgeman; p109 (r) © Robert Estall photo agency/Alamy; p110 (t) © Brian Atkinson/Alamy; p112 (tl) © Robert Harding Picture Library Ltd/Alamy; p113 (b) © Ted Spiegel/Corbis; p115 (t) © British Library Board. All rights reserved, Stowe 944, f.6; p116 (tl) © British Library Board. All rights reserved, Add. 33241, f.1v; p117 (b) Musee de la Tapisserie, Bayeux, France, With special authorisation of the city of Bayeux/Bridgeman.

The Middle Ages

p120-121 (t) © akg-images / Erich Lessing/Musée de la Tapisserie; p122-123 © Travelshots.com/Alamy; p124-125 Copyright 2006. Photo Pierpont Morgan Library/Art Resource/Scala, Florence; p128 (t) © Justin Kase zfourz/Alamy; p130 (t) © UPP/TopFoto; p132 (l) © British Library Board. All rights reserved, Add. 42130, f.158; p134-135 © British Library Board. All Rights Reserved/ Bridgeman; p137 © Howard Taylor/Alamy; p138 © British Library Board. All rights reserved, Royal 14 C. VII, f.9; p141 Copyright 2003. Photo Scala, Florence; p143 (t) Bibliothèque Nationale, Paris, France/Bridgeman; p145 V& A Images/Victoria & Albert Museum; p146 (t) © Paul Watson/Travel Ink/Alamy; p148 (tl) © The National Archives/HIP/TopFoto; p149 (b) The Royal Collection © 2008 Her Majesty Queen Elizabeth II; p150-151 © David Lyons/Alamy; p151 (t) © British Library Board. All rights reserved, Cotton Nero D. II, f.182; p153 (t) The Art Archive / British Library; p156 (t) Bibliothèque Royale de Belgique, Brussels, Belgium/Bridgeman, (bl) © British Library Board. All Rights Reserved/Bridgeman; p157 (br) © Adam Woolfitt/Corbis; p159 Copyright 2003. Photo Scala, Florence; p160 (t) English or French, The Wilton Diptych © The National Gallery, London; p161 (t) Copyright 2003. Photo Scala, Florence; p162 © British Library Board. All rights reserved, Yates Thompson MS11 f. 6v; p164 (b) Copyright 2003. Photo Scala, Florence; p165 (t) Private Collection/Bridgeman; p166-167 Bibliothèque Nationale de France; p169 © Green Bay Media Ltd; p171 Private Collection/Bridgeman; p173 (r) British Museum, London, UK/Bridgeman; p174 (b) Private Collection/Bridgeman; p175 (t) © Dick Clarke/Mayhem Photographics.

The early 20th century

p352 (l) © Topfoto; p353 (tr) Mary Evans; p354 © Hulton-Deutsch Collection/Corbis; p355 (r) By permission of The National Library of Wales; p356 (bl) © Museum of London /HIP/Topfoto; p356-357 (t) © Hulton-Deutsch Collection/Corbis; p358-359 © Bettmann/Corbis; p360-361 Mary Evans; p362 (t) © Bettmann/Corbis; p364 (t) © Roger-Viollet/Topfoto; p366 IWM Q49104; p368 (t) The Art Archive/Imperial War Museum; p369 The Art Archive/Imperial War Museum/Eileen Tweedy; p370 The Art Archive/Imperial War Museum; p372 (bl) © Hulton Archive/Getty Images; p372-373 (t) IWM Q58481; p373 (b) © Hulton-Deutsch Collection/Corbis; p374-375 © Corbis; p376 (tl) IWM Q27025A; p376-377 © akg-images; p378-379 The Art Archive/Imperial War Museum; p380-381 The Art Archive/Imperial War Museum; p382 (tl) © Bettmann/Corbis, (b) IWM E(AUS)001220; p383 (br) © Bettmann/Corbis; p384-385 © Michael St. Maur Sheil/Corbis; p386 (b) © Bettmann/Corbis; p387 (tl) © Science and Society/NRM - Pictorial Collection, (br) © Hulton Archive/Getty Images; p388 (t) © Bettmann/Corbis; p389 (tr) © Hulton Archive/Getty Images; p390 (t) © Hulton-Deutsch Collection/Corbis. Some of the photographs in this chapter were originally in black and white and have been digitally tinted by Usborne Publishing.

The Second World War

p394 (tl) © Corbis (Heinrich Hoffmann); p395 © Hulton Archive/Getty Images; 396 (bl) IWM D651; 397 (t) The Art Archive/Eileen Tweedy, (b) © Eric Harlow/Hulton Archive/2007 Getty Images; p399 (t) Hulton Archive/2007 Getty Images; p400 © Bettmann/Corbis; p401 (t) © David Low, Evening Standard, 14th May 1940, Solo Syndication/British Cartoon Archive, University of Kent; p402 © Bert Hardy/Hulton Archive/2007 Getty Images; p403 (tr) © POPPERFOTO/Alamy; p404 (b) © Fox Photos/Hulton Archive/Getty Images; p405 (t) © Skyscan/Corbis; p407 © David Pollack/Corbis; p408-409 Keystone/Hulton Archive/2007 Getty Images; p411 © Bettmann/Corbis; p412 (bl) © Corbis; p412-413 © Bettmann/Corbis; p414 (tl) © The Lordprice Collection/HIP/TopFoto; p415 IWM D8806; p416 © Zoltan Glass/Hulton Archive/2007 Getty Images; p417 (t) © Keystone/Hulton Archive/2007 Getty Images; p418 (t) © Keystone/Hulton Archive/2007 Getty Images; p419 © Keystone/Hulton Archive/2007 Getty Images; p420 (l) IWM D23727; p421 (br) © Volker Steger/SPL; p422 akg-images/ullstein bild; p423 (t) IWM A3532; p424-425 © Corbis; p425 (tr) © Swim Ink 2, LLC/Corbis; p426 (t) akg-images/ullstein bild; p427 (b) Copyright © Ronald Searle 1943, by kind permission of the artist and The Sayle Literary Agency; p428 (tl) IWM E18980, (b) © POPPERFOTO/Alamy; p430 IWM FLM002343; p431 IWM HU4594; p432 (tl) The Art Archive/Eileen Tweedy; p432-433 IWM C4363; p434 (tl) © ITV plc/Granada International/Source: BFI Stills, (b) IWM A14185; p435 (t) © Keystone/Hulton Archive Getty Images; p436 (bl) IWM MH3660; p438-439 IWM B5245; p440 (t) The Art Archive; p441 IWM BU11149; p443 (tr) © Reuters/Corbis, (b) © Keystone/Hulton Archive/Getty Images; p444 (t) © Keystone/Hulton Archive/Getty Images, (bl) © Hulton-Deutsch Collection/Corbis; p445 (b) © Hulton Archive/Getty Images; p446-447 © Corbis; p447 (tr) © John Van Hasselt/Corbis Sygma; p448 © Hulton-Deutsch Collection/Corbis; p449 (tr) © Bettmann/Corbis, (br) © Museum of London. Some of the photographs in this chapter were originally in black and white and have been digitally tinted by Usborne Publishing.

Post-war Britain

p452 (tl) © Hulton-Deutsch Collection/Corbis, (b) © Bettmann/Corbis; p454 (tl) © Hulton-Deutsch Collection/Corbis; p455 © Haywood Magee/Hulton Archive/Getty Images; p456 (t) © Fox Photos/Hulton Archive/Getty Images, (bl) The National Archives UK DN7525; p458-459 (background) © Jim Grant/Photodisc/Getty Images; p459 (main) © Everett Collection/Rex Features, (tr) © Bettmann/Corbis, (br) Michael Ochs Archives/Getty Images; p460 (tl) © PA Photos; p461 © PA Photos; p462 (tl) © Bettmann/Corbis, (bl) © PA Photos; p463 (t) © PA Photos, (br) The Band Aid Trust; p464-465 © PA Photos; p465 (tr) © Paul McErlane/epa/Corbis; p469 © Tim Ockenden/PA Photos; p470 (b) © UPP/Topfoto; p471 (t) © PA Photos; p472-473 © Tuohig Sion/Corbis Sygma.

Factfile

p476 © British Library Board. All rights reserved, Cotton Augustus I. i. 74; p479 (b) © Adam Woolfitt/Corbis; p480 (b) © J Marshall - Tribaleye Images/Alamy.

Consultants:

Dr. Timothy Taylor, University of Bradford; Dr. Andrew Gardner, University College London; Dr. Ryan Lavelle, University of Winchester; Professor Christopher Dyer, University of Leicester; Dr. Anne Millard; Janice Barter; Professor Stephen Conway, University College London; Professor Hilary Fraser, Birkbeck College, University of London; Terry Charman, Imperial War Museum; Dr. Peter Mandler, University of Cambridge.

First published in 2008 by Usborne Publishing Ltd., Usborne House, 83–85 Saffron Hill, London, EC1N 8RT, United Kingdom. www.usborne.com Copyright © 2008 Usborne Publishing Ltd. The name Usborne and the devices ⊕ ♀ are Trade Marks of Usborne Publishing Ltd. All rights reserved. No part of this publication may be reproduced, stored in any retrieval system, or transmitted in any form or by any means, electronic, mechanical, photocopying, recording or otherwise, without the prior permission of the publisher. Printed in Singapore. UE